Coastal zone management

Coastal zone management

Edited by
David R. Green
University of Aberdeen

Published by Thomas Telford Limited, 40 Marsh Wall, London E14 9TP.
www.icevirtuallibrary.com

Distributors for Thomas Telford books are
USA: ASCE Press, 1801 Alexander Bell Drive, Reston, VA 20191-4400
Australia: DA Books and Journals, 648 Whitehorse Road, Mitcham 3132, Victoria

First published 2010

Also available from Thomas Telford Limited
Future flooding and coastal erosion risks. C. Thorne, E. Evans and E. Penning-Rowsell.
ISBN 978-0-7277-3449-5
Manual on the use of timber in coastal and river engineering. M. Crossman and J. Sim.
ISBN 978-0-7277-3283-5
Whole life costs and project procurement in port, coastal and fluvial engineering. J. Simm and N. Masters.
ISBN 978-0-7277-3232-3

A catalogue record for this book is available from the British Library

ISBN: 978-0-7277-3516-4

FSC
Mixed Sources
Product group from well-managed
forests and other controlled sources
Cert no. SGS-COC-2953
www.fsc.org
© 1996 Forest Stewardship Council

Typeset by Academic + Technical, Bristol
Index created by Indexing Specialists (UK) Ltd, Hove, East Sussex
Printed and bound in Great Britain by CPI Antony Rowe, Chippenham

Contents

Preface

Several years ago I was approached by Thomas Telford Publishing to develop a proposal for a new book focusing on the broad theme of integrated coastal zone management. As many of you are already aware there is a number of well known and highly respected books on coastal management and integrated coastal zone management (ICZM) already on the library shelves and, in addition, many other texts that focus on specific aspects of ICZM, e.g. ICZM and the geospatial technologies. Some of these books have been based on collections of papers presented at international conferences and symposia, and usually cover many different and very diverse topics.

Rather than produce yet another such volume, primarily targeted solely at the coastal research community, the rationale for the current book was twofold. First, to provide a *course reader* for marine and coastal students that aims to cover some of the key issues and topics in coastal and marine resource management and ICZM; subjects that perhaps are to be found only in specialist collections or scientific journals, which may not always be readily accessible to the undergraduate or postgraduate student. Second, to provide an introduction to various different aspects of the coastal environment and coastal management that would have wider interest for coastal engineers, managers, and coastal practitioners in local authorities, who likewise may not have access to the scientific literature. Following this line of reasoning, the current volume was assembled to provide both an accessible and readable introduction to a wide range of issues and topics in coastal management considered to be relevant both today and into the future. In addition, the content was selected to provide a basic introduction to a subject, as well as stimulating the reader to pursue it in more depth, either by selective reading from the reference lists at the end of each chapter, or by pursuing the subject matter in the scientific journals.

Naturally there are many subjects that can be covered in books such as this and, given the obvious space constraints of any book, it is clearly necessary to be highly selective. The current book seeks to provide introductions to a number of subjects that were considered, on the basis of consultation at the outset with reviewers and colleagues, to be of direct interest to the wider coastal community. To summarise, these include the following:

- climate change and sea level rise
- maritime spatial planning
- catchment management
- coastal and marine boundaries
- natural capital
- marine protected area (MPAs)
- the role of coastal fora in coastal management
- coastal environments and geomorphology
- the urban coastline and waterfront development
- environmental and ICZM indicators
- coastal vulnerability
- coastal hazards and disasters
- carrying capacity for coastal management
- coastal and marine spatial data infrastructures (SDIs)
- modelling of the coast
- visualising the coastal environment.

One of the key components of any successful book lies with the subject matter covered that will be of interest to the expected readership. Ultimately, however, success also rests with the ability of the invited authors, all specialists in their respective fields, to be able to communicate the information to the potential reader – in this case likely to be quite wide ranging – and in a way that is appropriate to that readership, is at an introductory level, but one that necessarily includes more depth and specialisation than might be achieved in a standard textbook on coastal management. As many of the chapters in this book are likely to be read by people who perhaps have not been exposed to the wider literature and may be seeking an introduction to the material, the invited authors were also asked to present the material in such a way as to both stimulate interest and provide a broad coverage that would naturally cover the appropriate ground but would also lead them onto further reading.

I do hope this collection of chapters proves to be a useful text for people interested in the coastal environment and coastal management who might use the volume as a starting point to explore some of the key subject areas and issues that are important. I would also hope that this volume may be used to introduce students of coastal management programmes to some of these subject areas, perhaps to support their reading lists for a course or, as I plan to do, to provide a *reader* for a course on current issues in marine and coastal studies.

In compiling this collection of invited chapters, there is always the inevitable problem that things move on very quickly and the content of the book will soon become outdated. However, by choosing the subjects I have, I feel that they will form the basis of discussion for a number of years to come by providing a focus on the fundamentals that will perhaps not date quite so quickly.

Thanks are also due to Jenny Johnson and Alison Sandison for redrafting many of the figures in this book.

Last, but not least I would like to thank all the authors who have contributed to this book, as well as Thomas Telford Publishing, and in particular Matthew Lane, for helping to make this all possible.

David R. Green
University of Aberdeen

Contributors

Pamela A. Abuodha, *GeoQuest Research Centre, University of Wollongong, Australia*

Barry J. Bleichner, *Department of Geography & Environment, University of Aberdeen, UK*

Margaret Carlisle, *CMCZM, Department of Geography & Environment, University of Aberdeen, UK*

Philip A. Collier, *Department of Geomatics, University of Melbourne, Australia*

J. Andrew G. Cooper, *Centre for Coastal & Marine Research, University of Ulster, UK*

Peter J. Cowell, *School of Geosciences, University of Sydney, Australia*

Nicholas D. Cutts, *Institute of Estuarine & Coastal Studies, University of Hull, UK*

Alastair G. Dawson, *Aberdeen Institute for Coastal Science and Management, University of Aberdeen, UK*

Mark E. Dickson, *School of Environment, University of Auckland, Australia*

Fanny Douvere, *Marine Spatial Management Initiative, UNESCO, France*

Michael Elliott, *Institute of Estuarine & Coastal Studies, University of Hull, UK*

Roger W. Fraser, *Office of Surveyor General Victoria, Department of Sustainability and Environment, Australia*

David R. Green, *CMCZM, Department of Geography & Environment, University of Aberdeen, UK*

Christina C. Hicks, *Envision Management, Newcastle-upon-Tyne, UK*

Jeremy M. Hills, *School of Marine Science & Technology, University of Newcastle, UK*

Nicholas J.K. Howden, *Natural Resources Department, Cranfield University, UK*

Chris Lakhan, *Department of Earth & Environmental Sciences, University of Windsor, Canada*

Martin D.A. LeTissier, *School of Marine Science & Technology, University of Newcastle, UK*

Roger Longhorn, *Info-Dynamics Research Associates Ltd., UK*

Frank Maes, *Marine Institute at the Faculty of Law, Ghent University, Belgium*

John McKenna, *Centre for Coastal & Marine Research, University of Ulster, UK*

James Ortiz, *North Cornwal District Council, Bodmin, UK*

Alan H. Pickaver, *Coast & Marine Union (EUCC), UK*

William Ritchie, *Aberdeen Institute for Coastal & Marine Management, University of Aberdeen, UK*

Paola Salmona, *ICCOPS, Landscape, Natural & Cultural Heritage, Observatory, Italy*

Anna Trono, *Department of Arts & Heritage, University of Salento, Italy,*

Mick J. Whelan, *Natural Resources Department, Cranfield University, UK*

Sue M. White, *Natural Resources Department, Cranfield University, UK*

Colin D. Woodroffe, *School of Earth & Environmental Sciences, Unvirsity of Wollongong, Australia*

1

Understanding changes in relative sea level and storminess: views from Earth and space

Alastair G. Dawson
Aberdeen Institute for Coastal Science and Management, University of Aberdeen,
Scotland

This chapter explores some of the key ocean-atmosphere processes relevant to ways in which climate change processes affect the Earth's coastlines. The debate on how climate change is affecting coasts is very much in the public eye. Yet, many publically stated views demonstrate very clearly how misunderstanding of process is clouding judgement. This paper contrasts the perspective of coastal change as viewed from the land and contrasts this with the knowledge gained from satellite measurements. It is shown here that there is no such thing as a single global sea level. The discussion is thereafter broadened into a discussion of regional variations in storminess. An attempt is made to distinguish between storminess attributable to 'human-induced' climate change and storminess due simply to natural climate variability. The latter discussion focuses in particular on regional effects of La Niña and El Niño – in particular on the development of hurricanes and typhoons across low latitudes.

1.1   Introduction

Viewed from the coast, the ocean stretches to the horizon. This furthest visible limit of the sea adds to popular belief that the sea is flat – at least as far as the eye can see. Of course, with the exception of those in the 'flat Earth' society, it is recognised that the horizon represents an expression of the curvature of the Earth – the point beyond which can be seen no further. In some ways, this view of sea level from the coast is perpetuated in the popular and scientific literature. We invariably read about the issue of 'sea level rise' even 'global sea level rise' where we are presented with an extension of this concept of a horizontal sea level – namely that 'global sea level' is predicted to be a certain value by a given date in the future and that this value is a global average. The majority of scientific literature, therefore, clings to the notion that there is such a thing as a numerical value for 'global sea level' and that, in the future, each climate change scenario predicts 'sea level' to rise by a given amount over a fixed period of time.

This concept of a globally averaged sea level is illustrated in the various Intergovernmental Panel on Climate Change (IPCC) reports on climate change. The values of 'sea level rise' predicted in the IPCC accounts are, however, based on detailed scientific calculations on factors such as projected rates of melting of alpine glaciers and small ice caps around the world, rates of anticipated melting of parts of the Greenland and Antarctic ice sheets, as well as projections of how much the world's oceans will thermally expand as they absorb heat from a continually warmed atmosphere as a result of 'global warming'.

The view from space, however, is very different. In fact, the Earth's ocean surface is highly irregular. When measured from satellites it shows an uneven ocean that departs markedly from its 'average' description as an oblate spheroid. The ocean surface has a relief locally in excess of 150 m. Across the North Atlantic, for example, the ocean surface is in the order of +60 m above average while across parts of the Indian Ocean the geoidal ocean surface lowers to a minimum value in the order of −100 m below average. This geoidal sea surface owes its variability to regional variations in the Earth's gravity field – which varies regionally and is subject to small regional deformations on a daily basis. Viewed from a ship, the geoidal ocean topography still shows the same flat horizon. But, viewed from space, regional variations in the geoidal sea surface are very clearly in evidence.

From the standpoint of climate change, the volume of the world's oceans is subject to long-term change. Since the area of the world's oceans in ca. $360 \times 10^6 \, \text{km}^2$ simple arithmetic tells us that a 1 mm increase in sea level averaged worldwide is equivalent to the melting of $360 \, \text{km}^3$ of ice. Since the advent of satellites that are sufficiently accurate to measure such small changes in the sea surface across the world, the available data appear to indicate that, on average, since 1993, the sea level has risen by ca. 3 mm/yr. However, maps produced by graphical visualisation of the satellite data, show quite clearly that, whereas the majority of the world's oceans have indeed experienced sea level rise, there are many other areas of the ocean that have experienced a lowering of the sea surface over the same period. One ocean area that has experienced a systematic lowering is that across the central Indian Ocean. The cause of such a remarkable change (given that we are told the sea level is rising everywhere) is most probably due to changes in the temperature of ocean water. When ocean water is heated, as a result of rising air temperatures, it expands and the sea surface rises. Conversely, where ocean water is cooled it contracts and the sea surface falls. The principal cause of ocean cooling in the Indian Ocean is invariably associated with an increased flux of freshwater from the land. In the case of the northern Indian Ocean this appears to be river discharge through the Ganges and Brahmaputra rivers that drain the Indian subcontinent. Similarly, in the northern North Atlantic, large areas have experienced a cooling over recent decades linked to a freshening – perhaps related to increased ice melt on neighbouring landmasses while adjacent areas (e.g. the western North Atlantic) have experienced above average warming. In the central and North Pacific regions the juxtaposition of areas subject to cooling and warming may be related in complex ways to the recent history of regional El Niño and La Niña events.

The Intergovernmental Panel on Climate Change released its Fourth Assessment Report in 2007 (IPCC, 2007). While recognising that marked spatial variations in sea level change have occurred recently (both warming and cooling), the report focuses on a calculated average value and predicts that this value will rise between 0.18 m and 0.59 m by the year AD 2100. Over the twentieth century, global sea level has risen by on average about 1.8 mm per year, but since the early 1990s this rate has almost doubled (Cazenave and Nerem, 2004; Church and White, 2006; Gehrels, 2006).

The key elements in causing an overall increase in the volume of ocean water are not well understood. The IPCC (2007) attribute the majority of sea level rise in the future to the thermal expansion of ocean water. The world's oceans presently absorb ca. 80% of the heat associated with a warmer global atmosphere. A consequence of this heat uptake is that ocean water is heated and this increased heating causes ocean water to expand. The process of thermal expansion of ocean water is complicated, however, since on the one hand the majority of heat is absorbed within the top few metres of the ocean surface, yet on the other the expansion of ocean water involves heating and expansion of the entire ocean water column. Thus it is a mistake to consider that the world's oceans are warming everywhere and that the

3

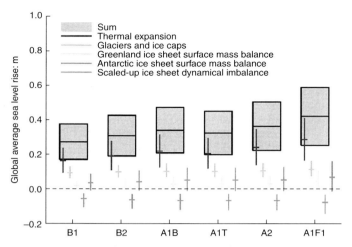

Fig. 1.1 *IPCC (2007) predictions of an average global mean sea level for the last decade of the twenty-first century, relative to 1980–1999. The different predictions refer to different climate change scenarios. Note the important influence that thermal expansion has on sea level values*

IPCC (2007) prediction of future sea level rise will be the same everywhere (Fig. 1.1).

In a detailed study by Dyurgerov and Meier (2005) the loss of ice from the world's glaciers and ice caps is estimated to have been, between 1961–2003, equivalent to an averaged sea level rise of $+0.51$ mm yr^{-1}, rising to $+0.93$ mm yr^{-1} between 1994–2003. For the Greenland and Antarctic ice sheets the calculated contributions to sea level for the period 2002–2005 are: $+0.36 \pm 0.04$ mm yr^{-1} (Greenland), $+0.3 \pm 0.06$ mm yr^{-1} (West Antarctica) and -0.19 ± 0.07 mm yr^{-1} (East Antarctica) (Ramillien *et al.*, 2006). The overall contribution of these ice sheets to sea level rise is therefore around 0.47 mm yr^{-1}, with the Greenland contribution somewhat more than the IPCC estimate, and the Antarctic contribution rather less (Benn, pers. comm.). Combining this figure with that calculated by Dyurgerov and Meier (2005) for glaciers and ice caps yields a total current glacio-eustatic contribution to sea level change of ~ 1.4 mm yr^{-1}. Add to this, the best estimates of the averaged increase in sea level due to the processes of thermal expansion (1.6 mm/yr) and we derive a net averaged recent sea level rise in the order of 3 mm/yr.

It is for this reason that future predictions of sea level rise are strongly linked to an anticipated increase in oceanic thermal expansion. This is because nearly all climate models for the future predict rising air temperatures. If this takes place, increased global air temperatures imply a commensurate increase in heat absorption by the oceans and therefore increased thermal expansion due to increased ocean water temperatures.

For any region, the estimation of changes in relative sea level over time describes the changing height of the sea with respect to the land and therefore includes both vertical land changes together with changes in ocean volume. Therefore, it is not possible to use IPCC sea level change data on their own to estimate regional values of relative sea level change for any coastal area. In some areas, significant vertical lowering (subsidence) of the land surface takes place and serves to exaggerate the amount of relative sea level rise. Typical are the world's deltas where long-term sediment compaction is associated with subsidence rates of tens of cm per year. By contrast there are some areas of the world's coastline that are still rebounding due to glacio-isostatic processes following the melting of the last great ice sheets. For example, the northern area of the Gulf of Bothnia is presently associated with a vertical uplift rate in the order of +8 mm/yr. If a sea level rise rate of +3 mm/yr is assumed for this area, the net effect is an annual rate of lowering of relative sea level of 5 mm/yr.

1.2 Regional perturbations of the sea surface

Whereas regional oceans and seas are subject to relatively small-scale (ca. 1–3 mm/yr) annual changes in sea level, they are also subject to much larger vertical changes due to changes in ocean-atmosphere circulation. Probably the most notable example of such changes is the El Niño Southern Oscillation (ENSO).

The definition of the term 'El Niño' is subject to a great deal of confusion. It has been so widely used by the media in recent years that the precise meaning of the term has become more and more obscure. Originally, the term 'El Niño' (Spanish for little boy) was used to describe a warm, seasonal ocean current that arrives along the coastline of Ecuador and Peru around Christmas – hence the celebration of El Niño as arrival of the Christ child. However, today the term is generally used as a description of a dual phenomenon that has closely linked oceanic and atmospheric elements. Hence, most analyses of El Niño describe the links between: (1) remarkable increases in sea surface temperature and an increase in regional sea surface elevation over the central and eastern equatorial Pacific region; and (2) associated periods of heavy rainfall in the central Pacific, and western

5

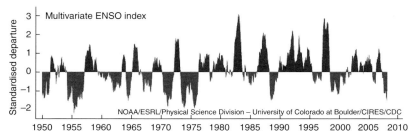

Fig. 1.2 ENSO index showing as positive values, time intervals characterised by El Niño circulation and (negative values) periods associated with La Niña circulation. Note the prominence of the last two major El Niño episodes during 1982–83 and 1997–98 (based on National Oceanic and Atmospheric Administration data)

South America and California, with corresponding droughts in Australia and Indonesia (Philander, 1989) (Fig. 1.2).

An El Niño is only one combined element (warm period) of a dual phase oscillation within the ocean-atmospheric system (Dawson and O'Hare, 2000). When the system switches to a cold phase, Pacific waters return to a cool state with cold water off the coast of Ecuador and Peru and warm water in the western Pacific in the vicinity of Indonesia and eastern Australia. As a result, dry conditions return to the central and eastern Pacific (Peru and Ecuador) with wet conditions in the western Pacific (Indonesia and Australia). Sometimes, in an El Niño's wake, eastern Pacific waters not only return to a cool state but also become unusually cold. When this happens a 'La Niña' (Spanish for little girl) occurs which causes, among other climate effects, extreme drought in coastal Peru and Ecuador and very heavy rains in the western Pacific. During periods of La Niña, the regional sea surface is lowered (due to the cooler water) across the eastern Pacific with a corresponding rise across the western Pacific, Australasia and Indonesia (Dawson and O'Hare, 2000). By contrast, periods of El Niño circulation are generally associated with a marked rise in relative sea level across the eastern Pacific Ocean. For example, the El Niño episodes that took place during 1982–83 and 1997–98, were associated with a rise in the average sea surface in the order of +30 cm. This pattern of change is well-illustrated in the tide gauge record for San Francisco where periodic increases in the elevation of the sea surface due to major El Niño events is superimposed upon a longer-term increase in sea level due to 'global warming' (Fig. 1.3).

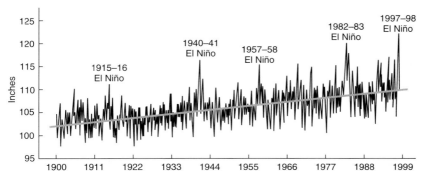

Fig. 1.3 Tide gauge for San Francisco, showing a series of sea surface rises attributable to former El Niño events superimposed upon a longer-term and sustained rise attributed to climate change (based on data from the United States Geological Survey) (http://www.cru.uea.ac.uk/cru/data/nao.htm)

1.3 El Niño and La Niña events: effects on Atlantic hurricanes

One of the effects of El Niño episodes on low-latitude atmospheric circulation is the creation of increased wind shear in the upper troposphere. This has the effect of impeding the development of large hurricanes. As a consequence, major ENSO events correlate well with decreased hurricane activity across not only the central Atlantic but also in the Bay of Bengal, the southern Indian Ocean and the northwest tropical Pacific (Diaz and Pulwarty, 1997; Gray, 1999; O'Hare, 1999).

Detailed analyses of oceanographic changes across the central Atlantic during El Niño events show a decrease in sea surface temperatures (SSTs) – indirectly related to increased wind shear in the upper troposphere. Such SST reductions reduce ocean evaporation and thus the main source of energy (latent heat) for hurricane generation (Gray, 1984; NOAA, 1998). Conversely, periods of strong La Niña activity are typically associated with increased hurricane activity across the central Atlantic and Caribbean.

Detailed reconstructions of ENSO events dating from circa AD 1500 have been undertaken by Quinn and Neal (1992). These authors used documentary sources to not only identify past ENSO events but they also devised a scale of ENSO severity. Inspection of the timing of strong, strong/very strong and very strong ENSO events for the last ca. 500 years shows some significant trends. For example, there is a very noticeable gap between AD 1830–65 during which time no major ENSO events appear to have taken place. Similarly, between

7

AD 1942–74 only one major ENSO event occurred in the category (S), i.e. strong or higher. Comparison between the timing of major ENSO events and the most destructive tropical Atlantic hurricanes is also instructive (Rappaport and Fernandez-Partagas, 1998). A test of the hypothesis described above would be that the most destructive Atlantic tropical cyclones occur during cold phase La Niña events, when tropical Atlantic sea surface temperatures are higher than average. Rappaport and Fernandez-Partagas (1998) compiled a detailed list of the 'deadliest' Atlantic tropical cyclones for the period AD 1492–present. They defined such cyclones as those reported to have caused 25 or more deaths in any part of the Atlantic basin. Comparison of the timing of major ENSO events with major hurricane events for the period between circa AD 1500–1800 shows an almost perfect inverse relationship, i.e. hurricanes rarely occur in the tropical Atlantic during El Niño periods. The significance of this data is not entirely clear, since complications in the interpretation are posed by the manner in which individual events were reported. Clearly, increased media reporting over time has resulted in an increase in the frequency of recording of cyclone events, particularly during the last century (Michaels, 1999).

These results are striking and point to a set of processes in the Earth's climate system demonstrating a 'see-saw' link between ocean-atmosphere processes in the tropical Pacific and those in the tropical Atlantic Ocean. The fact that these 'see-saw' patterns may extend back to circa AD 1500 (and possibly earlier) indicates that such processes were in operation prior to the Industrial Revolution, and that they may truly be considered part of a 'natural' global climate process. In addition, since major ENSO events appear to have been an important feature of the Earth's climate system during the last 500 years, there may be important discoveries to be made in determining the role that such events have played on patterns of climate change in parts of the world far distant from the Pacific Basin (Dawson and O'Hare, 2000).

The patterns of change described above illustrate well why it is a mistake to argue that 'global warming' has been associated with an increase in hurricane activity, since there is little doubt that the chronology of hurricane activity across low latitudes during recent centuries has more to do with El Niño and La Niña periodicity. It also makes abundantly clear that the risk of extreme marine flooding across low latitudes has much more to do with the timing of major La Niña/El Niño phases that any perceived changes due to 'global warming'.

1.4   El Niño and La Niña events: effects on Asian typhoon activity

The chronology of Asian typhoons is also related to the history of El Niño and La Niña changes. Here the effect of enhanced wind shear in the upper atmosphere during major El Niño phases has the effect of causing decreased typhoon activity and intensity across the northwest Pacific. Inspection of the tracks of major Asian typhoons for major El Niño and La Niña periods shows that the ocean area across the northwest Pacific in which typhoons are generated is greatly increased during La Niña phases compared with major El Niño episodes. Here, also, it may be profitable to consider coastal flood risk across southeast Asia as linked to major episodes of La Niña activity.

In respect of the Indian Ocean, the effects of El Niño and La Niña are less clear. Here, a complicating factor is that ocean surface temperature changes in the northern sector of the Indian Ocean are strongly affected by the flux of freshwater emanating from the major rivers (e.g. Ganges, Brahmaputra) from the Indian subcontinent. Furthermore, there is not a clear oceanic and atmospheric response to El Niño and La Niña phases within the Indian Ocean region with the effect that some major El Niño and La Niña periods are not recognisable across the Indian Ocean while others are. Perhaps the best known example of a major El Niño having affected the Indian Ocean is the 1997–98 event. During this period a major ocean warming took place that was sufficiently severe to have led to the destruction of large areas of coral.

1.5   Disentangling global warming and ENSO events

One of the most perplexing problems associated with understanding the Earth's climate system is how to distinguish natural factors such as ENSO events which may induce short-term or cyclical climate changes, from longer-term climate trends caused by human-induced 'global warming'. The climate change effects of 'global warming' and ENSO events are closely interwoven with regard not only to long-term averages, but also to extreme weather events. The above discussion illustrates very well how regional signals of warming sea surface temperatures and rising sea levels need not demonstrate proof positive of global warming. Clearly, major ENSO events are extremely important contributors to the natural variability of sea surface changes (Anderson *et al.*, 1998). Given such high-magnitude and rapid changes in the level of the sea surface across, for example, the Pacific, it is not surprising that attributing particular sea level rises to global warming (from ice melt and the expansion of heated water) is problematic.

1.6   North Atlantic changes in storminess

In the north Atlantic, the strength of the Gulf Stream and westerly winds blowing over the UK and Europe are influenced by pressure differences between semi-permanent low pressure over Iceland (Icelandic low) and semi-permanent high pressure off the coast of Portugal and Spain (Azores high). This pressure gradient has been shown to vary or oscillate every two to three decades over the last 150 years between two distinct phases: when in positive mode (e.g. between AD 1900–30, and also since the 1980s), pressure differences are high and both westerly winds and Gulf Stream advection are strong (Fig. 1.4). When the cycle switches to negative mode (for example, between AD 1930–60) pressure variations, westerly winds and ocean advection are much weaker (Wilby *et al.*, 1997). This decadal-scale cycle in surface pressure, winds and ocean currents has been called the North Atlantic Oscillation (NAO) (Hurrell, 1995). When in positive mode, westerly winds and frontal activity strengthen and shift northwards over the Atlantic bringing increased winter storminess. When in the opposite (cold) negative phase, the NAO encourages much colder drier weather over northwest Europe and reduced winter storminess across the North Atlantic.

During recent decades, increased air temperatures across the northern hemisphere have led to a decreased meridional (north to south) air temperature gradient between the polar regions and mid-latitudes. The effect of this process coupled with (and partly related to) changes in

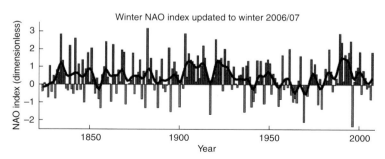

Fig. 1.4 Histogram showing fluctuations between periods of positive NAO Index values (increased winter storminess) and negative NAO Index values (decreased winter storminess) (based on data from Climatic Research Unit, University of East Anglia)

the NAO, have led to a recent decrease in regional storminess across the North Atlantic region. As a consequence, the risk of coastal flooding due to storminess across northern and northwest Europe, has decreased. It should be noted that these observations are not consistent with the well publicised view of IPCC (2007) that 'global warming' has led to a recent increase in storminess across the mid-latitudes of the northern hemisphere.

1.7   Summary

This paper represents an initial attempt to consider in more details the popularly held concept of 'global sea level rise' and 'increased storminess' caused by 'climate change'. When we look at both of these concepts we realise that both are illusory. There is no such thing as 'global sea level rise'. Instead, recent satellite data show that there are strong regional variations in patterns of sea level change. Whereas the majority of the world's oceans display evidence of recent relative sea level rise caused principally by thermal expansion effects, other areas of oceans have been characterised by oceanic cooling and sea surface lowering. In a similar manner, it is a mistake to consider that there exists a single trend of increased storminess caused by climate change. Patterns of storminess change exhibit marked regional differences, for example in the low latitudes they are linked to El Niño and La Niña perturbations. These factors are fundamental to any evaluation of coastal flood risk.

References

Anderson, D., Bengtsson, L., Delecluse, P., Duplessy, J.-C., Fichefet, T., Joussaume, S., Jouzel, J., Komen, G., Latif, M., Laursen, L., le Treut, H., Mitchell, J., Navarra, A., Palmer, T., Planton, S., Ruiz de Elvira, A., Schott, F., Slingo, J. and Willebrand, J. (1998) *Climate variability and predictability research in Europe, 1999–2004*, Euroclivar.

Cazenave, A. and Nerem, R.S. (2004) Present-day sea level change: observations and causes. *Review of Geophysics*, Vol. 42, RG3001.

Church, J.A. and White, N.J. (2006) A 20th century acceleration in global sea-level rise. *Geophysical Research Letters*, Vol. 33, LO1602.

Dawson, A.G. and O'Hare, G. (2000) Ocean-atmosphere circulation and global climate: the El Niño-southern oscillation. *Geography* (Millenium Special Issue), pp. 193–208.

Diaz, H.F. and Pulwarty, R.S. (eds) (1997) *Hurricanes: climate and socioeconomic impacts*. Springer, London.

Dyurgerov, M.B. and Meier, M.F. (2005) *Glaciers and the changing Earth system: a 2004 snapshot*. Institute of Arctic and Alpine Research Occasional Paper 58.

Gehrels, R. (2006) Sea level rise and coastal subsidence in SW England, *Report and Transactions of the Devonshire Association*, Vol. 138, pp. 25–42.

Gray, W.M. (1984) Atlantic seasonal hurricane frequency: Part 1: El Niño and 30 mb quasi-biennial oscillation influences. *Monthly Weather Review*, Vol. 112, pp. 1649–1668.

Gray, W.M. (1999) Past and future trends in US hurricanes and their destruction. In: Kinsman, J., Mathai, C.V., Mitchell, B., Holt, E. and Trexler, M. (eds) *Global Climate Change: science, policy and mitigation/adaptation strategies*, Vol. 1. Proceedings of the Second International Speciality Conference, pp. 61–66. Air and Waste Management Association, 13–15 October 1998, Washington, DC.

Hurrell, J.W. (1995) Decadal trends in the North Atlantic oscillation: regional temperature and precipitation. *Nature*, Vol. 269, pp. 676–679.

IPCC (Intergovernmental Panel on Climate Change) (2007) Climate change 2007: the science of climate change, report overview, contribution of Working Group 1 to the 4th assessment report of the Intergovernmental Panel on climate change. Cambridge University Press, New York. http://www.ipcc.ch.

Michaels, P. (1999) The discernible human influence on climate change: warming the frigid, reducing the variance, and modifying the models. In: Kinsman, J., Mathai, C.V., Mitchell, B., Holt, E. and Trexler, M. *Global Climate Change: science, policy and mitigation/adaptation strategies*, Vol. 1. Proceedings of the Second International Speciality Conference, pp. 234–268. Air and Waste Management Association, 13–15 October 1998, Washington, DC.

NOAA (1998) What is an El Niño? Online at: http://www.pmel.noaa.gov/toga-tao/el-nino-wstory.html, pp. 1–4.

O'Hare, G. (1999) Global warming and extreme weather; a cautionary note. *Geography*, Vol. 84, Issue 1, pp. 87–91.

Philander, S.G. (1989) El Niño, La Niña and the Southern oscillation, *International Geophysical Series* Vol. 46, R. Dmowska and J.R. Holton (eds), Academic Press, San Diego, CA.

Quinn, W.H. and Neal, V.T. (1992) The historical record of El Niño events, In: Bradley, R.S. and Jones, P.D. *Climate since 1500 AD*. Routledge: London and New York, pp. 623–648.

Ramillien, G., Lombard, A., Cazenave, A., Ivins, E.R., Llubes, M., Remy, F. and Biancale, R. (2006) Interannual variations of the mass balance of the Antarctica and Greenland ice sheets from GRACE. *Global and Planetary Change*, Vol. 53, Issue 3, pp. 198–208.

Rappaport, E.N. and Fernandez-Partagas, J. (1998) The deadliest Atlantic tropical cyclones, 1492–present. Available online at: http://www.nhc.noaa.gov/pastdeadlya2.html, 1–19.

Wilby, R.L., O'Hare, G. and Barnsley, N. (1997) The North Atlantic Oscillation and British Isles climate variability, 1865–1996. *Weather*, 52, pp. 266–276.

2

The contribution of marine spatial planning to implementing integrated coastal zone management

Fanny Douvere * *and Frank Maes*†
* *Marine Spatial Management Initiative, Intergovernmental Oceanographic Commission, UNESCO, France;* † *Maritime Institute at the Faculty of Law, Ghent University, Belgium*

Marine spatial planning is a novel approach to managing activities at sea and contributes to the implementation of the principles of integrated coastal zone management.

2.1   Introduction

Integrated coastal zone management (ICZM) aims at integrating the land and sea interface through rational planning of activities and better coherence between public and private activities that affect the use of the coastal zone. It should improve decision-making processes between the public authorities at national, regional and local levels by creating structured platforms for cooperation with stakeholders to discuss common policies and new developments. Governance failure and lack of statutory commitments are often cited as barriers for a successful application of ICZM by European Union (EU) member states. Others believe that the ICZM principles recommended by the Economic Community (EC) in 2002 are too vague to be successfully implemented or that ICZM is too much focused on local levels, ignoring the broader marine perspective. In this chapter it is argued that marine spatial planning (MSP) creates a new impetus for further implementing the ICZM principles by making them more tangible and operational.

2.2　Practice of integrated coastal zone management: fiction or reality in Europe?

In Europe and other countries there is already a long practice to strive to implement ICZM, with varying results (Cicin-Sain and Belfiore, 2005). The idea of ICZM, often called integrated coastal and ocean management (ICM) (Cicin-Sain and Knecht, 1998) or integrated management and sustainable development of coastal and marine areas, including exclusive economic zones (Chapter 17, Agenda 21) or integrated marine and coastal area management (IMCAM) under the Convention on Biological Diversity (CBD Decisions) already gained considerable international attention before the European Community recommended a set of eight principles for ICZM in 2002 (2002/413/EC). These principles were the result of the Commission's demonstration programme on ICZM that ran from 1996 to 1999, when a thematic expert group evaluated 35 projects. The ICZM principles are: (1) a broad overall perspective (thematic and geographic) that will take into account the interdependence and disparity of natural systems and human activities with an impact on coastal places (holistic approach); (2) a long-term perspective that will take into account the precautionary principle and the needs of present and future generations (future-oriented approach); (3) a gradual process that will facilitate adjustment as problems and knowledge develop, implying the need for a sound scientific basis concerning the evolution of coastal zones (adaptive approach); (4) local specificity and great diversity of European coastal zones, which will make it possible to respond to their practical needs with specific solutions and flexible mechanisms; (5) working with natural processes, respecting the carrying capacity of ecosystems, and conserving ecosystem structure and functioning, in order to maintain ecosystem services, and making human activities more environmentally friendly, socially responsible and economically sound in the long run (ecosystem approach); (6) involving all the parties concerned (economic and social partners, the organisations representing coastal zone residents, non-governmental organisations and business sector) in the management process (participatory approach); (7) support and involvement of relevant administrative bodies at national, regional and local level aiming at improved coordination; and (8) use of a combination of instruments designed to facilitate coherence between sectoral policy objectives and coherence between planning and management.

McKenna *et al.* (2008) divide these principles into three groups: (1) 'procedural' principles focusing on methods and procedures to advance ICZM (principles 7 and 8) that can be considered means rather than aims; (2) 'strategic' principles fitting in the sustainability discourse (principles 1, 2 and 5) and focusing on large spatial or temporal scales or considered as multi-sectoral; and (3) essentially 'local' principles to balance the strategic principles and fitting in the bottom-up approach, participation and consensus-based discourse (principles 3, 4 and 6). After a critical assessment of the ICZM principles, they conclude that the strategic and local principles are the core of the ICZM Recommendation. Their main critique for the poor functioning of the principles is due to their voluntary nature that leads to a non-prescriptive and non-prioritised focus of the principles and the lack of precise language. (McKenna *et al.*, 2008).

An evaluation in 2006 of the ICZM practice in the EU revealed successes in progress toward ICZM, as well as failures (Rupprecht Consult, 2006). Major failures were: (1) not all member states have implemented an ICZM national strategy or have an agreed ICZM policy; (2) unsatisfactory involvement of stakeholders; (3) threats to coastal areas are often seen on a local scale while they can be more effectively approached on a global scale, preferably a regional seas approach. Successes toward implementation of ICZM within the EU are: (1) new awareness and increased level of preparedness regarding long-term coastal challenges; (2) rethinking of traditional planning approaches by promoting sustainable management; (3) local ICZM-based processes created pressure to increase participation in decision making; (4) ICZM is considered the instrument to link terrestrial to marine legislation; (5) the proper implementation of ICZM can improve the livelihood and employment in coastal areas (Rupprecht, 2006). Although governance failure is considered a major obstacle in ICZM progress, the conclusions of the review also recognise that the principles of ICZM need to be made more operational and better communicated (Communication from the Commission, 2007).

Traditionally, ICZM focuses on a process-oriented approach that emphasises integration across agencies and across sectors. It has rarely addressed allocation of coastal space to achieve efficient economic development and effective protection of valuable ecological and biological areas. Meanwhile, marine spatial planning (MSP) has taken a different approach. While acknowledging the need for interagency and cross-sectoral integration, it has focused on determining a basis for the efficient and effective allocation of ocean space to economic activities and the designation of areas for conservation and protection. ICZM could use this new approach, with a focus on spatial planning, to produce more meaningful results.

This viewpoint was largely confirmed at the EU 'First European High-level Forum' on ICZM in 2002. The forum emphasised the possibility of using 'spatial planning integrated with sea-use planning, at the national, regional and local level, as a way to apply a holistic and dynamic perspective in ICZM in order to create a common vision of the sustainable development in the coastal zone and ensure dialogue and participation of local and regional stakeholders' (Spanish Presidency of the EU, 2002). The evaluation of ICZM in Europe, mentioned above, recognises MSP as one of the priority themes for the further implementation of ICZM in European coastal zones (Communication from the Commission, 2007).

2.3   Marine spatial planning: concept and application

2.3.1   *Defining marine spatial planning*

Despite numerous academic discussions and the application of MSP in various countries, no official or commonly accepted definition for MSP exists. Definitions and terms such as 'ecosystem-based marine zoning' (Sivas and Caldwell, 2008), 'marine spatial management' (Douvere, 2008), 'maritime spatial planning' (Commission of the European Communities, 2006, 2008), 'integrated maritime spatial planning' (Schultz-Zehden *et al.*, 2008) or 'marine planning' (Department for Environment, Food and Rural Affairs, 2008) can be found throughout the spatial planning literature and are not used consistently.

Essentially, MSP is a public process through which parts of three-dimensional marine spaces are analysed and allocated to specific uses or non-uses, to achieve ecological, economic and social objectives that are usually specified through the political process (Ehler and Douvere, 2007). It aims at 'creating and establishing a more rational organisation of the use of marine space and the interactions between its uses, to balance demands for development with the need to protect the environment, and to achieve social and economic objectives in an open and planned way' (Department for Environment, Food and Rural Affairs, 2008).

Marine spatial planning differs from current practice of allocating space in marine environments. Most countries already designate ocean and coastal space for certain uses or non-uses, such as exploitation of natural resources, marine protected areas, etc. This, however, does not necessarily lead to integrated management. Typically, current allocation of ocean space is done on a sector-by-sector basis, without much consideration of conflicts or compatibilities toward other sectors or the environment. Marine spatial planning, on the contrary, proposes a more comprehensive approach to the development and allocation of ocean space by considering the area as a whole and enabling governments to: (1) incorporate the heterogeneity of marine ecosystems into decision making in an operational manner; (2) influence the behaviour of humans and their activities in time and space; (3) make conflicts and compatibilities among human uses and between human use and the environment visible, and therefore tangible; and (4) guide single-sector management toward integrative decision making by visualising and projecting possible futures (Douvere, 2008).

2.3.2   Use and application of marine spatial planning

Practice and interest in MSP have risen considerably in the last years. Marine spatial planning, particularly its multi-objective approach is a new paradigm for the management of activities at sea. Early forms of MSP were used to manage marine protected areas. Some well-known examples include Australia's Great Barrier Reef Marine Park (GBRMP) (Australian Government, 2008) and the Florida Keys National Marine Sanctuary in the United States (United States Department of Commerce, 2007). Both have a long-standing experience in the application of MSP, in which different spaces with varying levels of access for use are identified, ranging from multiple-use zones where most offshore activity is allowed, to 'no-use zones' where virtually no use is permitted. The focus of these early plans was mainly to ensure that conservation objectives were not impaired by human activities.

Recently, a more multiple-objective approach to MSP has been taken, particularly in Europe. Belgium implemented a MSP system that covers both its territorial sea and exclusive economic zone (Calewaert *et al.*, 2005). Marine spatial planning in Belgium aims at achieving economic, social and ecological objectives (sustainable management) for human activities taking place at sea and for the protection and conservation of biological diversity. These objectives, together with past and ongoing research projects (Maes *et al.*, 2005a, 2005b; Calewaert and Maes, 2007), provided the basis for a Master Plan for MSP that has been implemented incrementally since 2003 (Douvere *et al.*, 2007; Plasman, 2008).

A similar approach has been taken in the Netherlands, Germany and Norway, and is underway in the United Kingdom and Sweden. In 2005, the Netherlands developed an overarching spatial policy for the Dutch part of the North Sea. The primary objective of the spatial policy was to enhance the economic importance of the North Sea and maintain and develop its ecological and landscape features. Implementation of the spatial policy is further defined and described in the 'Integrated Management Plan for the North Sea 2015' (Interdepartmental Directors Consultative Committee, 2005) where the aim of MSP is translated into the need for a healthy, safe and profitable sea. Currently, the Dutch MSP initiatives are being revised to adapt to the effects of sea level rise and to provide a better legal basis for MSP in the future.

In April 2006, the Norwegian government launched its integrated management plan for the Barents Sea and the sea areas off the Lofoten Islands (Royal Norwegian Ministry of the Environment, 2006). The management plan aims to establish holistic and ecosystem-based management of the activities in the area. It sets the overall framework for both existing and new activities in these waters to facilitate the co-existence of different industries, particularly the fisheries industry, maritime transport and petroleum industry (Olsen *et al.*, 2007). Similar plans are being developed for the Norwegian Sea and the Norwegian part of the North Sea.

In 2007, the German Federal Maritime and Hydrographic Agency drafted multiple-use marine spatial plans for the German exclusive economic zones in the North Sea and the Baltic Sea. The multiple objective approach to MSP in Germany is largely reflected in the guidelines that form the basis for spatial development in these zones. They include: (1) securing and strengthening maritime traffic; (2) strengthening economic capacity by orderly spatial development and optimisation of the use of space; (3) promotion of offshore wind energy use in accordance with the Federal Government's sustainability strategy; (4) long-term safeguarding and use of special characteristics and potential in the exclusive economic zone through reversibility of uses, economic use of space and priority for marine-specific uses; and (5) securing natural resources by avoiding disruptions to and pollution of the marine environment (Federal Maritime and Hydrographic Agency, 2008).

Both the United Kingdom and Sweden are preparing a statutory basis for the development of MSP. On 3 December 2008, HM the Queen of the United Kingdom announced that the current Parliamentary session, ending in autumn 2009, will include a Marine and Coastal Access Bill (formerly known as the Marine Bill released in April 2008). This announcement is a great stimulus for the necessary parliamentary procedures toward final approval of the Bill (Defra, 2009). The Bill introduces a statutory basis for marine plans for the English, Scottish, Welsh and Northern Ireland inshore and offshore regions and identifies marine planning authorities. Maintenance and protection of ecosystems are considered key components of future spatial planning initiatives, but are part of the broader aims of obtaining best value from different uses of marine resources (Defra, 2008). The UK planning system will encompass all activities and will be directed to deliver sustainable development by facilitating proactive decision making.

Recently, the Swedish government published the findings of its inquiry on how the planning and management of the Swedish marine environment can be improved, both nationally and together with other countries. The inquiry proposes the introduction of a new planning system, based on marine spatial plans, similar to the comprehensive plans for land areas. (Swedish Ministry of the Environment, 2008). Multiple-use MSP is also emerging in other parts of the world, including in the context of Australia's marine bioregional planning (Australian Government, 2009), Canada's 'Eastern Scotian Shelf Management Plan' (Fisheries and Oceans Canada, 2007), China's Sea Use Management Act (Li, 2006) and recently in the USA as part of a newly released Presidential memorandum that requires the development of coastal and marine spatial planning framework (US White House, 2009).

2.4 Making ICZM operational through marine spatial planning

Generally, the goals of MSP are not different from those of ICZM. Both MSP and ICZM propose to tackle problems inherent to single-sector management and the fragmentation in jurisdiction among levels of government and the land-water interface.

By focusing on the spatial and temporal aspects of management, MSP has been more pragmatic in its approach to tackle such problems. Despite variations in detail and inclusiveness, marine spatial plans typically identify and visualise where offshore uses occur and how they relate to the physical, biological and ecological composition of the planning area. Often, such plans also indicate conflicts and compatibilities among offshore uses and between uses and the environment in the planning area. The development of such spatial plans for an entire region enables the visualisation of the use of space and its implications, which, in turn, provides guidance to a range of decision makers, each responsible for a particular sector, activity or concern. Fisheries managers, for examples, will gain insight in the conflicts and compatibilities their management plans have with plans for offshore renewable energy initiatives, marine protected area management plans, and vice versa.

This experience of using spatial planning for ocean management, as applied in MSP, seems to provide a feasible method that could help making at least some of the principles of ICZM more operational. The strategic principles of ICZM, for example – as defined by McKenna *et al.* (2008) and described earlier in this chapter – could be made more operational by defining what they imply in space and time. Below, a short analysis is given of how this is being done in MSP.

2.4.1   A 'holistic approach' in marine spatial planning

The concept of a 'holistic approach' is often used in medical disciplines where it refers to the treatment of a disease by taking into consideration every part of the body to bring the full body into balance. In general terms, a holistic approach relates to, or is concerned with, complete systems rather than with the details or parts that make up the whole. When applied to ocean and coastal management, a holistic approach refers to taking a broad overall perspective, both geographic and thematic.

Geographically, a holistic approach implies that the boundaries of the management area are not based on political or administrative considerations only, but instead are also meaningful from an ecological perspective, e.g. consider the system as a whole. It also implies that the boundaries do not delimit the influences of exogenous marine processes on the management area. Both Australia's future 'Marine Bioregional Plans' (Australian Government, 2009a) and Canada's 'Eastern Scotian Shelf Integrated Management Plan' (Fisheries and Oceans Canada, 2007) apply a holistic approach in this sense. Both countries have defined marine regions or, alternatively, ecologically based planning and management units, on the basis of physical and ecosystem characteristics, including hydrographic, oceanographic and bio-geographic features, rather than relying on political or administrative boundaries only. To date, exogenous influences are incorporated only in the 'Great Barrier Reef Marine Park Zoning Plan' (Great Barrier Reef Marine Park Authority, 2003) and the 'Florida Keys National Marine Sanctuary Management Plan' (United States Department of Commerce, 2007). Both plans specify where activities occur outside the management area that are likely to influence the success of MSP within the area.

On the contrary, European MSP initiatives have set their boundaries on the basis of political and legal considerations, not ecological ones, and should, therefore, not be considered holistic from a geographic standpoint. In European seas, coastal states are closely bordered next to and in front of each other. Consequently, applying a holistic approach based on ecosystem considerations automatically requires trans-boundary cooperation that complicates the process of MSP. In the context of the EU Marine Strategy Directive (Commission of the European Communities, 2005) and EU Maritime Policy (Commission of the European Communities, 2006), discussion is ongoing how to facilitate such trans-boundary cooperation.

Thematically, a holistic approach implies that management is not focused on a single concern, sector, activity or species, but instead considers the interdependence and disparity of the system as a whole, including all human activities affecting it. From a thematic perspective, most MSP initiatives apply a holistic approach in the sense that they do not focus on a single sector, activity, species or concern. As discussed in the previous section, marine spatial plans in Europe are established to achieve multiple objectives, not to tackle just one concern such as, for example, nature protection or aquaculture only. In all four countries previously mentioned (Belgium, the Netherlands, Norway and Germany), MSP started with an analysis of the current conditions of the area that included ecological and biological features as well as human use and its impact in the area. This 'stocktake' of current conditions provided the necessary basis to determine how, where and when multiple objectives could be achieved. Essentially, through spatial planning, a range of multiple objectives – usually set through political processes – have been translated and interpreted in time and space. By doing so, they have been made operational and tangible.

A closer look at the focus of the plans illustrate that some differences can be emphasised. First, although marine spatial plans tend to be holistic they are not necessarily all-inclusive. Fisheries activities, for example, are often not addressed in current MSP initiatives. One explanation might lie in the way authority for fisheries management is distributed in various countries. For example, fisheries management has become an exclusive domain of the EU and is regulated through the Common Fisheries Policy (CFP) (European Council, 2002). No unilateral actions from member states are possible with regard to fisheries management that affects other member states (Maes, 2008). Other interpretations refer to the difficulties to incorporate fishing activities, needs and impacts into MSP because of their dynamic nature (Degnbol and Wilson, 2008) and lack of data. The latter might only be a temporary problem since new data sources (e.g. VMS) will contribute in identifying principal areas for fisheries (Fock, 2008). Second, some spatial plans give a larger focus to some components or concern. The German spatial plans have been designed with the attempt to achieve multiple objectives while giving a top priority to a few uses: offshore wind energy and maritime transport. This priority is largely reflected in the Act upon which the German spatial plans are based. The Act provides the German Maritime Transport and Hydrographic Agency the authority to develop spatial plans for the exclusive economic zone, while providing only a non-binding advisory role to other agencies, including the ones responsible for nature conservation (Raumordnungsgezetz, 2006).

2.4.2 A 'long-term perspective' in marine spatial planning

Spatial planning is, in general, a future-oriented, proactive exercise that focuses on planning for activities in the future, not simply documenting present activities and conditions, and extrapolating current trends (Rydin, 2003). Achieving sustainable development of sea uses is a key component of coastal and ocean management, while establishing a long-term vision is considered as one of the major functions (Cicin-Sain and Knecht, 1998). A proactive planning approach is necessary for a variety of reasons. Many coastal and ocean places face common challenges, such as potential impacts of climate change. At the same time, coastal and ocean areas have become significantly attractive for the development of some form of renewable energy that can contribute to the reduction of CO_2 emissions. Both climate change and renewable energy, along with growing coastal populations, are likely to have a considerable impact on the allocation of ocean space in the future (Communication from the Commission, 2007). Renewable energy, for example, increases claims for ocean space and potential conflict between uses and environmental protection. Climate change, on the other hand, is likely to affect the distribution of living species, and thereby influence locations and spaces needed for protection. The added value of MSP in this regard is its ability to create sea use scenarios that incorporate such assumptions and specify the spatial implications of alternative visions that are produced on the basis of certain goals and objectives.

A comprehensive method for developing alternative 'spatial sea use scenarios' has been proposed in Belgium to set the stage for a spatial structure plan for the Belgian part of the North Sea (Maes *et al.*, 2005a, 2005b). The concept of 'spatial sea use scenario' can be defined as 'a vision that projects the future use of ocean space based on a core set of goals and objectives and assumptions about the future'. By developing spatial sea use scenarios, future possibilities and conditions of the sea area are visualised in a clear way, in order to make well-grounded choices for the future. The method defined six steps, essential for the development of alternative MSP scenarios, including (1) defining current trends and demands for space and conditions; (2) defining key values of the marine area; (3) defining strategic objectives and goals for the marine area; (4) identifying general spatial and temporal constraints (e.g., on the basis of existing regulation, physical characteristics or political opportunities); (5) developing alternative spatial use scenarios, each reflecting a priority set of goals, objectives and values; and (6) defining the significance and implications of each spatial scenario for the different functions and activities in the marine area (Maes *et al.*, 2005a, 2005b). Two additional steps are necessary for this alternative spatial use scenario to guide a long-term and pro-active MSP process, e.g. (1) an evaluation of each scenario that interprets the costs and benefits of each scenario; and (2) the selection of a desired spatial use scenario and the measures to implement it.

In the context of the Dutch 'Integrated Management Plan for the North Sea 2015', efforts are made to underpin new decision making about the future use of space with a better, scientifically sound, basis. This is being done through an initial analysis of current and projected economic values of offshore activities (for a period of 2005–15) and its consequences in terms of spatial demands and impacts (Ministerie van Verkeer en Waterstaat, 2008). Additionally, three alternative estimates have been made of the potential impact of sea level rise in the Netherlands until the year 2100. Results of this work will be incorporated in the evaluation and adaptation of existing spatial plans and guide future management decisions about the use of space in the Dutch part of the North Sea.

2.4.3   An 'ecosystem approach' in marine spatial planning

The Convention on Biological Diversity defines the ecosystem approach as 'a strategy for integrated management of land, water, and living resources that promotes conservation and sustainable use in an equitable way. The ecosystem approach is based on the application of appropriate scientific methodologies focused on levels of biological organisation, which encompass the essential processes, functions and interactions among organisms and their environment' (Convention on Biological Diversity, 2000). Although the ecosystem approach means different things to different people, it essentially requires working with natural processes in ways that respect the carrying capacity of ecosystems and conserve ecosystem structure and functioning to maintain ecosystem services.

Australia is developing a comprehensive process to apply an ecosystem approach through MSP, called marine bioregional planning (MBP). Australia introduced the concept of MBP to enable better protection of the marine environment, conserve biodiversity and deliver greater certainty for industry and decision makers on marine conservation priorities (Australian Government, 2009). The MSP process, bioregional plan identifies: (1) conservation priorities for the regions; (2) appropriate measures available to address conservation priorities; (3) sites to include in a network of representative marine protected areas (MPAs) for the region; and (4) social and economic implications of proposed conservation measures, including MPAs. The development of the bioregional plan contains three steps: (1) the compilation of a bioregional profile that reflects the understanding of the ecology of the planning area and provides the necessary ecological and biophysical information base for the bioregional plan; (2) the compilation of a draft bioregional plan in which assessments are made of threats posed by current and emerging activities, and guidance for future decisions regarding threats; and (3) the development of the bioregional plan itself that identifies priorities for action and strategic guidance for decision makers.

The process to underpin MSP with an ecosystem approach is best illustrated in the bioregional profile that forms the basis of the bioregional plan. It includes four key steps. The bioregions are identified on the basis of their: (1) geomorphology; (2) oceanography; (3) biological communities; (4) ecosystem processes, including benthic productivity, recruitment and food web interactions for a range of species; and (5) key ecological features, including resident, breeding and nursery areas for protected species. Second, for each of the bioregions, components of marine biodiversity and heritage were identified and recognised as 'conservation values' by the Australian government. Conservation values refer to elements that are either specifically protected under Australian law (mainly listed marine species, but also historic shipwrecks) or key ecological features that were identified in the region through analysis. These conservation values form the underlying basis for decision making about proposed economic development or ongoing activities. Particularly, the key ecological features guide decisions about whether an action is likely to have a significant impact on the marine environment or whether the site needs to be included in a network of MPAs. Key ecological features of the marine environment are determined on the basis of criteria such as: (1) species, group of species or community with a regionally important ecological role (e.g. a predator, prey that affects a large biomass or number of other marine species); (2) species, group of species or community that is nationally or regionally important for biodiversity; (3) an area or habitat that is nationally or regionally important for enhanced or high productivity, aggregations of marine life, biodiversity and endemism; or (4) a unique seafloor feature with known or presumed ecological properties of regional significance. Third, a set of goals and principles is developed to guide the identification of a representative system of MPAs. These goals and principles aim to maximise conservation outcomes and refer to components of the coastal and marine environment (depth ranges, benthic/demersal biological features, types of seafloor features, etc.) that need to be part of the MPA network. Fourth, an analysis is made of the nature and scope of human activities that take place in the region. Special attention is paid to Aboriginal people and their relationship with offshore activities in the region. Efforts are also made to encompass the socio-economic value of human activity in the region (Australian Government, 2007, 2009b).

A somewhat similar approach has been taken in the Canadian 'Eastern Scotian Shelf Integrated Management Plan'. Prior to the development of Canada's plan, analysis and mapping of physical characteristics (e.g., circulation patterns, temperature, salinity, etc.), biological features of the Shelf, significant natural areas in the region, and the potential impacts of human activities (in particular fisheries and oil and gas exploitation) has been undertaken (Breeze *et al.*, 2002; Zwanenburg *et al.*, 2006).

Also in Europe, initiatives to underpin decisions with an ecosystem approach have emerged. In Belgium, for example, a scientific study on the biological valuation of the North Sea was completed. The study resulted in a set of maps showing the intrinsic biological value of different sub-areas within the Belgian part of the North Sea (Derous *et al.*, 2007). The maps were developed using available spatial data for macro-benthos and seabirds and, to a lesser extent, data on the spatial distribution of demersal fish and epi-benthos. These marine biological valuation maps are considered a unique and indispensable tool to develop objective and scientifically sound spatial plans. Although they have been developed after the 'Master Plan for the Belgian part of the North Sea' had been implemented, it is likely these biological valuation maps will provide a basis for spatial management actions in the future. As mentioned earlier, however, a more challenging task at hand in Europe is to connect marine spatial plans adjacent to one another. In various cases, plans developed at the national level are not embedded in the broader perspective of the North Sea ecosystem as a whole.

2.5   Conclusion

In Europe, ICZM has been practised with varying results. Although governance failure and lack of statutory commitments are often cited as barriers for successful implementation of ICZM, a number of assessments also recognise that the ICZM principles, recommended by the EC in 2002, are too vague and need to be made more operational and better communicated.

Since its inception, ICZM has focused primarily on a process-oriented approach, emphasising integration across agencies and sectors. It has rarely addressed allocation of coastal space to achieve its goals. Meanwhile, management in the marine environment has taken a different approach through the use of MSP. By focusing on the spatial and temporal aspects of management, MSP has been more pragmatic in tackling similar problems as those encountered in ICZM.

Multiple-use MSP, as is currently developing in Europe, Australia and Canada, seems to use at least certain ICZM principles. Application of the strategic principles of ICZM, e.g. those related to a holistic approach, long-term perspective and an ecosystem approach, could learn from the current experience with MSP. A holistic approach, for example, could be made specific and operational by determining what it implies in time and space. Examples can be found in Canada's Eastern Scotian Shelf Integrated Management Plan and the multiple-use marine spatial plans in Belgium, Norway, the Netherlands and Germany. A long-term perspective in MSP has been proposed in Belgium through the concept of 'spatial sea use scenarios' and is currently further evolving in the Netherlands. Such spatial sea use scenarios visualise future possibilities and conditions, and provide the basis and guidance for well-grounded decision making. Australia is developing a comprehensive process to apply an ecosystem approach through MSP. Results start to be apparent in the form of its bioregional profiles that are being designed for its marine regions.

ICZM could take a similar approach and use spatial planning to make its principles more tangible and operational by better defining what they imply in space and time.

Acknowledgements

Acknowledgement is expressed to Charles Ehler, co-principal investigator of UNESCO's Marine Spatial Planning Initiative (Intergovernmental Oceanographic Commission), for his insightful comments on earlier drafts of this text. Fanny Douvere expresses her grateful acknowledgement to the Gordon and Betty Moore Foundation and the David and Lucile Packard Foundation for their support to the UNESCO initiative on Ecosystem-based Marine Spatial Management. Dr Frank Maes is grateful to the Belgian Federal Science Policy (BELSPO) for the financial support of the GAUFRE research project 'Towards a Spatial Structure Plan for the Sustainable Management of the Sea' (2003–05).

References

Australian Government (2008) Great Barrier Reef Marine Park Authority. Available online at: http://www.gbrmpa.gov.au

Australian Government (2003) Great Barrier Reef Marine Park Authority. Great Barrier Reef Marine Park Zoning Park 2003. Available online at: http://www.gbrmpa.gov.au

Australian Government (2007) The South-west marine bioregional plan. Bioregional profile. A description of the ecosystems, conservation values, and uses of the south-west marine region.

Australian Government (2009a) Marine bioregional planning. Available online at: http://www.environment.gov.au/coasts/mbp/index.html

Australian Government (2009b) The South-east Regional Marine Plan. Available online at: http://www.environment.gov.au/coasts/mbp/south-east/previous-process.html

Bogaert, D. and Maes, F. (eds) (2008) *Who Rules the Coast? Policy Processes in Belgian MPAs and Beach Spatial Planning*, Ghent, Academia Press.

Bouamrane, M. (ed.) (2006) Biodiversity and stakeholders: concertation itineraries. *Biosphere reserves, technical notes 1.* UNESCO, Paris.

Breeze, H., Fenton, D.G., Rutherford, R.J. and Silva M.A. (2002) The Scotian Shelf: An ecological overview for ocean planning. *Fisheries and Oceans Canada.*

Calewaert, J.-B., Lescrauwaet, A.-K., Mees, J., Seys, J., Hostens, K., Redant, F., Raemaekers, M., Demaré, W., Belpaeme, K., Maelfait, H., Kyramarios, M., Tak, P., Maes, F., Overloop, S. and Peeters, B. (2005) Kust en Zee. Te weinig vis, teveel vervuiling, in VAN STEERTEGEM (red), MIRA-T 2005. Milieu- en natuurrapport Vlaanderen-Thema's. Leuven, Lannoo Campus, pp. 145–159.

Calewaert, J.-B. and Maes, F. (ed.) (2007) *Science and Sustainable Management of the North Sea: Belgian Case Studies*, Ghent, Academia Press.

CBD Decisions: Decision IV/5 on Conservation and sustainable use of marine and coastal biological diversity, including a programme of work CBD Handbook, 464–474; Decision VII/5 Marine and coastal biological diversity, UNEP/CBD/COP/7 at http://www.cbd.int/doc/decisions/ COP-07-dec-en.pdf; Decision VIII/22 on the implementation of IMCAM, UNEP/CBD/COP8, available online at: http://www.cbd.int/doc/decisions/COP-08-dec-en.pdf

Cicin-Sain, B. and Belfiore, S. (2005) Linking marine protected areas to integrated coastal and ocean management: a review of theory and practice. *Ocean and Coastal Management*, pp. 847–868.

Cicin-Sain, B. and Knecht R. (1998) *Integrated Coastal and Ocean Management. Concepts and Practices*, Washington, DC, Island Press.

Commission of the European Communities (2005) *Thematic strategy on the protection and conservation of the marine environment.* Communication from the Commission to the Council and the European Parliament. COM(2005)504 final, Brussels.

Commission of the European Communities (2006) Green paper: *Towards a future maritime policy for the union: A European vision for the oceans and seas.* COM(2006)275 final, Brussels, 7 June.

Commission of the European Communities (2007) Blue Paper: *An Integrated Maritime Policy for the European Union.* COM(2007)575, Brussels, 10 October.

Commission of the European Communities (2008) Communication from the Commission. *Roadmap for Maritime Spatial Planning: Achieving Common Principles in the EU.* COM(2008)791, Brussels, 25 November.

Communication from the Commission (2007) Report to the European Parliament and the Council: *An evaluation of integrated coastal zone management (ICZM) in Europe.* Commission of the European Communities. COM(2007) 308 final, Brussels, 7 June.

Convention on Biological Diversity (2000) COP 5, Decision V/6 of the Conference of the Parties to the Convention on Biological Diversity, Nairobi, 15–26 May.

Day, J. (2008) The need and practice of monitoring, evaluating and adapting marine planning and management. Lessons from the Great Barrier Reef. *Marine Policy*, Vol. 32, pp. 823–831.

Day, V., Paximos, R., Emmett, J., Wright, A. and Goecker, M. (2007) The Marine Planning Framework for South Australia: a new ecosystem-based zoning policy for marine management. *Marine Policy*, Vol. 32, pp. 535–543.

Degnbol, D. and Wilson, D. (2008) Spatial planning on the North Sea: A case of cross-scale linkages. *Marine Policy*, Vol. 32, pp. 189–200.

Department for Environment, Food and Rural Affairs (Defra) (2008) Draft Marine Bill. April. Available online at: http://www.defra.gov.uk/corporate/consult/marinebill/

Department for Environment, Food and Rural Affairs (Defra) (2009) Marine and Costal Access Bill. Available online at: http://www.defra.gov.uk/marine/legislation/index.htm

Derous, S., Verfaillie, E., Van Lancker, V., Courtens, W., Stienen, E., Hostens, K., Moulaert, I., Hillewaert, H., Mees, J., Deneudt, K., Deckers, P., Cuvelier, D., Vincx, M. and Degraer, S. (2007) A biological valuation map for the Belgian part of the North Sea. BWZee. Research in the framework of the BSP programme 'Sustainable management of the sea'. Belgian Federal Science Policy Office, Brussels.

Douvere, F. (2008) The importance of marine spatial planning in advancing ecosystem-based sea use management. *Marine Policy*, Vol. 32, pp. 762–771.

Douvere, F. and Ehler, C. (2009) New perspectives on sea use management: initial findings from European experience with marine spatial planning. *Journal for Environmental Management*, Vol. 90, pp. 77–88.

Douvere, F. and Ehler, C. Ecosystem-based marine spatial management: an evolving paradigm for the management of coastal and marine places. *Ocean Yearbook*, Vol. 23.

Douvere, F., Maes, F., Vanhulle, A. and Schrijvers, J. (2007) The role of marine spatial planning in sea use management: the Belgian case. *Marine Policy*, Vol. 31, pp. 181–191.

Ehler, C. and Douvere, F. (2007) Visions for a Sea Change. Report of the *First International Workshop on Marine Spatial Planning*. IOC-IMCAM Dossier 3, UNESCO, Paris.

European Parliament and the Council (2002) Recommendation concerning the implementation of integrated coastal zone management in Europe, 2002/413/EC, Brussels, 30 May 2002, OJ L 148 of 06.06.2002.

European Council. Regulation of the European Council 2371/2002 of 20 December 2002 on the conservation and sustainable exploitation of fisheries resources under the Common Fisheries Policy, OJ·L 358 of 31 December 2002.

European Parliament and the Council (2008) Directive 2008/56/EC of 17 June 2008 establishing a framework for community action in the field of marine environmental policy (Marine Strategy Framework Directive). OJ L 164/19 of 25.06.2008.

Federal Maritime and Hydrographic Agency (2008) Marine spatial plan for the German exclusive economic zone in the North and Baltic Seas, June 2008. Available online at: http://www.bsh.de/en/The_BSH/Notifications/Spatial_Planning_in_the_German_EEZ.jsp

Fisheries and Oceans Canada (2007) *Eastern Scotian Shelf Integrated Ocean Management Plan*, Dartmouth, Nova Scotia, Canada.

Fock, H.O. (2008) Fisheries in the context of marine spatial planning: defining principal areas for fisheries in the German EEZ. *Marine Policy*, Vol. 32, pp. 728–739.

Gilliland, P. and Laffoley, D. Key elements and steps in the process of developing ecosystem-based marine spatial planning. *Marine Policy*, Vol. 32, pp. 787–796.

Government of Canada (2005) *Canada's Federal Marine Protected Areas Strategy*, Ottawa, Canada.

Holling, C. (ed.) (1978) *Adaptive Environmental Assessment and Management*, Wiley, Chichester.

Interdepartmental Directors' Consultative Committee (2005) Integrated Management Plan for the North Sea 2015 (IMPNS 2015), The Netherlands.

Li, H. (2006) The impacts and implications of the legal framework for sea use planning and management in China. *Ocean and Coastal Management*, Vol. 49, pp. 717–726.

Lindeboom, H., Geurts van Kessel, J. and Berkenbosch, L. (2005) *Areas with Special Ecological Values on the Dutch Continental Shelf*, Ministerie van Verkeer en Waterstaat. Rijkswaterstaat, The Netherlands.

Maes, F. (2008) The international legal framework for marine spatial planning. *Marine Policy*, Vol. 32, pp. 797–810.

Maes, F., Schrijvers, J. and Vanhulle, A. (eds) (2005a) A flood of space. *Belgian Science Policy*.

Maes, F., Schrijvers, J., Van Lancker, V., Verfaillie, E., Degraer, S., Derous, S., De Wachter, B., Volckaert, A., Vanhulle, A., Vandenabeele, P., Cliquet, A., Douvere, F., Lambrecht, J. and Makgill, R. (2005b) Towards a spatial structure plan for sustainable management of the North Sea (GAUFRE). Belgian Science Policy; Brussels. Report and maps on http://www.belspo.be_publications_final reports_mixed actions

McKenna, J., Cooper, A. and O'Hagan, A.M. (2008) Managing by principle: a critical analysis of the European principles of integrated coastal zone management (ICZM). *Marine Policy*, Vol. 32, pp. 941–955.

Ministerie van Verkeer en Waterstaat (2008) *Verkenning van economische enruimtelijke ontwikkelingen op de Noordzee*, The Netherlands.

Olsen, E., Gjosaeter, H., Rottingen, I., Dommasnes, A., Fossum, P. and Sandberg, P. (2007) The Norwegian ecosystem-based management plan for the Barents Sea. *ICES Journal of Marine Science*, Vol. 64, pp. 599–602.

Plasman, C. (2008) Implementing marine spatial planning: A policy perspective. *Marine Policy*, Vol. 32, pp. 811–815.

Pomeroy, R. and Douvere, F. (2008) The engagement of stakeholders in the marine spatial planning process. *Marine Policy*, Vol. 32, pp. 816–822.

Raumordnungsgezetz (ROG) vom (2006) 18 August 1997 (BGB1. IS. 2081, 2102), zuletzt geändert durch Artikel 10 des Gesetzes vom 9 December (BGB1. IS 2833).

Royal Norwegian Ministry of the Environment (2006) *Integrated Management of the Marine Environment of the Barents Sea and the Sea Areas off the Lofoten Islands*, Oslo, Norway.

Rupprecht Consult – *Forschung Urban and Environmental Planning in the UK*, Palgrave Macmillan, New York.

Schultz-Zehden, A., Gee, K. and Scibior, K. (2008) *Handbook on Integrated Maritime Spatial Planning*, INTERREG IIIB CADSES PlanCoast Project, Berlin.

Sivas, D. and Caldwell, M. (2008) A new vision for californian ocean governance: comprehensive ecosystem-based marine zoning. *Stanford Environmental Law Journal*, Vol. 27, pp. 209–270.

Spanish Presidency of the EU (2002) First European ICZM High Level Forum on Community Strategies for Integrated Coastal Zone Management, La Vila Jolosa, Alicante, Spain, 18–20 April.

St Martin, K. and Hall-Arber, M. (2008) The missing layer: geo-technologies, communities, and implications for marine spatial planning. *Marine Policy*, Vol. 32, pp. 779–786.

Swedish Ministry of the Environment (2008) The marine environment inquiry. *Better management of the marine environment*. Sweden, June 2008.

United States Department of Commerce, National Oceanic and Atmospheric Administration, National Ocean Service and National Marine Sanctuary Program (2007) *Florida Keys National Marine Sanctuary revised management plan*, United States of America.

United States White House (2009) Memorandum for heads of executive departments and agencies on national policy for the oceans, coasts and great lakes, Washington DC.

Zwanenburg, K., Bundy, A., Strain, P., Bowen, W., Breeze, H., Campana, S., Hannah, C., Head, E. and Gordon, D. (2006) Implications of Ecosystem Dynamics for the Integrated Management of the Eastern Scotian Shelf. *Fisheries and Oceans*, Canada.

3

River catchment contributions to the coastal zone

Mick J. Whelan, Sue M. White and Nicholas J.K. Howden
Natural Resources Department, School of Applied Sciences, Cranfield University, UK

River catchments deliver water, sediment, chemical pollutants, carbon and nutrients to the coastal zone. The impact of this delivery on coastal environments depends on the relative magnitude of these fluxes compared with other sources (and sinks). Factors such as river flow regime, pollutant loading, and land and river management practices are often important. Impacts will also depend on the relative magnitudes of coastal zone factors such as tidal range, estuary type and coastal currents (which will influence transport and mixing). This chapter considers a number of potential catchment influences on the coastal zone using an international set of examples to illustrate the possible role of management intervention. The scope is principally limited to land upstream of the tidal limit, although estuarine processes are briefly considered because they can be important modifiers for the magnitude and temporal patterns of material fluxes from the catchment system. After a brief introduction, the chapter discusses generic controls over river flow regimes and the transport of sediment, nitrogen, phosphorus, carbon, metals, organic contaminants and micro-organisms to the coastal zone. The influence of human activities (such as land use and river management) is discussed in relation to potential environmental problems arising and to the array of solutions available, including some of the challenges we are likely to face as a consequence of climate change.

3.1   Introduction and scope
River catchments deliver water, sediment, chemical pollutants, carbon and nutrients to the coastal zone. This delivery is an essential component of global biogeochemical cycling and has shaped the development

Coastal zone management
978-0-7277-3641-1

of estuarine deltas and food production throughout human history. There are many examples (the Nile, Ebro and Danube) of civilisations which have developed on fertile delta regions formed from the supply of sediments from river basins and many contemporary nations, for example Vietnam, Bangladesh, Egypt and the Shanghai region of China, are still heavily dependent on agricultural production from deltas.

The extent of the impact of fluvial fluxes (water and dissolved and particulate material) on coastal environments depends on the relative magnitude of these fluxes compared with other sources (and sinks). Factors such as river flow regime, pollutant loading, and land and river management practices are often important. Impacts will also depend on the relative magnitudes of coastal zone factors such as tidal range, estuary type and coastal currents (which will influence transport and mixing). It is clear that human activities (such as land use and management) have the potential to enhance fluvial fluxes of carbon, nutrients and sediment (Raymond *et al.*, 2008). In some parts of the world this has led to problems in the coastal zone such as algal blooms in the Gulf of Mexico which have been attributed, at least in part, to hydrochemical fluxes from the Mississippi River.

This chapter considers a number of potential catchment influences on the coastal zone using an international set of examples to illustrate the possible role of management intervention. Our scope is principally limited to land upstream of the tidal limit, although estuarine processes are briefly considered because they can be important modifiers for the magnitude and temporal patterns of material fluxes from the catchment system.

3.2   Introduction to the catchment system

The river catchment is a fundamental unit of landscape organisation and process integration. The term is often used interchangeably with 'river basin' and 'watershed'. Climatic, hydrological, ecological, edaphic and biogeochemical processes interact within the catchment boundary, and contribute to the magnitude and temporal patterns of material fluxes to the catchment outlet. The influences of land management, industrial activity and other human interventions are also integrated at the catchment scale.

River catchments are usually topographically-delineated such that water and material fluxes can be accounted for within a given, well-defined boundary. This is shown schematically in Fig. 3.1. Inputs, such as water or nutrients arriving at the land surface within the

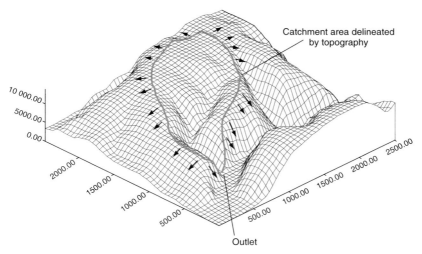

Fig. 3.1 Schematic outline of a catchment delineated topographically. Water and material fluxes should be accountable within the catchment boundary

catchment boundary, sometimes known as the watershed or divide, have the potential to be transferred to the catchment outlet. Inputs falling outwith this boundary are moved elsewhere and become part of the budgets for adjacent areas. A catchment may be defined at any scale from small headwater valleys to continental river basins. In general, the larger the area drained, the greater the potential for spatial and temporal integration and the lower the potential for activities with limited spatial and temporal extent to influence overall hydrological and water quality responses at the outlet.

Water is the main vehicle for material transfer (both in the solid phase and as solutes) from land to water and then subsequently through the river network to the coastal zone. As water moves through the various stores of the hydrological cycle, it reacts chemically and interacts physically with its surroundings (e.g. vegetation, soil and rock matrices) picking up and/or depositing materials along its path. Particles are entrained and/or deposited, while solutes are released, retained or transformed. These fluxes occur naturally, but are supplemented by human activity by way of, for example, the emission of wastes (e.g. sewage effluent), mining operations, the use of synthetic organic chemicals (e.g. pesticides) and the modification of biogeochemical cycles in agriculture (Fig. 3.2). Furthermore, human activity can significantly modify the hydrological regime through water abstraction, waste water discharge, damming, inter-catchment water transfers, or by

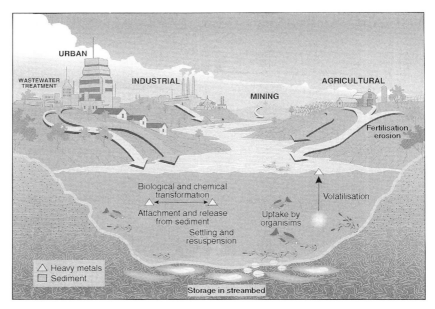

Fig. 3.2 The catchment system illustrating many of the potential sources of surface water pollutants and some of the processes which can affect their fate (from Meade, 1995)

modification of land surfaces by urban and industrial development (e.g. construction using impermeable surfaces such as concrete and tarmac results in reduced infiltration). So, fluxes at the catchment outlet result from an integration of both natural processes and human activities.

Often, by observing inputs and outputs at the catchment scale, we can construct material 'budgets' (e.g. Likens and Borman, 1995) and gain an integrated understanding of the processes operating, including the role of geology, soil, vegetation, topography, hydrological processes, human activities and the effectiveness of management. We can also spot important environmental changes (perturbations) which may be manifested only at the catchment scale.

To ensure mass balance in catchment budgets, all inputs to the catchment and all outputs (either to the atmosphere or in water flowing out of the catchment) need to be quantified. Significant departures of outputs from inputs can indicate the magnitude of sources or sinks. For pollutants which originate principally on the land (diffuse-source pollutants), transfer from land to water depends on two groups of processes (e.g. Whelan *et al.*, 1995): (1) material 'supply', which is affected by sources, sinks and transformations and (2) material transport (chiefly the hydro-logical processes acting to move material from one location to another). Either or both of these factors can limit the material flux.

Material fluxes (often referred to as loads) transported through river catchments, either in dissolved form or associated with suspended particles, can be quantified in a number of ways. In principal, the average flux at any location can be defined (after Walling and Webb, 1985) as:

$$J = \frac{1}{T} \int_0^T C.Q \, dt$$

where J is the average flux ($kg \, d^{-1}$) over period T(d), C is the concentration of the material of interest ($kg \, m^{-3}$), Q is the river discharge ($m^3 \, d^{-1}$) and t is time (d). Both Q and C vary continuously. However, continuous measurements are usually only available for Q. Variations in C are often estimated from discrete samples. A number of methods have been proposed for combining measurements of Q and C which have been summarised by Walling and Webb (1985). Some methods use the mean discharge calculated from continuous flow records, whereas others use discharge measurements taken at the same time as samples were collected. Methods which employ time-weighted, rather than flow-weighted, concentration are generally thought to be inferior in principle, although in practice the accuracy of flux estimates will depend mainly on the frequency of sampling relative to the variability in concentrations.

Hydrochemical sources within the catchment can often be identified as originating from point – or diffuse – sources from analyses of solute rating curves (i.e. the relationship between concentration and discharge: see, e.g., Gregory and Walling, 1973; Bowes *et al.*, 2008; Howden *et al.*, 2009). Dilution effects (i.e. reduced concentration with increasing flow) are commonly observed for materials for which the source is not runoff-dependent. For example, the flux of pollutants derived from sewage effluent (such as orthophosphate) is relatively constant in time and so will be diluted by higher flows in the receiving water body. Some solutes derived from rock weathering may also be diluted in high flows if they are predominantly transported by way of groundwater, provided that concentrations in near-surface hydrological pathways (which are active during storm events) are low (e.g. dissolved silica; see Petry *et al.*, 2002).

For those materials that are mobilised by rainfall, runoff and/or by high in-channel discharge, such as suspended solids, there is often a positive relationship between discharge and concentration. For these cases, good flux estimates will depend on obtaining a representative sample of storm event concentrations. This may not be captured efficiently using regular periodic or random grab sampling strategies, unless the frequency of sampling is high.

Where a combination of point and diffuse sources is present, a composite relationship may be observed displaying dilution with increasing discharge at relatively low flows, when concentrations are dominated by point sources, but increasing concentrations with discharge at very high flows, resulting from the mobilisation of diffuse source material. A schematic illustration of these relationships is shown in Fig. 3.3. A key part of establishing such relationships requires monitoring with sufficiently high frequency and over a long enough period, in order to capture the full range of load and flow conditions experienced at the site in question.

Even in cases where there is generally a dilution effect, i.e. where there is a negative relationship between river discharge and concentration, there is often still a positive relationship between discharge and contaminant flux, since emissions are normally at least constant seasonally and usually increase to some extent during high flows (e.g. in combined sewers receiving both foul sewage and storm drainage). For contaminants with widely distributed sources, which are mobilised by runoff, such as nitrate, particulate phosphorus and suspended solids, a positive relationship usually exists between river discharge and concentration. The relationship between discharge and flux is, therefore, more pronounced. A good example of these patterns was presented by Sanders *et al.* (1997) who showed pronounced seasonality in nitrate and dissolved phosphate concentrations at the tidal limit of the River Trent at Dunham (UK). In the case of nitrate there was a winter maximum concentration and in the case of phosphate there was a winter minimum, owing to the fact that most of the phosphate in the Trent originates from sewage (generated in highly urbanised population centres in the English Midlands). The corresponding estimates of nitrate and phosphate flux, however, both show distinct peaks during high flow periods. It should be noted that, in the case of nutrients, flux peaks are often not coincident with nutrient demand (plants and algae) in the river channel, estuary and coastal environments. Eutrophication is, thus, more likely to be controlled by high concentrations during periods of high primary productivity, at least in the case of lotic systems (e.g. Holman *et al.*, 2008).

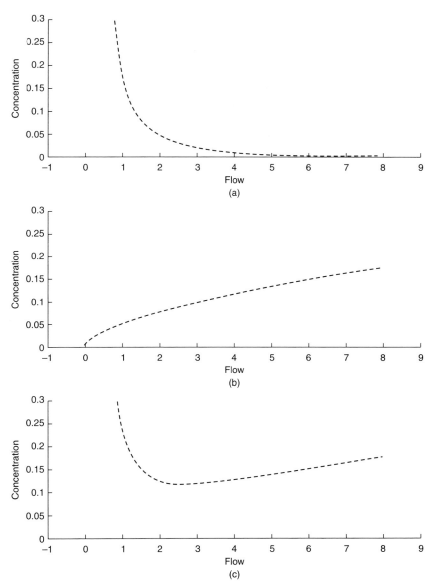

Fig. 3.3 Typical forms for solute rating curves for: (a) a point source pollutant, such as orthophosphate in an urbanised catchment; (b) a diffuse-source pollutant, such as nitrate and (c) a solute with combined point and diffuse sources, such as phosphate in a mixed urban and rural catchment dominated by point sources at low flow and diffuse sources at high flow

3.3   River flow regime and its modification

River flow regime (the long-term seasonality of river discharge) influences the timing and magnitude of material fluxes from the catchment to the coastal zone. Flow regimes are mainly affected by climatic factors in the catchment such as precipitation (amount and temporal distribution) and evapotranspiration (in turn, controlled by the solar radiation flux density, temperature, atmospheric humidity, wind speed, vegetation architecture and soil moisture availability). The edaphic and hydro-geological composition of the catchment may also play an important role. The flows in catchments underlain by permeable strata often receive significant contributions from groundwater. In these catchments low flows are relatively high compared with the mean flow and flow peaks associated with specific storm events are relatively minor. On the other hand, in catchments with thin soils underlain by impermeable strata, groundwater contributions to stream flow are relatively minor and flow peaks are often more 'flashy' – responding relatively rapidly to storm events (e.g. Ward and Robinson, 2000). For large catchments, the flow regime at the outlet will be a net result of flows from different parts of the catchment which might have different seasonal patterns in flow peaks and troughs. For example, the flow regime in high mountain head-waters may be dominated by spring snow melt, whereas at lower altitudes the regime may reflect low runoff in summer (due to high soil moisture deficits resulting from high evapotranspiration) and high rainfall-driven runoff in winter.

Flow regimes can be modified by human activity in a number of ways. Examples of significant modifications include large water diversion schemes, the construction of impoundments and abstractions for domestic water supply and irrigation. Dam construction can have a particularly strong effect on flow regime – usually 'homogenising' flows, i.e. reducing the typical flow range by damping peaks and increasing drought flows (e.g. Poff *et al.*, 2007) and decreasing fluvial fluxes of suspended sediment (Vericat and Batalla, 2006).

3.4   Sediment transport

In all catchments, hillslopes naturally erode and sediment is transported towards the sea. The supply and transfer of sediment within a river basin is highly variable in both time and space. In general, comparison of quantified sources of sediment with the amount of material being moved through the river system shows that a high proportion of supplied (eroded) sediment is not delivered to the downstream end of the river

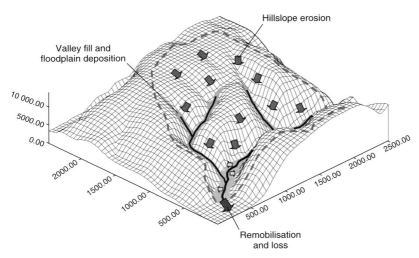

Fig. 3.4 *Schematic illustration of the catchment sediment cycle showing hillslope erosion, valley fill and floodplain deposition (grey shaded areas), sediment remobilisation and transfer out of the catchment at the outlet*

system, at least over the timescales over which it is possible to make direct flux observations. Instead, much of the sediment which is mobilised in erosion events is re-deposited in a range of in-catchment stores with different mean residence times (e.g. Walling, 1999). Sediment can also be counted multiple times as a source as it is detached, deposited and then remobilised on its way down through the catchment system (Fig. 3.4). Within-catchment retention of sediment can be conceptualised in terms of a sediment delivery ratio, i.e. the ratio between the sediment load transferred out of the catchment to that estimated to erode from the hillslopes within it (see, e.g., Walling, 1983; Richards, 1993). Sediment delivery ratios are often very low – particularly for large catchments, suggesting that the potential for within-catchment sediment storage (on hillslopes, on floodplains and in channels) is high. This is well illustrated by the high rates of alluvial deposition, suggested by dated valley fill depths, in catchments such as Coon Creek in Wisconsin, USA, which has an estimated long-term (century-scale) delivery ratio of only about 6% (see, e.g., Trimble, 1983, 1999). It should be noted, however, that erosion, sediment storage and remobilisation are spatially and temporally discontinuous and are probably never in steady state.

Rates of sediment transfer can be dramatically affected by human activity, such as land use change or the construction of river infrastructure. For example, major deforestation of the Spanish Pyrenees in the last 2000 years led to formation of the Ebro delta (Guillén and Palanques, 1997) but, today, estimates suggest that 97% of the sediment supply of the Ebro River may be trapped behind the many dams and barrages which have been constructed throughout the catchment in the twentieth century (Vericat and Batalla, 2006). Such reductions in sediment flux, sometimes referred to as 'sediment starvation', have been identified for many other rivers around the world, perhaps most dramatically in the large impoundment schemes which have been developed in China in recent years (e.g. on the Yangtze River; Yang *et al.*, 2005 and the Pearl River; Dai *et al.*, 2008). Other well-known examples include dams on the rivers Nile (see, e.g., Stanley, 1996) and Danube (see, e.g., Klaver *et al.*, 2007). In the case of the Nile, Stanley (1996) has argued that sediment trapping in the irrigated agricultural areas downstream of the Aswan dams – particularly on the Nile delta plain – has been at least as important as sediment trapping in the dams themselves, in terms of depriving the delta and coastal areas of sediment.

In addition to dams, changes in sediment yield can potentially be affected by climate change, river dredging (particularly in lower river reaches), deforestation and agricultural intensification. However, we should note that, in order for land use changes to have a major impact on sediment yield, the areal extent of such changes, relative to the size of the catchment, needs to be significant. It is also important to remember that changes in erosion rates may not always be manifested as significantly altered sediment yields at the catchment outlet because of the 'buffering' potential of in-catchment sediment storage.

Sediment transport in most rivers, is usually 'supply-limited' – i.e. the river could carry more sediment than they currently do, if it became available. Periodically, however, extreme events, such as landslides, earthquakes and tropical storms, can result in an increased sediment supply which cannot all be transported by the river immediately after the event. For example, a series of floods in the winter of 2000–01 caused extensive bank erosion in the River Tees in northern England, increasing sediment supply. Three years later, sediment transport rates were still in excess of those observed pre-flood.

In addition to increasing turbidity, mobilisation of 'new' sediment sources also carries another risk. Many of the floodplain sediment sources accessed during recent European floods have been contaminated as a result of historical mining and industrial activity. In some catchments (such as in northern England and South Wales) floodplain sediments, the current river banks, were deposited during times of widespread mining activity. When these sediments are re-mobilised during flood events, the contaminants are also transported, enhancing the potential for exposure to people and wildlife, usually temporarily (e.g. Dennis *et al.*, 2003).

3.5   Nutrient transfers

In addition to sunlight (see, e.g., Colijn and Cadée, 2003), ecosystems depend on the availability of nutrient elements for primary production (plant and algal growth). The rate of plant or algal growth will be limited by the nutrient which is in shortest supply relative to demand, such that quite small changes in availability result in marked increases in primary productivity. Although a range of elements is required (in different proportions), there are two principal macro-nutrients which are frequently limiting: nitrogen and phosphorus (Cartensen *et al.*, 2005). Nutrient transfers from river catchments can provide important contributions to maintaining coastal ecosystems, often with economic benefits, such as fisheries (e.g. Baisre and Arboleya, 2006). However, excess nutrients can result in 'eutrophication', a condition characterised by algal blooms and an associated deterioration of water quality. Instances of eutrophication have been widely documented in both freshwaters (see, e.g., Moss, 1998) and marine systems (see, e.g., Degobbis *et al.*, 2000; Gobler *et al.*, 2004). In the coastal zone, the intensity and spatial extent of eutrophication can vary widely, from small hot spots in enclosed bays to significant fractions of whole seas, such as the Baltic (Artioli *et al.*, 2008).

The degree to which nutrient transfers from land to the coastal zone contribute to such problems depends on the magnitude of the fluvial flux relative to atmospheric inputs, internal nutrient cycling, imports from the open sea by way of the prevailing currents and on the residence time of the coastal waters (Håkanson, 2008). Enclosed coastal zones (such as coastal lagoons and embayments) tend to have longer residence times and thus higher sensitivity to nutrient inputs. One of the best known cases of coastal eutrophication, in the so-called 'dead-zone' off the coast of Louisiana in the northern Gulf of Mexico, is thought to result, in large part, from nutrient contributions from the Mississippi River (e.g. Lohrenz *et al.*, 2008). Rydberg *et al.* (2006) have also reported correlations between primary productivity in the entrance region of the Baltic Sea and annual terrestrial nutrient loads over a 50-year period, although such correlations are not observed everywhere in the Baltic.

It is now recognised that coastal eutrophication is not simply a function of nutrient loading, but also depends on the relative availability of nitrogen (N) and phosphorus (P) with respect to silica (Si) (see, e.g., Sanders *et al.*, 1997; Billen and Garnier, 2007). Riverine N fluxes have increased markedly in many parts of Europe, mainly as a result of land-use change. Globally, western Europe has long been considered to be a hot spot of nitrogen flux (Meybeck, 1993). P fluxes have not increased as rapidly as N and in some areas have been reduced (e.g. as a result of improved sewage treatment). This has resulted in an increase in the N:P ratio of waters entering many marine systems. In general, the transfer of Si is not believed to have changed over recent decades, so that changes in N:Si and P:Si ratios have been controlled by changes in N and P concentrations (e.g. Jickells, 1998). However, it has also been proposed that in some catchments Si transfers from land to marine systems have been restricted by the construction of large dams (see, e.g. Conley *et al.*, 1993; Humborg *et al.*, 2006). This has resulted in an even greater increase in the N:Si ratio in the coastal zone, reducing the role of diatoms in favour of other (non-siliceous) algal species (see, e.g., Riegman *et al.*, 1992).

3.5.1 Sources

Terrestrial fluxes of N and P generally originate from either point or diffuse sources or a combination of the two. Point sources are those where nutrient-rich effluent is discharged to surface waters via a pipe (such as the discharge from sewage treatment plants or factory effluents). Diffuse sources refer to materials which are distributed throughout the landscape (e.g. in agricultural soils) and which are transported to the fluvial system by way of a range of hydrological processes, although it has recently been suggested that many sources previously identified as diffuse may in fact be a combination of large numbers of land-based point sources. The relative contribution of point and diffuse sources varies markedly between catchments, depending on a number of factors including the overall population density, the level of sewage treatment provision, current and historical land use (and agricultural practices), soil type, climate and river regime. The contribution also differs for nitrogen and phosphorus.

3.5.2 Nutrient cycling

Nutrients in aquatic systems are subject to a range of transformation processes. In addition to nutrient inputs from diffuse and point sources, nutrients can be released from the decomposition of plant detritus and the associated mineralisation of organic N and P. Inorganic nutrients can, in turn, be taken up by plants and algae. Some nutrient forms have a propensity to associate with particulates, for example ammonium and phosphate, and in these cases their fate is closely connected with the behaviour of the particles to which they are attached. Others, such as nitrate, are likely to be present predominantly in solution and will be transported out to the estuary unless taken up by plants and algae or transformed into nitrous oxide and nitrogen gas in the process of denitrification (by facultative anaerobic micro-organisms), which can occur in anaerobic sediments (see, e.g., Burns, 1998; Mulholland *et al.*, 2008). In lotic ecosystems, such as rivers, the idea of the nutrient cycle has been referred to in terms of a 'spiral' in which the cycle is translated longitudinally downstream as material is transported, in solution or attached to sediment. Nutrients can be taken up from the water column and stored in plant biomass but may be released in mineral form once plants die back and their litter is decomposed. Thus, plant uptake may only represent a temporary (seasonal) removal mechanism for nutrients in the water column. Similarly, deposition of particle-associated N and P is often temporary, since sediment stores can be remobilised in subsequent storm events.

3.5.3 Fluxes

Fluxes of nitrogen from river catchments in many parts of the world have increased significantly in the last 60 years – often due to more intensive agricultural practices (e.g. McIsaac *et al.*, 2002). In the UK, a number of long-term records exist that show similar features. An example is given in Fig. 3.5 which shows annual nitrate concentrations in the River Stour at Langham Bridge, in East Anglia, UK (Burt *et al.*, 2008). A pronounced increase in fluvial nitrate concentrations and loads in the period 1940–80 is apparent, followed by a stabilisation of concentrations in the last 20–25 years. Sharp discrete rises in nitrate concentration were observed in the years following severe droughts (e.g. following 1976 and 2003). These increases are consistent with enhanced production of soil mineral nitrogen in the year of the drought – possibly by way of enhanced mineralisation of microbial-derived nitrogen on rewetting dry soils (Birch, 1960; Powlson and Jenkinson,

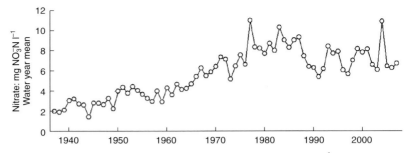

Fig. 3.5 Annual mean nitrate concentrations (mg $NO_3^-NL^{-1}$) for the River Stour in East Anglia, UK from 1937–2007. All are calculated for water years beginning 1 October. Reproduced from Burt et al. (2008). Data supplied by the Environment Agency of England and Wales

1976; Haynes and Swift, 1989) and possibly due to physical disturbance induced by the drying and wetting event itself. A very similar temporal pattern of flux estimates of dissolved inorganic nitrogen (DIN) from the Mississippi River from 1950 to 2004 is presented by Lohrenz *et al.* (2008). These data show a pronounced increase in DIN flux between the mid-1960s and the 1980s after which the flux has levelled out and may now even be decreasing.

Fluxes of dissolved nitrogen from the terrestrial environment have recently been estimated for the island of Great Britain by Worrall *et al.* (in press) using long-term data from 270 stations collected under the UK Harmonised Monitoring Scheme (HMS) from 1974–2005 (Simpson, 1980). These analyses suggest the total annual nitrogen flux (dissolved and particulate) from the British Isles varies annually between approximately 504 and 1004 ktonnes N yr^{-1} (i.e. 20 and 42 kg N ha^{-1} yr^{-1}) and is dominated (>70%) by DIN (mainly as nitrate). The study also showed that the dissolved N flux is still currently increasing at a rate of about 6.3 ktonnes N yr^{-1}, despite an overall reduction in nitrogen inputs to terrestrial systems.

The apparent inconsistency between the flux trend and concurrent estimates of nitrogen inputs (to agriculture) reflects a common phenomenon in catchment systems: that of temporal lags in system responses to perturbation. Such lags result from a combination of long-term adjustments in material supply (the amount of material available for transport) and the transport process itself, which can sometimes delay the transfer of material from its source (e.g. the soil) to the catchment outlet (Howden and Burt, 2008). An example of the former is the adjustment in organic nitrogen levels in soils ploughed out of permanent pasture in the UK during and after World War II. According to Whitmore *et al.* (1992) in some eastern counties of England up to two-thirds of the area of long-term pasture was brought into arable production in the 50 years post 1940. This resulted in a loss of almost 4 tonnes N ha^{-1} over a period of approximately 25 years after ploughing, as the soil organic matter levels declined to new equilibria. Much of this loss of N is believed to have been due to enhanced mineralisation followed by leaching out of the soil as nitrate. The pasture to arable conversion may have been a significant contributor to rising nitrate concentrations in ground and surface waters in the post-war period. Increases in nitrate leaching (whether resulting from additional mineralisation or additional N inputs) have been particularly slow to manifest themselves in ground and surface waters in catchments with long unsaturated zone solute travel times. This is evident in lowland areas underlain by permeable geology, where river flow regimes are dominated by groundwater inputs and, consequently, solute transfers from land may be subject to long delays in both the unsaturated zone and in the saturated groundwater system itself. Transfer times in some groundwater systems can amount to decades or even centuries. While characterisation of such residence times have long been the focus of hydrological investigation (e.g. Jackson *et al.*, 2006) it has recently been shown that such catchments experience a delayed solute 'breakthrough' phenomenon resulting in nitrate concentration changes in groundwater-fed streams decades after the changes in land-based source availability (Howden and Burt, 2008).

3.6   Carbon

Transfers of particulate organic (POC), dissolved organic (DOC) and dissolved inorganic (DIC) carbon from land to sea have been extensively studied (e.g. Schlesinger and Melack, 1981; Meybeck, 1993). Organic carbon is of interest in the coastal zone because it represents a potential resource for microbial populations mediating a range of biogeochemical processes (such as denitrification). Carbon fluxes are of interest more widely because of the role of carbon (as atmospheric carbon dioxide and methane) in the global radiation budget. Soil carbon represents an important terrestrial carbon store; more than twice as much carbon is stored in soil as in vegetation or the atmosphere (e.g. Batjes, 1996). Soils can sequester atmospheric carbon under conditions favouring organic matter accumulation or act as an atmospheric carbon source, if soil organic matter levels decline. Recent evidence

(Bellamy *et al.*, 2005) suggests that soil carbon stores in some areas may be decreasing – possibly due to a combination of land-use changes and increased mineralisation with respect to litter inputs from primary production. However, increases in fluvial transfers of carbon from land to water have also been observed (e.g. Worrall and Burt, 2004; Worrall *et al.*, 2007) and may also play a role in regulating the soil carbon stock. A number of factors could be responsible for these increases in carbon transfer, including increasing temperatures, increased incidence of drought and changes in land management (particularly changes in burning practices in the uplands). The flux of organic and inorganic carbon from the world's rivers to the oceans has been estimated to be of the order of $542 \, \text{Tg} \, \text{C} \, \text{year}^{-1}$ with an approximate contribution of 37%, 18% and 45% from DOC, POC and DIC respectively (Worrall *et al.*, 2007).

3.7 Contaminant transfers

In addition to sediment, carbon and nutrients, a range of contaminants, both organic and inorganic, is transferred through the fluvial system to the sea. These have many sources which, again, can be both point and diffuse. In some cases, legacy contaminants, such as heavy metals (often originating from historical mining activities) or persistent organic pollutants such as polychlorinated biphenyls (PCBs) or polycyclic aromatic hydrocarbons (PAHs) can be retained in sediment stores within the river catchment long after their emission has ceased. These stores can be periodically mobilised and sometimes represent the dominant pollution source for some contaminants (e.g. Dennis *et al.*, 2003). As with nutrients, the relative importance of riverine pollutant sources compared with other inputs (such as the atmosphere or the open sea) is case-specific.

3.7.1 *Organic contaminants*

River water contains a range of naturally occurring and synthetic organic compounds. Synthetic chemicals originate variously from agricultural use or from industrial processes – purposefully discharged to waste water or air or accidentally released in spillages or from inadequate waste containment. Pesticides used on farms and for weed control in road and railway maintenance are usually considered diffuse-source contaminants, although point-sources also exist (e.g. sheep-dip stations and in effluent from textile industries employing moth-proofing; House *et al.*, 2000). Other chemicals may be used in personal or domestic applications such as pharmaceuticals or cleaning products which have a significant 'down-the-drain' disposal scenario, after use. Most organic chemicals discharged to water are degradable (some more quickly than others) and many are not present at toxic concentrations. However, a few chemicals do present significant environmental risks (such as PAHs which can be generated during combustion and which are often present in urban runoff) and it is these that have been targeted for legislative action (e.g. the priority hazardous substances list developed under the European Water Framework Directive). Riverine fluxes have been shown to make a very significant contribution to the oceanic PAH levels (e.g. Wang *et al.*, 2007).

3.7.2 Metals
Like organic contaminants, metals have a wide range of sources, diffuse and point. For any metal, a proportion of the environmental load will originate from natural sources. However, the extraction (mining and quarrying) and processing industries, along with domestic and industrial uses, can significantly enhance background levels and potentially cause deleterious environmental effects.

Note that, as for many organic contaminants, metals can enter marine systems from the atmosphere, as well as via rivers and internal recycling. For example, river inputs of most metals are believed to be smaller than atmospheric inputs for the western Mediterranean (Elbaz-Poulichet *et al.*, 2001). This is also the case for PAHs in the eastern Mediterranean (Tsapakis *et al.*, 2006).

3.7.3 Microbiological pollutants
Many near-shore coastal waters have historically been affected by microbiological transfers from land to water. Water contamination with pathogenic micro-organisms can pose a health risk to recreational users, such as swimmers, surfers and other water sports enthusiasts. In the past this contamination was mainly associated with the emission of (often untreated) sewage to coastal waters. However, there is now increasing evidence that a number of diffuse bacterial sources exist in coastal catchments, such as grazing livestock. Bacteria and other pathogens can be transferred from these sources to beach areas, particularly during storm events, and result in periodic breaches of

bathing water quality standards (see, e.g., Kay *et al.*, 2005; Wilkinson *et al.*, 2006).

3.8   Estuarine processes

The estuary is an important transitional environment between rivers and the sea. Often, the tidal limit, which marks the start of the estuary and the end of the river-proper is a significant distance from the coast, so that many estuaries are, spatially, quite extensive. Processes occurring within estuaries include sorption and desorption of contaminants to suspended solids, uptake by algae and bacteria, sediment (and associated contaminant) deposition (and, potentially, subsequent burial) and denitrification. These processes can be affected by steep gradients in salinity, pH, temperature and redox potential and can significantly modify the net flux of materials to the coastal zone (e.g. Pastuszak *et al.*, 2005; Sanders *et al.*, 1997). In addition, in the short term, the direction of material fluxes changes with the tidal cycle such that pollutants can be transported backwards and forwards many times within the estuary before settling out or being emitted to the open sea (e.g. Brooks *et al.*, 1999). Pastuszak *et al.* (2005) have estimated that the Oder estuary retains approximately half and one-third of total nitrogen and total phosphorus fluxes, respectively, from the River Oder to the Baltic Sea. Denitrification in anaerobic sediments was the most significant loss mechanism for nitrogen. Phosphorus was believed to be retained mainly by deposition of particulates followed by dredging. Adsorption to suspended particles can be enhanced by resuspension caused by tidal currents as well as potential destabilisation of colloids resulting from increased ionic strength (e.g. Zwolsman, 1994; Sanders *et al.*, 1997). Primary production is unlikely to be a significant removal mechanism in many estuaries because of the relatively low depth of the photic zone relative to water depth (Sanders *et al.*, 1997). The retention of sediment-associated contaminants means that, in some estuaries, nutrient and pollutant levels in the sediment store may represent historical, rather than present-day, fluxes, and can act as potential sources of toxic stress for both the pelagic and benthic ecosystems for years to come (see, e.g., Grant and Middleton, 1990). Note that in some estuary and coastal environments, import of nutrients from the open sea may be relatively high. This is the case in the North Sea, where import of P from the north Atlantic is estimated to be four to five times greater than the P flux from land (Artioli *et al.*, 2008). In these cases, eutrophication may be relatively insensitive to changes in riverine nutrient loads.

3.9   Managing material transfers in the catchment

Many of the examples discussed here suggest that fluvial transfers of dissolved and sediment-associated materials to estuarine and coastal environments can be affected by human activity. Significant changes in suspended sediment, carbon, nutrient and trace-element transfers can be triggered by major land-use change (such as widespread deforestation) and by the construction of large dams. Land-use change and land management practice is also believed to be responsible, at least in part, for recent increased transfers of dissolved inorganic nitrogen and dissolved organic carbon from river catchments. In addition, point-source emissions can have a significant role to play in controlling fluvial concentrations and loads of phosphorus in many catchments. Such (unintentional) anthropogenic phenomena suggest that it is also possible to bring about changes in material transfers intentionally by way of concerted catchment management. The feasibility of effective management depends on the pollutants under consideration and, particularly, the nature and relative strength of their sources.

Pollutants that are emitted mainly from point sources are generally considered to be easier to manage than those with diffuse origins because of the potential for enhancing end of pipe treatment. This has been reflected in significant reductions in point-source contributions to nutrient budgets in a number of European countries in recent years. The urban waste water treatment directive (UWWTD: 91/271/ EEC) came into full force in 2002 and requires any population centre with more than 10 000 inhabitants to be served by secondary sewage treatment. This has reduced the discharge of untreated effluent to many European surface waters and has significantly reduced associated point-source P loads. In parallel, the use of sodium tripolyphosphate (STPP) as a builder in laundry detergents has also decreased in recent years as a combined result of enforced restrictions in some countries, such as Germany and Italy, and voluntary switches by the detergent industry to alternative phosphate-free formulations (see, e.g., Morse *et al.*, 1995). Finally, many waste-water treatment facilities now have tertiary treatment which includes phosphate stripping to reduce residual phosphate levels in the effluent stream. Efficient stripping can remove up to 95% of soluble P influx (Reynolds and Davies, 2001). While such treatment options may be expensive to implement,

49

they are technically feasible. Widespread implementation of tertiary sewage treatment for phosphorus removal for major population centres in much of the Baltic Sea catchment, combined with a reduction in phosphate use in detergents and some reduced inputs from agriculture, in response to land use controls, have significantly decreased terrestrial phosphorus transfers (Carstensen *et al.*, 2005). Reductions in nutrient fluxes to the Baltic have been accompanied by a moderate decrease in primary production in some areas (e.g. Rydberg *et al.*, 2006), although it should be noted that responses to changes in inputs may be masked by internal recycling of nutrients – particularly exchanges between the water column and the sediment (which, in turn, may have high nutrient levels as a consequence of historically elevated inputs; see, e.g., Artioli *et al.*, 2008). The Baltic Proper (the central region of the Baltic Sea) is an example of a water body where sediments are the predominant nutrient source (Artioli *et al.*, 2008), although other regions of the Baltic Sea are more influenced by riverine inputs (see Rydberg *et al.*, 2006).

In the case of diffuse-source pollutant problems, solutions tend to be less obvious and are often less immediately effective. This stems, in part, from the need to implement land use or land management practices over large areas containing multiple stakeholders (e.g. land owners and farmers). In order to achieve reductions in pollutant transfers, action (such as reductions in fertiliser inputs) is required by the majority of land managers in the catchment. Although this can, in principle, be achieved voluntarily by way of financial incentives (compensation schemes), it is probably more effective in practice to have compulsory rules (such as those imposed on farmers in so-called nitrate vulnerable zones or NVZs in England and Wales). Rules in NVZs include a limit on livestock manure application rates, a closed season for manure and inorganic fertiliser applications, a minimum manure storage capacity and a requirement to tailor applications of inorganic N in line with crop requirements (with avoidance of application in areas designated to be particularly vulnerable to diffuse-source transfers from land to water). Some NVZs have been in place since 1996, with additional areas added in 2002 and 2008. The current extent of NVZs is shown in Fig. 3.6. Despite the fact that a significant fraction of England is now designated as an NVZ, nitrate concentrations in surface and ground waters in much of the country remain high and, according to Worrall *et al.* (in press), the terrestrial flux of N from Great Britain still appears to be increasing. It may be that a major reversal in the nitrate concentration trends observed during the 1960s, 1970s and

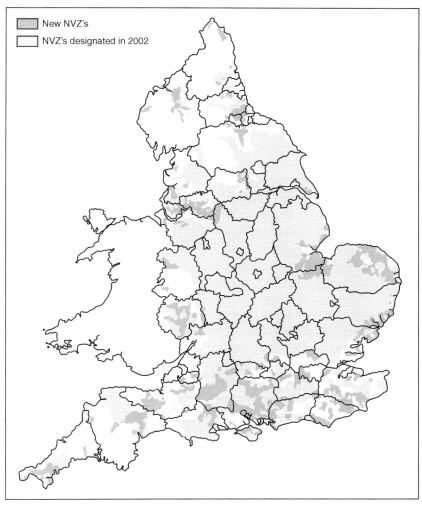

Fig. 3.6 Nitrate vulnerable zones in England and Wales (Source: http://www. defra.gov.uk/environment/water/quality/nitrate/)

1980s will not be possible without more radical measures (such as taking land out of intensive agricultural production). Such measures could potentially result in reduced domestic food security and increased food prices and would, therefore, be politically unpopular.

A number of European Directives has been influential in attempting to manage water pollution. These include the Drinking Water Directive (98/83/EEC), the Nitrates Directive (91/676/EEC), the Urban

51

Wastewater Treatment Directive (91/272/EEC), the Habitats Directive (92/43/EEC) and the Pesticide Authorisation Directive (91/414/EEC). While these directives remain in place, most active management of the quality of water resources in the European Union now falls under the auspices of the Water Framework Directive (WFD) (2000/60/EC). The WFD requires all inland and coastal waters within defined river basin districts to reach at least 'good' status by 2015. This will be achieved by way of bespoke measures for individual water bodies which target ecosystem-specific pressures in an attempt to meet environmental targets (typically expressed in terms of ecological quality). The extent to which the WFD is able to mitigate deleterious material fluxes from river catchments to the coastal zone is currently unknown. However, the integrated nature of the directive is likely to provide a more effective framework for tackling the multi-faceted issues which surround water pollution, at least in principle.

3.10   Climate change

Many of the environmental processes operating within river catchments which control the supply and transport of contaminants to the coastal zone are likely to be subjected to some modification under climate change scenarios. Such modifications will take place in parallel with changes in human activities (land management practices, irrigation demands, population increases, migration, industrial activity, etc.). Some modified practices will be independent of climate shifts and some will be in response to them (so-called adaptations). Examples of processes which are likely to be most affected by changing climate include the intensity and seasonality of rainfall and evapotranspiration and associated soil moisture deficits and runoff. This could, in turn, lead to changes in the transfer of suspended sediment and diffuse-source pollutants from land to water and to changes in dilution offered by rivers. In many catchments, suspended sediment loads to the estuary are buffered by in-catchment sediment storage and appear to be transport-limited (i.e. significant shifts in sediment supply have a relatively minor effect on sediment transfers at the catchment outlet; Phillips, 1991). It is possible that in these cases, sediment transport may be more sensitive to changes in runoff than to changes which affect sediment supply (such as deforestation). There is already some evidence that major river flows are influenced by the global climate system. For example, Lohrenz *et al.* (2008) report that long-term trends in the discharge of the Mississippi River are correlated with the intensity of the El Niño–Southern Oscillation (ENSO) phenomenon. However, it is uncertain whether or not this phenomenon is likely to intensify with global warming. In addition to changes in rainfall patterns and to the driving influence of temperature on the physics of surface to atmosphere water transfers, enhanced atmospheric CO_2 concentrations may result in reductions in evapotranspiration, *ceteris paribus*, because of a reduction in plant stomatal apertures required to achieve a given rate of photosynthesis (Idso and Brazel, 1984). Indeed, recent (post 1960) increases in global river flows have already been attributed, somewhat controversially, to this phenomenon (Gedney *et al.*, 2006). This said, we should stress here that predictions of future climate change, coincident changes in human activity and catchment responses to these changes remain highly uncertain.

3.11 Conclusions

River catchments transfer water and materials (sediment, carbon, nutrients, pollutants) from land to sea and can exert strong controls over physical and ecological phenomena operating in coastal zones. Management of many coastal zones must, therefore, include a consideration of processes and human activities in contributing catchments in order to be effective. River catchments act to integrate a range of processes: physical, chemical, biological and anthropogenic, to deliver fluvial loads. Often these loads are modified in estuaries and deltas and sometimes they may make relatively minor short-term contributions compared with internal cycling of materials from sediment stores or with imports from the open sea. However, in the long term, these transfers represent an essential component of global biogeochemical cycling. Human activities in river catchments can significantly alter material transfers. Examples include the effects of agricultural intensification on increased nitrogen fluxes from many river basins and the reduction of suspended sediment delivery caused by major dam construction. Management of fluvial fluxes is usually challenging and requires widespread concerted action over long periods – often in different countries. Management intervention may be easier where pollutants are principally released from point sources. In the case of sewage-associated phosphorus transfers, for example, end of pipe treatment solutions exist, in addition to legislation to limit the use of P in detergents. However, successful management tends to be more difficult in cases where pollutant sources are more widespread and where their delivery to and transfer through fluvial systems is not well understood.

Many diffuse-source pollutants fall into this category and bringing them under control requires national or international scale action which may be expensive and which may be in conflict with other desirable objectives (such as the production of affordable food). Such action is particularly difficult to justify where water quality responses to land use changes in the catchment are not likely to be seen for some considerable time after implementation.

References

Artioli, Y., Friedrich, J., Gilbert, A.J., McQuatters-Gollop, A., Mee, L.D., Vermaat, J.E., Wulff, F., Humborg, C., Palmeri, L. and Pollehne, F. (2008) Nutrient budgets for European seas: a measure of the effectiveness of nutrient reduction policies. *Marine Pollution Bulletin*, Vol. 56, pp. 1609–1617.

Baisre, J.A. and Arboleya, Z. (2006) Going against the flow: effects of river damming in Cuban fisheries. *Fisheries Research*, Vol. 81, pp. 283–292.

Batjes, N.H. (1996) Total carbon and nitrogen in the soils of the world. *European Journal of Soil Science*, Vol. 47, 151–163.

Bellamy, P.H., Loveland, P.J., Bradley, R.I., Lark, R.M. and Kirk, G.J.D. (2005) Carbon losses from all soils across England and Wales 1978–2003. *Nature*, Vol. 437, 245–248.

Billen, G. and Garnier, J. (2007) River basin nutrient delivery to the coastal sea: assessing its potential to sustain new production of non-siliceous algae. *Marine Chemistry*, Vol. 106, pp. 148–160.

Birch, H.F. (1960) Nitrification in soils after different periods of dryness. *Plant and Soil*, Vol. 12, pp. 81–96.

Bowes, M.J., Smith, J.T., Jarvie, H.P. and Neal, C. (2008) Modelling of phosphorus inputs to rivers from diffuse and point sources. *Science of the Total Environment*, Vol. 395, pp. 125–138.

Brooks, D.A., Baca, M.W. and Lo, Y.T. (1999) Tidal circulation and residence time in a macrotidal estuary: Cobscook Bay, Maine. *Estuarine, Coastal and Shelf Science*, Vol. 49, pp. 647–665.

Burns, D.A. (1998) Retention of NO_3^- in an upland stream environment: a mass balance approach. *Biogeochemistry*, Vol. 40, pp. 73–96.

Burt, T.P., Howden, N.J.K., Worrall, F. and Whelan, M.J. (2008) Importance of long-term monitoring for detecting environmental change: lessons from a lowland river in south east England. *Biogeosciences*, Vol. 5, pp. 1529–1535.

Carstensen, J., Conley, D., Andersen, J. and Erteberg, G. (2005) Coastal eutrophication and trend reversal, a Danish case study. *Limnology and Oceanography*, Vol. 51, pp. 398–408.

Colijn, F. and Cadée, G.C. (2003) Is phytoplankton growth in the Wadden Sea light or nitrogen limited? *Journal of Sea Research*, Vol. 49, pp. 83–93.

Conley, D.J., Schelske, C.L. and Stoermer, E.F. (1993) Modification of the biogeochemical cycle of silica with eutrophication. *Marine Ecology Progress Series*, Vol. 81, pp. 121–128.

Dai, S.B., Yang, S.L. and Cai, A.M. (2008) Impacts of dams on the sediment flux of the Pearl River, southern China. *Catena*, Vol. 76, pp. 36–43.

Degobbis, D., Precali, R., Ivanic, I., Smodlaka, N., Fuks, D. and Kveder, S. (2000) Long term changes in the northern Adriatic ecosystem related to anthropogenic eutrophication. *International Journal of Environmental Pollution*, Vol. 13, pp. 495–533.

Dennis, I.A., Macklin, M.G., Coulthard, T.J. and Brewer, P.A. (2003) The impact of the October–November 2000 floods on contaminant metal dispersal in the River Swale catchment, North Yorkshire, UK. *Hydrological Processes*, Vol. 17, pp. 1641–1657.

Elbaz-Poulichet, F., Guieu, C. and Morley, N.H. (2001) A reassessment of trace metal budgets in the western Mediterranean Sea. *Marine Pollution Bulletin*, Vol. 42, pp. 623–627.

Gedney, N., Cox, P.M., Betts, R.A., Boucher, O., Huntingford, C. and Stott, P.A. (2006) Detection of a direct carbon dioxide effect in continental river runoff records. *Nature*, Vol. 439, pp. 835–838.

Gobler, C.J., Boneillo, G.E., Debenham, C.J. and Caron, D.A. (2004) Nutrient limitation, organic matter cycling, and plankton dynamics during an *Aureococcus anophagefferens* bloom. *Aquatic Microbial Ecology*, Vol. 35, Issue 1, pp. 31–43.

Grant, A. and Middleton, R. (1990) An assessment of metal contamination of sediments in the Humber estuary. *Estuarine, Coastal and Shelf Science*, Vol. 31, pp. 71–85.

Gregory, K.J. and Walling, D.E. (1973) *Drainage Basin Form and Process. A Geomorphological Approach*, Edward Arnold, London.

Guillén, J. and Palanques, A. (1997) A historical perspective of the morphological evolution in the lower Ebro River. *Environmental Geology*, Vol. 30, pp. 174–180.

Håkanson, L. (2008) Factors and criteria to quantify coastal area sensitivity/ vulnerability to eutrophication: presentation of a sensitivity index based on morphometrical parameters. *International Review of Hydrobiology*, Vol. 93, pp. 372–388.

Haynes, R.J. and Swift, R.S. (1989) Effect of air dried soils on pH and accumulation of mineral N. *Journal of Soil Science*, Vol. 40, pp. 341–347.

Holman, I.P., Whelan, M.J., Howden, N.J.K., Bellamy, P.H., Willby, N.J., Rivas-Casado, M. and McConvey, P. (2008) Phosphorus in groundwater – an unacknowledged contributor to eutrophication? *Hydrological Processes*, Vol. 22, Issue 26, pp. 5121–5127.

House, W.A., Long, J.L.A., Rae, J.E., Parker and Orr, D.R. (2000) Occurrence and mobility of the insecticide permethrin in rivers in the Southern Humber catchment, UK. *Pest Management Science*, Vol. 56, pp. 597–606.

Howden, N.J.K. and Burt, T.P. (2008) Temporal and spatial analysis of nitrate concentrations from the Frome and Piddle catchments in Dorset (UK) for water years 1978 to 2007: evidence for nitrate breakthrough? *Science of the Total Environment*, Vol. 407, pp. 507–526.

Howden, N.J.K., Bowes, M.J., Clark, A.D.J., Humphries, R.N. and Neal, C. (2009) Water quality, nutrients and the European Union's Water Framework Directive in a lowland agricultural region: Suffolk, south-east England. *Science of the Total Environment*, Vol. 407, pp. 2966–2979.

Humborg, C., Pastuszak, M., Aigars, J., Siegmund, H., Morth, C.M. and Ittekot, V. (2006) Decreased silica land–sea fluxes through damming in the Baltic Sea catchment. Significance of particle trapping and hydrological alterations. *Biogeochemistry*, Vol. 77, pp. 265–281.

Idso, S.B. and Brazel, A.J. (1984) Rising atmospheric carbon dioxide concentrations may increase streamflow. *Nature*, Vol. 312, pp. 51–53.

Jackson, B.M., Wheater, H.S., Mathias, M.A., McIntyre, N. and Butler, A.P. (2006) A simple model of variable residence time flow and nutrient transport in the chalk. *Journal of Hydrology*, Vol. 330, pp. 221–234.

Jickells, T.D. (1998) Nutrient biogeochemistry of the coastal zone. *Science*, Vol. 281, pp. 217–222.

Kay, D., Wyer, M.D., Crowther, J., Wilkinson, J., Stapleton, C. and Glass, P. (2005) Sustainable reduction in the flux of microbial compliance parameters from urban and arable land use to coastal bathing waters by a wetland ecosystem produced by a marine flood defence structure. *Water Research*, Vol. 39, pp. 3320–3332.

Klaver, G., van Os, B., Negrel, P. and Petelet-Giraud, E. (2007) Influence of hydropower dams on the composition of the suspended and riverbank sediments in the Danube. *Environmental Pollution*, Vol. 148, pp. 718–728.

Likens, G.E. and Borman, F.H. (1995) *Biogeochemistry of a Forested Ecosystem*, Springer-Verlag, New York.

Lohrenz, S.E., Redalje, D.G., Cai, W.J., Acker, J. and Dagg, M. (2008) A retrospective analysis of nutrients and phytoplankton productivity in the Mississippi River plume. *Continental Shelf Research*, Vol. 28, pp. 1466–1475.

McIsaac, G.F., David, M.B., Gertner, G.Z. and Goolsby, D.A. (2002) Nitrate flux in the Mississippi River. *Nature*, Vol. 414, pp. 166–167.

Meade, R.H. (1995) Contaminants in the Mississippi River. *1987–1992 US Geological Survey Circular 1133*, USGS, Denver, CO.

Meybeck, M. (1993) Riverine transport of atmospheric carbon sources, global typology and budget. *Water Air Soil Pollution*, Vol. 70, pp. 443–463.

Morse, G.K., Perry, R. and Lester, J.N. (1995) The impact of sodium tripolyphosphate substitution in western Europe. *Ambio*, Vol. 24, Issue 2, pp. 112–118.

Moss, B. (1998) *Ecology of Freshwaters: Man and Medium, Past to Future*, 3rd ed., Blackwell Science, Oxford.

Mulholland, P.J., Helton, A.M., Poole, G.C., Hall, R.O., Hamilton, S.K., Peterson, B.J., Tank, J.L., Ashkenas, L.R., Cooper, L.W., Dahm, C.N., Dodds, W.K., Findlay, S.G., Gregory, S.V., Grimm, N.B., Johnson, S.L., McDowell, W.H., Meyer, J.L., Valett, H.M., Webster, J.R., Arango, C.P., Beaulieu, J.J., Bernot, M.J., Burin, A.J., Crenshaw, C.L., Johnson, L.T., Neiderlehner, R.R., O'Brien, J.M., Potter, J.D., Sheibley, R.W., Sobota, D.J. and Thomas, S.M. (2008) Stream denitrification across biomes and its response to anthropogenic nitrate loading. *Nature*, Vol. 452, pp. 202–206.

Pastuszak, M., Witek, Z., Nagel, K., Wielgat, M. and Grelowski, A. (2005) Role of the Oder estuary (southern Baltic) in transformation of the riverine nutrient loads. *Journal of Marine Systems*, Vol. 57, pp. 30–54.

Petry, J., Soulsby, C., Malcolm, I.A. and Youngson, A.F. (2002) Hydrological controls on nutrient concentrations and fluxes in agricultural catchments. *The Science of the Total Environment*, Vol. 194, pp. 95–110.

Phillips, J.D. (1991) Fluvial sediment delivery to a coastal-plain estuary in the Atlantic drainage of the United States. *Marine Geology*, Vol. 98, pp. 121–134.

Poff, N.L., Olden, J.D., Merritt, D.M. and Pepin, D.M. (2007) Homogenization of regional river dynamics by dams and global biodiversity implications. *Proceedings of the National Academy of Sciences of the United States of America*, Vol. 104, pp. 5732–5737.

Powlson, D.S and Jenkinson, D.S. (1976) The effects of biocidal treatments on metabolism in soil. II. Gamma radiation, autoclaving, air drying and fumigation with chloroform or methyl bromide. *Soil Biology and Biochemistry*, Vol. 8, pp. 179–188.

Raymond, P.A., Oh, N.H., Turner, R.E. and Broussard, W. (2008) Anthropogenically enhanced fluxes of water and carbon from the Mississippi River. *Nature*, Vol. 451, pp. 449–452.

Reynolds, C.S. and Davies, P.S. (2001) Sources and bioavailability of phosphorus fractions in freshwaters: a British perspective. *Biology Review*, Vol. 76, pp. 27–64.

Richards, K. (1993) Sediment delivery and the drainage network. In Beven, K. and Kirkby, M.J. (eds) *Channel Network Hydrology*, John Wiley and Sons, Chichester.

Riegman, R., Noordeloos, A.A.M. and Cadée, G.C. (1992) Phaeocystis blooms and eutrophication of the continental coast zones of the North Sea. *Marine Biology*, Vol. 112, pp. 479–484.

Rydberg, L., Ertebjerg, G. and Edler, L. (2006) Fifty years of primary production measurements in the Baltic entrance region, trends and variability in relation to land-based input of nutrients. *Journal of Sea Research*, Vol. 56, pp. 1–16.

Sanders, R.J., Jickells, T., Malcolm, S., Brown, J., Kirkwood, D., Reeve, A., Taylor, J., Horrobin, T. and Ashcroft, C. (1997) Nutrient fluxes through the Humber estuary. *Journal of Sea Research*, Vol. 37, pp. 3–23.

Schlesinger, W.H. and Melack, J.M. (1981) Transport of organic carbon in the world's rivers. *Tellus*, Vol. 33, pp. 172–181.

Simpson, E.A. (1980) The harmonization of the monitoring of the quality of rivers in the United Kingdom. *Hydrological Sciences Bulletin*, Vol. 25, pp. 13–23.

Stanley, D.J. (1996) Nile delta: extreme case of sediment entrapment on a delta plain and consequent coastal land loss. *Marine Geology*, Vol. 129, pp. 189–195.

Trimble, S.W. (1983) A sediment budget for Coon Creek in the Driftless Area, Wisconsin 1853–1977. *American Journal of Science*, Vol. 283, pp. 454–474.

Trimble, S.W. (1999) Decreased rates of alluvial sediment storage in the Coon Creek, Wisconsin, 1975–93. *Science*, Vol. 285, pp. 1244–1246.

Tsapakis, M., Apostolaki, M., Eisenreich, S. and Stephanou, E.G. (2006) Atmospheric deposition and marine sedimentation fluxes of polycyclic aromatic hydrocarbons in the eastern Mediterranean basin. *Environmental Science and Technology*, Vol. 40, pp. 4922–4927.

Vericat, D. and Batalla, R.J. (2006) Sediment transport in a large impounded river: the lower Ebro, NE Iberian Peninsula. *Geomorphology*, Vol. 79, pp. 72–92.

Walling, D.E. (1983) The sediment delivery problem. *Journal of Hydrology*, Vol. 65, pp. 209–237.

Walling, D.E. (1999) Linking land use, erosion and sediment yields in river basins, *Hydrobiologia*, Vol. 410, pp. 223–240.

Walling, D.E. and Webb, B.W. (1985) Estimating the discharge of contaminants to coastal waters by rivers: some cautionary comments. *Marine Pollution Bulletin*, Vol. 16, pp. 488–492.

Wang, J.Z., Guan, Y.F., Ni, H.G., Luo, X.L. and Zeng, E.Y. (2007) Polycyclic aromatic hydrocarbons in riverine runoff of the Pearl River delta (China): concentrations, fluxes and fate. *Environmental Science and Technology*, Vol. 41, pp. 5614–5619.

Ward, R.C. and Robinson, M. (2000) *Principles of Hydrology*, McGraw-Hill, Maidenhead, UK.

Whitmore, A.P., Bradbury, N.J. and Johnson, P.A. (1992) Potential contribution of ploughed grassland to nitrate leaching. *Agriculture, Ecosystems and Environment*, Vol. 39, pp. 221–233.

Whelan, M.J., Kirkby, M.J. and Burt, T.P. (1995) Predicting nitrate concentrations in small catchment streams. In Trudgill, S.T. (ed.) *Solute Modelling in Catchment Systems*, John Wiley and Sons, Chichester, pp. 165–192.

Wilkinson, J., Kay, D., Wymer, M. and Jenkins, A. (2006) Processes driving the episodic flux of faecal indicator organisms in streams impacting on recreational and shellfish harvesting waters. *Water Research*, Vol. 40, pp. 153–161.

Worrall, F. and Burt, T.P. (2004) Time series analysis of long-term river dissolved organic carbon records. *Hydrological Processes*, 18, 893–911.

Worrall, F., Guilbert, T. and Besien, T. (2007) The flux of carbon from rivers: the case for flux from England and Wales. *Biogeochemistry*, Vol. 86, pp. 63–75.

Worrall F., Burt, T.P., Howden, N. and Whelan, M.J. (in press) The fluvial flux of nitrate from Great Britain 1974–2005 in the context of an overall terrestrial nitrogen budget. *Global Biogeochemical Cycles*.

Yang, S.L., Zhang, J., Zhu, J., Smith, J.P., Dai, S.B., Gao, A. and Li, P. (2005) Impact of dams on Yangtze River sediment supply to the sea and delta intertidal wetland response. *Journal of Geophysical Research – Earth Surface*, Vol. 110, p. F03006.

Zwolsman, J.G. (1994) Seasonal variability and biogeochemistry of phosphorus in the Scheldt Estuary, south west Netherlands. *Estuarine, Coastal and Shelf Science*, Vol. 39, pp. 227–248.

4

Defining coastal and marine boundaries

*Philip A. Collier** and *Roger W. Fraser*†
* *Department of Geomatics, The University of Melbourne, Australia;* † *Office of Surveyor General Victoria, Department of Sustainability and Environment, Australia*

Legally defined and enforceable marine boundaries are critical to the governance and sustainable management of the oceans and the coastal zone. The basic principles that allow such boundaries to be established at law and physically realised form essential knowledge for all who work professionally in the marine environment.

4.1   Introduction

In our everyday world, we are confronted by the reality that we cannot simply go where we choose, when we choose. For example, there are some countries we cannot freely visit, there are some places within our own country that we cannot go, and we cannot just wander into our neighbour's back yard and treat it as if it were our own. But one may ask, 'How do I know whether I can go here or there?' Restrictions on our movements and the right or denial of access to a certain place is generally governed by legally defined boundaries or borders. A well known historical example is the famous Berlin Wall, shown in Fig. 4.1, which, in the era from 1961 to 1989, prevented those living in communist East Berlin from fleeing to the West.

Most of us are familiar with boundaries on land. We see a fence or a wall and we know implicitly that it delineates an area where some restrictions apply to our movements and perhaps our behaviour. But rights and restrictions imposed through the proclamation and enforcement of legal boundaries are not limited to the terrestrial environment. Boundaries are very common in the marine environment as well. But the concept of marine

Coastal zone management
978-0-7277-3641-1

Fig. 4.1 The once-famous Berlin Wall
(Source: http://www.essential-architecture.com/G-BER/BER-029.htm)

boundaries is less familiar to many, first because the marine environment is vast and largely inaccessible and, second because offshore boundaries, more often than not, cannot be seen. Except on rare occasions, there are no fences or boundary markers at sea. Nonetheless, legally enforceable boundaries exist in the marine environment and they are crucial to the process of ocean governance, particularly in the highly exploited and environmentally delicate coastal zone.

Readers who have had dealings in land (for example, buying or selling property) may be familiar with the concept of the land *cadastre*, for which the International Federation of Surveyors (FIG) has produced the following definition (FIG, 1995):

> A cadastre is normally a parcel based and up-to-date land information system containing a record of interests in land (i.e. rights, restrictions and responsibilities). It usually includes a geometric description of land parcels linked to other records describing the nature of the interests, and ownership or control of those interests, and often the value of the parcel and its improvements. It may be established for fiscal purposes (e.g. valuation and equitable taxation), legal purposes (conveyancing), to assist in the management of land and land use (e.g. for planning and other administrative purposes), and enables sustainable development and environmental protection.

Thus, the land cadastre exists to register, record, manage and administer individual and corporate interests and dealings in land.

The cadastre is fundamentally reliant on the definition and practical realisation of legally defined boundaries for the delimitation of the land parcels. Without legally defined and enforceable boundaries, there can literally be no cadastre, no land dealings and no register of interests in land.

The concept of the cadastre can of course be extended to the marine environment and, in recent years, a number of researchers have been investigating the feasibility of developing a *marine cadastre*. The marine cadastre emerges as a logical extension to the land cadastre, although, as we shall see, there are some significant differences that must be considered.

The purpose of this chapter is to expose the reader to some of the most critical issues relating to the role of legally defined boundaries in the management, administration and governance of the marine environment. To achieve this objective, the chapter begins with a brief review of land boundaries to provide a basis for comparison and contrast to the marine case. The reader is then introduced to the concept of the marine cadastre as a means of formally managing offshore areas in a spatial context. This is followed by a description of the main types of marine boundaries and how they are delimited. The basic principles of realising marine boundaries and offshore positioning are then discussed to bring the chapter to a conclusion.

4.2 Some basic principles

4.2.1 Land boundaries

As an introduction to our later consideration of marine boundaries, it may be useful to review the basic principles that govern the definition and realisation of land boundaries. As illustrated in Fig. 4.2, often such boundaries may be visually recognised by means of fences, walls or other physical markers such as survey pegs. Such 'monuments' provide realisation to the limits of a land parcel. From a legal perspective, land boundaries are most often defined by a combination of a deed of grant, a survey plan and government regulations or other documents of legal standing. Figure 4.3 shows an example of a Certificate of Title and its accompanying Title Plan used to establish the intent of the spatial extent of a Crown allotment. In general, land boundaries can only be challenged, modified or removed through the application of well defined legal principles and procedures. For example, the creation of new boundaries or the modification of existing boundaries for the

Fig. 4.2 Fences and walls give physical realisation to land boundaries

purposes of land subdivision, is a common but very closely regulated process that can only be undertaken by licensed land (cadastral) surveyors. Indeed, only a licensed surveyor has the right under law to place pegs showing the location of the corners of a land parcel and it is illegal for those pegs to subsequently be removed.

The most common, and sometimes the most contentious, land boundaries are those that divide parcels of privately owned land from other privately owned land or public land. Other familiar land boundaries include those that distinguish between:

- different countries (international borders)
- different states within a country (national borders)
- local government areas (municipalities)
- state or government owned land (Crown land)
- easements and other encumbrances
- rights of way, roads and carriageways
- parks, reserves, sanctuaries and other protected areas.

With these basic and quite familiar features of land boundaries in mind, let us now consider some basic principles of boundaries in the marine environment.

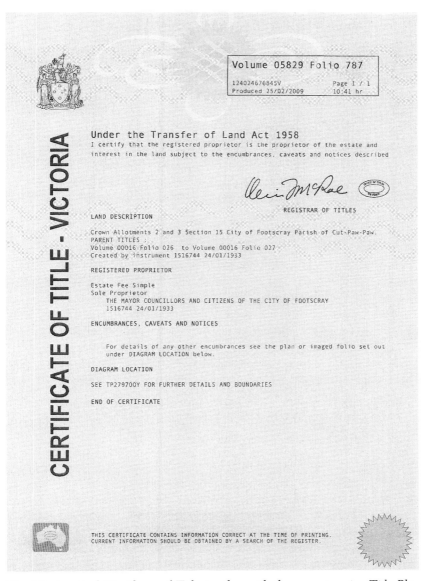

Fig. 4.3 A typical Certificate of Title together with the accompanying Title Plan (Reproduced by permission of The Registrar of Titles, Victoria)

4.2.2   Marine boundaries

Boundaries at sea are generally not visible to the human eye, nor are they routinely marked in any physical way, simply because of the practical difficulties associated with placing pegs or other permanent monuments in

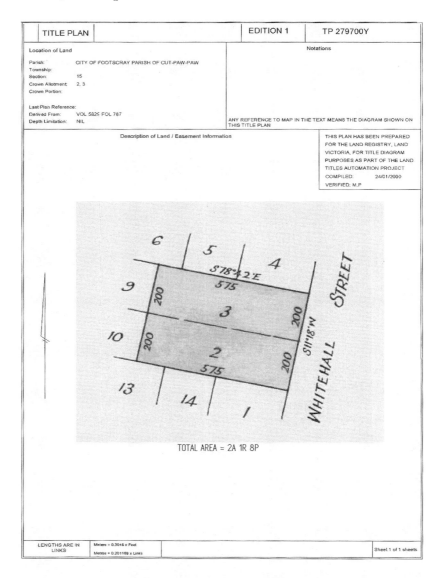

| TITLE PLAN | | | EDITION 1 | TP 279700Y |

Location of Land

Parish: CITY OF FOOTSCRAY PARISH OF CUT-PAW-PAW
Township:
Section: 15
Crown Allotment: 2, 3
Crown Portion:

Last Plan Reference:
Derived From: VOL 5829 FOL 787
Depth Limitation: NIL

Notations

ANY REFERENCE TO MAP IN THE TEXT MEANS THE DIAGRAM SHOWN ON THIS TITLE PLAN

Description of Land / Easement Information

THIS PLAN HAS BEEN PREPARED FOR THE LAND REGISTRY, LAND VICTORIA, FOR TITLE DIAGRAM PURPOSES AS PART OF THE LAND TITLES AUTOMATION PROJECT
COMPILED: 24/01/2000
VERIFIED: M.P

TOTAL AREA = 2A 1R 8P

| LENGTHS ARE IN LINKS | Metres = 0.3048 x Feet | | | Sheet 1 of 1 sheets |
| | Metres = 0.201168 x Links | | | |

Detailed print of TP279700Y, Page 1 of 1, Printed 10:49 25/02/2009, Customer rj13

Fig. 4.3 Continued

water or on the sea floor. There is, nonetheless, a plethora of boundaries in the marine environment and, in many ways, the inter-relationship between these boundaries can be more spatially and legally complex and more difficult to administer, than land boundaries.

Like boundaries on land, marine boundaries are normally defined in a legally binding way through, for examples an Act of Parliament, an International Treaty or some other legal instrument. By way of illustration, Fig. 4.4 shows an extract from the 2003 Great Barrier Reef Marine Park Zoning Plan (GBRMPA, 2003), which textually describes the spatial extent of the Ninian Bay marine protected area off the north Queensland coast. A graphical representation of the area is also shown (in the darker tint), having been extracted from the corresponding Great Barrier Reef Marine Park Zoning Map. Boundaries at sea usually define areas or zones (such as marine national parks, fishing zones, shipping channels, dumping grounds, etc.) which have associated with them clearly defined rights, restrictions and responsibilities. These interests may, of course, overlap in both space and time in complex ways that are quite foreign to the terrestrial case (Grant, 1999; Robertson *et al.*, 1999; Treml *et al.*, 1999; Collier *et al.*, 2001; Ng'ang'a *et al.*, 2001; Todd, 2001). The concept of a *marine parcel* is familiar when one considers the parallel of a land parcel in the terrestrial realm, as discussed in Section 4.2.1. However, in the marine environment, there is a clear distinction that must me made: with only a few exceptions, there is no such thing as *ownership* or *freehold title* over marine parcels and therefore no issuance of Certificates of Title to individuals, corporations or other legal entities.

Because most marine boundaries are not physically marked or monumented, they must be realised each time their location is required in a real world application. For example, if the operator of a fishing vessel needs to know whether his or her boat is inside or outside a proclaimed fishing area, this can only be determined in real time by comparing the vessel's current location (usually determined by satellite positioning technology such as the global positioning system – GPS) to the mathematical and/or legal description of the boundary. This is normally done either graphically, by plotting the boundary and the vessel's position on a nautical chart (digitally or manually), or computationally by calculating whether the vessel is inside or outside the polygon defining the prescribed fishing zone. The process of realising the marine boundary for such purposes can be performed by the vessel operator or navigator, it does not require particular training, special qualifications or legal endorsement as in the case of marking land boundaries.

Marine boundaries can exist for a variety of purposes. The following is a list of some common examples:

[CP-14-4015] Ninian Bay

The area bounded by a line commencing at 14° 20.040' S, 144° 36.942' E then running progressively:

1. east along the parallel to its intersection with longitude 144° 38.820' E
2. east along the parallel to its intersection with longitude 144° 39.253' E
3. south-easterly along the geodesic to 14° 20.842' S, 144° 39.720' E
4. south along the meridian to its intersection with latitude 14° 21.960' S
5. west along the parallel to its intersection with the mainland coastline at mean low water (at or about 14° 21.960' S, 144° 38.992' E)
6. along the mainland coastline at mean low water to its intersection with the meridian 144° 35.763' E (at or about 14° 21.920' S, 144° 35.763' E)
7. north-easterly along the geodesic to the point of commencement

---

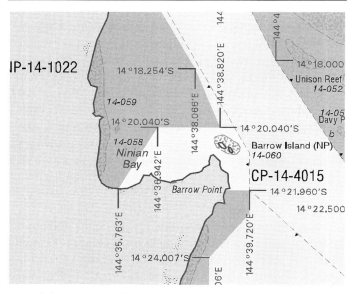

Fig. 4.4 Legal description and map extracts of Ninian Bay from the 2003 Great Barrier Reef Marine Park Zoning Plan and Zoning Map (Sources: http://www.gbrmpa.gov.au/_data/assets/pdf_file/0016/10591/Zoning_Plan.pdf http://www.gbrmpa.gov.au/_data/assets/pdf_file/0017/10673/mpz_04.pdf)

- international boundaries (e.g. exclusive economic zone)
- national boundaries (e.g. contiguous zone)
- lease boundaries
- marine parks
- fishing zones
- pipelines and cables
- native title areas

- exploration areas
- shipping channels.

4.2.3   The place of marine boundaries in coastal zone management

It is important to be clear about the role of legally defined boundaries in the process of coastal zone management in particular, and ocean governance more generally. Something like 70% of the Earth's surface is covered by water. In the case of Australia, the nation's land mass is some 7.7 million km^2, while the 200 nautical mile exclusive economic zone (EEZ) surrounding the Australian mainland is approximately 8.6 million km^2. (This figure excludes external territories such as the Australian Antarctic Territory, as well as the vast areas of extended continental shelf to which Australia has seabed rights as determined by the United Nations Commission on the Limits of the Continental Shelf – see Fig. 4.5.) Thus, Australia has sovereign rights over a significantly greater area of ocean than it does over land. This is not an unusual situation for countries with long coastlines such as Australia, New Zealand and Canada and serves to illustrate the strategic, security, economic and environmental imperatives that emerge with regard to the management of the world's oceans and ocean resources.

The boundary of Australia's EEZ has been determined using internationally agreed criteria prescribed under the United Nations Convention on the Law of the Sea (UNCLOS, United Nations, 1982) and is generally 200 nautical miles from the coast. But as we move from the open oceans towards the coast, the complexity and density of marine boundaries begins to increase. In some cases these boundaries are declared through international instruments such as conventions or treaties, but more commonly they are proclaimed under Federal or State legislation. In the coastal zone, they may also be more local in nature and purpose such as those imposed by local government for planning, zoning and other management reasons. What becomes abundantly clear is that effective management, control and administration of the marine environment implicitly demands the use of legally defined and enforceable boundaries in much the same way as boundaries are used on land. Without boundaries there will be uncontrolled exploitation of the marine environment and its resources. Boundaries are simply a means to an end in this respect. They provide a legal mechanism and a spatial framework by which behaviour can be controlled and specific rights, restrictions and responsibilities can be imposed and enforced.

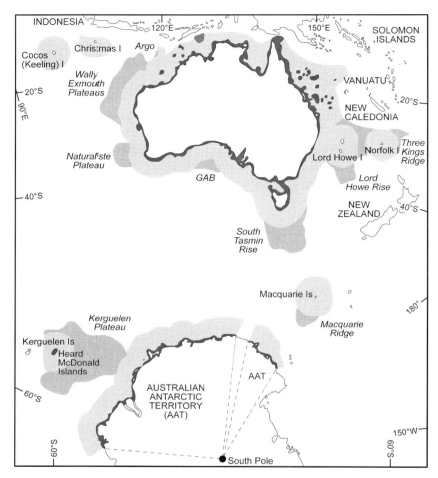

AUSTRALIA'S CONTINENTAL SHELF CONFIRMED BY THE COMMISSION ON THE LIMITS OF THE CONTINENTAL SHELF

■ Territorial sea and internal waters	Area of Australia's continental shelf beyond 200M as confirmed by the Commission on the Limits of the Continental Shelf
□ Areas of marine jurisdiction within 200M of Australia and its external territories	■ Joint Petroleum Development Area under Timor Sea Treaty 2002

Fig. 4.5 Australia's maritime jurisdiction (© Commonwealth of Australia, Geoscience Australia, 2008) (Source: http://www.ga.gov.au/image_cache/GA11214.pdf)

4.3   The marine cadastre principle

In this section, the basic concept of the marine cadastre will be discussed and some of the major similarities and differences between the more familiar and well established land cadastre will be identified.

As discussed in Section 4.1, the land cadastre exists to register, record, manage and administer interests in land. It serves fiscal, legal, management and environmental functions and is the very cornerstone of all dealings in land. The land cadastre is built on the premise that legally defined boundaries delimit the location, size and extent of land parcels and that those boundaries can be established, marked and re-established on the ground in a consistent and repeatable way through the process of measurement. In developed countries, the right to own, use, occupy or otherwise exploit a parcel of land for private or commercial purposes is a strictly controlled process.

In maintaining a land cadastre, distinctions are normally made between land held privately and that which rests with the government (variously referred to as Crown land or public land). Private land can be bought and sold and confers rights of exclusive use and occupation, introducing the concepts of *ownership* and *freehold title*. The boundaries of private land are normally fenced or otherwise conspicuously marked so that the physical extent of the parcel is clearly, permanently and unambiguously evident. Thus, a casual walk down a residential street or a flight over the suburbs of a major city (e.g. Fig. 4.6) will reveal the practical reality of the land cadastre and the boundaries that distinguish one land parcel from another.

When it comes to publicly owned (or government) land, the boundaries are equally well defined and have comparable legal status to land held privately, although dealings in public land only take place when that land is being converted to private ownership through the process of alienation. While some government land will be fenced for the purposes of delineating its boundaries and restricting access (e.g. military bases and other government installations), much government land is unfenced and the boundaries – while being defined legally – are not so visible or obvious to the casual observer. Such land is generally open to the public, although restrictions of use often apply. A national park is a familiar example of government-controlled land where access to the public is permitted, but use and enjoyment of the land is controlled by rules and regulations that will limit what can be done, where and when. For example, camping may be confined to certain areas and the use of firearms and the taking of firewood may also be prohibited. Public land can sometimes be leased for private use by individuals and corporations, subject to certain conditions. For example, government-owned land in rural areas is sometimes leased for pastoral or agricultural purposes or mining operations.

69

Fig. 4.6 Visible evidence of the land cadastre (Caroline Springs, Victoria)
(Source: Google Earth (maps.google.com.au))

There is a clear analogy between the principles and purposes of the land cadastre and the existence and role of boundaries in the marine environment. Both on land and at sea, legally defined boundaries exist to delimit 'parcels' with specified rights, restrictions and responsibilities associated with them. The basic concept of the marine cadastre is illustrated in Fig. 4.7, which shows some typical marine boundaries and the inter-relationships between them. The marine environment is the subject of much human activity, particularly in the coastal and near-coastal zone. Activities range from recreational uses such as fishing, swimming and boating through to commercial operations such as oil and gas extraction and aquaculture. There are also environmental protection zones and sanctuaries as well as native title areas and commercial shipping operations, to name but a few of the familiar uses. In many cases, these diverse and sometimes competing interests, must co-exist. Sitting as an overarching requirement on the management of the marine environment is the need to preserve the delicate and inherently valuable ecological balance, while at the same time allowing reasonable and equitable use and the sustainable exploitation of natural resources. The marine cadastre has the potential to provide the tool to register, record and manage these diverse interests.

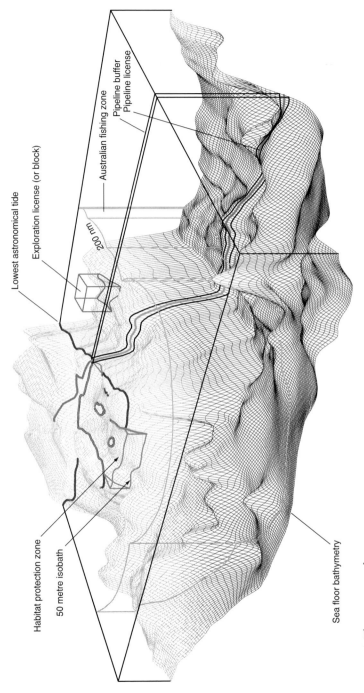

Fig. 4.7 The marine cadastre concept

Lowest astronomical tide

Australian fishing zone

Pipeline buffer

Pipeline license

Exploration license (or block)

200 nm

Habitat protection zone

50 metre isobath

Sea floor bathymetry

4.4 Distinctions between the land and marine cadastre

Now we will consider some of the distinctions between the land cadastre and the concept of the marine cadastre.

4.4.1 Marine boundaries are virtual

Standing on the sea shore, sailing across the ocean or travelling by submarine below the sea surface will not reveal the multitude of boundaries that exist, nor the potentially complex spatial, temporal and legal interactions between them, simply because marine boundaries are not normally visible. Indeed, it is rare in the marine environment for a boundary to be monumented in any physical way at all. Occasionally, such a boundary may be identified by a series of buoys, but, of necessity, the location of the buoys will be approximate as they drift and move under the influence of currents, waves, wind and tides (e.g. Fig. 4.8). Furthermore, the exact location of the boundary formed by the interconnection of the buoys can only be estimated by the mariner as obviously no line is drawn on the water surface or the ocean floor to delineate the exact location of the boundary.

The absence of physical demarcation of marine boundaries leads inevitably to the conclusion that such boundaries must be regarded as *virtual* entities for the purposes of ocean use, management and governance.

Fig. 4.8 Buoys can only approximately show the location of a marine boundary (Source: Lise Glaser)

4.4.2　*The marine environment is truly 3D*

The legal description of a land parcel is normally given in 2D (horizontal) terms. While the mode of description may vary (e.g. it may be by coordinates or by bearings and distances) it is the horizontal location and extent of the parcel that forms the essence of the description. This is not to say that rights for normal use and enjoyment do not exist vertically (both above and below ground level), nor that parcels cannot be defined in three dimensions in certain cases (e.g. strata titles). However, as a general rule, the vertical extent of a land parcel does not form part of the legal description.

Offshore, though, the situation can be very different. In terms of use and exploitation, the marine environment must be regarded as truly 3D. The sea surface, water column, seabed and sub-seabed are all distinct and subject to different forms of activity and use, either separately or simultaneously (Fowler and Treml, 2001; Ng'ang'a *et al.*, 2001). This means that, in practice, overlapping rights, restrictions and responsibilities can co-exist, often without interference or conflict. For example, the right to fish requires access to the sea surface and the water column, but does not preclude other co-existent uses such as shipping, the laying of undersea cables and pipelines or the extraction of oil and gas. To further illustrate the truly 3D nature of the marine environment, it should be noted that when aquaculture leases are granted for the purposes of fish farming it is often the case that the lease will have a specified depth limit, as governed by the physical dimensions of the fish pens, so that use of the water column and sea floor below the lease boundary remains unencumbered for all practical purposes.

4.4.3　*Freehold title does not exist*

A principal reason for the existence of the land cadastre is to register private ownership and other interests in land. When a person purchases a property, that transaction is registered, they become the proprietor and, perhaps subject to certain encumbrances and other limitations, are entitled to the exclusive use and enjoyment of that parcel of land. They are then said to have freehold title or ownership of the property and can prosecute those who trespass or infringe on their rights. Except in some very rare circumstances, no such systems of ownership, exclusive use or scheme of trading occur in relation to marine parcels. Subject to certain restrictions and limitations, the oceans represent something more akin to public open space. It is true that certain

73

areas can be designated or set aside for a particular use, the extent of which will be governed by legally defined boundaries, but rarely are such areas confined to a single or exclusive use. So, for example, a proclaimed fishing area assigns rights to commercial fishing fleet operators, but that proclamation does not prohibit other uses such as, recreational fishing, boating or scuba diving. Further, in the case of an aquaculture lease, exclusive use may be granted to the lessee but, strictly speaking, not freehold title or ownership. It should be pointed out that while freehold title is not granted in the marine environment, it is possible to buy and sell lease areas in the marine environment (e.g. aquaculture leases or oil and gas exploration leases).

4.4.4 Marine boundaries can change temporally

In many cases, boundaries in the marine environment are time (temporally) variable. For example, fishing in a particular area may be banned at certain times of the year, but not at others. Thus, marine boundaries can come and go temporally, depending on the purpose they serve. While such flexibility in the imposition and removal of boundaries and the rights, restrictions and responsibilities associated with them has legitimate practical justification, it introduces significant complexity when it comes to management and governance of the oceans.

Marine boundaries can also be *ambulatory*. This pertains to temporal variations in location as discussed above, but due to a different cause. In the first case, temporal change is introduced through the process of boundary proclamation, it is deliberate, purposeful, controllable and of human origin. However, temporal change in the location of marine boundaries can take place – and sometimes in quite a dramatic fashion – as a result of natural processes. For example, many marine boundaries are explicitly related to the position of the coastline. But the coastline itself is very much an ambulatory feature. Storm surges, wave action, the natural processes of erosion and accretion, as well as humanly induced changes can have significant impacts on the location of the coastline over time. As a consequence, the location of any marine boundary directly related to the coastline will also change. In many ways, society struggles to cope with the concept of ambulatory boundaries and there is a line of legal reasoning that argues once a boundary has been proclaimed, it becomes fixed in time, regardless of the fact that if the boundary was to be redetermined it would fall in a different place. However, the reality is that the dynamic nature of the oceans and coastal zone can make static boundary definition somewhat nonsensical and sometimes totally impractical.

4.4.5   Summary

As a tool to register, manage and administer the use of marine parcels, the marine cadastre is a useful concept that can draw significantly from experiences in the development and implementation of the land cadastre. However, the marine cadastre must be sufficiently flexible and different from its terrestrial counterpart to deal with the peculiarities and complexities of the marine environment, as discussed above.

At the time of writing (2009) there is not a country in the world that has an operational marine cadastre, although various jurisdictions have been considering and investigating the idea for a number of years. Among these are Canada, Australia, the United States of America and New Zealand. It does seem likely that these leading nations will move down the path of implementing a marine cadastre in some form, though explicit details remain unresolved. The workload required for full implementation of a register of marine interests should not be underestimated and this is one of the major practical limitations that will impede adoption. In any case, the fact that the marine cadastre is topical indicates an increasing awareness of the importance of systematic governance of maritime jurisdictions for the benefit of all and for the sustainable exploitation of the delicate and inherently valuable marine environment.

4.5   Types of marine boundaries

To this point we have seen that legally defined boundaries are comon in the marine environment. Such boundaries are critical to the management, administration and governance of the oceans. An analogy has been drawn between the way interests in land parcels are administered through the land cadastre and how a marine cadastre could serve a similar function offshore, notwithstanding some of the distinct and important differences between the terrestrial and marine cases. The objective of this section is to discuss the different ways in which marine boundaries can be established and their various categories. In this respect, the natural hierarchy of marine boundaries will become apparent.

4.5.1   *Ways of establishing marine boundaries*

Given the multitude of boundaries in place throughout the world's oceans, it would be impossible to describe here all the different ways in which a marine boundary may be established. Instead, this section will focus on some key delimitation principles and will provide some typical examples for the purposes of illustration.

Coastline boundaries

Perhaps the most important marine boundary in the coastal zone is the coastline itself. The coastline plays a significant role in the delineation of various land and marine parcels abutting the coastline, as well as a number of offshore boundaries. Accordingly, one of the key tasks for government in managing the coastal zone and its broader marine jurisdiction generally, is to establish and maintain an accurate determination of the coastline.

In principle, the coastline may be regarded as a string of points along the foreshore where the sea intersects the land. However, such a simple definition is inadequate when it comes to establishing the *exact* location of the 'coastline'. The delineation of the coastline is intrinsically linked to the definition of different tidal planes and is complicated by the fact that, in the statutory regime used for establishing land and marine boundaries, several different tidal planes are used, each giving rise to a different realisation of the coastline. The following examples, taken from the Australian context, illustrate some of the different definitions that exist for the 'coastline'.

In relation to land parcels adjoining tidal waters, there is a well defined heirarchy of law and practice for establishing and reinstating tidal (or littoral) boundaries. In most cases, the generally (though not universally) adopted tidal datum for this purpose is ordinary (or mean) high water (MHW). In the case of Queensland legislation, MHW is defined as:

> The average of all high waters over a sufficiently long period (preferably over the National Tidal Datum Epoch). (Queensland Government, 2008, p. 216)

While this definition appears succinct and relatively clear in its meaning and intent, the practical realisation of boundaries based on this and other similar definitions has been fraught with difficulties relating to legal–technical interpretations (Fraser, 2008). As a consequence, many protracted disputes have been carried out over the exact position of a tidal boundary in a particular location and at a given point in time.

In relation to offshore boundaries, the coastline is often defined as the line of 'low water' and this line is subsequently used in the delineation of numerous maritime boundaries. On the international scene, the definition of 'low water' is ambiguous. In Australia, multiple definitions for 'low water' exist within the relevant legislation. For instance, in relation to the establishment of national and international boundaries under the provisions of UNCLOS (discussed in Section 4.5.2), such boundaries are to be delineated based upon the location of what is described as the 'normal baseline'. Article 5 of UNCLOS defines the normal baseline as follows:

> Except where otherwise provided in this convention, the normal baseline for measuring the breadth of the territorial sea is the low-water line along the coast as marked on large scale charts officially recognised by the coastal State. (United Nations, 1982, p. 27)

UNCLOS does not provide explicit definitions for 'low water' and 'large scale'. As such, opinions are divided as to which tidal datum should be adopted. For most purposes, in Australia, the low water line has been officially defined as the line of lowest astronomical tide (LAT).

As can be appreciated from these examples, the establishment of the coastline is no simple nor straightforward matter. The coastline may be based upon one of a number of tidal planes. Therefore, when attempting to define the spatial extent of areas along the coastal zone, it is imperative that the term 'coastline' be interpreted according to the legal instrument and context in which the area has been defined. To illustrate the complexity of the problem, Fig. 4.9 shows the delimitation of highest astronomical tide (HAT), mean high water springs (MHWS), Australian height datum (AHD), and lowest astronomical tide (LAT) along the foreshore of the Coolum Beach region in Queensland.

Explicit geometric constructors
Frequently, the location and spatial extent of marine areas are specified by explicit geometric constructors. Such constructors include the geographic coordinates of a point, arc boundaries defined by centre-point and radius, and boundary corners described by the intersection of particular meridians, rhumb lines, geodesics and/or parallels. Typical purposes for which this method of delimitation are used include offshore

77

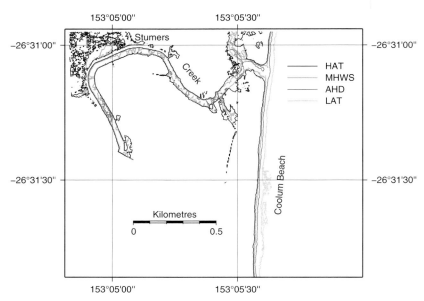

Fig. 4.9 The intersection of various tidal planes along the foreshore of Coolum Beach, Queensland

petroleum blocks, aquaculture leases, marine parks, research areas, marine protected areas, traffic separation schemes, restricted and dangerous areas.

As an example, consider the following extract from the 2003 Great Barrier Reef Marine Park Zoning Plan (GBRMPA, 2003) which defines the boundaries of the Pickersgill Reef Conservation Park Zone:

Pickersgill Reef (15–093)
The area bounded by a line commencing at 15° 50.400' S, 145° 30.000' E then running progressively:

1. east along the parallel to its intersection with longitude 145° 36.600' E
2. south along the meridian to its intersection with latitude 15° 55.200' S
3. westerly along the geodesic to 15° 55.201' S, 145° 30.000' E
4. north along the meridian to the point of commencement. (p. 125)

Figure 4.10 shows the graphical representation of the Reef, extracted from the 2003 Great Barrier Reef Marine Park Zoning Map.

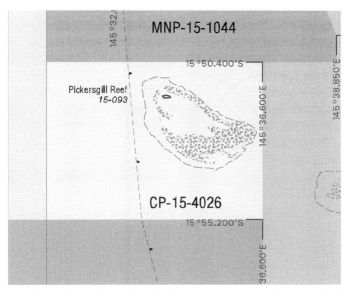

Fig. 4.10 Pickersgill Reef from the 2003 Great Barrier Reef Marine Park Zoning Map

Zone width from the coastline

Many marine boundaries are established by computing a line at a specified distance (zone width) from the coastline. Indeed, this is the primary means by which national boundaries are established under UNCLOS (discussed in more detail in Section 4.5.2). The adopted technique for delimiting boundaries offset from the coastline is the method of *envelopes of arcs* (Boggs, 1930), described as follows:

> ... envelope of all arcs of circles having a radius of three nautical miles drawn from all points on the coast. (Boggs, 1930, p. 544)

While the method was originally developed for delimiting the territorial sea using a 3 nautical mile zone width, it remains valid regardless of the distance and therefore may be used to delimit boundaries using any offset. The concept of delimiting zone boundaries by way of the envelopes of arcs method is shown in Fig. 4.11.

It is worth noting that, when a legal description defines the position of a boundary relative to the location of a naturally occurring marine feature (such as the coastline), uncertainty will inevitably arise in the delimitation of that boundary as a result of not being able to accurately and precisely locate the marine feature. The predominant source of

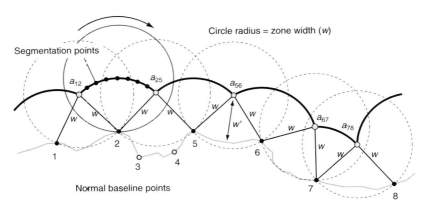

Fig. 4.11 Zone boundary points generated by the method of envelopes of arcs

error and uncertainty comes from errors in the original survey measurements taken to locate the marine feature.

From a rigorous point of view, ignoring information about uncertainty in a measurement is not legitimate. Since all measurements are subject to error, it follows that all measurements and measurement results are only an estimate of the true value and are therefore complete only when they are accompanied by a statement of uncertainty. This is particularly the case if assertions are to be made on the location of marine boundaries which in turn are based upon the location of marine features. In this light, effort should be made to quantify as reliably as possible the uncertainty that exists in the delimitation of marine boundaries (Fraser, 2008).

Natural features and named places

Numerous marine boundaries are defined using references to natural features and named places. Typical examples include harbours, bays, ports, marine parks, marine reserves, and natural, cultural and indigenous heritage areas. Common features and places that may be referenced for this purpose include harbours, gulfs, passages, rivers, reefs, headlands, points, cliffs, banks and the foreshore. In many instances, the natural feature to which a boundary is referenced is a legally defined entity in its own right, such as 'the normal baseline' or 'the line of lowest astronomical tide'. The location of marine boundaries (or more accurately their terminal points) relative to natural features and named places may be described using topological relationships such as 'northern point of', 'mouth of', 'a distance of x nautical miles from', 'the coastal 1 km line', 'from the x metre isobath', 'seaward of', 'landward of', 'extension of', and 'above and below'.

As an example, the Queensland Marine Parks Regulation 1990 uses the following spatial descriptions to define part of the limits of the Rodds Bay segment of the Mackay/Capricorn Management Area (Queensland Government, 1990, pp. 75–76):

- from where the mainland at high water intersects latitude 24° 24.910' south
- then generally northerly along the coastal line along the mainland to where it intersects latitude 24° 25.904' south
- then generally northerly along the mainland at high water to the most eastern point where it intersects latitude 23° 56.405' south
- then easterly along a geodesic to the most northern point where the coastal 500 m line around the mainland intersects the longitude that runs through the most northern point of Richards Point at low water
- then generally south-easterly along the coastal 500 m line around the mainland to the most northern point where it intersects long-itude 151° 43.063' east
- . . .
- then south-easterly along a geodesic to where the coastal 500 m line around the mainland intersects the longitude that passes through the most northern point of Round Hill Head at low water
- . . .
- then west along latitude 24° 24.910' south to where it intersects the mainland at high water.

An interesting point to note is that a considerable level of ambiguity can arise in the delimitation and/or positioning of legal descriptions based on natural features and place names. For instance, unless the exact location of 'Round Hill Head' has been published, the longitude estimated by the mariner may be different from the intended longitude. Furthermore, if the foreshore is unstable, it is probable that 'the most northern point' will be in a different location today to that of the original intention. Clearly, the significance of this difference will also change with time.

Artificial features and objects
Less commonly, references to artificial features and objects may be used to define the location and spatial extent of marine boundaries. Typical

features and objects to which reference is made include registered land parcels, artificial islands, marinas, jetties, bridges, shipwrecks, navigation beacons and buoys, submarine cables and pipelines, and floating oil and gas production facilities. The topological relationships to artificial features and objects may be described in numerous ways, not dissimilar to those for natural features cited above.

As an example, the 1982 Petroleum (Submerged Lands) Act and 1994 Offshore Minerals Act make provision for the proclamation of safety zones around offshore structures and installations as shown by the following example (Commonwealth Australia, 1994):

> The safety zone may extend not more than 500 metres from the outer edge of the structure or equipment. (Commonwealth Australia, 1944, p. 233)

Time

Another principle applicable to defining domestic marine boundaries is the use of time. Time is most commonly used in association with the protection of living resources in defined areas, and is generally specified in advance by means of zoning plans and regulations. For instance, time is often specified to commence or terminate the operation of a commercial fishery or aquaculture farming agreement, to regulate over-fishing of certain species, to protect seasonal egg production and the migratory habitation of protected species.

As an example, Part 2(6) of the Fisheries (Spanner Crab) Management Plan 1999, in pursuance of the Queensland Fisheries Act 1994, uses the following description to declare a State-wide closed season on the removal and/or possession of Spanner Crabs in Queensland waters:

> Spawning closure
> The period from midnight on 20 November to midnight on 20 December in every year is a closed season for spanner crabs. (Queensland Government, 1999, p. 10)

4.5.2 National and international boundaries

The United Nations Convention on the Law Of the Sea (UNCLOS) (United Nations, 1982) is the principal legal instrument that recognises and defines the rights of a coastal state to have an interest in and

sovereign rights over its adjacent waters. UNCLOS provides a foundation for establishing a state's maritime claims, the rules and procedures
for delimiting the spatial extent of those claims, and the jurisdictional
regime for a state to assert its sovereignty within those claims. The
two categories of boundaries to which UNCLOS applies are national
and international maritime boundaries.

National maritime boundaries
National maritime boundaries are those which are established to delimit
the spatial extent of a country's sovereign claims over the ocean. The
basis upon which national maritime claims and the boundaries which
delimit them are defined within UNCLOS is a series of maritime
zones which are defined using prescribed distances (or zone widths)
from a predefined coastal baseline. In Australia, the coastal baseline
coincides with the line of lowest astronomical tide and is called the
territorial sea baseline (TSB). In practice, the TSB is a series of points
along the coast (or foreshore) that marks the seaward limit of the
mainland and islands at LAT, and separates the country's internal
waters (such as harbours, rivers and bays) from its national maritime
jurisdiction.

Proceeding seaward from the baseline, the national maritime zones
defined under UNCLOS are defined in the following paragraphs.
Figure 4.12 shows a cross-section of the relevant maritime zones.

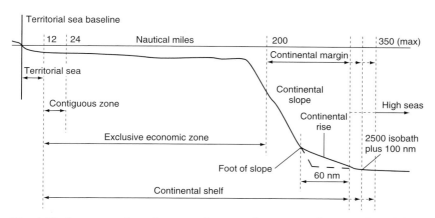

Fig. 4.12 A cross-section of a county's national maritime claims (Adapted from Prescott, 1985, p. 37)

Territorial sea

As defined in Article 2 of UNCLOS, the territorial sea is a belt of water adjacent to the baseline over which a coastal state may extend its jurisdictional sovereignty. Articles 3 and 4 of UNCLOS define the principles for delimiting the outer limit of the territorial sea as follows:

> Article 3
> Every State has the right to establish the breadth of its territorial sea up to a limit not exceeding 12 nautical miles, measured from baselines determined in accordance with this Convention.

> Article 4
> The outer limit of the territorial sea is the line every point of which is at a distance from the nearest point of the baseline equal to the breadth of the territorial sea. (p. 27)

As stated under Article 3, the maximum claimable width for the territorial sea is 12 nautical miles. The adopted technique for implementing boundaries defined under Article 4 is Boggs' method of envelopes of arcs (see Section 4.5.1).

Contiguous zone

Article 33 of UNCLOS defines the outer limit of the contiguous zone as follows:

> Article 33
> The contiguous zone may not extend beyond 24 nautical miles from the baselines from which the breadth of the territorial sea is measured. (p. 35)

As defined under Article 33, the contiguous zone is a belt of water 12 nautical miles wide, extending from the outer limit of the territorial sea to a maximum distance of 24 nautical miles from the territorial sea baseline. Within the contiguous zone, a country is legally empowered to deal with infringement of customs, tax, immigration and sanitary laws. The method for delimiting the contiguous zone is the same as that for delimiting the territorial sea.

Exclusive economic zone

The exclusive economic zone extends from the outer limit of the territorial sea to a maximum distance of 200 nautical miles from the territorial sea baseline. Articles 55 and 57 of UNCLOS define the spatial extent of the exclusive economic zone as follows:

Article 55
The exclusive economic zone is an area beyond and adjacent to the territorial sea, subject to the specific legal regime established in this Part, under which the rights and jurisdiction of the coastal State and the rights and freedoms of other States are governed by the relevant provisions of this Convention. (p. 43)

Article 57
The exclusive economic zone shall not extend beyond 200 nautical miles from the baselines from which the breadth of the territorial sea is measured. (p. 44)

The method for delimiting the exclusive economic zone is the same as that for delimiting the territorial sea. Within the exclusive economic zone, coastal states are granted sovereign rights over all activities relating to living and non-living resources, whether in the water, on the seabed or in the subsoil. These rights apply to artificial islands, marine scientific research, and the protection and preservation of the marine environment. A coastal state has no control over the airspace above the exclusive economic zone.

Extended (or juridical) continental shelf
The final national maritime boundary is the outer limit of the extended continental shelf. In distinction to the physical continental shelf, the juridical continental shelf defined under UNCLOS is that which is comprised of the seabed and subsoil, beginning at the seaward limit of the territorial sea and extending to a maximum limit at or beyond the exclusive economic zone. Paragraph 1 of Article 76 of UNCLOS defines the continental shelf as follows:

The continental shelf of a coastal State comprises the seabed and subsoil of the submarine areas that extend beyond its territorial sea throughout the natural prolongation of its land territory to the outer edge of the continental margin, or to a distance of 200 nautical miles from the baselines… where the outer edge of the continental margin does not extend up to that distance. (p. 53)

Based upon this definition, the spatial extent of rights to the continental shelf can be extended wherever there is a protrusion of the outer edge of the continental margin beyond the limit of the exclusive economic zone. In such a case, a country is entitled to claim an extended continental shelf out to a maximum distance of 350 nautical miles from the TSB or 100 nautical miles from the 2500 m isobath, which ever is most landward. Figure 4.5 shows the area of Australia's extended continental shelf.

International marine boundaries

In instances where the maritime claims from two countries overlap, a common, international maritime boundary must be established to provide jurisdictional certainty. Often cited as lateral boundaries, international maritime boundaries are established by unilateral action, bilateral negotiation or arbitration through the International Court of Justice (ICJ) and the International Tribunal for the Law of the Sea. The settlement of international maritime boundaries is a complex and sometimes contentious issue faced by many countries, some of which still have their common boundaries unresolved after decades, even centuries, of negotiation and dispute.

There are two circumstances under which an international maritime boundary must be established. The first case occurs when two countries are *adjacent* to each other (i.e. they share a common international land border that needs to be extended offshore). In this case, the lateral boundary will likely be drawn from a point beginning at the coastline (at the intersection of the land-based international border and the territorial sea baseline) and will extend seaward through the respective maritime zones. Since Australia has no *adjacent* international neighbours, there is no requirement for Australia to determine a lateral boundary of this type.

The second circumstance occurs when two countries are *opposite* each other. In this case the maritime claims of the opposing countries overlap, giving rise to the need for a negotiated common boundary. If the boundary so determined is chosen to be equidistant from each coastal state, the result is often referred to as the median line solution. There are seven countries whose maritime claims overlap one or more zones surrounding Australia's mainland and external territories. For example, Fig. 4.13 shows the negotiated lateral maritime boundary between Australia and New Zealand according to the Treaty negotiated between the Australian and New Zealand Governments (Commonwealth of Australia, 2004). This boundary has predominantly been based on an equidistant or median line solution.

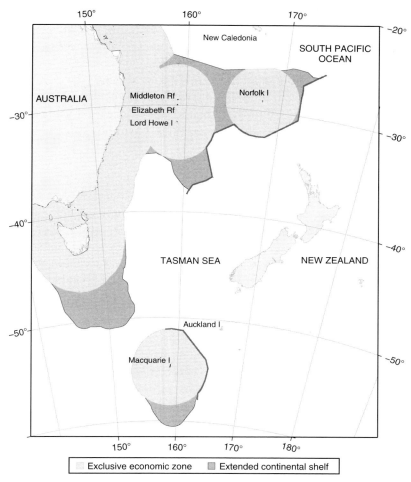

Fig. 4.13 Australia/New Zealand Treaty boundary

4.5.3 Other categories of marine boundaries

Once a country has secured sovereignty over areas of sea and seabed (according to the relevant provisions of UNCLOS), domestic marine boundaries are often required to assist in administering diverse marine interests and associated activities at a more local level. To this end, domestic boundaries are used to delimit areas of political, social, environmental and commercial interest, each of which has various legally binding rights, restrictions and responsibilities associated with them. Typical purposes for which such areas have been defined include jurisdictional sovereignty and administration, marine parks, conservation

87

areas, prohibited activity areas, protected fishing zones, aquaculture leases, petroleum, oil and gas leases, pipelines and cables, military training areas, submarine testing grounds, shipping and transport routes, native title areas, ammunition, chemical and boating waste (or disposal) dumps, artificial islands and jetties, and historic wrecks.

The ways in which such boundaries are established are varied. However, most, if not all of these boundaries are defined using one or more of the principles described in Sections 4.5.1 and 4.5.2.

4.6   Realising marine boundaries

From a purely legal perspective, the unambiguous legal description of a marine boundary is the cornerstone to maintaining legal integrity and certainty. However, the legal description is of little use in a practical sense if the spatial extent cannot be realised at sea in a tangible way. That is, it must be possible to visualise and realise the intent and meaning of the words of a legal spatial description – clearly and unambiguously – for the law to have any effect in the real world. The following examples illustrate this need:

- Government authorities with legislative powers to manage and administer the marine environment must have access to an unambiguous view of the boundaries for which they are responsible.
- Public and commercial stakeholders with an interest in the marine environment must be able to visualise and/or realise the spatial extents within which they may legally conduct an activity.
- Law enforcement agencies must know exactly what rights, restrictions and responsibilities apply, what legislation is involved and what powers are enforceable in a specific area, whether on a map or in the real world.

There are numerous other examples but, in almost every case, a technical implementation is required if the spatial extent of an interest, which is described in words, is to be visualised or realised. A visual representation of a boundary, whether on a map, chart, survey plan or electronic device, involves the process of boundary delimitation. Similarly, realisation involves the process of positioning (or locating) a boundary in the real world. Typically, the process of positioning boundaries in the marine environment will simultaneously require a visual representation so that the location of the mariner in relation to a boundary may be seen.

The requirement for positioning a marine boundary stems from the previously stated reality that marine boundaries are *virtual*. For the mariner, this necessitates the use of a positioning technology whenever the physical location of a boundary is required. Most commonly today, the global positioning system (GPS) is used for this task. GPS and the emergence of other global navigation satellite systems (GNSS), along with ground- and space-based augmentation systems, allow for an unprecedented level of accuracy and simplicity in the task of offshore positioning and navigation. They also serve the useful purpose of allowing non-experts to determine position at sea with relative ease. So for example, even a recreational fisher can routinely determine whether or not he or she is fishing inside or outside a restricted fishing zone with a high level of confidence and with the press of a single button.

A word of caution must conclude this section on realising marine boundaries. While GPS has largely revolutionised the task of offshore positioning, like any measuring system, positions at sea derived from GPS are not error free and GPS equipment can, from time to time, malfunction and report an incorrect position. Thus, when it comes to the critical task of realising legally defined marine boundaries, the wise mariner will always take into consideration the limitations of the measurement system and weight *position-critical* decisions accordingly.

4.7   Conclusion

We began this chapter by pointing out that while legally defined boundaries in the marine environment may not be as visible and as immediately obvious as they are on land, they nonetheless exist and are critical to the process of coastal zone management. Marine boundaries fall into different categories, such as international, national and domestic boundaries. In each case though, such boundaries exist by virtue of explicit legal and spatial description to convey rights, restrictions and/or responsibilities upon the human use, enjoyment or exploitation of the marine environment. It has been suggested that the marine cadastre concept offers a useful way to think about ocean governance in a spatial context and this concept has been illustrated by comparison with the more familiar land cadastre.

Acknowledgements

The authors would like to express their thanks to Dr Russell Priebbenow, Department of Natural Resources and Water, Queensland and Dr Abbas Rajabifard, Department of Geomatics, The University of Melbourne for their assistance in proof reading and providing expert comment on this chapter. Copyright approvals granted by various individuals, organisations and agencies are also gratefully acknowledged.

References

Boggs, W. (1930) Delimitation of the territorial sea: the method of delimitation proposed by the delegation of the United States at the Hague Conference for the Codification of International Law. *American Journal of International Law*, Vol. 24, Issue 3, pp. 541–555.

Collier, P., Leahy, F. and Williamson, I. (2001) Defining a marine cadastre for Australia. *Proceedings of the 42nd Australian Surveyors Congress*, Brisbane. Institution of Surveyors.

Commonwealth of Australia (1994) Offshore Minerals Act. Number 28 of 1994 as amended. Commonwealth of Australia, Canberra, Australia. Includes amendments up to Act No. 140 of 2001.

Commonwealth of Australia (2004) Treaty Between the Government of Australia and the Government of New Zealand Establishing Certain Exclusive Economic Zone Boundaries and Continental Shelf Boundaries. Commonwealth of Australia.

FIG (1995) *The FIG Statement on the Cadastre*, FIG Publication No. 11.

Fowler, C. and Treml, E. (2001) Building a marine cadastral information system for the United States – a case study. *International Journal on Computers, Environment and Urban Systems*, Vol. 24, Issue 4–5, pp. 493–507.

Fraser, R. (2008) A Rigorous Approach to the Technical Implementation of Legally Defined Marine Boundaries. PhD thesis, Department of Geomatics, The University of Melbourne, Melbourne, Australia.

GBRMPA (2003) *Great Barrier Reef Marine Park Zoning Plan*, Great Barrier Reef Marine Park Authority, Townsville.

Grant, D. (1999) Principles for a seabed cadastre. *Proceedings of the New Zealand Institute of Surveyors Conference* (FIG Commission VII Conference), pp. 15–22, Bay of Islands, New Zealand.

Ng'ang'a, S., Nichols, S., Sutherland, M. and Cockburn, S. (2001) Toward a multidimensional marine cadastre in support of good ocean governance. *Proceedings of the International Conference on Spatial Information for Sustainable Development*, Nairobi.

Prescott, J.R.V. (1985) *The Maritime Political Boundaries of the World*, Meuthen & Co. Ltd, London.

Queensland Government (1990) *Marine Parks Regulation*, Queensland Parliamentary Council. Includes commenced amendments up to 2005 SL No. 13.

Queensland Government (1999) *Fisheries (Spanner Crab) Management Plan*, Office of Queensland Parliamentary Council. Reprint No. 3.

Queensland Government (2008) *The Official Tide Tables and Boating Safety Guide*, Queensland Department of Transport, Brisbane.

Robertson, W., Benwell, G. and Hoogsteden, C. (1999) The marine resource: administration infrastructure requirements. *Proceedings of the United Nations – International Federation of Surveyors International Conference on Cadastral*

Infrastructures for Sustainable Development, Melbourne. International Federation of Surveyors (FIG).

Todd, P. (2001) Marine Cadastre – Opportunities and Implications for Queensland. *Proceedings of the Institution of Surveyors 42nd Australian Surveyors Congress*, Brisbane, 25–28 September.

Treml, E., Neely, R., Smillie, H., Fowler, C. and LaVoi, T. (1999) Spatial policy: geo-referencing the legal and statutory framework for integrated regional ocean management. Technical Report, NOAA Coastal Services Center. Available online at: http://www.csc.noaa.gov/opis/html/esri99.htm

United Nations (1982) *United Nations Convention on the Law of the Sea*, Publication No. E97.V10. United Nations, New York.

5

Natural capital – valuing the coast

Christina C. Hicks,[*][†] *Jeremy M. Hills*[*] *and Martin D.A. LeTissier*[*]
[*] *Envision Management, Horsley, Newcastle-upon-Tyne, UK;* [†] *School of Marine Science and Technology, Newcastle University, UK*

The concept of natural capital has evolved greatly since the days of pre-classical economics; these developments reveal a pivotal role for natural capital in economic development and justify its incorporation as a key management tool. While economic approaches and methodologies have provided advances in this area, integrated coastal zone management (ICZM) managers now need to fully integrate assessments of ecological and social features responsible for the generation of natural capital in order to better assess tradeoffs in management choices.

5.1   Introduction

Coastal marine fringes have the greatest concentration of human populations and represent some of the most impacted and altered ecosystems worldwide (Adger *et al.*, 2005). Here multiple stakeholders compete for finite coastal resources within a narrow coastal band. Burgeoning societies associated with coral reefs, for example, are heavily dependent on the extraction of natural resources for their livelihoods. The exponential rates of human population growth and the limits to ecological and fisheries production, as well as other climate mediated threats, leave these environments both ecologically and socially vulnerable to disturbance. These anthropocentric impacts, which are driven by economic forces, permeate every ecosystem, in spite of the wealth of ecological knowledge. The degradation of natural resources and threat of species extinction remains a consequence of socio-economic circumstances that motivate human actions (Armsworth and Roughgarden, 2001; McClanahan *et al.*, 2006). Thus, analysis of individual motives and values should be critical to a solution (Ehrlich and Kennedy, 2005).

This chapter will examine the evolving concept of natural capital and its role in ICZM.

The next section explores the historical role of land and nature as a form of capital. In the late 1980s economists revisited old concepts of 'land' and realised that economics had moved to an era where natural capital, rather than human capital, was the limiting factor. Justification for economic valuation based on the notion that societies will make the best decisions about ecosystems if they possess the best available information on ecosystem values will be put forward. This new approach of combining ecology with economics broadens the conventional goal of economic theory for optimum allocation of resources through efficiency, to include ecological sustainability and social equity.

The third section continues with this ecosystem services approach rationale to categorise ecosystem goods and services, and describe the variety of economic valuation methods and approaches used. This will include consideration of limitations of the associated valuation techniques and criticisms raised in the literature.

The concept of linking natural capital to human welfare, assumes that choices will be made based on preferences to achieve optimum efficiency, sustainability and equity. However, preferences change on temporal and spatial scales depending on factors such as education, advertising and culture. Individual choices may be made to achieve maximum efficiency, as stated in conventional economic theory. However, equity and sustainability need community and global consensus. The role society plays, and the levels of social capital and institutions available to facilitate sharing of information and learning, is a crucial link to building our ability to manage natural resources. The final section examines the links between social capital and ecosystem services capturing tradeoffs within ecological–economic– human systems at different scales. In this section a management framework is put forward to aid ICZM decision making.

5.2   Natural capital – a historical perspective

The concept 'capital' refers to the production function that links inputs, such as stocks of labour, to the output of goods and services. Therefore, natural capital, first distinguished as a separate category of capital in the late 1980s, can be thought of as stocks of natural assets (e.g. fish, land or CO_2), or delivering ecosystem goods and services (e.g. food or climate regulation which support most aspects of human existence) (Pearce, 1988). The need for a separate category of capital arose as economics had passed from an era in which human capital (financial or knowledge), could be interchangeably the limiting factors to growth, to one in which increasingly the limiting factor was natural capital. Increasing scarcity of natural assets, or ecological limits to growth, is apparent in observed trends of increasing species extinctions, temperature variability and weather related damages. Combined with the pressures of continued population growth rates, economic growth is increasingly uneconomic growth, with costs outweighing benefits.

5.2.1 Scarcity and decision making

Economics studies the scarcity of goods, with neoclassical economics concerning itself with what can be considered relatively scarce. The concept of relative scarcity assumes a substitute exists for all goods and services, in this way economics evaluates issues of human preference or choice for one good over another. However, not all goods and services can be substituted; many are considered 'absolutely scarce'. For example, once a species becomes extinct, if no other species exist that can fulfil its functional role; the loss will likely affect the viability of other species (Balvanera *et al.*, 2001). This was the case leading to the early 1990's Caribbean phase-shift from a coral to an algal dominated reef unable to support a healthy fishery. It is thought that the removal by fishing of the herbivores and the subsequent disease induced Diadema die-off led to macro algal overgrowth limiting space and opportunity for new coral colonisation (Hughes, 1994). While the distinction between relative and absolute scarcity is important to make, as it is to recognise that we are not actually dealing with economic problems of choice but are facing problems of absolute scarcity, human action remains dictated by choice. Economics therefore can provide us with a framework to address issues of absolute scarcity using relative scarcity as a decision-making tool. Armed with information on ecosystem values, the rational for valuing natural capital is that action or inaction can be better evaluated against the costs and benefits to promote consensus on conservation planning (Baumgartner *et al.*, 2006). As information on ecosystem values becomes widespread, these values can become integrated into everyday decision making. There is no greater need for a proper and continuous evaluation of the consequences of our relationships with the environment than in the narrow finite band of the coastal zone where multiple stakeholders compete for space, resources and a diversity of goods and services. This approach, combining ecology with economics, broadens the conventional goal of economic theory for optimum allocation of resources through efficiency to include ecological sustainability and social equity.

5.2.2   The evolution of concepts of 'land' in economic theory

The idea that the environment features as a unique component of capital is not a new one. Land, labour and capital were the three primary inputs of economics; the term land encompassed the natural environ-ment including the atmosphere and oceans. However, over time, the concept of land in economics became increasingly narrow in its contri-bution to human well being. Only recently, with the environmental crisis and awareness of the late twentieth century has it resurfaced as an important concept. What is evident is how the views of old economics are resurfacing in today's discourse.

In pre-classical economics (1500–1776) the basis of the economy and growth was land and agriculture. Understandably, land and labour were considered critical to the economy. The earlier Mercantilists saw labour as the limiting factor to growth whereas the Physiocrats saw it to be land but neither attacked the foundations on which they saw their economy based: land and labour. With the arrival of the industrial revolution came the beginning of classical economics (1776–1850s). As economic thought developed, land retained its crucial role as the principle source of revenue and wealth for every country (Smith, 1776). One point of divergence at this time was whether rent, or the value of land, was based on its scarcity (Malthus, 1798), or its diversity (Ricardo, 1817). In 1798, Malthus wrote of population growth being ultimately limited by the natural environment, as population growth would always far exceed the rate at which we could increase agricultural output. The ideas of the time led to the ultimate conclusion that economic growth must come to a halt due to the scarcity of land (Becker *et al.*, 2005). Malthus saw the confrontation between the human mind and nature as certain and constant, with man's role as attempting to control nature and nature being ultimately unconquerable. However Words-worth at the same time recognised a fundamental conflict between nature and the economy seeing nature as fundamentally endangered (Hubacek and van den Bergh, 2006). Other major developers of classical economic thought, Mill and Marx, also recognised the intrinsic value of land or nature in its attributes and quality and the importance of retaining undisturbed land (Becker, 2005).

95

With the decline of the importance of the landlord class during the industrial revolution, and the development of industrialism, capitalism and industrial labour as the dominant class, neoclassical economics emerged (~1870). New economic thought was characterised by the length (~60 years) of the industrial revolution and the pace at which technologies developed. The value for a good came to be described as the value to the user rather than the nation. Shifts in economic theory and analysis were:

1. Land and other capital inputs regarded as capital and labour alone.
2. Physical measures of capital were replaced by monetary measures.
3. The theory of production was replaced by a theory of allocation and prices.
4. Individual factors of capital were viewed as commensurable, their complementarities ignored, and therefore considered as substitutable.
5. Units of efficiency were replaced by concepts of marginal value of utility (Hubacek and van den Bergh, 2006).

Land as a factor of capital lost its unique role in this framework and had no reason to be set aside in economic analysis. With 'land' unprotected in neoclassical economics, various sub-fields of economics emerged from the 1920s to address particular concerns over aspects of land including *agricultural economics, land economics,* and *environmental and resource economics.*

5.2.3   The emerging 'spaceship' economy

The 1960s saw the beginnings of a shift from resource allocation in an economic system to interdependencies of economic-ecological systems. Previously the general belief had been that the economy exists in an open inexhaustible environment with no 'limits to growth'. Now the reality that it existed in a closed system with a fixed amount of energy input from the outside in the form of solar energy was becoming apparent (Boulding, 1966). The 'limits to growth' report (Meadows *et al.*, 1972), although heavily criticised at the time, reiterated classical economic concerns over the consequences of unabated growth. These ideas led to the development of the concept of sustainable development; brought to global attention by the Brandt (1980) and Bruntland (1987) commissions, where two forms of sustainability were put forward. The first, so called 'weak' sustainability containing neo-classical economic ideals, aimed to maintain the aggregate stock of human and man-made capital. However, this again assumed these two forms of capital are interchangeable offering no rational to preserve natural stocks of capital. In the second form, 'hard' sustainability, a minimum necessary condition is that the stock of natural capital is maintained. The economic valuation of biodiversity was pioneered by David Pearce and aimed to develop existing economic theories to include more ecologically sensitive concepts and address two goals (Pearce, 1988):

- First to demonstrate that biodiversity generates values sufficient to motivate its own preservation.
- Second to show how local peoples whose actions determine the fate of indigenous biodiversity can capture or appropriate enough of the value of biodiversity to compensate them for the opportunity cost of preserving it (Simpson, 2007).

Ecological economics also emerged as a separate field in the late 1980s using the concept of natural capital, and argues against mainstream economic thinking through linking in ecosystem thinking (Akerman, 2003). As such ecological economics studies the relationship between economy and nature using interdisciplinary methods in an attempt to develop new solutions to the causes of modern environmental problems. (Costanza, 1989; Becker *et al.*, 2005; Farber *et al.*, 2006). Regardless of which academic label is worn, the common theme through environment, natural resource and ecological economics is the analysis of interactions between ecological and human production and consumption systems.

5.2.4   Management implications

Intelligent management of any natural resource system requires quantification of all the costs and benefits, and an evaluation of the tradeoffs, of the various management choices (Arrow *et al.*, 1995). The concept of value lends itself well to evaluating well-defined changes to ecosystems as it concerns itself with marginal changes. It is within this rational that the valuation of biodiversity provides an effective tool to quantify the relative importance of different components of an ecosystem. Ecosystem services, which are used to encompass elements of biodiversity in valuation studies, refer variously to the benefits humans obtain from ecosystems (Millenium Ecosystem Assessment, 2005), this includes the benefits people perceive and those they do not. Increasingly, calls are to focus on ecosystem services in conservation planning (Balvanera *et al.*, 2001; Chang *et al.*, 2006). Adopting an ecosystem services approach, means that human preferences and wellbeing will be incorporated, thereby increasing the likelihood of cooperation and effective conservation. While the importance of such an approach for conservation planning has been widely accepted, a recent study found only 8% of randomly selected conservation assessments to include ecosystem services (Egoh *et al.*, 2007). Many constraints exist to the application of this approach so that a generally accepted method of planning for ecosystem services does not exist and there are methodological disagreements across disciplinary boundaries, (Balvanera *et al.*, 2001; Kremen, 2005). The most powerful approach to such an analysis would involve a model or framework. This would include a definition of the system and its boundaries, the sources and consumers of the ecosystem services, their conservation or management requirements and the benefits to humans.

5.3 Ecosystem service valuation – methods and approaches

The basic philosophy behind ecosystem service valuations can be illustrated with a simplistic look at the supply and demand for conservation (Fig. 5.1). The x-axis measures some flow of ecosystem services and the y-axis the economic value. D_M is the demand curve for the marketed ecosystem services and $D_{M\&NM}$ is the demand for the marketed and non-marketed ecosystem services (Pearce, 2007).

The more ecosystem services there are, the less we are willing to pay for each additional unit of the marketed and non-marketed ecosystem services. However, at very low levels of ecosystem services the amount we are willing to pay for an additional unit of ecosystem service becomes very high. At some point, close to zero flow of ecosystem services, the amount we are willing to pay for an additional unit is unbounded. The point at which demand for ecosystem services increases dramatically reflects some ecological limit beyond which we cannot survive ES_{min}. In order to maintain ecosystem services, some costs are incurred; these are referred to as the supply curve. MC_M reflects the marginal costs associated with managing ecosystem services.

One potential cost of maintaining ecosystem services is lost opportunity costs, such as through foregone revenue from fishing. MC_{OC} reflects the opportunity costs of maintaining one additional unit of ES, therefore the overall marginal cost of conservation of ecosystem services is $MC_M + MC_{OC} = MC_{M\&OC}$. As the aggregate costs of

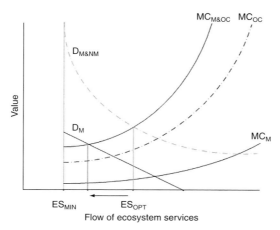

Fig. 5.1 A simplistic look at the supply and demand for conservation. The x-axis measures some flow of ecosystem services and the y-axis the economic value (adapted from Pearce, 2007)

conservation is reflected by the area under $MC_{M\&OC}$ and the global benefits are reflected by the area under $D_{M\&NM}$, then ES_{opt} reflects the economically optimum level of ecosystem services provision. Any point to the left of ES_{opt} means that benefits are greater than the costs of their supply (demand is greater than supply) and, unless we confine our measurement arbitrarily to points between ES_{min} and ES_{opt}, we have infinite or undefined total benefits. Moreover, while $D_{M\&NM}$ reflects the true global benefit, unless the un-marketed goods are captured or some form of quantitative restrictions are imposed then the demand curve that matters is D_M. In this instance a market failure will occur and there is a real danger of serious under provision of the ecosystem services. The valuation of non-marketed goods and the creation of hypothetical markets can provide a solution for the goods or services for which the original market failed D_{NM}. In this way we can all be made accountable for our externalities. This section is intended as an introduction to the tools necessary to address these issues.

5.3.1 Definition of economic goods and services

Multiple classification systems exist to address ecosystem service valuations. While this may seem confusing and over-complicated, they are necessary to address the various purposes of valuations and the complex nature of the systems we operate in. This situation is also characteristic of an evolving research area and here we will look at two such systems:

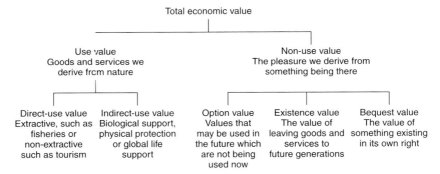

Fig 5.2 A conventional goods and services classification system (adapted from Barton, 1994)

- The more conventional goods and services approach (Barton, 1994, Table 5.1).
- That adopted by the Millennium Ecosystem Assessment (2003, Table 5.2).

Ecosystem services refer to the benefits people obtain from ecosystems. The conventional economic approach to benefit includes only those people perceive and are willing to pay for. This is reflected in the environmental economic classification of goods and services that combine environmental values with an ecosystem-function approach. The first general separation is made between (1) *use* and (2) *non-use* values. Use values typically refer to the goods and services we derive from nature, and can further be split into (a) *direct* and (b) *indirect* uses. Non-use values refer to the pleasure we derive from something being there and include (a) *bequest* and (b) *existence* values, although individuals may derive little or no actual value (Barton, 1994; Spurgeon, 1992; Moburg and Folke, 1999). A final category, *option*, can be classified as a use and a non-use value, as it refers to all the values that may be used in the future which are not being used now (Fig. 5.2).

A more biocentric approach more common in ecological economics includes the benefits people perceive as well as those they do not. The over-arching classification system applied in the Millennium Ecosystem Assessment (2003; Hein *et al.*, 2006) groups goods and services into five categories: (1) *production services*; (2) *regulation services*; (3) *cultural services*; (4) *supporting services*; and a fifth category as added by Beaumont *et al.* (2007), (5) *option use services* (Table 5.1 shows this classification system and how the goods and services approach may fit in this system).

Table 5.1 An overarching classification system as adopted by the Millennium ecosystem assessment (2003). Services are classified by the relevant spatial scale they are likely to be provided at

Category	Good or service	Definition	Spatial scale
Production services (*direct use values; extractive*)	Food provision	The extraction of marine organisms for human consumption	**Micro** Meso
	Raw materials	The extraction of marine organisms for all purposes	**Micro** Meso
Cultural services (*direct use values; non-extractive*)	Cultural heritage and identity	Benefit of biodiversity that is of founding significance or bears witness to multiple cultural identities of a community	**Micro** Meso
	Cognitive benefits	Cognitive benefit including education and research, resulting from marine organisms	Micro **Meso** Macro
	Leisure and recreation	The refreshment and stimulation of the human body and mind through the perusal and study of, and engagement with marine organisms in their natural environment	Micro Meso **Macro**
	Feel good warm glow (non-use values)	Benefit which is derived from marine organisms without using them (existence, bequest)	**Micro** Meso Macro
Regulation services (*in direct-use values*)	Gas and climate regulation	Balance and maintenance of the chemical composition of the atmosphere and oceans by marine organisms	**Macro**
	Disturbance prevention (flood and storm protection)	The dampening of environmental disturbances by biogenic structures	Micro **Meso**
	Bioremediation of waste	Removal of pollutants through storage, burial and recycling	Micro **Meso**
Overarching support services (*in direct-use values*)	Resilience and resistance (life support)	The extent to which ecosystems can absorb recurrent natural and human perturbations and continue to regenerate without slowly degrading or unexpectedly flipping to alternate states	**Macro**
	Biologically mediated habitat	Habitat which is provided by living marine organisms	Micro **Meso** Macro
	Nutrient cycling	The storage and cycling and maintenance of nutrients by living marine organisms	**Macro**
Option use value	Future unknown and speculative benefits	Currently unknown potential future uses of marine biodiversity	Micro Meso Macro

5.3.2   Economic valuation

Environmental economists have developed various methods for constructing values for the goods and services described although each method is associated with issues and constraints (Table 5.2).

5.3.3   Valuation classification

In welfare economics the price of a commodity will be determined by the most efficient relationship between the quantity available and the demand for that commodity. A demand curves depicts this relationship in a graph representing the amount consumers are willing to buy at any given price. Environmental economics have developed methods for valuing many of the non-extractive services that ecosystems offer (such as bequest and existence values). Two basic distinctions exist between economic valuation methods, those which use a 'Hicksian' or 'Marshallian' demand curve, and those which do not and so fail to value the commodity in a 'true' welfare measure (Fig. 5.3) (Turner *et al.*, 1994). The latter category, however, still provides valuable information for policy on certain indirect use values.

Demand-side valuation methodologies are based on the subjective preference theory of value where value originates in the minds of individuals and involve the construction of a demand curve. However, these methods cannot consider objective biophysical properties.

Non-demand-side valuations (or supply) are based on the actual costs of production where value originates from the actual things from which goods are made from. However, these cannot provide true welfare measures and, instead, value the outcome of policies not the good or service. An example is the cost of construction of a sea wall to counter the increased rates of erosion caused from the loss of the coral reef which previously buffered the impacts of the waves.

5.3.4   Valuation methodologies (Table 5.2)

Non-demand-side valuations (supply)

Replacement cost calculates the value of ecosystem services based on the cost of replacing or restoring a damaged asset, such as with physical protection services. **Avoided cost** similarly, calculates the value based on the cost of preventing damages due to lost services. **Substitute cost** calculates the value based on the cost of providing a substitute service. As these do not reflect true welfare values they are best applied

Table 5.2 A list of economic valuation methods, listing curve produced and issues and constraints associated with the method

Method	Demand curve	Issues	Summarised issues
Replacement cost: RC	Imputed WTP	Not social preferences, assume costs = benefits, few direct substitutes	Not true welfare value, reliant on assumptions, subjective valuation
Avoided costs: AC	Imputed WTP		Not true welfare value, reliant on assumptions, subjective valuation
Substitute cost: SC	Imputed WTP		Not true welfare value, reliant on assumptions, subjective valuation
Market value: MV	Revealed WTP	Limited goods, market imperfections, overstate or understate	Only extractive resources, subjective valuation
Productivity method: PM	Revealed WTP	Limited goods, underestimate as not all services related to marketed good, information on scientific relationship between actions to improve quality/quantity may be lacking	Only extractive, inferring value, subjective valuation
Travel cost: TC	Revealed WTP	Opportunity cost of time missed, availability of substitute sites, need considerable difference in distances travelled	Reliant on assumptions, limited to marketed services, subjective valuation
Hedonic pricing: HP	Revealed WTP	People may not be aware of the linkages, outside influences to housing market, data intensive	Reliant on assumptions, limited to things related to house price, subjective valuation
Contingent valuation: CV	Stated WTP	Controversy over whether it actually measures WTP as a hypothetical situation may not adequately reflect the choices made in a market situation, difficult to validate non-use categories, may be valuing services the respondent is unaware of	Non-tangible services, subjective valuation
Value transfer: VT	Imputed WTP	Adequacy of initial study difficult to assess, only as accurate as the initial measure, value will vary depending on site, location and user specific specifications	Reliant on assumptions subjective valuation

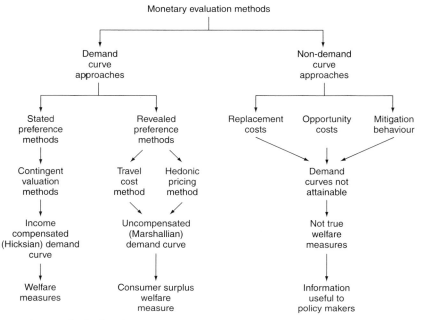

Fig. 5.3 Methods for the monetary evaluation of ecosystem goods and services (adapted from Turner, 2000)

where damages have actually been incurred or replacements have or will be made.

Demand-side valuation

Market value methods can be used for goods such as fisheries which are bought and sold in conventional markets. The values of goods are calculated using standard economic techniques based on the price and quantity of goods. **Productivity methods** are used when ecosystem goods or services are used in conjunction with other goods to produce a marketed good. When environmental quality directly affects the cost of producing a marked good, such as drinking water where the benefits of purer water can be directly related to the reduced purification costs. **Travel cost** methods can be used to value non-extractive services that have a market value, such as recreation, indirectly by using a revealed preference based method. A zonal travel cost method (TCM) uses the actual number of visitors travelling to an area aggregated by their country of origin to calculate a recreation service (equation 1) (Freeman, 2003; Bateman *et al.*, 2004). These numbers are standardised by the country populations giving a standardised visitor number. The linear relationship between the standardised visitor numbers and the cost of travel is established. This relationship is then used to calculate a 'marshallian' consumer surplus curve. Where a countries' GDP at the purchasing power parity is also taken into account, a 'Hicksian' consumer surplus is produced, which attempts to compensate for income (Bateman *et al.*, 2004; Freeman, 2003).

$$V^* = \frac{V}{P \times GDP} \tag{1}$$

Where: V^* = number of visitors standardised, P = population of country of origin, GDP = gross domestic product of country of origin.

However, problems exist with differences in the availability of alternative sites, time costs, repeat visitors or actual cost of each visit.

Hedonic pricing methods (HPM) are used to establish aesthetic values. Hedonic pricing method attempts to account for outside influences to land price leaving a value based on aesthetic qualities alone. Land and property prices with similar characteristics are compared in order to determine the difference in price attributable to the physical characteristics of a site. This method assumes the price, when standardised for other factors, indirectly reflects the value of the aesthetic characteristics of the site (Turner *et al.*, 1994; Brouwer, 2000).

TCM and HPM provide a straightforward technical approach to the monetary valuation of natural or environmental characteristics based on people's actual behaviour, avoiding many of the biases found in expressed or stated preference approaches. However, these models rely on assumptions the validity of which can be questioned (Brander *et al.*, 2007). Although both methods are considered reasonably robust (Turner *et al.*, 2003).

Contingent valuation methods (CVM) are used for non-use values. This approach uses a hypothetical choice scenario where market behaviour and private willingness to pay (WTP) can be considered indicators of people's preferences and values respectively (Turner *et al.*, 1994; Bateman *et al.*, 2004), are the only means of eliciting a value. Practitioners share the view that closed-ended questions are superior to an open-ended approach, as a discrete choice situation is more similar to a traditional market situation (Andersson *et al.*, 2007). As the payment situation has an impact on the accuracy, the payment vehicle needs to be realistic and understandable as the ability to pay strongly affects the WTP (Andersson *et al.*, 2007). The risk for misspecification bias is considered smaller for on-site surveys (White-head *et al.*, 1995), although this is not always feasible.

Value transfer methods use values established for goods and services elsewhere and assume that values can be equated to the new situation adjusting for factors such as inflation. While many criticisms exist for this method, such as differences in the state of the goods and services being valued for financial constraints, this may be the best option. One of the assumptions in economic value theory is that preferences are given and it does not matter why we value things. However, differences in underlying motives and reasons may enable us to better explain differences in valuation outcomes, and hence come up with a model which has a sufficiently high explanatory power to validly and reliably predict values across sites and groups of people. How individuals construct these values is based on their socio-cultural setting. Together with the shortfalls of the methods discussed, valuations will vary across superficially similar sites and across methods chosen. A meta-analysis comparing recreation values across sites found hedonic pricing to produce the lowest values followed by CVM then travel cost, all varying across sites. Significant differences in the impact of coral bleaching using stated preference and revealed preference valuations have been explained by differences in scales of reference. Stated preferences dealt with the individual, returning no loss in welfare from the impacts of coral bleaching whereas revealed preference dealt with populations of the world resulting in marginal changes in estimates that are often approximations and returned high losses in welfare (Andersson *et al.*, 2007).

5.3.5 *Economic approaches*

These methods and conventional economic tools can be used in a variety of approaches dependent on the objective of assessment.

Economic impact analysis traces spending through an economy and measures the cumulative effects of the spending.

Financial analysis assesses the viability, stability and profitability of a project.

Cost–benefit analysis is a relatively simple technique, based on economic efficiency, in which the costs and the benefits of a course of action are weighed up. In its simplest form only financial costs and benefits are used, in more sophisticated forms the costs and benefits of more intangible things can be evaluated, such as the value of stress-free travel to work. Stakeholder analysis is an important component of CBA in revealing who benefits and who gains from a particular conservation measure. However, when based on hypothetical scenarios the practitioner needs to consider that preferences develop and change over time.

Multi-criteria analysis is a decision-making tool designed for choosing from a set of alternative scenarios where multiple criteria or objectives exist. MCA incorporates quantitative and qualitative, social, environmental and economic criteria in a process orientated manner (Brown *et al.*, 2001). This approach engages stakeholders in a scenario-type situation where the resource users are provided with information on the criteria and impacts of a certain project. The relationships between social conditions and the values people hold are examined as there are limits to data and information available.

Habitat equivalency analysis (HEA) is used in a natural resource damage assessment process (NRDA). The purpose is restoration after environmental damage occurs where the extent of resource injury, suitable restoration methods, and appropriate amounts of restoration needed are established. HEA specifically, concerns itself with less accounted for uses, primarily ecological and biological. It determines the appropriate scale of compensatory restoration by estimating the interim ecological service loss based on an ecological metric as an indicator. A range of compensatory measures is identified and one is chosen that will provide a present value service gain equal to the service value loss (Roach and Wade, 2006). In this way HEA aims to maintain a baseline of ecological functioning rather than human welfare.

Total economic value (TEV) is the aggregation of all components of Table 5.1. In a seminal, though controversial work in 1997, Costanza *et al.* provided the first valuation of all the Earth's ecosystems. However, in using economic valuation methodologies to construct a TEV, this value is not to be assumed as the same as the total system value, as ecosystem services are synergistic with the value in the continued functioning of a healthy system more than the sum of its parts (Turner, 2000).

5.3.6 *Considerations in application*

Like any process, the approach and methodology must be specific to the question being addressed. Additionally, the socio-cultural setting of the location needs to be incorporated and the limitations of the methodology considered in evaluating the results. From an environmental perspective the economic value theory underlying economic valuation techniques can seem overly restrictive with many assumptions, and there is the danger that economic efficiency criterion is promoted as the sole decision-making criterion. Similarly, from an economic perspective, environmental valuation is considered a social process relying upon social agreements, and as such only loosely coupled, if at all, to technical economic valuation method.

Environmental economics presents a model for conducting an economic valuation of ecosystem services that has been well tested. While criticisms exist to the integrity of the methods, their use have gained acceptance as demonstrated by their inclusion in policy and compensation claims paid out in courts based on environmental valuations. However, in conducting these studies, the aggregate of values (TEV) is not to be considered a measure of the aggregate producer and consumer surplus, or even some indicator of overall economic performance. It is, rather, the measure of the economy wide incremental change in biological diversity or the habitat which supports it (Pearce, 2007). Increasingly, however, ecological economists have argued for a more biocentric approach, including an intrinsic value for ecological services, alongside the well established subjective valuations (Table 5.2). This stresses the need to incorporate biological processes, carrying capacities and indicators of resilience (Arrow *et al.*, 1990). While this philosophy may be agreed on in principle among those concerned for the degradation of our natural environment, scepticism over too bold claims for the values of ecosystem services exist (Pearce, 2007). Developments are being made in ecosystem services frameworks (Turner and Daily, 2008) incorporating spatial modelling software programs such as MARXAN, that call for a framework which addresses the biophysical and ecological reality of how ecological resources contribute to value (intrinsic) with the notion of a subjective value to an individual (Straton, 2006).

5.4   Enabling an ecosystem services approach

Capital is generally categorised into human, built, natural and social. All these forms of capital, related by complex feedback mechanisms, contribute to human welfare (Costanza, 2003). Human capital refers to both the labour force, as well as the intellectual capacity possessed within that labour force, whereas built capital concerns itself with technology and infrastructure. These two forms of capital are well measured and easily quantifiable in economic terms. Natural capital, as discussed earlier, refers to the capacity for production within the natural environment whereas social capital refers to 'features of social organisation such as networks, norms and social trust that facilitate coordination and cooperation for mutual benefit' (Putnam, 1993). These less tangible forms of capital have a significant role to play in our patterns of production, consumption and wellbeing and are far more problematic to study and measure. In addition to this complexity, as the scale of interest increases the definition of the ecosystem services and the role of these different forms of capital merge. This section will concern itself with the interdependencies of these latter two forms of capital and set forward an interdisciplinary approach to addressing resource use within an ecosystem service valuation framework appropriate as a tool in ICZM.

5.4.1   Property rights and scale

Ecosystem services work at varying temporal and spatial scales (CO_2 regulation operates at small rapidly changing scales whereas C sequestration operates at a long-term global scale). Complex property rights and regimes operating at these various scales make a broad economic definition problematic. Local costs and benefits of small scale processes have little relevance to those operating at global scales. Biodiversity conservation is no different as it effectively operates as: (1) a global commons that is important for humanity as a whole; (2) a regional commons important for ecotourism and other benefits; and (3) a local commons that produces ecosystem services for human wellbeing and livelihoods (Berkes, 2007). As such, the problems of managing common pool resources are felt at and across multiple scales. Benefits derived at one level may result in disproportionate losses at another (Andrews *et al.*, 2005). As ecosystem services flow and interact across spatial and temporal scales, it is important to account for these flows, and address biodiversity conservation as a complex and multilevel system understanding the tradeoffs involved in their relevant social-ecological system.

Property rights affect who has access to these values, in effect controlling the scale at which the values can be utilised. Ecosystem services have historically been abundant so there have been limited incentives to develop property rights. As we expand our appropriation over ecosystem services and they become limited there is an incentive to establish property rights (Pearce, 2007). Within conservation policy the dominant assumption that natural resource ownership lies with the state has altered the complex property rights which have developed in association with natural resources (Mertz *et al.*, 2007). Conservation

109

measures, which have traditionally focused on biodiversity conservation and not the maintenance of human welfare, have resulted in the benefits being assigned to future generations and the global, not local, community (Balmford and Whitten, 2003). This approach has the potential of disempowering and oppressing people, enforcing state or global ownership and breaking down local property rights (Chan *et al.*, 2007). The resultant lack of clear or defined ownership leads to the unsustainable use and harvest of these resources (Hardin, 1968). As economic theory relates value to the quantity (Malthus) and the quality (Ricardo) of available natural capital altering property rights also alters the quantity and quality of natural capital available, thus dissipating the potential rent.

5.4.2   Interdependencies

Due to the difficulties of managing across spatial scales and ecosystem services, management has preferred to focus on managing for a specific ecosystem service, such as maintaining a biologically mediated habitat service; commonly the aim of many marine protected areas. However, coastal managers need to integrate management across a range of services and scales. Ecosystem goods and services are synergistic in nature, in that the value of the continued provision of all ecosystem services is greater than the sum of the individual services. It is important to recognise that losses in ecosystem goods and services may result in unexpected tradeoffs and disproportionate losses in ecosystem functioning. These complex systems require integrated responses with multiple-objective approaches that incorporate tradeoffs across services and society (MA, 2005). However, to implement such an approach we need an understanding of the mechanisms and feedbacks operating between social conditions and ecosystem values, thereby enabling a more informed and adaptive governance system.

Such an approach should aim to analyse the governance structure in place as the existing structures will dictate the flow of resources or ecosystem services, and dictate whether the natural capital is realised in an efficient equitable manner or whether the natural capital will be degraded and lost to the system. Policy and legal considerations are commonly incorporated into decisions involving management intervention, however the role social capital plays is rarely taken into account. The challenge is to build a fully communicative and deliberative multilevel system that deals with tradeoffs between social and ecological objectives in an optimal fashion without being skewered by disciplinary biases, or the political economy of power relations (Berkes, 2007; Adger *et al.*, 2005).

5.4.3   Social capital

Experiencing disturbance and change contribute to building knowledge and developing a societies learning capacity; both are necessary conditions in enabling the adaptive management of natural resources (Folke *et al.*, 2005). However, in a world that is rapidly becoming globalised, external markets and management conditions may have masked these experiences, damaging the ability for society to learn and change (Hicks *et al.*, 2009). Part of the justification for ecosystem service valuations is rectifying these market failures by realising and appropriating values for ecosystem services. The concept of linking natural capital to human welfare, assumes that choices will be made based on preferences to achieve optimum efficiency, sustainability and equity. However, preferences change on temporal and spatial scales dependent on factors such as education, advertising and culture (Constanza, 2001). Essentially, individual choices (WTPs) may be made to achieve maximum efficiency, as stated in conventional economic theory. However, equity and sustainability need community and global consensus.

The role society plays, the levels of social capital and institutions available to facilitate the sharing of information and learning, crucially links to building our ability to manage the world's natural resources. The value in social capital was first identified by Tonnies (1887) and has received increasing amounts of attention in the past couple of decades. Social capital has been widely recognised as important for conservation and resource management (Pretty and Ward, 2001; Putnam, 1993; Bodin and Crona, 2008) and is regarded as the glue for adaptive capacity and collaboration (Pretty and Ward, 2001). The idea of social capital is that there is a value in social arrangements, which means that people can act to realise their personal aims and interests. Key features identified as representative of social capital include:

1. Relationships of trust.
2. Reciprocity and exchange.
3. Common rules, norms and sanctions.
4. Connectedness (Pretty and Smith, 2004).

Reciprocity and exchange increase trust which lowers the costs of interactions and also facilitate coordination, making individuals less

111

likely to treat goods as common pool and less likely to invest in unfettered actions resulting in costs borne to others including resource degradation. Rules and norms give people the confidence to invest in the collective good, knowing others will do so too. Connections refer to the links in, between and beyond communities.

As natural capital is predominantly a common pool resource it is not sufficient to realise the value of natural capital. For values to be suitably appropriated through time, opportunity costs and changing management practices, people need to be convinced that the benefits derived from collective approaches outweigh those from individual ones. The presence of social capital helps new ideas spread and without sufficient levels of social capital amongst people ideas will not spread and practices will not change.

5.4.4   An adaptive governance framework

Adaptive management provides an approach which focuses on ecosystem dynamics and feeding ecological knowledge into management organisations. When this approach involves the social domain it is defined as adaptive co-management (Folke *et al.*, 2005). Such an approach would be needed for information on ecosystem service valuations to be fed into management, and for correct ecosystem service appropriation to be implemented. However, for this to be maintained the channels that enable information on the levels of natural capital, and maintain their appropriation, need to operate with effective feedback mechanisms. An adaptive co-management framework would not necessarily link between social actors, across the multiple scales or possess the capacity to evaluate the tradeoffs and facilitate conflict resolution. An overarching framework is necessary to address issues at and across multiple scales.

Governance has been described as the structures and processes by which individuals in society make decisions and share power (Lebel *et al.*, 2005). An informed and trusted governance system would have the ability to distribute information on ecosystem services and sanction adaptive approaches to resource use. Adaptive systems of governance have been described as polycentric forms of social coordination in which actions are coordinated voluntarily by individuals and organisations with self-organising and self-enforcing capabilities (Folke *et al.*, 2005). Any governance system possesses social and natural capital; however, the structuring of the system reflects how the values are appropriated and the resultant levels of capital realised.

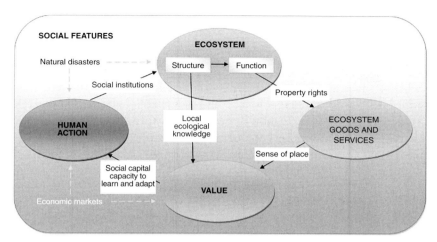

Fig. 5.4 *A conceptual framework representing the flow of ecosystem goods and services and the role governance structure plays*

Figure 5.4 shows a conceptualisation of such a relationship, summarising the various factors discussed above and their interactions with ecosystem service value. At the ecosystem level, *ecosystem structure* determines *ecosystem function* which in turn determines the *ecosystem goods and services* available to us. The *value* of these ecosystem goods and services is a construct of both the value derived from these goods and services through valuation studies as well as a result of the underlying ecosystem structure. *Value* motivates *human action* which ultimately affects *ecosystem structure*. The existing social features of the governance structure interact with these relationships. *Property rights* can affect access to or the ability of people to benefit from the ecosystem services. A *sense of place* can alter the value of these ecosystem services to the resource user and *local ecological knowledge* may affect the perceived value of the ecosystem structure. *Social capital* or one's ability to learn and adapt can affect human action and human action may be affected by the *social institutions* in place altering their effect on the ecosystem structure.

While it may be desirable to control all the components of this conceptual model, as managers we have limited influence. Although our actions will influence the ecosystem and the ecosystem goods and services they provide, we cannot control this ecosystem. However, through social capital, it may be possible to affect value and the interplay of the components of total economic value resulting in altered long term human action.

113

5.4.5 The role of an ICZM manager

As discussed, total economic value can be split into the broad functional groupings of direct, indirect, option, existence and bequest (Fig. 5.3). It is generally accepted that an increase in an ecosystem good or service will result in tradeoffs with other goods or services (Steffan-Dewenter *et al.*, 2007). Additionally, it is accepted that these changes in ecosystem goods and services have non-linear responses (Barbier *et al.*, 2008). Therefore, it would be reasonable to expect these tradeoffs to change the overall total economic value. Social capital has been recognised as productive, either in giving an individual the competitive advantage or in permitting a community to 'add value' to something by enabling them to make more of some benefit than would be possible without that particular form of social capital (Inkeles, 2000). Therefore, social capital also influences the TEV. The interplay of these goods and services, and resultant tradeoffs, can be depicted along a scale of social capital with social capital affecting specific values and increasing, or decreasing, the overall total economic value (Fig. 5.5). Recognising the role of social capital in affecting the interplay of ecosystem goods and services is key to enabling optimal management of ecosystem services by ICZM managers.

Figure 5.5 depicts this relationship, where, at low levels of social capital, tradeoffs exist between direct use values and indirect use values leading to the degradation of the stocks of natural capital that support the whole ecosystem. Tradeoffs also exist between option value and existence and bequest values where rights of access outweigh the value of maintaining those services either for future generations or in their own right. The total economic value of a system with low levels of social capital will be lower than possible as use is very egocentric and inefficient. Stocks of natural capital are likely to erode and dissipate

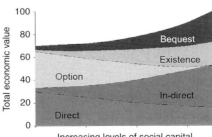

Fig. 5.5 The interplay of the functional value groupings for ecosystem goods and services with the resultant tradeoffs shown along a scale of increasing social capital

through the maximisation of direct-use values, which represent unsustainable use. As social capital increases, and there is cooperation to realise mutual aims and interests, conservation practices are likely to develop associated with higher bequest and existence values, with a corresponding increase in indirect-use values. A more efficient appropriation of values is likely to lead to an associated decrease in option values as all potential uses are maximised. With the increase in indirect use values, which are responsible for supporting the whole ecosystem, and increased cooperation from higher levels of social capital the long-term sustainability of the whole system will be increased, thereby building confidence in existing management and resource use. The total economic value of a system with high social capital will also be maximised.

This relationship has been seen to hold in Kenya, where differing levels of social capital exist, affected in part by the choice of management strategy. At low levels of social capital, TEV is dominated by direct use values where each resource user is maximising their individual benefit with little long-term perspective. This is seen adjacent to a national marine protected area (MNPA) where top-down management has eroded the community values and levels of social capital. Here TEV is dominated by direct use values, predominantly 'recreation' and 'fisheries' goods and services. Levels of non-use values (existence and bequest) are low though option values may be high as many of the potential ecosystem goods and services are not being used or are being used inefficiently. Conversely, in areas where a community based marine protected area has been established (CBMPA), levels of social capital are higher as a result of arrangements of trust reciprocity and exchange within the community. Here direct-use values are lower with higher values for existence and bequest. Human action in these areas is orientated towards long term sustainability and indirect use values benefit from this conservationist action (Fig. 5.6) (Hicks *et al.*, 2009).

For the ICZM manager, understanding how tradeoffs are likely to occur will enable them to include these costs and benefits into the evaluation of any proposed management intervention. Recognising the role social capital has to play provides the manager with a tangible strategy for intervention strategies to follow. A final dimension for consideration is spatial scales. Ecosystem goods and services are provided at and across scales. In a management context the benefactors of the ecosystem goods and services represent the stakeholders at various scales such as user, local, regional, national and global. Depending

115

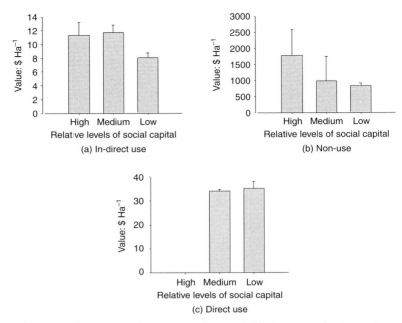

Fig. 5.6 (a) Indirect use, (b) non-use values and (c) direct use (option, existence, bequest) in three management scenarios, characterised by decreasing social capital, in the coral reef fisheries of coastal Kenya (adapted from Hicks et al., 2008)

on the governance structure in place different stakeholders will have differing levels of social capital.

A 'power' curve can represent this relationship (Fig. 5.7); we use the word 'power' to describe this curve as it directly related to governance which is closely related by the distribution of decision-making etc. power. For example, in a government imposed no-take area, levels of social capital will be lowest for the resource user at a local level, as they have had their traditional rules and norms disrupted. At the national level social capital will be higher, supported by commitments by governments through international conventions, international organisations and NGO communities to protect biodiversity. Conversely, where there is local co-management, social capital will be highest at the resource user and local level as this is where decisions are made. These high levels of social capital will decrease at the regional level, and even more so by the national level, as management is to protect local values not national targets. In an extreme case, such as managed realignment of the Humber estuary in the UK, highest levels of social

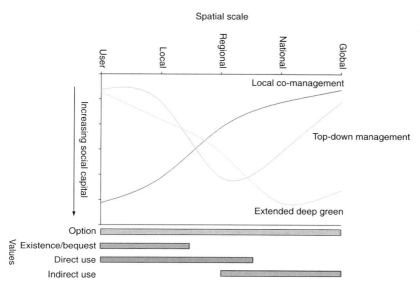

Fig. 5.7 A power curve depicting the effect of governance on the spatial scale of social capital and the relevant spatial scale at which goods and services will be generated and supplied at

capital exist at the global and national level and lowest at the user's level. As discussed previously, the levels of social capital will have an influence on specific values, which can be seen to relate to the scale at which the services are provided (Table 5.1). Different goods and services will be generated and supplied at different scales (Hein *et al.*, 2006). The benefits from the majority of indirect use values, such as climate regulation, are felt at a global scale, whereas the benefits from the majority of direct use values, such as fisheries, are felt at a local scale.

Consequently an effective approach to coastal management would be to assess the levels of social capital at the various scales, conduct a total economic valuation and focus on rebuilding social capital where the largest tradeoffs in ecosystem services are occurring. This coupling of social capital with management interventions for optimising TEV leads to a two-step approach:

1. identify what is to be achieved, and
2. enhance social capital at the governance scale at which we want the benefits to be secured.

For example, in instances where management has favoured global or national initiatives, indirect use values will likely have resulted in conflicts at the local scale. Strategies aimed at promoting community level social capital will promote cultural and direct use values reducing conflict, which will result in benefits being felt at the local level. Thus, maximising natural capital and promoting sustainability of the coast must be done in conjunction with building levels of social capital at and across relevant scales.

5.4.6 Conclusions

It is widely recognised and generally accepted that economic valuation methodologies for environmental resources are flawed; the literature critiquing and improving these approaches is considerable and growing (Turner *et al.*, 2003). However, their value in decision making should not be overlooked. Each method and approach is associated with constraints; consequently their individual suitability should be appraised within each project based on a number of factors including cost, time, location, use, stakeholders involved and levels of social capital. The values and benefits we derive from environmental resources, or ecosystem services, are dependent on both social and ecological features for their generation (Andersson *et al.*, 2007). Considerable research has gone into the linkages between biodiversity, functioning and services (Naeem and Wright, 2003), and social and ecological information is increasingly integrated into coastal management (Cinner, 2007). However, studies on ecosystem services which consider social features responsible for their generation are lacking. We present an approach aimed at integrating existing economic methods and approaches which focus on identifying the value derived from ecological features of coastal systems with the value derived from social features, specifically social capital.

Acknowledgements

The authors would like to thank Eva Michalena (Sorbonne University, France) for reviewing and providing comments on this chapter and to the editors for their support in producing this chapter.

References

Adger, N.W., Hughes, T.P., Folke, C., Carpenter, S.R. and Rockstrom, J. (2005) Social-ecological resilience to coastal disasters. *Science*, Vol. 309, pp. 1036–1039.

Akerman, M. (2003) What does 'natural capital' do? The role of metaphor in economic understanding of the environment. *Environmental Values*, Vol. 12, pp. 431–448.

Andersson, E., Barthel, S. and Ahrne, K. (2007) Measuring Social-Ecological Dynamics behind the generation of ecosystem services. *Ecological Applications* Vol. 17, pp. 1267–1278.

Andrews, J.E., Burgess, D., Cave, R.R., Coombes, E.G., Jickells, T.D., Parkes, D.J. and Turner, R.K. (2005) Biogeochemical value of managed realignment, Humber estuary, UK. *Science of the Total Environment*, Vol. 371, pp. 19–30.

Armsworth, P.R. and Roughgarden, J.E. (2001) An invitation to ecological economics. *Trends in Ecology and Evolution*, Vol. 16, pp. 229–234.

Arrow, K., Bolin, B., Costanza, R., Dasgupta, P., Folke, C., Holling, C.S., Jansson, B.O., Maler, K.G., Perrings, C. and Pimentel, D. (1995) Economic growth, carrying capacity, and the environment. *Science*, Vol. 268, pp. 520–521.

Balmford, A. and Whitten, T. (2003) Who should pay for tropical conservation, and how should the costs be met? *ORYX*, Vol. 37, pp. 238–250.

Balvanera, P., Daily, G.C., Erlich, P.R., Ricketts, T.H., Baily, S.A., Kark, S., Kremen, C. and Pereira, H. (2001) Conserving biodiversity and ecosystem services. *Science*, Vol. 291, pp. 2047–2047.

Barbier, E.B., Koch, E.W., Silliman, B.R., Hacker, S.D., Wolanski, E., Primavera, J., Granek, E.F., Polansky, S., Aswani, S., Cramer, L.A., Stoms, D.M., Kennedy, C.J., Bael, D., Kappel, C.V., Perillo, M.E. and Reed, D.J. (2008) Coastal ecosystem-based management with non-linear ecological functions and values. *Science*, Vol. 319, pp. 321–323.

Barton, D.N. (1994) Economic factors and valuation of tropical coastal resources. *SMR-Report*, 14/94, Bergen, Norway.

Bateman, I., Lovett, A.A. and Brainard, J.S. (eds) (2004) *Applied Environmental Economics: A GIS Approach to Cost Benefit Analysis*, Cambridge University Press, Cambridge.

Baumgartner, S. (2006) The ecological economics of biodiversity, methods and policy applications. *Ecological Economics*, Vol. 59, No. 1, pp. 181–182.

Beaumont, N.J., Austen, M.C., Atkins, J.P., Burdon, D., Degraer, S., Dentinho, T.P., Derous, S., Holm, P., Horton, T., van Ierland, E., Marboe, A.H., Starkey, D.J., Townsend, M. and Zarzycki, T. (2007) Identification, definition and quantification of goods and services provided by marine biodiversity: Implications for the ecosystem approach. *Marine Pollution Bulletin*, Vol. 54, pp. 253–265.

Becker, C., Faber, M., Hertel, K. and Manstetten, R. (2005) Malthus vs Wordsworth: perspectives on humankind, nature and economy. A contribution to the history and foundations of ecological economics. *Ecological Economics*, Vol. 53, pp. 299–310.

Berkes, F. (2007) Community-based conversation in a globalized world. *PNAS*, Vol. 104, pp. 15188–15193.

Bodin, O. and Crona, B. (2008) Management of natural resources at the community level – exploring the role of social capital and leadership in a rural fishing community. *World Development*, Vol. 36, No. 12, pp. 2763–2779.

Boulding, K. (1966) The economics of the coming spaceship earth. In Jarrett, H. (ed.) *Environmental Quality in a Growing Economy. Resources for the Future.* John Hopkins University Press, Baltimore, MD, pp. 3–14.

Brander, L.M., van Beukering, P. and Cesar, H.S.J. (2007) The recreational value of coral reefs: a meta-analysis. *Ecological Economics*, Vol. 63, pp. 209–218.

Brandt, W. (1980) *North–South: a programme for survival: report of the Independent Commission on International Development Issues*, MIT Press, Cambridge, MA.

Brouwer, R. (2000) Environmental value transfer: state of the art and future prospects. *Ecological Economics*, Vol. 32, pp. 137–152.

Brown, K., Adger, N., Tompkins, E., Bacon, P., Shim, D. and Young K. (2001) Tradeoff analysis for marine protected area management. *Ecological Economics*, Vol. 37, pp. 417–434.

Bruntland Commission (1987) World Commission on Environment and Development (1987) 'Our Common Future', Oxford University Press, Oxford.

Chan, K.M.A., Pringle, R.M., Ranganathan, J., Boggs, C.I., Chan, Y.L., Erlicht, P.R., Haff, P.K., Heller, N.E., Al-Khafaji, K. and MacMynowski, D.P. (2007) When agendas collide: human welfare and biological conservation. *Conservation Biology*, Vol. 21, pp. 59–68.

Chan, K.M.A., Shaw, M.R., Cameron, D.R., Underwood, E.C. and Daily, G.C. (2006) Conservation planning for ecosystem services. *PLOS Biology*, Vol. 4, pp. 2138–2152.

Cinner, J.E. (2007) Designing marine reserves to reflect local socio-economic conditions: lessons from long-enduring customary management systems. *Coral Reefs*, Vol. 26, pp. 1035–1045.

Costanza, R. (1989) What is ecological economics? *Ecological Economics*, Vol. 1, pp. 1–7.

Constanza, R. (2001) Visions, value, valuation and the need for ecological economics. *BioScience*, Vol. 51, pp. 459–468.

Costanza, R. (2003) A vision of the future of science: reintegrating the study of humans and the rest of nature. *Futures*, Vol. 35, Issue 6, pp. 651–671.

Costanza, R., d'Arge, R., de Groot, R., Farber, S., Grasso, M., Hannon, B., Limburg, K., Naeem, S., O'Neill, V., Paruelo, J., Raskin, R.G. and Sutton, P. (1997) Value of the world's ecosystem services and natural capital. *Nature*, Vol. 387, pp. 253–260.

Egoh, B., Rouget, M., Reyers, B., Knight, A.T., Cowling, R.M., van Jaarsveld, A.S. and Welz, A. (2007) Integrating ecosystem services into conservation assessments: a review. *Ecological Economics*, Vol. 63, pp. 714–721.

Ehrlich, P.R. and Kennedy, D. (2005) Millenium assessment of human behaviour. *Science*, Vol. 309, pp. 562–563.

Farber, S., Costanza, R., Childers, D.L., Erickson, J., Gross, K., Grove, M., Hopkin, C.S., Kahn, J., Pincetl, S., Troy, A., Warren, P. and Wilson, M. (2006) Linking ecology and economics for ecosystem management. *Bioscience*, Vol. 56, Issue 2, pp. 121–133.

Folke, C., Hahn, T., Olsson, P. and Norberg, J. (2005) Adaptive governance of social ecological systems. *Annual Review of Environment and Resources*, Vol. 30, pp. 441–473.

Freeman, A.M. (2003) *The Measurement of Environmental and Resource Values: Theory and Methods*, 2nd ed., Resources for the Future, Washington, DC.

Hardin, G. (1968) The tragedy of the commons. *Science*, Vol. 162, p. 1244.

Hein, L., van Koppen, K., de Groot, R.S. and van Ierland, E. (2006) Spatial scales, stakeholders and the valuation of ecosystem services. *Ecological Economics*, Vol. 57, pp. 209–228.

Hicks, C.C., McClanahan, T.R., Cinner, J.E. and Hills, J.M. (2009) Trade-offs in values assigned to ecological goods and services associated with different coral reef management strategies. *Ecology and Society*, Vol. 14, No. 1.

Hubacek, K. and van den Bergh, J.C.J.M. (2006) Changing concepts of 'land' in economic theory: from single to multi-disciplinary approaches. *Ecological Economics*, Vol. 56, pp. 5–27.

Hughes, T.P. (1994) Catastrophic phase-shifts and large-scale degradation of a Caribbean coral-reef. *Science*, Vol. 265, pp. 1547–1551.

Inkeles, A. (2000) Measuring social capital and its consequences. *Policy Sciences*, Vol. 33, pp. 245–268.

Kremen, C. (2005) Managing ecosystem services: what do we need to know about their ecology? *Ecology Letters*, Vol. 8, pp. 468–479.

Lebel, L., Anderies, J.M., Campbell, B., Folke, C., Hatfield-Dodds, S., Hughes, T.P. and Wilson, J. (2005) Governance and the capacity to manage resilience in regional social-ecological systems. *Ecology and Society*, Vol. 11, p. 19.

MA (2005) *Ecosystems and human well-being: synthesis*, ME Assessment, Island Press, Washington, DC.

Malthus, J. (1798) *An Essay on the Principle of Population*, J. Johnson, London.

McClanahan, T.R., Verheij, E. and Maina, J. (2006) Comparing the management effectiveness of a marine park and a multiple-use collaborative fisheries management area in East Africa. *Aquatic Conservation: Marine and Freshwater Ecosystems*, Vol. 16, pp. 147–165.

Meadows, D.L., Randers, J., Meadows, D.L. and Behrens, W.W. (1972) The limits to growth: a report for the Club of Rome's project on the predicament of mankind, Potomac Associates Book, Signet, New York.

Mertz, O., Ravenborg, H.M., Lovei, G.L., Nielsen, I. and Konijnendijk, C.C. (2007) Ecosystem services and biodiversity in developing countries. *Biodiversity Conservation*, Vol. 16, pp. 2729–2737.

Millenium Ecosystem Assessment (2003) *Ecosystems and Human Well Being: A Framework for Assessment*, Island Press, Washington, DC.

Millenium Ecosystem Assessment (2005) Ecosystems and Human Well Being: Synthesis' Island Press, Washington, DC.

Moberg, M. and Folke, C. (1999) Ecological goods and services of coral reef ecosystems. *Ecological Economics*, Vol. 29, pp. 215–233.

Naeem, S. and Wright, J.P. (2003) Disentangling biodiversity effects on ecosystem functioning: deriving solutions to a seemingly insurmountable problem. *Ecology Letters*, Vol. 6, No. 6, pp. 567–579.

Pearce, D. (1988) Economics, equity and sustainable development. *Futures*, Vol. 20, pp. 598–605.

Pearce, D. (2007) Do we really care about biodiversity? *Environment Resource Economics*, Vol. 37, pp. 313–333.

Pretty, J. and Smith, D. (2004) Social capital in biodiversity conservation. *Conservation Biology*, Vol. 18, pp. 631–638.

Pretty, J. and Ward, H. (2001) Social capital and the environment. *World Development*, Vol. 29, pp. 209–227.

Putnam, R.D. (1993) *Making Democracy Work*, Princeton University Press, Princeton, NJ.

Ricardo, D. (1817) On the Principals of Political Economy and Taxation, John Murray, London.

Roach, B. and Wade, W.W. (2006) Policy evaluation of natural resource injuries using habitat equivalency analysis. *Ecological Economics*, Vol. 58, pp. 421–433.

Simpson, D.R. (2007) David Pearce and the economic value of biodiversity. *Environmental Resource Economics*, Vol. 37, pp. 91–109.

Smith, A. (1776) *An Inquiry Into the Wealth of Nations*, Methuen and Co., London.

Spurgeon, J.P.C. (1992) The economic valuation of coral reefs. *Marine Pollution Bulletin*, Vol. 24, pp. 529–536.

Steffan-Dewenter, I., Kessler, M., Barkmann, J., Bos, M.M., Buchori, D., Erasmi, S., Faust, H., Gerhold, G., Glenk, K., Gradstein, S.R., Guhardja, E., Harteveld, M., Hertel, D., Hohn, P., Kappas, M., Kohler, S., Leuschner, C., Maertens, M., Marggraf, R., Migge-Kleian, S., Mogea, J., Pitopang, R., Schaefer, M., Schwarze, S., Sporn, S.G., Steingrebe, A., Tjitrosoedirdjo, S.S., Tjitrosoemito, S., Twele, A., Weber, R., Woltmann, L., Zeller, M. and Tscharntke, T. (2007) Tradeoffs between income, biodiversity, and ecosystem functioning during tropical rainforest conversion and agroforestry intensification. *PNAS*, Vol. 104, pp. 4973–4978.

Straton, A. (2006) A complex systems approach to the value of ecological resources. *Ecological Economics*, Vol. 56, pp. 402–411.

Tonnies, E. (1887) *Germienschaft und gessellschaft*, Routledge & Kegan Paul, London.

Turner, R.K., Pearce, D. and Bateman, I. (eds) (1994) *Environmental Economics: An Elementary Introduction*, Harvester Wheatsheaf Publishing, New York.

Turner, R.K. (2000) Ecological-economic analysis of wetlands: scientific integration for management and policy. *Ecological Economics*, Vol. 35, No. 1, pp. 7–23.

Turner, R.K. and Daily, G.C. (2008) The ecosystem services framework and natural capital conversion. *Environmental and Resource Economics*, Vol. 39, pp. 25–35.

Turner, R.K., Paavola, J., Cooper, P., Farber, S., Jessamy, V. and Georgiou, S. (2003) Valuing nature: lessons learned and future research directions. *Ecological Economics*, Vol. 46, pp. 493–510.

Whitehead, J.C., Blomquist, G.C., Hoban T.J. and Clifford, W.B. (1995) Assessing the validity and reliability of contingent values – a comparison of no-site and off-site users and non-users. *Journal of Environmental Economics and Management*, Vol. 29, pp. 238–251.

6

Marine protected areas legislation in the Caribbean Lesser Antilles

Barry J. Bleichner
Department of Geography & Environment, University of Aberdeen,
Scotland, UK

Marine protected areas (MPAs) have garnered increasing attention as a means to effectively protect and conserve marine resources. Marine protected areas are typically established through implementing legislation that provides a legal basis for enforcement of MPA rules and regulations. This chapter explores whether a link exists between MPA legislation and effective conservation of marine resources, using coral reef protection in the Caribbean as a case study. The first component of the research delineates a set of legislative provisions, or guidelines, which should be included within MPA legislation, as determined by a review of literature written by protected areas legislative experts and managers. The second phase of the chapter compares those guidelines against the legislation of two separate island groups within the Caribbean Lesser Antilles – the Windward (or Northern) Netherlands Antilles and the US Virgin Islands. The results of the legislative analysis were then compared with the actual state of coral reefs found within the maritime boundaries of the respective countries to establish whether effective MPA legislation results in better protection of coral reefs. The analysis revealed that effective legislation alone is not sufficient to maintain healthy coral reef ecosystems. However, the chapter does offer suggestions as to which components of MPA legislation are most crucial to sustainable coral reefs, such as self-financing, coverage area, and legislative authorisation to control activities outside of MPA boundaries.

Coastal zone management
978-0-7277-3641-1

6.1   Introduction

Scientists have estimated that 30% of existing coral reefs are severely endangered, with possibly 60% being completely destroyed by 2030 (Hughes *et al.*, 2003, p. 929). The destruction of coral reefs is facilitated through a number of factors – both natural and anthropogenic. These causes include hurricanes and severe storms, global climate change, overfishing, fishing with poisons and explosives, marine and land-based pollution, and coastal development. The numerous threats faced by coral reefs around the globe, both land based and sea based, ensure that there is no single solution that will alleviate the danger of further morbidity. However, scientists and analysts have supported the establishment of marine protected areas, which are delimited zones in which marine species and/or ecosystems are sheltered from the harmful activities that threaten survival. Research indicates that marine protected areas (MPAs) can greatly benefit the ecosystems and species found within their boundaries.

To successfully establish and manage an MPA, governments are generally required to adopt legislation formulated for both the implementation and management of marine protected areas. The aim of

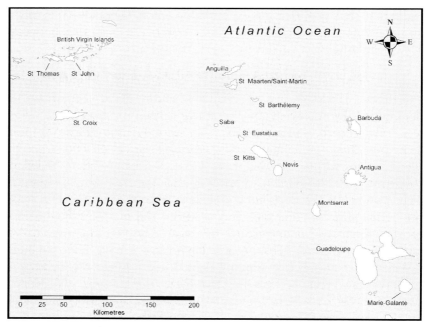

Fig. 6.1. Map of Caribbean Leeward Islands (data courtesy of US Defense Mapping Agency)

this chapter is to analyse selected marine protected areas legislation to determine which provisions are crucial to effective marine protected areas legislation and how that legislation translates into effective management and preservation of marine resources. The two island groups selected for analysis are within the Caribbean Leeward Islands – the Netherlands Antilles and the US Virgin Islands.

Section 6.2 briefly details several of the environmental threats confronting coral reefs in the Lesser Antilles, the purported benefits of MPAs, and the historic political challenges to the creation of MPAs. Section 6.3 summarises previous works on marine protected areas legislation and provides a comprehensive catalogue of important legal provisions. Section 6.4 is devoted to an assessment of the MPA legislation of two island groups mentioned above – the US Virgin Islands and the windward group of the Netherlands Antilles (comprising St Maarten, St Eustatius and Saba). Finally, Section 6.5 applies the results of Section 6.4 against the actual state of coral reefs of the selected islands and thereby seeks to identify those provisions most crucial to reef sustainability.

6.2   The argument for MPAs

Within the Caribbean Lesser Antilles, one of the primary sources of coral reef damage is land-based activities, which endanger coastal environments from 'sewage, alteration and destruction of habitats, sediment mobilisation, nutrient pollution, heavy metals and hydrocarbons' (Barker, 2002, p. 75). The two predominant economic activities among the islands of the Lesser Antilles – tourism and agriculture – are responsible for much of the threat. Irresponsible development within the tourist industry leads to destruction of the marine and coastal environment on which much of the industry depends (Barker, 2002). Intensive agriculture demands the clearing of forested habitats and, in turn, can result in erosion and sediment loss. Sedimentation and eutrophication degrade the coastal environment and leave certain habitats, such as coral reefs and seagrass beds, less able to thrive.

Ecosystem degradation from agriculture and coastal development are not exclusive to the Caribbean region nor are they the only dangers to the sustainability of coral reef habitats. Orams (2004, p. 199) listed the five major threats as: 'pollution of the seas, over exploitation of living things, physical alteration of the environment, the introduction of alien species, and finally, increased ultraviolet radiation and alteration of climatic conditions.' Blake (1998, p. 507) also notes that, along

125

with tourism, fisheries and the oil and gas industry exert ecological stresses on the coastal environment.

Although tourism is supplanting export agriculture as the dominant economic activity on many of the islands, agriculture is still very prevalent. The clearing of lands for agriculture increases the incidence of erosion and run-off. Moreover, Debrot and Sybesma (2000, p. 598) note that past and current grazing practices on some of the islands of the Netherlands Antilles has led to deforestation. The result is that sediment run-off and other pollution associated with poor or irresponsible agricultural practices degrades coastal waters. Sedimentation from erosion can limit reef development, as noted in a survey of Saban reefs by Klomp and Kooistra (2003).

The consequences of widespread destruction of coral reefs are especially serious when one recognises the integral part that coral reefs play in the economies of many small island nations, such as those located in the Eastern Caribbean. Countries most affected are frequently those that are least capable of handling the economic and ecological impacts. Depondt and Green (2006, p. 188) write that the 'economic value of coral reefs is of extreme importance, notably as due to their physiological requirements they are predominantly concentrated along the coasts of developing countries'. Burke and Maidens (2004, p. 58) estimated that the total annual value of coral reefs to the economies of countries within the Wider Caribbean Region is from 3.1 to 4.6 billion USD. The same study also estimates that future annual losses from continued degradation of the region's coral reefs could total as much as 870 million USD (Burke and Maidens, 2004, p. 58). The fundamental necessity of protecting coral reefs in the Caribbean (as well as elsewhere) was aptly stated by Barker (2002, p. 75), where he asserted that the 'hallmarks of Caribbean tourism – living coral reefs, brightly coloured fish, clear water and sandy beaches – are components of healthy ecosystems that are easily damaged or destroyed by "tourism development" activities that depend on them'.

Recent science has focused on the efficacy of marine protected areas in protecting marine resources, which are considered by some to represent the best management tool for conserving marine ecosystems (Hughes *et al.*, 2003). The International Union for Conservation of Nature (IUCN) (1998) defines a marine protected area as 'any area of the intertidal or subtidal terrain, together with its overlying water and associated flora, fauna, historical and cultural features, which has been reserved by law or other effective means to protect part or all of

126

the enclosed environment'. Sobel and Dahlgren (2004, p. 166) state that a marine protected area is essentially 'a set of rules that collectively govern human interactions with a specified portion of the marine environment'.

Marine protected areas can come in all shapes and sizes and restrictions. Although the delineation of types of MPA may differ across organisations, they can generally be classified into three broad categories: (1) multiple use; (2) no-take; and (3) no impact/access. A multiple-use MPA generally allows some extractive activities within its limits, although the amount of extraction will be limited according to the resource being protected. A no-take MPA is just as its name implies – no extraction of resources is allowed within the limits of the MPA. No-take MPAs generally accommodate tourist-friendly activities, such as scuba diving or snorkelling. They will also typically allow recreational boating, although regulations seek to ensure that ecosystems, such as coral reefs, are not disturbed through negligent operation or anchoring of the vessel. Thus, there is usually some level of human activity within a no-take MPA.

No impact and no access MPAs place the severest restrictions on activity under their jurisdiction, where the only type of human interference allowed is scientific research and is thus completely off-limits to the public at large. Sobel and Dahlgren (2004, pp. 19–20) acknowledge the particular advantage of marine reserves (incorporating those MPAs where extraction is outlawed) in protecting an entire ecosystem as opposed to a single species. They state that marine no-take areas are among the most essential tools required to protect and restore the health of our oceans from multiple stressors.

Marine protected areas may provide important ecological and biological benefits, such as enhancement of the reproduction potential of fishery stocks, maintenance of species diversity, preservation of important habitats, and conservation of ecosystem functions (Bergen and Carr, 2003, pp. 10–11). More specifically, studies have revealed that MPAs may be instrumental in protecting valuable coral reef ecosystems and fishery stocks. For instance, MPAs may prove invaluable to the global struggle to combat the consequences of coral bleaching events, widely attributed to the effects of climate change (Lewsey *et al.*, 2004). While MPAs are obviously incapable of halting an increase in water temperatures, they *can* help to relieve coral reefs from human-induced pressures, which thereby enable the reefs to better cope and recover from coral bleaching events (Hughes *et al.*, 2003, p. 932).

Overall, MPAs are associated with higher values of species density, biomass, organism size, and diversity of species (Halpern 2003, S122). The importance of MPAs in protecting shallow-water ecosystems has been especially noted (Ogden, 1997). Ogden (1997, p. 1414) states that coral reefs protected by a reserve of only several hectares 'will develop larger populations of organisms composed of larger individuals within periods as short as a few years'. One study has posited that at least 30% of the world's coral reefs should be protected within strict 'no-take areas' to ensure long-term protection of coral reefs and associated fishery stocks (Hughes *et al.*, 2003, p. 933). Other research argues that a network of reserves covering 20% of all biogeographic regions and habitats should be fully protected to meet conservation goals (Roberts *et al.*, 2003, S216). Issues of size and percentage coverage notwithstanding, Gjerde (2001, pp. 516–517) relates that:

> 150 of the world's leading marine scientists issued a scientific consensus statement proclaiming there is now compelling evidence that providing protection on an area basis works. It urged the immediate application of fully protected marine reserves as a central ocean management tool.

Still, a broad consensus within the scientific community does not ensure implementation (Gillespie, 2000, p. 300). Despite their noted benefits and recognition of the need for more MPAs, they still cover less than 1% of the world's ocean, with even less (<0.01%) designated as strict no-take areas that forbid any resource extraction (Bergen and Carr, 2003, p. 10). It is thus readily apparent that more needs to be done to ensure that sustainable uses are developed to guarantee that future generations have access to the ocean resources enjoyed by today's populations.

The difficulty in establishing MPAs stems from out historical perception of the sea as possessing an unlimited reserve of resources. Lodge (2004, p. 302) notes that the only international rule currently governing exploitation of marine resources is the rule of 'capture', which provides that ownership of a common resource is enjoyed by the party first able to exert 'dominion and control' over the resource. Many current attempts to adopt meaningful regulations and standards for the use of oceans and marine resources have been met with hostility, both in the US and throughout the world (Frontani, 2006). Accordingly, commentators have noted that the largest obstacle to MPA establishment has generally been political (Salomon *et al.*, 2001; Ogden, 1997). Several studies on MPA creation in the US have looked at conflicts between key groups, such as politicians, scientists, MPA managers, and stakeholders (Mascia, 1999; Morin, 2001; Lundquist and Granek, 2005; Frontani, 2006). For example, in the Florida Keys, organisations of local fishermen were instrumental in bringing about a decrease in the total area of no-take area within the Florida Keys National Marine Sanctuary (Ogden, 1997; Frontani, 2006). Marine reserves are seen as limiting their 'right' to extract marine resources at will (Ogden, 1997, p. 1415).

On a positive note, research has also shown that Americans are beginning to realise the importance of protecting our natural ocean resources. Brailovskaya (1998, p. 1237) notes a 1996 poll where 84% of the respondents acknowledged that 'ocean protection was part of society's responsibility to future generations'. Lindholm and Barr (2001, p. 1443) cite a 2001 survey indicating that US citizens understand that the marine environment faces serious pressures and generally support both additional regulations and the expansion of marine protected areas.

6.3   Recommended legislative provisions

Despite a recognised need for an increase in the number and size of MPAs, establishment of marine protected areas is often difficult to achieve. Because of the long-held belief that ocean resources are both a limitless and common resource, proposed MPAs are often challenged by local stakeholders. Moreover, in the event that marine protected areas are established, they are often so-called 'paper parks' with little or no management or enforcement. To some extent, the problem is one of financing, as the small island states have scant financial resources to enforce what is generally an unpopular measure to begin with. However, the problem may also stem from ineffective implementing legislation. For example, MPA regulations may be ignored if too many restrictions are enacted, whereas too few restrictions coupled with questionable enforcement practices results in continued degradation of the resources the law seeks to protect. Well-constructed marine protected areas laws and regulations can achieve a crucial balance between respect of traditional uses of the sea and enabling of appropriate mechanisms for enforcement and funding in order to realise the objectives behind establishment.

This section lists those legislative provisions deemed important to MPA establishment and management and draws heavily upon previous work on MPA legislation by Lausche[i] (1980), Kelleher and Kenchington (1992), and Salm *et al.* (2000). The Lausche publication, titled *Guidelines for Protected Areas Legislation*, is, as the title suggests, specifically devoted to explication of the provisions crucial to the effectiveness of a protected area. The one caveat is that the book encompasses proposed guidelines for both marine *and* terrestrial protected areas, and thus several of the proposed guidelines are inapplicable to management of marine areas.

Nevertheless, the majority of the provisions found in *Guidelines for Protected Areas Legislation* are relevant to the present analysis and the publication is the primary source for the elements included herein. Significantly, Lausche has worked as a consultant to the Organisation of Eastern Caribbean States assessing environmental legislation in the Caribbean, as well as drafted national parks legislation for the British Virgin Islands. Furthermore, Lausche notes that the guidelines 'have the benefit of scientific and legal review from experts working with protected areas' and 'represent some consensus as to essential legal elements important to both disciplines' (1980, p. 9).

The second and third publications utilised are *Guidelines for Establishing Marine Protected Areas*, and specifically, the chapter titled 'Legal Considerations for Protection of Marine and Estuarine Areas and Resources' (Kelleher and Kenchington, 1992); and *Marine and Coastal Protected Areas: A Guide for Planners and Managers*, and more specifically, the chapter titled 'Institutional and Legal Framework' (Salm *et al.*, 2000). Unlike Lausche (1980), the Kelleher and Salm publications are devoted specifically to marine protected areas. Although the books are not quite as comprehensive as Lausche (1980), they are useful to supplement those guidelines where the unique nature of the marine environment requires special considerations.

The author's review of the guidelines set forth in these publications identified 15 key elements for successful MPA legislation. However, as noted by Salm *et al.* (2000, p. 134), every country is different and the form and content of legislation will differ according to the needs, traditions, and institutions of the individual country. Accordingly, it is highly unlikely that a country's laws will incorporate each of the identified elements. For that and other reasons, Lausche writes that the elements presented in her book are 'presented as guidelines rather than a Model Act' (Lausche, 1980, p. 21). Each of the elements are listed below, along with a brief description of its purpose and/or relevance to the establishment and administration of marine protected areas.

6.3.1 Statement of policy

Legislation should include a statement of policy on the 'management, sustainable use and conservation' of marine areas (Kelleher and Kensington, 1992, p. 18). To that end, the policy should specify, *inter alia*, a country's economic, social, political, development, and land use considerations (Lausche, 1980, p. 22). Lausche (1980, p. 23) also suggests that, when applicable, the policy statement should include whether the legislation: (1) is adopted to comply with multilateral obligation or international convention; or (2) is guided by a particular international principle or concern. Formation of a comprehensive policy statement may also help increase national recognition of the need to protect and conserve marine resources (Kelleher and Kensington, 1992, p. 18).

6.3.2 Statement of objectives

The legislation should specifically indicate the goals that the country hopes to achieve through the establishment of marine protected areas. Generally, the objectives should include 'conservation, recreation, education and scientific research' goals, with resource conservation being of primary importance (Kelleher and Kensington, 1992, p. 18). Clearly-stated objectives will also help to guide the activities and decisions of MPA managers and officers (Lausche, 1980, p. 23). Examples of general objectives are:

(a) to safeguard and maintain representative samples of the natural ecosystems and endangered species occurring therein;
(b) to propagate, protect, conserve, study, and manage those ecosystems, flora and fauna . . . of particular national or local significance for the benefit and enjoyment of the inhabitants of the country;
(c) to conserve ecosystems or species of particular international value for the preservation of important representative ecosystems, species, or genetic resources, or for the management of shared resources;
(d) to provide educational and recreational services that will allow the public to appreciate and enjoy the values of protected areas;
(e) to provide for multiple-use resource areas which offer protection to ecosystems and resources as well as some secondary social and economic benefit;
(f) to establish buffer zones outside the periphery of a particular protected area to lessen disturbances that may be caused by human activity outside that area (Lausche 1980, pp. 24–25).

6.3.3 Definitions
Definitions of the terms used in MPA legislation help to avoid confusion over comprehension and application of legislative provisions. Definitions are also important when using standardised terms. For example, Lausche (1980, p. 26) notes that the classification for a 'national park' in one jurisdiction may often differ from that of a different jurisdiction.

6.3.4 Establishment of protected areas
One of the most critical aspects of MPA legislation is the method adopted for establishment of marine protected areas, which will involve several components. Lausche (1980, p. 31) writes that the powers and procedures to establish, amend and abolish protected areas should rest with the 'highest body responsible for legislative matters in the country or region...'. Lausche also recommends that decisions affecting the MPA boundaries and classifications be altered only through legislation coming from the top (1980, p. 31). Such high-placed authority may be necessary in order to ensure that the restrictions of the MPA are not limited or reduced at lower levels of administration. However, Lausche does recommend that the governing authority consult the public about critical decisions affecting the MPA (Lausche, 1980, p. 32). Last, the legislation should contain management provisions that 'ensure fulfilment of each area's purpose and objectives' (Lausche, 1980, p. 33).

6.3.5 Jurisdiction
A protected area may be subject to the authority of different agencies, and so it is important that the legislation delineate management and enforcement responsibilities among the various groups when such an eventuality exists. Additionally, responsibility for areas and activities outside the protected area that impact the MPA also needs to be clearly defined (Lausche, 1980, p. 30).

6.3.6 Demarcation of boundaries
It is quite important to define clearly the boundaries of the marine protected area. As with the establishment and amendment of MPAs, the boundaries should be set forth in the general legislation coming from the highest governing authority. Salm *et al.* (2000, p. 141) maintain that the boundaries 'must be broad enough to encompass the critical areas it aims to protect,' and 'must also be small enough that

enforcement is possible'. Furthermore, they note that equitable considerations demand that MPA boundaries not be so extensive that
traditional users reject the limitation of their rights. MPAs whose
boundaries are set according to a justifiable rationale are more likely
to be 'accepted, and respected, by the stakeholders' (Salm *et al.*,
2000, p. 141).

Legislation should seek to regulate activities both inside and outside
the marine protected area that may impact protection and conservation
of the ecosystems and species within the MPA. Thus, the legislation
should, whenever possible, include buffer zones in which activities are
controlled and regulated. The buffer zone should be clearly delimited
and the proscribed activities within the buffer zone clearly defined
(Lausche, 1980, pp. 40–41).

6.3.7   *Management plan*

For an MPA to be successful, it is often vital that the protected area
develop and abide by a comprehensiveness management plan. The
management plan will govern nearly all aspects of actual administration
of the protected area, such as conservation and protection measures,
maintenance, buildings, roads, monitoring, research surveys, recreational activities and facilities, visitors fee amounts, etc. (Lausche,
1980, p. 35). Thus, any legislation regulating MPAs should require
that a management plan be produced. One of the key provisions of
the plan, especially for large MPAs, is delimitation and regulations
inside different zones within the MPA. Kelleher and Kensington
(1992, p. 21) recommend that 'zoning arrangements be described in
sufficient detail to provide adequate control of activities and protection
of resources'.

Lausche notes several other components of the management plan
that should be dealt with in the legislation:

(a) a detailed description of the manner in which management of the
protected area is to be undertaken;
(b) the interval of time within which and manner by which public
comments may be made to the authorities in connection with the
plan;
(c) when the plan allows for certain uses or developments in the
protected area (e.g. recreation, building of certain facilities, etc.),
it should clearly set out any conditions which are applicable to
those uses or developments;

(d) in preparation of the plan, objectives and purposes for the general program area should be recognised and followed;

(e) a clear description of the zoning category and the conditions under which each zone should be maintained; and

(f) the interval of time during which it will be effective and date on which it will cease to have effect (Lausche, 1980, p. 36).

6.3.8 Financing

Even with well-structured management plans and well-intentioned managers and officers, an MPA will be unsuccessful if the administration of the MPA is not adequately financed. The legislation must provide for the allocation of adequate revenues for the MPA to achieve its conservation goals. When possible, the legislation should create a special fund specifically reserved to finance MPA activities (Salm *et al.*, 2000, p. 157).

In addition (or alternatively), the legislation should require that fees collected by the park itself, such as funds acquired through visitors' fees or park concessions, be used for park administration and management. Successful marine parks, such as those in Bonaire and Saba, have nearly achieved self-sufficiency through this method. Such an arrangement is further recommended because it assures that the MPA will be supported if the government ever votes to reduce or abolish government financing. The one drawback in self-supporting MPAs, however, is that the need to maintain its funding may lead the MPA to focus more on obtaining revenue than conservation.

6.3.9 Institutional arrangements

Each established MPA will have its own managers and officers; however, the government must also develop 'institutional mechanisms' to oversee implementation of legislative rules and objectives (Lausche, 1980, p. 41). Consistent with the objective of protecting marine resources and areas, the institutional mechanism with overarching responsibility for marine protected areas should be given powers 'to adopt such protective measures as may be necessary for each area' (Lausche, 1980, p. 42). Kelleher and Kenchington (1992, p. 20) state that, in order to avoid interorganisational conflict, the 'arrangements should grow from existing institutions' and that the 'creation of new agencies should be minimized'. For newly established countries, Salm *et al.* (2000, p. 136) maintain that non-governmental organisations, which will often have the experience and expertise lacking in a young government, can be beneficial as overseers of MPA legislation and management.

Even if new agencies are not created, it is inevitable that disputes between agencies may arise (Kelleher and Kenchington, 1992, p. 20). To minimise potential conflict, the legislation should, to the extent possible, delineate the relationships between, and respective powers and duties of, the various agencies and include either (1) mechanisms for dispute resolution, or (2) clearly identify the agency having ultimate authority over MPA matters (Kelleher and Kenchington, 1992, p. 20). The government may want to consider creation or appointment of an advisory body of appropriate scientific and technical merit to make recommendations to the oversight agency.

6.3.10 *Prohibited and regulated activities*

Legislation should include the types of activities allowed and prohibited within marine protected areas and related buffer zones. Restrictions on activities will define, or be defined by, the type of MPA established (e.g. no-take reserve, marine park, multiple-use area). The following are general and specific activities that should be regulated:

(a) prohibiting or strictly regulating access to the whole or part of an area;
(b) prohibitions against distraction or alteration of the marine ecosystem;
(c) prohibitions against [or permitting of] the killing, capturing, taking away, damaging or disturbing of any resource, or other object for exploitation or any other purpose;
(d) regulating or prohibiting the collecting or taking of animals or plants into or out of the protected area;
(e) prohibitions against damage of ecosystems or species from pollution;
(f) prohibitions against introduction of alien or exotic species; prohibiting the use of explosives and poisons in the protected area;
(g) conducting of scientific research;
(h) removal or alteration of any flora or fauna... in any protected area (Lausche, 1980, pp. 52–55).

6.3.11 *Enforcement*

The success of an MPA may often be linked to effective enforcement of the rules and regulations laid out in legislation and the management plan. Thus, the legislation should include provisions governing the duties and powers of enforcement officers (Lausche, 1980, p. 59). The law should also specify the fines and penalties to be levied against those that break MPA rules and regulations. Three key elements of enforcement that should be specified are:

(a) the types of officers that have the various enforcement duties and powers;
(b) the kind of enforcement powers which should be granted;
(c) a strong focus on public participation in enforcement and on public education about the law and the protected areas program (Lausche, 1980, p. 59).

Considering the last element, Salm *et al.* (2000, p. 156) state that legislation should provide 'as many incentives as possible for the enforcement of rules and regulations by local people who use and benefit from the area'.

6.3.12 Monitoring and research

Legislation should give the oversight agency authority 'to undertake or contract out and supervise research and surveys relevant to planning and management..., and should include detailed socio-economic analysis of neighbouring communities' (Salm *et al.*, 2000, p. 137). Monitoring allows the management and advisory bodies to gauge the success of marine protection measures, while research can help identify those factors that influence most heavily the success of legislative measures.

6.3.13 Equity and compensation

Creation of an MPA will often require restricting use of the area by local stakeholders. Both Salm *et al.* (2000) and Kelleher and Kenchington (1992) recommend that legislation provide compensation to stakeholders for the loss of use of protected areas. Moreover, as already stated, the legislation should seek to consider the traditional uses and rights of local stakeholders when setting MPA restrictions and delimiting MPA boundaries (so as not to create overly large areas).

6.3.14 Legal proceedings

Legislation should provide for the manner in which transgressors will be dealt with legally, which may include proceedings before the appropriate court of law. Penalties for rule-breaking can be defined under either this section or under 'Enforcement', and may include fines, imprisonment and/or forfeiture. Forfeiture without compensation should apply to 'any objects or devices (whether mechanical or non-mechanical) taken, used or involved in the commission of the offense', or 'all natural flora or fauna taken as well as any... proceeds of sale of any such objects' (Lausche, 1980, p. 65). Lausche further recommends that the burden of proof be defined and, where possible, shift the burden to the defendant to rebut the presumption of guilt (1980, p. 66).

6.3.15 *Public participation and education*
Within the preceding elements are many instances where the public is encouraged to assist with management and enforcement of MPA rules and regulations. MPAs should implement education and outreach programmes in order to notify the public about the benefits of marine resource conservation and the strategic role that an effective MPA can play to achieve conservation goals. Provisions to encourage public participation might include:

(a) public opportunity to review and comment on proposed protected area designations, management plans, regulations, etc.;
(b) public involvement and management activities, enforcement programs and administration, when appropriate, with local programs;
(c) public representation on advisory committees at all appropriate levels;
(d) local participation in decisions of disbursement of certain revenues for local operation of a protected area (Lausche, 1980, p. 67).

Engaging local stakeholders will help to avoid conflict over use of protected areas and foster relationships between stakeholders and MPA officers and officials, generally resulting in more successful protected areas.

6.4   Analysis of marine protected areas legislation
The legislative guidelines presented in Section 6.3 form the basis for analysis of the marine protected areas laws of the three island groups. The first step is to identify the specific provisions within each law or ordinance which are deemed crucial to successful MPA establishment and management. Accordingly, Section 6.4 is devoted to a simple outline of the relevant provisions from the selected legislation of each

island group.[ii] The consequences for protection of marine resources will be dealt with in Section 6.5.

6.4.1 *Netherlands Antilles*

Within the Windward group of the Netherlands Antilles, the only meaningful marine protected areas legislation is the Marine Environment Ordinance of Saba (A.B. 1991 Nr 8), and the Marine Environment Ordinance of St Eustatius (A.B. 1996 Nr 3).[iii] Both ordinances, passed by the island's governing bodies, establish the marine parks surrounding each island. St Maarten has yet to pass a similar ordinance or formally establish a marine park. In this chapter, only the Saba Marine Environment Ordinance will be reviewed.

Marine Environment Ordinance (A.B. 1991 Nr 8)
Preamble: states that the ordinance is passed in order to:

> establish regulations for managing the marine environment of the Island Territory Saba, in order to preserve the natural resources of that environment for both commercial, as well as educational, recreational and scientific purposes.

The preamble is deficient as a statement of policy and statement of objective, but it can be viewed as incorporating elements of both.

Part I, Art. 1: Part 1 is entitled 'Definitions' and lists the terms used in the Marine Ordinance, including descriptions of coral, conch, turtles and scuba. Significantly, the first definition establishes the limits of the Saba National Marine Park (SMP), which are:

> the sea floor and overlying waters around and adjacent to the island Saba, with the high water tidemark as the upper limit and the 60 m depth contour as the lower limit.

Thus, by definition, the SMP completely surrounds the island, encompassing all marine areas up to a 60 m depth.

Part II, Art. 2: declares unlawful any acts that violate the SMP zoning plan as set forth in the Island Resolution Containing General Provisions (IRCGP). The general provisions are incorporated as amendments to the Marine Ordinance and are discussed below. The article does not include details on the types of regulations to be enforced or the penalties for violations, however, these matters are dealt with in other sections.

138

Part II, Arts 3, 4: these two articles prohibit spearfishing with scuba gear or hookah equipment and the use of poisons, chemicals or explosives for fishing.

Part II, Arts 5, 6: restricts the number of turtle and conch that can be extracted from the park. Persons who choose to collect either turtle or conch are obligated to report their catch to the SMP manager.

Part II, Art. 7: Article 7 is an important provision because it allows for the passage of new regulations affecting catch and collection of marine organisms. Significantly, however, it states that these additional regulations are to be issued by Island Resolution, and thus it is the island government that has ultimate authority regarding protection of marine species. This provision most closely relates to Guideline 4 (Establishment of Protected Areas), insofar as changes in regulations may represent a downgrade or withdrawal in classification.

Part II, Art. 8: Article 8 contains a general statement that it unlawful to engage in activities that harm the marine environment, or to intentionally destroy the marine environment of the SMP. Subsection 3 specifically prohibits anyone to 'kill, break, catch or collect corals or other bottom-dwelling invertebrates and plants on or in the sea floor'. However, subsection 4 relaxes the restrictions for Sabans, who are, within limits, permitted to take snails, squids and octopus, and crustaceans for personal use.

Part II, Arts 9, 10, 11: these articles detail several other prohibited activities within the SMP, such as anchoring in coral (except during an emergency), the discharge of substances into the waters of the SMP, and the construction or destruction of mooring sites within the SMP. Furthermore, boats are not to occupy existing mooring sites any longer than is needed to complete a dive.

Part II, Art. 12: provides that 'developments or modifications of the coastal zone which may influence the marine environment of SMP must be preceded by an independent environmental impact assessment'. This is the only provision in the reviewed legislation for regulation of activities outside a protected area which may potentially harm the environment within the MPA. Saba is a popular diving destination within the Caribbean and considered to have well-maintained reefs. It is likely that Article 12 is partly responsible for effective protection of the surrounding marine resources.

Part III, Art. 13: Saba Marine Park is at or near self-sustainability as far as financing its own operations is concerned. Self-financing has been achieved through the imposition of visitors' fees on scuba divers and snorkellers in the park. Article 13 requires that operators transporting visitors into the park obtain permits and they in turn are responsible for collecting fees from their clients. Adequate financing for park management and maintenance could well prove one of the most important elements for MPA success.

Part III, Art. 14: authorises the Executive Council to grant exemptions from regulations for scientific, commercial or educational purposes, but provides that the council must seek expert advice before doing so. Article 14 specifically grants Executive Council authority to grant exemptions to subsection 3 of Article 8 (prohibiting taking of coral and other bottom-dwelling invertebrates) for commercial purposes.

Part III, Arts 16, 17: both articles outline penalties to be assessed under the ordinance. However, Article 16 is unique in that it provides for specific charges against the director of a 'legal body' should he/she fail to 'ensure that the legal body directed by him does not violate any regulations of this ordinance'. Presumably, the legal body is some authority vested with responsibility for administering or making regulations for the park. Should the director fail in his duties, he may be imprisoned for up to one month. Article 17 states that other violations will be punished by imprisonment of up to one month or fines.

Article 20: provides for forfeiture of objects used or acquired during violation of ordinance. As noted above, forfeiture can be seen as an effective way of discouraging violations, as the loss of a boat or vehicle can be much more severe than payment of the maximum fine.

Island Resolution (A.B. 1987, Nr 10), Amendment 3.1.2

Article 1: establishes the different zones within the Saba National Marine Park. The Island Resolution creates one multiple use zone, five recreational diving zones, three anchoring zones and an all-purpose recreational zone. Zoning can be beneficial because it allows for access to the Park (which in this case are all waters surrounding the island) but creates areas that can be restricted in order to preserve particularly significant or valuable marine areas.

Article 2: prohibits most fishing within recreational diving zones.

There are several other amendments to the Marine Environment Ordinance but they deal primarily with an increase in visitors' fees and how they are to be assessed, imposition of yachting fees, and a prohibition on anchoring in recreational areas. In this regard, the amendments more closely resemble those types of day-to-day management issues that might typically be dealt with in the park's management plan.

6.4.2   US Virgin Islands

As a territory of the United States, the legislation regulating marine protected areas in the US Virgin Islands is formulated by the US Congress. As such, the legislation governs the establishment and management for all marine protected areas designated by the US government. While dozens of federal laws apply to marine areas and resources, the National Marine Sanctuaries Act, 16 U.S.C. §1431 *et seq.*, and the National Parks Act, 16 U.S.C. §1 *et seq.*, are the most comprehensive legislation for MPAs. Additionally, the American Antiquities Act of 1906, 16 U.S.C. §§431–433, grants the president authority to establish national monuments on federal lands and waters (which is the authority for establishment of Buck Island National Monument off the coast of St Croix), but that law is not analysed here.

National Marine Sanctuaries Act, 16 U.S.C. §1431 *et seq.*

Sec. 301(a): titled 'Findings', this section notes that most resource protection legislation has, in the past, been limited to mostly terrestrial areas. The section recognises that marine areas of special significance also exist and similarly require special consideration. The section notes further that past legislation has dealt primarily with a specific resource rather than a particular area and that a coordinated approach to conservation is needed. A sanctuaries program incorporating areas of significance (which include conservation, ecological, scientific, and educational qualities) will:

(a) improve the conservation, understanding, management, and wise and sustainable use of marine resources;
(b) enhance public awareness, understanding, and appreciation of the marine environment; and
(c) maintain for future generations the habitat, and ecological services, of the natural assemblages of living resources that inhabit those areas.

The language in §301(a) is analogous to a policy statement, insofar as it spells out the reasons for the sanctuary programme.

Sec. 301(b): while §301(a) provides the policy behind the programme, §301(b) clarifies the objectives that the programme hopes to achieve. They include, *inter alia*:

(1) to identify and designate as natural marine sanctuaries areas of the marine environment which are of a special national significance;

(2) to provide authority for comprehensive and coordinated conservation and management of these marine areas, and activities affecting them, in a manner which complements existing regulatory authorities;

(3) to maintain the natural biological communities in the national marine sanctuaries, and to protect, and, where appropriate, restore and enhance natural habitats, populations, and ecological processes;

(4) to enhance public awareness, understanding, appreciation, and wise and sustainable use of the marine environment;

(5) to support, promote, and coordinate scientific research on, and long-term monitoring of, the resources of these marine areas;

(6) to facilitate to the extent compatible with the primary objective of resource protection, all public and private use of the resources of these marine areas not prohibited pursuant to other authorities;

(9) to cooperate with global programs encouraging conservation of marine resources.

Considering that part of the purpose of the statement of objective is intended to guide administration of the Act, §301(b) does a thorough job of establishing the intent of the government in order to direct management decisions.

Sec. 303: this section lays out the standards for designation of protected areas under the sanctuary program. The section provides that the Secretary of Commerce may designate:

> any discrete area of the marine environment as a national marine sanctuary and promulgate regulations implementing the designation if the Secretary determines that ... the area is of special national significance due to (A) its conservation, recreational, ecological, historical, scientific ... qualities; (B) the communities of living marine resources it harbors; or (C) its resources or human-use values.

To determine whether the discrete area meets the standards for designation, the Secretary is to consider:

> the area's natural resource and ecological qualities ... ; the present and potential uses of the area that depend on maintenance of the area's resources ... ; the existing State and Federal regulatory and management authorities applicable to the area and the adequacy of those authorities to fulfill the purposes and policies of [the act] ...

The section further requires the secretary of commerce to consult with other federal committees, state agencies, local government entities and other interested persons when making these findings. Thus, Section 303 details the qualities an area must possess in order to receive consideration for placement in the programme.

Sec. 304: Section 304 is one of the most important within the Marine Sanctuary Act, since it details procedures for designation, requires drafting of a management plan and further mandates interagency cooperation before final designation. First, the secretary issues a notice of the proposed designation, regulations and summary of the draft management plan in the Federal Register, newspapers and other media. Before designation, the secretary must make available for public inspection the: (1) draft environmental impact statement; (2) resource assessment that documents present and potential uses of the area, including commercial and recreational fishing, research and education, minerals and energy development, subsistence and uses; (3) a draft management plan; (4) maps depicting the boundaries of the proposed sanctuary; (5) the basis for the determinations made under §303(a) (standards for designation); and (6) an assessment of the considerations under §303(b)(1) (criteria for determining if standards are met).

Within the management plan, the secretary must include proposed regulations, responsibilities, costs and 'appropriate strategies for managing sanctuary resources, including interpretation and education, innovative management strategies, research, monitoring and surveys, etc.'. Under the Act, the plan is to be reviewed at least every five years. The sanctuary proposal must include the geographic area of the proposed sanctuary and proposed fishing regulations within the area. Finally, the secretary is to conduct public hearings near the designated area, consult with various congressional committees on the proposed designation, and review federal agency actions 'internal and external to a national marine sanctuary... that are likely to destroy, cause the loss of, or injure any sanctuary resource'.

Sec. 305: this section states that the regulations promulgated under §304 should 'be applied in accordance with generally recognised principles of international law, and in accordance with treaties, conventions, and other agreements to which the United States is a party'. In general, the section creates an obligation to cooperate with other governments and international organisations. Although not included in §301, the reference to international cooperation and principles falls under the policy guideline in Section 5.3.

Sec. 306: in conjunction with the specific regulations that should be included in the management plan, the Act contains a general list of prohibited activities within the marine sanctuary. The Act makes it unlawful to:

(1) destroy, cause a loss of, or injure any sanctuary resource managed under law or regulations for that sanctuary;

(2) possess, sell, offer for sale, purchase, import, export, deliver, carry, transport, or ship by any means any sanctuary resource taken in violation of this section;

(3) interfere with the enforcement of this chapter by

   (a) refusing to permit any officer authorized to enforce this chapter to board a vessel...

   (b) resisting, opposing, competing, intimidating, harassing, bribing, interfering with, or forcibly assaulting any person authorized by the Secretary to implement this chapter or any such authorized officer in the conduct of any search for inspection reforms under this chapter; or

   (c) knowingly and willfully submitting false information to the secretary or any officer authorized to enforce this chapter.

   (d) violate any provision of this chapter or any regulation or permit issued pursuant to this chapter.

Sec. 307: this section includes the powers and duties of park enforcement officers, as well as the penalties for violating park regulations. Under the Act, officers are allowed to board and search vessels, seize sanctuary resources, evidence of violations, and make arrests of violators. According to §307, those found guilty of an offence are subject to imprisonment for up to six months, fines or both. If a person uses a dangerous weapon, causes bodily injury, causes or fear of bodily injury, he/she can be fined and/or imprisoned for up to ten years. Last, §307 allows for forfeiture of vessels and other items used during or for the commission of an offence within the sanctuary.

Sec. 309: This section is titled 'Research, Monitoring, and Education' and contains general provisions requiring the secretary to 'conduct, support, or coordinate research, monitoring, evaluation, and education programs'. This includes long-term monitoring of sanctuary resources, which includes exploration, mapping, and environmental and socioeconomic assessment. Research and monitoring results are to be made available to the public.

Subsection (c) allows the secretary to 'support, promote, and co-ordinate efforts to enhance public awareness, understanding, and appreciation of national marine sanctuaries', with an emphasis on 'conservation goals and sustainable public uses of national marine sanctuaries'. Activities under subsection (c) are to include education of the general public, teachers, students, national marine sanctuary users, and ocean and coastal resource managers.

Sec. 310: allows the secretary to issue special use permits to conduct specific activities within the sanctuary if permission is necessary to: (1) establish conditions of access to and use of any sanctuary resource; or (2) to promote public use and understanding of the sanctuary resource. Under §310, the secretary is authorised to collect fees for activities under the special use permit, which are to be used for issuing and administering permits and expenses related to managing national marine sanctuaries.

Sec. 313: of the legislation reviewed thus far, §313 contains the only provision specifically authorising exact appropriation amounts from the government. In 2005, the legislature allocated 40 million dollars for the sanctuary programme.

Sec. 315: the act states that the secretary 'may' establish one or more advisory councils to make recommendations regarding designation and management of sanctuaries. Council members may come from just about any group; however, membership is limited to 15 members per sanctuary. The meetings of the advisory council are open to the public.

National Parks Act, 16 U.S.C. §1 *et seq.*

Sec. 1: creates the National Park Service within the Department of the Interior and creates position of Director of National Park Service, who is required to possess 'substantial experience and demonstrated competence in land management and natural or cultural resource conservation'.

Sec. 1a-1: contains the declaration of findings and purpose, which includes that areas of 'superb environmental quality [be] preserved and managed for the benefit and inspiration of all the people of the United States'. While preservation of resources is an important aspect of the National Park System, the Act is also designed to promote and foster public use of protected areas.

Sec. 1a-6: the secretary is given power to designate officers or employees to maintain law and order and protect persons and property within areas of the National Park System. Officers or employees are authorised to make arrests, execute warrants and conduct investigations of offences against the US committed and the National Park System.

Sec. 1a-7: requires the director of the National Park Service to prepare and revise, in a timely manner, general management plans for the preservation and use of each unit of the National Park System. The management plans shall include:

(1) measures for the preservation of the area's resources;
(2) indications of types in general intensities of development associated with public enjoyment and use of the area;
(3) identification of and implementation commitments for visitor carrying capacities for all areas of the unit;
(4) indications of potential modifications to the external boundaries of the Unit, and the reasons therefore.

Sec. 1a-12, 13: the Act provides for the consideration of boundary changes to park limits. The secretary is charged with developing criteria to evaluate any proposed changes to the existing boundaries of individual park units, including:

(a) analysis of whether or not the existing boundary provides adequate protection and preservation of the natural, historic, cultural, scenic and recreational resources integral to the unit;
(b) evaluation of each parcel proposed for addition or deletion to the unit based on the analysis under paragraph (1) [sic];
(c) an assessment of the impact of potential boundary adjustments taking into consideration the factors in paragraph (c) [sic] as well as the effect of the adjustments on the local communities and surrounding area.

After the assessment, the secretary may propose boundary changes to park areas, but must first consult affected agencies of state and local governments surrounding communities, affected landowners, and private national, regional and local organisations. The requirement to consult local officials and public brings equity considerations into the equation, as the potential effects on these parties must be factored into the analysis.

Sect. 1c: contains the general provision that 'each area within the National Park System shall be administered in accordance with the provisions of any statute made specifically at that area'. Under the Act, each park is designated under the statute and contains provisions for establishment and management. For instance, the Virgin Islands National Park is established under 16 U.S.C. §398.

Sec. 2: the executive powers of the president include the authority to designate federal lands as national monuments. Under this section, responsibility for management of national monuments, as well as national parks, is given to the Director of the National Park System, under the direction of the Secretary of the Interior.

Sec. 3: provides that 'the Secretary of the Interior shall make and publish such rules and regulations as he may deem necessary or proper for the use and management of the parks, monuments and reservations under the jurisdiction of the National Park Service, and any violation of any of the rules and regulations authorised by the section in sections 1, 2 and 4 of this title shall be punished by a fine of not more than $500 or imprisonment for not exceeding six months, or both, and be judged to pay all costs of the proceedings'.

Sec. 19jj: includes a few definitions related to resource protection under the National Park System. The section defines 'Marine or aquatic park system resource' as 'any living or non-living part of a marine or aquatic regimen within what is a living part of a marine or aquatic regimen within the boundaries of a unit of the National Park System, except for resources owned by a non-Federal entity'.

Sec. 398: as mentioned above, this section established the Virgin Islands National Park in 1956. It directs the secretary to preserve the area 'in its natural condition for the public benefit and inspiration, in accordance with the laws governing the administration of the national parks'.

Sec. 398d: this section is significant because it directs the secretary to 'employ and train residents of the Virgin Islands to develop, maintain, and administer the Virgin Islands National Park'. Thus, not only are local inhabitants provided jobs through the establishment of the park (which might possibly include those whose livelihoods are threatened or injured through park regulations), but the section also contributes to the objective of encouraging public participation.

Sec. 398e: protects traditional uses of park resources, such as bathing and fishing rights, stating that:

(a) Nothing in sections 398c to 398f of this title shall be construed as authorizing any limitation on customary uses of or access to the areas specified in section 398(c) of this title for bathing and fishing (including setting out of fish pots and landing boats), subject to such regulations as the Secretary of the Interior may find reasonable and necessary for protection of natural conditions and prevention of damage to marine life and formations.

(b) Notwithstanding any provision of law to the contrary, no fee or charge shall be imposed for entrance or admission to the Virgin Islands National Park.

This section is ambiguous in that it preserves the traditional rights of local stakeholders but only to the point where they do not interfere with park regulations designed to conserve the resource. Taken as a whole, it can be construed as directing the Secretary to consider these traditional uses when issuing regulations, such that at least some areas of the park remain open to fishing and recreational use.

6.4.3 Summary of marine legislation

According to the review of legislation, the MPA legislation of the US goes furthest in implementing the elements deemed necessary for effective marine protected area, with the Marine Sanctuaries Act containing approximately 13 of the proposed guidelines from Section 3, and the National Park Act implementing 11. Conversely, Saba's MPA legislation included only seven of the recommended guidelines in the Marine Environment Ordinance and accompanying Amendments/Regulations. The result is surprising, since, as discussed below, the waters and reefs off the Saba coast are generally regarded as among the most pristine within the wider Caribbean region.

6.5 Application of legislative analysis

According to the legislative review in Section 4, the MPA legislation covering the US Virgin Islands was more successful in implementing the recommended guidelines than was the island government of Saba. If one assumes that larger populations, increased financial resources and longer legislative histories beget better legislation, then the fact that the Netherlands Antilles falls short in its MPA legislation is not surprising. Not only does the US have a larger population from which to draw personnel, but, as the world's largest economy, it also has the financial resources to fund more scientific research and studies into marine resources and ecosystems. Accordingly, given the larger pool of expertise, greater funding capabilities and legislative history, it is not surprising that the US would produce what appears to be more effective MPA legislation.

Compared with the US, the islands comprising the Windward group of the Netherlands Antilles have far fewer inhabitants and a much lower GDP. Furthermore, the Netherlands Antilles became autonomous entities of the Kingdom of the Netherlands in 1954. While some legislation is passed down from the central Netherlands' government in Europe, the islands of the Netherlands Antilles are generally responsible for management of their own environmental affairs. Thus, the citizens of the Netherlands Antilles have less legislative experience from which to draw.

Despite less comprehensive implementing legislation, the Saba Marine Park is noted not only for the healthy state of its coral reefs but also for effective management. Table 6.1 provides details on the marine protected areas of the individual countries reviewed in the present research, including size, management level, management, effectiveness and the percentage of coral reefs within marine protected areas boundaries. Table 6.2 shows the percentage of coral reefs at risk for each country according to four threats – coastal development, inland sources of pollution, marine-based pollution and overfishing.

6.5.1   *Netherlands Antilles*

The assessment by the Australian Institute of Marine Sciences (AIMS) (Wilkinson, 2002, p. 329) acknowledges that anthropogenic causes of stress on Saban reefs have historically been low, which can be traced in part to limited coastal development. The limited anthropogenic threat is largely due to Saba's steep topography, which allows for little agriculture and also accounts for the absence of suitable beaches (Smith *et al.*, 1999). Still, the AIMS study (Wilkinson, 2002, p. 329) did note instances of degradation, finding that 'shallower reefs have deteriorated badly, possibly due to disease and bleaching'.

Statia is somewhat similarly situated, insofar as the coastline is relatively undeveloped. AIMS does note the presence of an 'oil terminal on the north-western coast, and some developments on the mid-leeward coast' (Wilkinson, 2002, p. 329). The study also states that there are only five fishermen on the island (ten others fish to supplement income) (Wilkinson, 2002, p. 331) and so there is little danger from overfishing. This fact is borne out by Burke and Maidens, who assess only a 27% medium threat level from fishing pressures (Table 6.2). The outlook for reefs around St Maarten, however, is less sanguine. Smith *et al.* (1999, p. 353) observe that 'rapid population growth and a dramatic expansion of tourism have resulted in major infrastructure development' and that surrounding reefs are 'seriously threatened by pollution, devegetation, siltation and eutrophication from sewage input and the very high level of recreational boating'.

Despite the rampant coastal development noted by Smith, only 41% of the reefs in the Netherlands Antilles are under a medium threat from coastal development (Table 6.2). In fact, of the countries reviewed in

149

Table 6.1 Data on marine protected areas in selected countries

Country	Marine protected areas (year established)[a]	Size: ha	Terrestrial component[a]	Active management/level of management[a]	Management effectiveness[b]	Fisheries management[a]	Area of coral Reefs in MPA: %[b]
Netherlands Antilles	Saba Marine Park (1987)	1000[b]	No	Yes High	Good	Regulated and restricted	67
	St Eustatius Marine Park (1996)	2750[c]	No	Yes Moderate	Partial	Zoned and regulated	
	St Maarten Marine Park*	5128[d]	Yes	Yes Moderate	Partial	Zoned	
US Virgin Islands	Virgin Islands National Park (1956)	5308[b]	Yes	Yes High	Good	Regulated	8
	Buck Island Reef National Monument (1956)	356[b]	Yes (offshore island)	Yes High	Partial	Prohibited	

* Actively managed but not legally established

Source: a. Geoghegan et al. (2001); b. Burke and Maidens (2004); c. STENAPA (2008); d. Dutch Caribbean Nature Alliance (2008)

Table 6.2 Threats to coral reefs from human activities. Risk levels represent percentage of country's total reef area under either medium or high risk

Threats	Risk level	Countries	
		Netherlands Antilles	US Virgin Islands
Coastal development: %	Medium	41	39
	High	0	18
Inland sources of sediment and pollution: %	Medium	24	34
	High	0	0
Marine-based pollution: %	Medium	9	22
	High	26	22
Fishing pressure: %	Medium	27	13
	High	1	87
Cumulative threat: %	Medium	21	9
	High	31	73
	Very high	0	18

Source: Burke and Maidens (2004)

the present thesis, the Netherlands Antilles face the least danger from the anthropogenic risks reported by Burke and Maidens (2004). Paradoxically, according to the analysis in Section 4, the Netherlands Antilles legislation contains the fewest number of MPA guidelines. In fact, St Maarten has yet to pass legislation legally establishing its proposed marine park.

The contradiction is likely explained, for one, by the effective management of the established marine protected areas. Table 6.1 indicates that the Saba Marine Park gets the highest marks for both management level and management effectiveness. The other parks do not fare quite as well, receiving medium grades under the two categories. However, a key element to note is that 67% of Netherlands Antilles reefs are placed under protection. Thus, a far greater percentage of marine habitats receive protection than do those of the US Virgin Islands. Last, the legislation for the Saba Marine Park specifically provides for payment of visitors fees by scuba divers and snorkellers that use the SMP (Part III, Art. 13). Thus, SMP is assured of adequate financing to finance management activities, which, as was discussed above, is often a primary impediment to effective protection of marine resources within the park. The benefits of user fees to self-finance have been recognised by park managers. Depondt and Green (2006, p. 189) state that 'using dive tourism as a source of funding, in the form of diving user fees is ... an excellent way to enable self-financing [since] recreational scuba diving is becoming a substantial component of the international tourism market'.

Because the reefs of the Netherlands Antilles are not under serious threat, little will be said about how effectively the legislation accounts for those risks. However, given that coastal development is such a pervasive threat throughout the Caribbean, one provision of the legislation bears pointing out. Part II, Article 12 states that 'developments or modifications of the coastal zone which may influence the marine environment of SMP must be preceded by an independent environmental impact assessment'. Other countries would be well advised to follow the example of Saba's marine ordinance and adopt a similar provision in their own laws to assuage future threats from coastal development.

6.5.2 US Virgin Islands

Of the countries reviewed for this thesis, the legislation of the US Virgin Islands scored the highest in terms of implementing the recommended guidelines. However, the Virgin Islands also rated lowest in terms of the cumulative threat to its reefs (Table 6.2). Surveys of Virgin Island reefs have found widespread degradation from various causes. Anthropogenic causes include 'destruction from boat anchors and boat groundings, careless land use, dredging, pollution, and overfishing' (Smith *et al.*, 1999, p. 351); groundwater depletion and contamination, increased sediment loads, and the displacement of traditional resource users (Wilkinson, 2004, p. 440); and sand extraction, groyne construction and sewage effluent (Wilkinson, 2000, p. 245). Sediment from coastal development is especially problematic on St John due its steep slopes (Wilkinson, 2004, p. 440). Wilkinson (2002, p. 258) observed that 'accelerating development, 56 km of unpaved roads, and poor land management on St John result in increased sediment runoff onto the reefs'. Unfortunately, the Virgin Islands also experienced several destructive hurricanes over the last 30 years, which resulted, in part, in a 5–85% reduction in live cover of elkhorn coral (Smith *et al.*, 1999, p. 351).

For the US Virgin Islands, then, legislation with adequate incorporation of recognised guidelines has not resulted in successful protection of marine resources. Of the risks detailed in Burke and Maidens, overfishing is far and away the most severe threat to coral reefs (Table 6.2). Coastal development also threatens nearly 60% of the reefs at a medium or higher level. Overall, 73% of Virgin Island reefs are under high risk, with an additional 18% under very high risk.

Table 6.2 indicates that the park management in St John and Buck Island National Parks were generally assessed high marks for both management level and management effectiveness. The effectiveness of management is somewhat of a contradiction considering the numerous problems faced by marine habitats. One problem may be that, unlike the Netherlands Antilles, only 8% of the total reef area within Virgin Island waters are covered by MPAs. Furthermore, while the MPA legislation meets many of the guidelines in Section 6.5.3, it fails to account for the most serious risks – overfishing and coastal development. Fisheries protection does not fall under the Marine Sanctuaries Act or National Parks Act, nor does the legislation contain any provisions requiring environmental impact statements for coastal construction and other potentially harmful activities. Perhaps the lesson to be learned from the US Virgin Islands is that meaningful MPA legislation must address the core problems faced by the protected habitat and not rely on parallel laws or agencies to meet this need.

6.6   Conclusion

While effective MPA legislation may result in successful protection of marine resources, it is certainly not a guarantee. The research illustrates that other factors can play as important a part in coral reef conservation as does the laws used to regulate activities in and around MPAs. It need not be gainsaid that additional research into the role of national legislation in achieving meaningful conservation needs to be studied in greater detail. Nonetheless, the analysis presented herein did reveal a few salient points that might help to guide future legislation.

(1) As has already been noted by other commentators, MPA legislation must include financing provisions in order to ensure capable management and enforcement of MPA regulations. The successful example of the Saba Marine Park helps to bear this out. To be sure, Saba is relatively fortunate in that the island does not possess the coastal development problems hampering protection efforts on other islands. Nevertheless, the self-financing provision seems well adapted to resource protection for a couple of reasons. First, as mentioned earlier, imposing users' fees ensures that funding will remain continuous. Also, in the case of the Saba Marine Park, one cannot help but think that the

self-reliance established by such a provision helps park management and local inhabitants believe that they have a stake in park affairs. Public participation is viewed as important to successful MPAs and thus the self-financing provision scores on more than one point.

(2) If governments and their legislators are truly concerned about protecting marine habitats and species, they must ensure through legislation that more of the ecosystems that require protection are placed within MPA boundaries. The disparity between the threat levels experienced by Netherlands Antillean reefs and those of the Virgin Islands can be partially explained by the area of coral reefs under MPA protection. Of course, Saba and Statia do not suffer from the same degree of tourism-related hazards, such as construction runoff and sewage pollution, as does the Virgin Islands. However, St Maarten is one of, if not the, most heavily developed, small island. And yet, only 41% of total reef area is under a medium threat from coastal development.

(3) MPA legislation needs to sufficiently account for activities occurring outside MPA limits. While fishing pressure is one of the chief causes of coral deterioration, the surveys of scientific experts presented herein lament the effects of coastal development, runoff, land-based pollution, and other threats that occur outside MPA boundaries. The Saba Marine Environment Ordinance scored lowest of the reviewed legislation, yet the provisions for self-financing and completion of environmental impact assessments are likely responsible for a large part of the success of the Saba Marine Park.

Notes

i   The author of the *Guidelines* is an environmental lawyer of note, having worked for such organisations as the World Bank, World Wildlife Fund, US Environmental Protection Agency, and Natural Resources Defense Council. Biographic information from http://www.irf.org/about/staff.php

ii The author would note that not every law having a marine component is reviewed – only those one or two laws of a country that directly provide for establishment of marine protected areas.

iii Both ordinances can be found on the website for the Netherlands Antilles Department of Environment and Nature at http://www.mina.vomil.an/policy/legislation.php, although only the Saba ordinance is translated into English.

References

Barker, D.R. (2002) Biodiversity conservation in the Wider Caribbean Region. *Reciel*, Vol. 11, pp. 74–83.

Bergen, L.K. and Carr, M.H. (2003) Establishing marine reserves: how can science best inform policy? *Environment*, Vol. 45, No. 2, pp. 8–19.

Blake, B. (1998) A strategy for cooperation in sustainable oceans management and development, Commonwealth Caribbean. *Marine Policy*, Vol. 22, pp. 505–513.

Brailovskaya, T. (1998) Obstacles to protecting marine biodiversity through marine wilderness preservation: examples from the New England region. *Conservation Biology*, Vol. 12, No. 6, pp. 1236–1240.

Burke, L. and Maidens, J. (2004) *Reefs at Risk in the Caribbean Data CD*. World Resources Institute, Washington, DC.

Debrot, A.O. and Sybesma, J. (2000) The Dutch Antilles. In Sheppard, C. (ed.) *Seas at the Millennium: An Environmental Evaluation. Vol. I: Regional Chapters: Europe, The Americas and West Africa*, Elsevier Science, Oxford.

Depondt, F. and Green, E. (2006) Diving user fees and the financial sustainability of marine protected areas: opportunities and impediments. *Ocean and Coastal Management*, Vol. 49, pp. 188–202.

Dutch Caribbean Nature Alliance (2008) *St Maarten*. Online at: http://www. dcnanature.org/ conservation/st_maarten.html

Frontani, H.G. (2006) Conflicts in marine protected area management. *Focus on Geography*, Vol. 48, No. 4, pp. 17–24.

Geoghegan, T., Smith, A.H. and Thacker, K. (2001) *Characterization of Caribbean Marine Protected Areas: An Analysis of Ecological, Organization, and Eocio-economic Factors. CANARI Report No. 287*. Online at: http://www.canari.org/ thacker.pdf

Gillespie, A. (2000) The Southern Ocean Sanctuary and the evolution of international environmental law. *International Journal of Marine and Coastal Law*, Vol. 15, Issue 3, pp. 293–316.

Gjerde, J. (2001) Current legal development: high seas marine protected areas. *The International Journal of Marine and Coastal Law*, Vol. 16, Issue 3, pp. 515–528.

Halpern, B.S. (2003) The impact of marine reserves: do reserves work and does reserve size matter? *Ecological Applications*, Vol. 13, No. 1, Supplement, pp. S117–S137.

Hughes, T.P., Baird, A.H., Bellwood, D.R., Card, M., Connolly, S.R., Folke, C., Grosberg, R., Hoegh-Guldberg, O., Jackson, J.B.C., Kleypas, J., Lough, J.M., Marshall, P., Nyström, M., Palumbi, S.R., Pandolfi, J.M., Rosen, B. and Roughgarden, J. (2003) Climate change, human impacts, and the resilience of coral reefs. *Science*, Vol. 301, pp. 929–933.

IUCN (1988) *Resolution 17.38 of the 17th General Assembly of the IUCN*, ICUN, Gland, Switzerland and Cambridge.

Kelleher, G. and Kenchington, R. (1992) *Guidelines for Establishing Marine Protected Areas*, ICUN, Gland, Switzerland.

Klomp, K. and Kooistra, D. (2003) A post-hurricane, rapid assessment of reefs in the Windward Netherlands Antilles. In *Status of coral reefs in the Western Atlantic: Results of initial surveys, Atlantic and Gulf Rapid Response Assessment Program*, ed. Judith Lang, 404-437. Atoll Research Bulletin 496. Washington, DC: Smithsonian Institution.

Lausche, B.J. (1980) *Guidelines for Protected Areas Legislation*, ICUN, Gland, Switzerland.

155

Lewsey, C., Cid, G. and Kruse, E. (2004) Assessing climate change impacts on coastal infrastructure in the eastern Caribbean. *Marine Policy*, Vol. 28, pp. 393–409.

Lindholm, J. and Barr, B. (2001) Comparison of marine and terrestrial protected areas under federal jurisdiction in the United States. *Conservation Biology*, Vol. 15, Issue: 5, pp. 1441–1443.

Lodge, M.W. (2004) Improving international governance in the deep sea. *International Journal of Marine and Coastal Law*, Vol. 19, Issue 3, pp. 299–316.

Lundquist, C.J. and Granek, E.F. (2005) Strategies for successful marine conservation: integrating socioeconomic, political, and scientific factors. *Conservation Biology*, Vol. 19, Issue 6, pp. 1771–1778.

Mascia, M.B. (1999) Governance of marine protected areas in the wider Caribbean: preliminary results of an international mail survey. *Coastal Management*, Vol. 27, pp. 391–402.

Morin, T. (2001) Sanctuary Advisory Councils: involving the public in the National Marine Sanctuary Program. *Coastal Management*, Vol. 29, pp. 327–339.

Ogden, J.C. (1997) Marine managers look upstream for connections. *Science*, Vol. 278, pp. 1414–1415.

Orams, M.B. (2004) The use of the sea for recreation and tourism. In Smith, H.G. (ed.) *The Oceans: Key Issues in Marine Affairs*, Kluwer Academic Publishers, Dordrecht, the Netherlands.

Roberts, C.M., Branch, G., Bustamante, R.H., Castilla, J.C., Dugan, J., Halpern, B.S., Lafferty, K.D., Leslie, H., Lubchenco, J., McArdle, D., Ruckelshaus, H. and Warner, R.R. (2003) Application of ecological criteria in selecting marine reserve and developing reserve networks. *Ecological Applications*, Vol. 13, Issue 1, pp. S215–S228.

Salm, R.V., Clark, J. and Siirila, E. (2000) *Marine and Coastal Protected Areas: A Guide for Planners and Managers*, IUCN, Washington, DC.

Salomon, A.K., Ruesink, J.L., Semmens, B.X. and Paine, R.T. (2001) Incorporating human and ecological communities in marine conservation: an alternative to Zacharias and Roff. *Conservation Biology*, Vol. 15, Issue 5, pp. 1452–1455.

Smith, A.F., Rogers, C.S. and Bouchon, C. (1999) Status of western Atlantic coral reefs in the Lesser Antilles. *Proceedings of the 8th International Coral Reef Symposium*, Vol. 1, pp. 351–356.

Sobel, J. and Dahlgren, C. (2004) *Marine Reserves: A Guide to Science, Design, and Use*, Island Press, Washington, DC.

STENAPA (St Eustatius National Parks) (2008) Statia Marine Park. Online at: http://www.statiapark.org/ parks/marine/index.html

Wilkinson, C. (ed.) (2000) *Status of Coral Reefs in the World*, Australian Institute of Marine Sciences, Townsville, Queensland.

Wilkinson, C. (2002) *Status of Coral Reefs in the World*, Australian Institute of Marine Sciences, Townsville, Queensland.

Wilkinson, C. (2004) *Status of Coral Reefs in the World*, Australian Institute of Marine Sciences, Townsville, Queensland.

7

Geomorphological models and their role in coastal management

Mark E. Dickson, * *Peter J. Cowell*† *and Colin D. Woodroffe*‡
* *School of Environment, University of Auckland, Australia;* † *School of Geosciences, University of Sydney, Australia;* ‡ *School of Earth and Environmenatal Sciences, University of Wollongong, Australia*

Prolific population growth and associated development over recent decades have placed enormous pressures on coastal areas. Over this period of time much of the Earth's sandy coasts are thought to have been eroding. The response has often been to build coastal defences, which are necessary in many areas but can have far-reaching effects. Coupled with concerns regarding sea-level rise and changing climate, these issues pose a considerable challenge for coastal managers. Scientists and engineers have the formidable responsibility of providing transparent advice upon which appropriate management decisions can be based. A quantitative measure of future coastal behaviour, usually from a numerical model, is often seen as preferable to the qualitative opinion of specialists and coastal stakeholders. However, not all agree that this is the right approach and the value of quantitative modelling in coastal management has been keenly debated. This chapter discusses issues pertaining to the use of numerical geomorphological models for coastal management. Discussion is focused using examples of models from two contrasting coastal systems. An overview is first provided of the formalisation of conceptual morphodynamic models from southeastern Australia in the Shoreline Translation Model. Lessons learned on wave-dominated depositional coasts are then extended to rocky coasts using a broad systems-based approach that links several models. Under various scenarios of climate change and shoreline management, the approach facilitates analysis of the contingent effects of cliff erosion, beach sediment transport and coastal flooding. Forecasts such as these are highly prized by coastal managers,

Coastal zone management
978-0-7277-3641-1

and yet models will always be imperfect, their representations deficient in some ways.

Understanding and communicating model uncertainty to those that use model outcomes is an active area of research. Geomorphological modelling has made significant progress since the focus on coastal process studies began after World War II. Such models can be viewed as an additional tool that can add to the collective geomorphological experience to assist in more prudent coastal management.

7.1   Introduction

Prolific population growth and associated development over recent decades have placed enormous pressures on coastal areas. Over this period of time there has been much evidence of coastal degradation and more than 70% of the Earth's sandy coasts are thought to have been eroding (Bird, 1985). The response has often been to build coastal defences. While these are necessary in many areas, they can have far-reaching effects on the behaviour of coastal systems and they are a major contributor to observed 'coastal squeeze', the gradual elimination of intertidal habitats (French, 1997). Coupled with concerns regarding sea-level rise and changing climate, it is clear that these issues pose a considerable challenge for coastal managers (Nicholls and Mimura, 1998). Scientists and engineers have the formidable responsibility of providing transparent advice upon which appropriate management decisions can be based (Dubois, 2002). A quantitative measure of future coastal behaviour, usually from a numerical model (Nicholls and Stive, 2004), is often seen as preferable to the qualitative opinion of a few specialists or the widely held 'common wisdom' of a wide suite of casual coastal stakeholders. However, not all agree that this is the right approach and the value of quantitative modelling in coastal management has been keenly debated (e.g. Pilkey and Cooper, 2004; Cooper and Pilkey, 2004, 2007).

Geomorphological models have their origin in the observed morphological characteristics of coastal landforms, and the co-adjustment of process and form, termed coastal morphodynamics (Wright and Thom, 1977). In their simplest form they presume that the coast adjusts to adopt a regular but highly simplified geometric shape. The earliest examples of such 'morphological states' were developed in the context of sandy shorelines; the idea of an equilibrium profile was initially conceived by Cornaglia (1889) and since adopted in various forms. Perhaps the best known and most widely applied is the Bruun model, whereby Per Bruun considered that the shoreface adopts a concave-up cross-section, and that the re-adjustment of this profile under rising sea level follows conservation of mass (sediment), enabling a slope-based prediction of the rate of retreat (Bruun, 1962). The concept of an equilibrium morphology underlies many coastal geomorphological studies, and the Bruun Rule that relates the rate of retreat of a shoreline in response to sea-level rise (and which is described in greater detail by Abuodha and Woodroffe, Chapter 12, this volume) has been widely applied by engineers in the context of anticipated future sea-level rise, despite continued criticism (e.g. Cooper and Pilkey, 2004). The mechanisms that control such morphology are complex and remain incompletely understood. In individual cases, it is often difficult to parameterise the profile and to accommodate the vagaries exerted by exogenous factors, such as bedrock outcrops, meaning that the concept is still regarded as contentious by some researchers (Thieler *et al.*, 2000).

Coastal managers require advice on how a coast may behave at the scale of several decades (Cooper *et al.*, 2001). This chapter focuses on the formulation and use of geomorphological models that are grounded in assumptions that there is an equilibrium morphology to which coasts are adjusting. It is concerned with models that have been developed to study aspects of coastal evolution at timescales of a few months to hundreds or thousands of years. Such models contrast with more detailed simulation models that are used in coastal engineering design (e.g. UNIBEST and LITPACK) and which typically find application over timescales of days to years (e.g. Stive and Batjes, 1984; Brøker-Hedegaard *et al.*, 1991). Unfortunately, as de Vriend *et al.* (1993) explain, several substantial difficulties have constrained efforts to extend the predictive capacity of these more detailed coastal engineering models.

The chapter outlines the development of conceptual models that focus on beach, barrier and estuarine systems of southeastern Australia, and their parameterisation in the numerical Shoreline Translation Model (STM). It then considers the modelling of cliffed shorelines. These examples help to develop concepts regarding approaches to modelling at different scales. This then feeds a discussion of the various issues associated with the practice of making quantitative forecasts in coastal geomorphology.

7.2 Modelling the coastal environments of southeastern Australia

Numerical models use simplified formulations of the principal inter-relationships that exist between the main components of a system.

These help to capture a small number of representative conditions. Such models ignore much of the detail, but the mark of a good model is that it embodies the major variations that a coastal system can undergo. In order to build models across annual to millennial timescales, it is necessary to organise and simplify the complexity of coastal systems, to test assumptions with observations and improve the determination of key parameters. The coast of southeastern Australia provides a good example of where this has been undertaken. In this section we briefly summarise three independent, but inter-related, conceptual models that were derived for three different aspects of the coast of southeastern Australia: morphostratigraphy of sand barriers, morphodynamics of beaches, and the infill of estuaries. This section focuses on how robust conceptual models of each of these have been developed, refined and elements combined into a computer simulation model, termed the STM.

The coast of southeastern Australia has served as a natural laboratory; it consists of a series of coastal compartments with different degrees of closure or interchange, each of which has experienced a similar history of climate and sea-level change, but has reached a different stage in the evolutionary pathway, driven by local variations in topographic, catchment, and wave characteristics. The morphostratigraphy of sand barriers along this coast was comprehensively investigated in the 1970s and 1980s through a programme of drilling and radiocarbon dating (summarised in Thom, 1984). These studies indicate that the majority of sand barriers along the New South Wales (NSW) coast first assumed their present form as a consequence of sea-level stabilisation towards the end of the postglacial marine transgression, around 6000 years ago (Chapman *et al.*, 1982). A number of different barrier types can be discriminated, ranging from receded barriers which are still experiencing shoreline recession, to prograded barriers, across which radiocarbon dates on shells indicate continual progradation during the Holocene, to more complex dune barriers (Fig. 7.1).

The case of the prograded barrier at Moruya provides a good example: the successive beach ridges can be seen in planform recording incremental progradation over the mid and late Holocene, with radiocarbon dates providing a chronology of progressive shoreline positions. A similar approach has been applied to sediment bodies on the continental shelf (Roy *et al.*, 1994). While there are substantial sand bodies in places on the inner continental shelf, the majority of sand is inferred to have been worked landwards across the shelf during sea-level rise to form the modern sand barriers. Along the NSW coast the stratigraphy implies

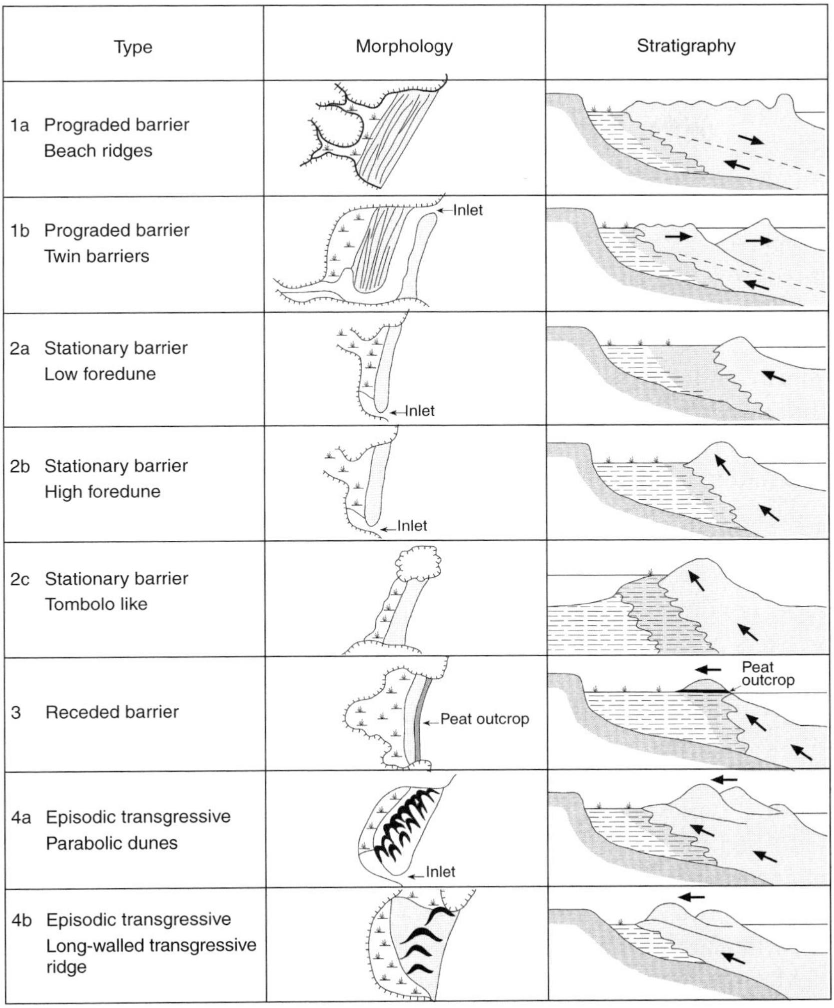
Type
Morphology
Stratigraphy
1a Prograded barrier
Beach ridges
1b Prograded barrier
Twin barriers
Inlet
2a Stationary barrier
Low foredune
Inlet
2b Stationary barrier
High foredune
Inlet
2c Stationary barrier
Tombolo like
3 Receded barrier
Peat outcrop
Peat
outcrop
4a Episodic transgressive
Parabolic dunes
Inlet
4b Episodic transgressive
Long-walled transgressive
ridge

Fig. 7.1 Different barrier types along the NSW coast indicate different evolutionary pathways (after Chapman et al., *1982)*

that there has been onshore movement of sediment during sea-level rise, in contrast to the Bruun premise that under such conditions the beachface is eroded with sand transport to the nearshore (Thom and Roy, 1988).

At the same time that the Holocene history of barrier formation was being examined, detailed studies of the morphology and dominant processes of wave-dominated beaches were being undertaken in the Sydney region (Wright and Short, 1984). Beaches change in response to wave energy, but it is possible to recognise a modal beach state, the morphology that a particular beach adopts for most of the time (Short, 1999). Six beach states were identified spanning a range of energy conditions from high-energy, dissipative beaches, which are broad and flat with fine sand and a wide surf zone, to low-energy, steep reflective beaches on which waves surge, often forming beach cusps from the coarser sediments (Fig. 7.2). Four intermediate beach types have been identified with various types of bar and rip currents. This classification of wave-dominated beaches has proved remarkably robust, and has been extended to 15 types of beaches around the entire Australian coastline (Short, 2006). These ideas have also been incorporated into beach models that have been applied in a broader, international context (Lippman and Holman, 1990).

The morphostratigraphy of barriers represents evolutionary stages over the geological timescale, whereas beach states represent short-term (weeks to months) responses of the beach and nearshore to wave conditions and antecedent state. Following a storm, a beach recovers from the erosion of sand and its deposition in nearshore bars, with the beach volume gradually being restored over subsequent weeks. The beach states have particular application in the recognition of beach safety ratings based on the occurrence of strong rip currents that endanger bathers during the intermediate beach states (Short, 2006). Studies along this part of the Australian coastline have also addressed the decadal time scale that is so important in a planning or engineering context. The impacts of short but extreme events (storm cut) as opposed to long-term mean adjustments, have been examined, in particular, by regular surveys across several decades of the foreshore at Moruya, demonstrating the significance of major erosional episodes (Thom and Hall, 1991). Storms in 1974 resulted in an erosion-dominated period during which the volume of sediment removed was comparable to about 200 years of mean-trend change as determined from radiocarbon-dated morphostratigraphic studies of this barrier. Erosion has been followed by a subsequent accretion-dominated period during which the development of the foredune has become evident (McLean and Shen, 2006). Similar continual monitoring on Narrabeen Beach in Sydney has revealed a pattern of beach rotation associated with wind changes that accompany the El Niño-Southern Oscillation (ENSO) phenomenon (Ranasinghe *et al.*, 2004), and detailed study still further north on the NSW coast implies that

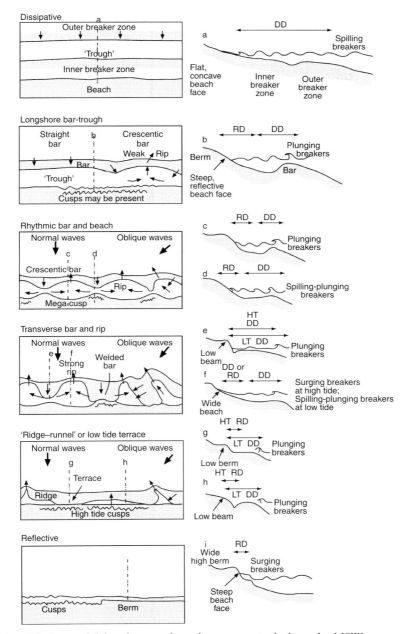

Fig. 7.2 Six modal beach states have been recognised along the NSW coast. At one end of the spectrum are high energy dissipative beaches composed of fine sediments, and at the other low energy reflective beaches usually composed of coarse sediments (after Wright and Short, 1984)

163

progradation history also contains a signal modulated by ENSO-PDO (Pacific Decadal Oscillation) components (Goodwin *et al.*, 2006).

Southeastern Australia has also provided an appropriate field laboratory for the development of models of estuary infill. The simultaneous formation of sand barriers along most of the New South Wales coast around 6000 years ago as sea level stabilised at a level close to its present, served to occlude a series of estuaries and coastal lagoons. The stratigraphy and infill of these estuarine embayments has been examined in detail by Roy *et al.* (1980), and a conceptual model of each of the three principal types, drowned river valley, barrier estuary, and saline coastal lake, described by Roy (1984). The notion of gradual infill of estuaries through immature to mature stages builds on the conceptual foundation of a geographical cycle and the development of landforms from youthful to mature stages. Based on a tripartite facies classification, marine sand barrier and flood tide delta, fluvial delta and central mud basin, different systems along the coast can be seen to be at different stages in the evolutionary sequence (Fig. 7.3). These ideas have led to a series of further developments in our understanding of estuarine geomorphology within Australia and overseas (Dalrymple *et al.*, 1992; Woodroffe *et al.*, 1993; Harris *et al.*, 2002). More significantly, in the context of coastal management, the type of estuary and the stage that it has reached in its evolution are seen to have important implications for ecological conditions, the availability and distribution of habitats, geochemical functioning and the potential of the system to cope with stresses such as pollution (Roy *et al.*, 2001; Harris and Heap, 2003).

The lessons from a consideration at a longer timeframe have been incorporated into the STM which builds upon both the Quaternary perspective and the process models of beach behaviour (Short, 1999). This coast lends itself to such modelling because the history of natural processes is relatively accessible, largely without interference by tectonic or anthropogenic complications. The STM is therefore consistent with established principles regarding the underlying processes, but also grounded in the longer-term behaviour of the coast, and involves the computational capacity to undertake conventional forward simulations (Cowell *et al.*, 1995). Testing of this model approach includes hindcasting details of coastal evolution as reconstructed for the transgressive and strandplain deposits in southeastern Australia where it was shown that the model produced morphostratigraphic outputs with high fidelity (Thom and Cowell, 2005). Figure 7.4 shows that model behaviour under falling and rising sea levels is consistent with stratigraphic

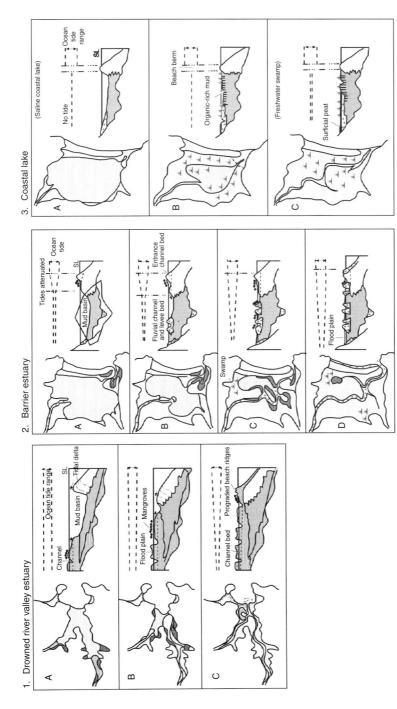

Fig. 7.3 Conceptual model of estuary infill on the wave-dominated shorelines of NSW, Australia (after Roy, 1984)

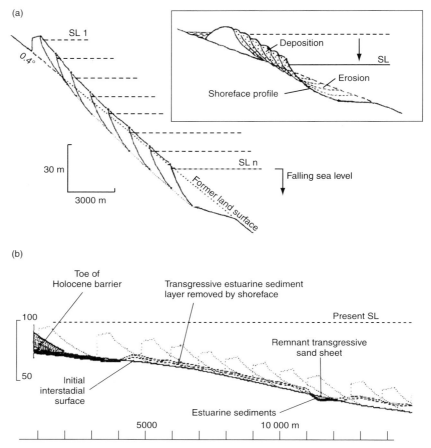

Fig. 7.4 Simulations with the Shoreline Translation Model accord with the strati-graphic record along the NSW coastline. (a) Regressive barriers develop under falling sea-level, whereas (b) barrier roll-over exposes relict estuarine sediments during the post-glacial transgression (after Cowell et al., 1995)

reconstructions along the coast of NSW that show the growth and decay of sand bodies over a full glacial–interglacial cycle. Over a period of slow, irregular falling sea level (up until about 30 ka) the model responded through a seaward and downward translation of the shoreface, resulting in a progradational sand plain constructed from sediments reworked from seaward. By contrast, rising sea level during the post-glacial transgression forced the modelled shoreface to translate through barrier roll-over. Notably, translation of the shoreface exposed estuarine mud on the seafloor, which is consistent with sedimento-logical evidence along this shoreline (Cowell et al., 1995, see Fig. 7.4).

166

7.3   Rocky coast models

Numerical models have only recently been developed to assist the geomorphologist to understand process-form interactions on cliffs, marine terraces and shore platforms over a range of different scales. At large scale (i.e. Quaternary), it is understood that tectonics and sea-level change impose fundamental controls on the evolution of rocky shorelines (Trenhaile, 1987). Anderson *et al.* (1999) explored this using a model that was designed to illustrate the variety of processes involved in producing terrace morphology on the uplifted coast of California, rather than replicating the evolution of particular terrace sequences. With such an approach the different mechanisms of land-scape change can be represented in a highly idealised way. For instance, their model adopts the simple view that marine erosion operates horizontally at a given rate, cutting through the hinterland. However, the model emphasises that over time the vertical locus of this attack has moved up and down according to the position of sea with respect to the land. Another simplification is made through a decision to simu-late a landscape that has been tectonically uplifted at a uniform rate. On this landscape the absolute position of sea level is superimposed (using sea-level data from Huon Peninsula), thereby deriving a time-series of vertical positions at which wave erosion has carved the landscape.

With this simple scheme, the model produced a staircase of terraces (Fig. 7.5) in which the distance of cliff retreat, or width of terrace

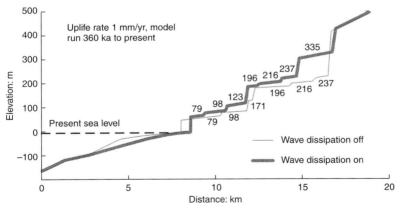

Fig. 7.5 In the absence of wave-energy dissipation, terrace width is proportional to the duration of a sea-level high-stand. Under these conditions the last inter-glacial (123 ka) terrace is not preserved. If wave energy dissipation is accounted for, there is less frequent destruction of previously formed terraces, and including the last interglacial terrace (after Anderson et al., 1999)

formation, is proportional to the length of time at which sea level remained at that position. Hence, when the level of the sea remains high for a relatively long period of time, erosion may obliterate older terraces. This is apparent in Fig. 7.5 through the absence of a terrace corresponding to oxygen isotope stage 5e (i.e. 123 ka). In reality, the stage 5e terrace is preserved on many uplifting shorelines (e.g. Ku and Kern, 1974; Pillans, 1983), which implies that the model is likely over-simplifying some aspect of reality. In particular, the effect of wave-energy dissipation was not considered in the first version of the model. The speed of ocean waves decreases as waves enter shallow water, while wave height increases. Wave energy is subsequently dissipated during breaking and surf-zone processes. As discussed in the previous section, very steep beaches have been termed 'reflective', because waves break close to the beachface and energy is dissipated across a narrow surf zone. By contrast, 'dissipative' beaches occur, where a combination of high wave energy and a gently sloping seafloor lead to wide surf zones. These concepts have relevance for terrace formation, because the gently sloping terrace that forms at the current sea level (i.e. shore platform) dissipates wave energy and so controls the amount of residual wave energy that is available to erode the cliff toe. To explore this effect, Anderson *et al.* (1999) add a dissipation component to the model, such that the rate of cliff retreat becomes linearly proportional to the amount of wave energy that remains at the shoreline. Re-running the original simulations with dissipation turned on shows that terrace survival is highly dependent on the rate of wave energy dissipation. For instance, Fig. 7.5 shows a very different flight of terraces, including a preserved stage 5e (123 ka) terrace. This simple model clearly illustrates the important role of wave energy dissipation in the development of marine terraces on shorelines that have been uplifted.

The development of rocky shore morphology is somewhat more complicated in areas that are tectonically stable, because Quaternary sea-level oscillations have resulted in marine erosion processes repeatedly visiting similar elevations to those that were planated by previous still-stands. Hence, the shore morphology becomes over-printed and partially inherited from previous erosion phases. A numerical shore platform evolution model has been developed in an attempt to clarify this circumstance (Trenhaile, 2000, 2001). Shore platforms form close to sea level and on tectonically active coasts they may be preserved as terraces once they are uplifted beyond the influence of marine processes. By contrast, on stable coasts, shore platforms are repeatedly visited by marine processes during sea-level oscillations. Like the terrace model, Trenhaile's shore platform model includes terms to account for the nearshore dissipation of wave energy. However, when the vertical position of the land is un-changing, then the vertical zonation of wave attack takes on an increased importance. Whereas the terrace model presumes a single vertical locus of wave attack, a function is included within the shore platform model that takes account of the oscillating tidal level. Other differences are demanded by the different scales of the models. For instance, within the shore platform model terms are included to account for the time required to remove debris that accumulates from cliff collapse, and also a threshold term below which waves are incompetent to erode rock. With these factors taken into account, modelling experiments guided Trenhaile (2001) to the conclusion that many of the rocky shore platforms that exist today are essentially protected from erosion of the rock face due to the extent of wave attenuation that occurs across the wide shore platform surfaces. The model implies that many shore platforms may have been inherited largely in their present form from previous interglacial stages when sea level was at a similar elevation to today (Trenhaile *et al.*, 1999).

The shore platform model has implications mainly for coasts that have been carved in hard rocks, because on soft-rock coasts (e.g. soft mudstones, clay, glacial till, etc.) shore platform development is on-going and cliff erosion rates of centimetres to metres per year represent a considerable management problem (EUROSION, 2004). Moreover, there are concerns that the rate of recession of soft-rock cliffs may increase under future sea-level rise. Bray and Hooke (1997) reviewed various approaches to dealing with this issue, including historical trend analysis and a geometrical model developed by Sunamura (1992). They concluded that, despite being designed for sandy coasts, the Bruun rule in a modified format is most suitable for testing the sensitivity of eroding cliffs to future climate change. An application of the rule to cliffs on the south coast of England indicated that by 2050 recession rates could increase by 22 to 133% under sea-level rise. They noted that erosion rates would be site specific with less erosion occurring where cliff release sediments that build-up beaches.

Since the review by Bray and Hooke (1997), the study of soft-rock coasts has been advanced through the development of a numerical model termed SCAPE (Soft-Cliff and Platform Erosion model). Walkden and Hall (2005) developed this model using a systems-based approach, but with the express purpose of examining coastal behaviour over timescales of concern to coastal management (i.e. decades). In this way, the purpose of the model differs from the terrace and shore platform models, where the emphasis was on trying to understand aspects of coastal evolution. Like a detailed reductionist model, SCAPE accepts that there are many interacting components within a geomorphological system that require numerical description. However, in SCAPE the modelling emphasis is on providing a robust description of the interactions within the model system, rather than on the detailed physics of the processes taking place. In order to fulfil its management focus, the model must consider many more aspects of the coastal system than purely exploratory models (e.g. the terrace model). For instance, SCAPE simulates the accretion and erosion of beaches during long-shore and cross-shore sediment transport, whereas beaches are omitted from the terrace model. However, reasonably simplistic treatment of physical processes means that SCAPE remains computationally inexpensive, and the internal feedbacks that emerge between interacting model components ensures model stability over long run times. A good example is provided by the relationship between the thickness of beach sediments within a SCAPE model, and the rate of cliff recession that emerges: when there is a very small beach at the toe of a cliff, then the shore platform and cliff receive little protection from wave attack and erosion rates are high; however, with an increased rate of cliff retreat the amount of beach-forming sediment also increases (assuming the cliff rock contains sediment of the appropriate grade), which means that beaches build and protect the cliff toe thereby reducing the rate of cliff erosion. As beaches build and rates of cliff retreat decrease, so less material is supplied to the beach. During the course of model runs this negative feedback leads to the development of a dynamic equilibrium in the rate of cliff retreat and the average-fluctuating size of the fronting beach.

The SCAPE model is typically initiated from a vertical plunging cliff. This situation is deliberately unrealistic: in reality, the sub-aerial part of a soft-rock cliff may be vertical, but the intertidal and sub-tidal portion of the profile (i.e. the shore platform) is generally very gently sloping. In SCAPE model runs, the initial profile erodes very rapidly because the steep nearshore profile ensures that a high portion of wave energy is available to erode the rock profile. Cliff erosion over time results in a gently sloping shore platform, the shallower profile of which causes waves to break further from the cliff toe, thereby resulting in wave energy dissipation across a wide surf zone. The effect of this progression from steep to gently sloping profile is that cliff erosion rates decay over

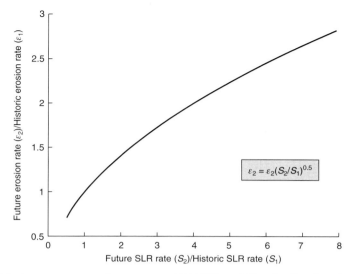

Fig. 7.6 Across a range of parameters, SCAPE modelling implies that the future rate of soft-cliff recession (in the case of small or absent beaches) can be estimated through a simple square-root dependency on future and past rates of sea-level rise and the historical cliff-recession rate (after Walkden and Dickson, 2008)

time and eventually oscillate around an average value. Having achieved this state, the model can be perturbed in ways that mimic various management concerns. For instance, Walkden and Dickson (2008) used the model to consider the development of an equilibrium rock shore profile under increasing rates of sea-level rise. The experiments showed that increased rates of sea-level rise produce a new equilibrium rock profile shape and a different equilibrium erosion rate. This is a notable difference to the Bruun rule, which assumes a translating but constant profile shape. Multiple simulations with the SCAPE model across a range of model parameters showed a surprisingly simple relationship between increased rates of sea-level rise and increased rates of cliff recession (Fig. 7.6). If several important constraints are observed, this relationship provides an opportunity for managers to rapidly estimate rates of recession of certain types of soft-rock coasts under future sea-level rise. The estimates are likely to be more realistic than those that would be achieved using a modified version of the Bruun rule, which cannot mimic the response of the rock profile to sea-level variation. Likewise, the estimates are likely to be more realistic than those obtained from an extrapolation of historical trends, because it would be difficult with such an analysis to consider the consequence of accelerating sea-level rise.

In the previous example, an increase in the rate of sea-level rise represents a perturbation on the model equilibrium. The model responds by eroding a new profile shape and eventually reaching a new average rate of cliff recession. This is an important 2D profile response, but the model can also be run in quasi-3D by taking multiple 2D profiles and connecting the beaches on the profiles with alongshore sediment transport. In this mode opportunities are presented to examine the effects of building coastal defence structures within a coastal system. Dickson *et al.* (2007) explored this along 50 km of the Norfolk coast by spacing 101 profiles at 500 m increments. In this study the model was run to equilibrium, which was realised when across the model domain the rate of cliff erosion, beach volume, and longshore sediment transport had stabilised on dynamically fluctuating averages. Again, the model was perturbed, this time to approximate the historical construction and effect of seawalls, timber revetments and groynes. Whereas seawalls stopped cliff recession (but not shore platform lowering), revetments slowed recession rates, and groynes interrupted longshore sediment transport thereby building beaches and slowing erosion rates.

Figure 7.7 shows the substantial effects of coastal defences on erosion rates modelled by SCAPE. Notably, the modelled rates of recession are

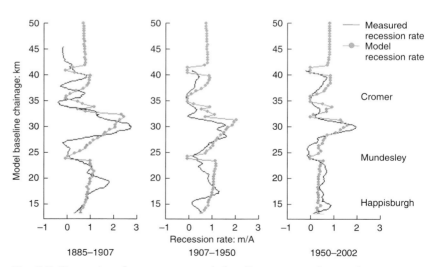

Fig. 7.7 Comparison between measured shoreline recession data and retreat rates modelled by Dickson et al. (2007)

similar to the rates of recession that were actually measured over the same time period. This illustrates that model results can be compared with reality and some measure of 'validation' can be achieved. The issue of model validation is an important one (Oreskes *et al.*, 1994), and considered further in the final section of this chapter. Dickson *et al.* (2007) took the view that because the behaviour of the model is consistent with the observed behaviour of the natural system, there is some basis on which to estimate the future behaviour of the system. This assumes that the process-form interactions that drove the past behaviour (on which the model is based) are likely to also control the future behaviour. In this way, the model is expected to be able to provide useful estimates of the effects of sea-level rise, changing storm frequency or direction of wave attack, and changing management policies. Conversely, aberrant extreme events are beyond the capabilities of the model.

Dickson *et al.* (2007) simulated the future rate of shoreline recession on the Norfolk coast under scenarios of climate change and varying management styles. Interestingly, some model behaviour was not immediately intuitive. For instance, increased rates of sea-level rise accelerated erosion rates on some sections of shoreline, as expected. Conversely, other areas actually eroded less quickly under future sea-level rise. Such model behaviour is not consistent with simple geometric models like the Bruun rule, where sea-level rise will always result in coastal recession. To explore the behaviour, the sea-level rise scenario was re-run on the Norfolk coast assuming that coastal structures had never been built. This simpler scenario showed that under sea-level rise an increase in recession rate in the central region of the study site means that additional sediments are supplied to adjacent 'down-drift' sections of coast. In some areas these sediments accumulate because the gradient in the longshore component of wave energy flux is insufficient to transport all of the additional sediment. Hence, beaches become larger and protect the adjacent cliff from erosion. Such a conclusion has interesting implications for coastal management decisions and shows the value of employing a broad systems model as opposed to a Bruun-type analysis.

Managers of eroding cliffed areas are typically interested in future cliff-top positions. The SCAPE model simulates the evolution of the shore platform and estimates the position of cliff *toe*. Erosion at the cliff toe steepens the cliff face, and in soft rocks the slope eventually becomes unstable and failure results. The timing of a landslide cannot be predicted precisely, but knowledge of the rate of cliff-toe retreat can be combined with an assessment of the geotechnical characteristics of the slope to generate a probability distribution of the cliff-top location following failure (Hall *et al.*, 2000). This approach was adopted in the Norfolk case study and then extended using a broad-scale risk analysis framework. As Dawson *et al.* (2009) describe, cliff-erosion risk can be evaluated by combining probabilistic cliff-top erosion forecasts with maps of the location of coastal properties. Simultaneously, the risk of coastal flooding in an adjacent area of low-lying land is evaluated using a GIS-based flood-inundation model. The flooding model is dependent on the outputs from the modelling on the cliffed coast. Specifically, under different scenarios of management and climate change, SCAPE produces different estimates of the amount of cliff recession and the volume of sediment transported alongshore. The area of low-lying land at risk to coastal flooding is included within the SCAPE modelling domain, such that there is information made available on the amount of sediment being provided to the beaches in this area. In scenarios

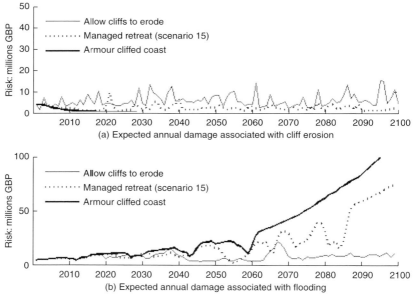

Fig. 7.8 Expected damage (calculated as risk) associated with coastal cliff recession (top) and coastal flooding (bottom) under three management scenarios. Defending cliffs reduces damages associated with erosion, but leads to heavy increases in risk associated with coastal flooding. Allowing cliffs to erode increases risk associated with erosion, but this is more than offset by the reduction in flood-related costs (after Dawson et al., *2009)*

174

which have led to high rates of cliff recession, large volumes of sand are moved into the area at risk to coastal flooding. In the flood-risk model, such large volumes of sand are considered to lower the risk of coastal flooding due to effects such as an increased size of sand dunes and a lower risk of undermining coastal flood defences.

This integrated approach provides an opportunity for managers to consider the risks associated with cliff erosion and coastal flooding in unison. One of the results of the integrated assessment of flood and erosion risk is shown in Fig. 7.8. In a scenario of complete coastal protection, the cost of cliff erosion decreases toward zero, but the impact in terms of flooding is dramatic. By contrast, the cost of cliff erosion increases if coastal defences are not maintained, but the overall effect on cost is lower, because flood risk reduces dramatically. There are more factors than cost taken into account when making decisions about how to manage a coastal area, and there are many uncertainties inherent in the modelling process that has been adopted. Nonetheless, this example is valuable in respect to the clarity of the message that it provides in the face of a highly complex morphodynamic system in which there are many interacting dependencies. It seems unlikely that this understanding would have been realised to the same extent without the aid of modelling.

7.4   The management challenge

There has been strong criticism of the use of geomorphological models for quantitative prediction (e.g. Thieler *et al.*, 2000; Cooper and Pilkey, 2004). The objections are specifically in respect to the use of models in which the intention is to provide useful predictions over engineering timescales (i.e. years to several decades). Cooper and Pilkey (2004, p. 642) '... are not concerned with the use of more qualitative or research models that are used to predict or explain the nature or direction of events on beaches.' They believe that qualitative models can play an important role in the study of beach processes. Murray (2003) contextualises the different uses of numerical models by placing individual models on a spectrum between simplified 'exploratory' models and detailed reductionist simulation models. Similarly in ecological modelling the basic purposes of modelling have been described in terms of 'exploration' and 'consolidation', where in the latter one attempts to compile all available information in the creation of a realistic surrogate of the investigated system (Bankes, 1993; Perry, 2009). For exploratory models the objective is usually to investigate fundamental geomorphological behaviour (e.g. the terrace model). By contrast, simulation models are designed to anticipate future change. Consolidated simulation models require that the modelled system be described in much finer detail, which usually requires inclusion of many non-linear elements that lead to instability in model behaviour over long-run times (de Vriend *et al.*, 1993). Anticipating coastal behaviour over the scale of decades remains beyond the capacity of the state-of-the-art reductionist models.

In this section we discuss prospects for the use of geomorphological models to aid coastal management at multi-decadal scales. For context, it is worth noting that on a spectrum between 'exploratory' and 'simulation' models, the SCAPE model could be placed midway or perhaps closer to the exploratory end. In principle, every kind of model can be used for every purpose (Batty and Torrens, 2001). SCAPE can be used in a qualitative mode to help understand various aspects of coastal behaviour, as preferred by Cooper and Pilkey. Alternatively, the model can be calibrated, compared with empirical data from some site (i.e. validation), and then used in forward prediction under different scenarios. This latter use is highly contentious.

Coastal geomorphologists have distinguished landforms, or suites of landforms, that are distinctive in terms of their shape, adopting morphological states that can be seen to recur in the landscape and through time. Some of the geomorphological models described in this chapter build on these equilibrium morphologies to offer the chance to anticipate the behavioural trends of coasts. These numerical models offer capacity beyond that achieved using a highly simplified geometric approach, but there is clearly a need to demonstrate that the premises underlying these approaches are appropriate to the coast under study.

It is entirely appropriate that the simple premises on which heuristics, such as the Bruun rule, are founded should be scrutinised and where necessary refined, especially in the context of anticipated future greenhouse-related sea-level rise. This is still more imperative if the principles on which such equilibrium concepts are based are to be extended to other types of shorelines, such as wetlands or estuaries (Pethick, 2001). For instance, the Bruun rule has been modified and applied to eroding cliffed shorelines (Bray and Hooke, 1997). It is possible that such an application could hold in the case of cliff and shore platform profiles that are overlain by large beaches in which an equilibrium profile might be sustained during sea-level rise. However, in the case of an eroding soft-rock shoreline where beaches are limited in size or absent, an application of the SCAPE model showed that the Bruun rule does not produce realistic estimates of future retreat rates (Walkden and Dickson, 2008). A further application of this model showed that platform shoreline response may also be highly complex under climate change, showing that the Bruun rule could produce highly unreliable estimates under many conditions (Dickson *et al.*, 2007). Hence, while considerable research has focused on managing constraints to applying a Bruun-type approach, particularly along the eastern coast of North America (Zhang *et al.*, 2004), it is clear that coastal response to sea-level rise is a complex morphodynamic issue (Stive, 2004).

To some extent the controversy surrounding use of the Bruun rule reflects the differences of goals between science and engineering. Science is about discovering and communicating new knowledge, whereas engineering is about applying that knowledge to real-world problems. No model should be viewed as complete or verified, but its underlying theory temporarily remains the most appropriate until the weight of evidence shows it to be false, or inadequate, and provides a better formulation (Baker, 1994; Brimicombe, 2003). Such is the case with the Bruun rule. While it has its detractors (Cooper and Pilkey, 2004), it has been widely adopted, particularly by engineers who are tasked with addressing real-world problems. In part this fact may relate more to the simplicity of the calculation and the perceived value of the quantitative prediction rather than its appropriateness. However, it has also resulted from a lack of suitable alternatives on a topic where managers desire quantitative predictions of future trends.

There are many fundamental difficulties associated with the practice of supplying quantitative model predictions to coastal managers. By definition, a model prediction cannot be correct, and yet to the coastal manager a quantitative prediction of a future shoreline position implies a level of model precision. Some of this precision is implied by the process of model validation (assessment of how accurately a model reproduces observed dynamics) or verification (assessment of a models structure). The geomorphological models described in this chapter (e.g. SCAPE and STM) are based on conceptual models, but their behaviour is parameterised to reflect different characteristics of the environment that they are supposed to represent. Their outputs are then compared with measurable quantities from the proto-type environments. This is typical of the classical approach to model valida-tion, which hinges on model assessment using real-world data. Whether models are truly validated or verified is a contested issue. For instance, to what extent is it useful to compare model behaviour with empirical data when there are assumptions associated with the empirical data themselves (Oreskes *et al.*, 1994)? Additionally, it has been noted that many hypotheses might explain the observations of a given set of data, or many multiple model representations could provide acceptable simulations of the observed system (Bevan, 2002). Hence, even if model predictions match observations, a model cannot be deemed 'true' or 'correct' (Perry, 2009). Despite these limitations, it is apparent that a simplistic model prediction of a shoreline position at some point in the future is readily useable to a coastal planner/manager. Hence, even if a modeller is aware of the various limitations and uncertainties associated with a model prediction, those tasked with making management decisions on the coast may not be. Clearly, there are substantial challenges associated with communicating model limitations.

Models are inherently false and model predictions should never be considered to be 'true'. Nevertheless, models may still be *approximately* true (Beven, 2002). Given that there is undoubtedly a pressing need for reliable prediction to inform environmental decision making (Perry, 2009), it can be argued that the problem is not so much with the models, but with the way that they are applied (Cowell *et al.*, 2006). There is no question that a huge variety of uncertainty exists in the modelling process. However, the notion of environmental forecasting (as opposed to prediction) provides a pragmatic framework within which coastal geomorphic models can meaningfully contribute to coastal management. In the context of ecological modelling, Clark *et al.* (2001, p. 657) define forecasting as 'the process of predicting the state of ecosystems ... with fully specified uncertainties'. They pragmatically add that 'forecastable' ecosystem attributes '... are ones for which uncertainty can be reduced to the point where a forecast reports a useful amount of information' and caution that the information content of a forecast is inversely proportional to forecast uncertainty. Uncertainty within coastal geomorphological models can be traced to a number of sources, including the actual physical description of process interactions, but also the values of various parameters and input variables. However, as Cowell *et al.* (2006) point out, the relatively computationally inexpensive models described in this chapter have a strong advantage, because rapid model run times mean that parameter and input values can be sampled from probability distributions during multiple simulations, thereby providing a range of model outputs. Hence, the coastal manager can be provided with a model *forecast* rather than a model prediction.

Some authors argue that the nature of shoreline response is too complex to allow meaningful quantitative modelling (Cooper and

Pilkey, 2004; Pilkey and Cooper, 2006). Instead they advocate an approach to coastal management that combines an examination of past patterns of accretion and erosion, and the use of expert judgement to assess likely future change at any given site. Do we rely on the judgement of experts and the associated subjectivity, or is it preferable to use a numerical model that is known to be imperfect, but provides a capacity to manage complexity in a systematic framework?

The issue of how best to use numerical models to study the behaviour of highly complex systems is an active area of research in many disciplines. A number of ideas of model use have emerged. Some ideas have a long lineage. For instance, more than a century ago Chamberlin (1897) recognised the value of research based on multiple hypotheses, and it is now apparent that in many instances it might be preferable to study a problem using multiple highly simplified models (Carpenter, 2003), rather than continually refining a single detailed model, which provides only one possible representation of a system. By embracing such ideas in geomorphological modelling, future development and application of geomorphological models to coastal management problems may change and improve. Certainly the relatively recent use of probabilistic methods in the forecasting of future shoreline positions can be seen as a significant improvement in the use of geomorphological models, because the apparent precision of a model prediction is replaced by a range of outcomes that provides an indication of the uncertainty inherent in the modelling process. Hence, while numerical geomorphological models are not a panacea for decision making in coastal management, there is reason to expect that future enhancements in the way that models are developed and used will translate into improved use of models for management purposes.

7.5   Conclusion

A good observational record of coastal systems has always underpinned sound geomorphological understanding of how the coast behaves. Recurring morphology (in time, through space, or both) has been inferred to represent equilibrium or near-equilibrium conditions, and provides a foundation for the development of conceptual models of coastal morphodynamics, as in the case of barrier systems, beach state or estuary infill in southeastern Australia. Understanding the response of landforms to variations in wave climate forms an important basis for each of these models, with tide and river conditions also significant in the case of estuarine sedimentation. The challenge for coastal scientists is the formalisation of exploratory models, based on investigations into geomorphological behaviour, and the development of simulation models that may be used to anticipate change. The STM provides one example that has been developed for use in southeastern Australia. Extending the lessons learned on sandy, wave-dominated coasts to rocky coasts provides further challenges. These coasts are more resilient to erosion, but in contrast to beach environments that recover through re-deposition of sand, rock erosion is irreversible. Despite this, over long periods of time erosion of rocky shorelines does result in recurrent morphologies, which implies that morphological models based on average forms may also have value on these coasts.

Rarely have numerical geomorphological models been fully verified in terms of their internal consistency, and all too infrequently has it been possible to evaluate their performance against observed behaviour. Even where natural changes on the coast coincide with the outcomes forecast by a model, it is important that modellers are mindful of the limitations of their model, and that those who use the model outcomes exercise a healthy scepticism and recognise those components of system behaviour which are outside of a model's capabilities. The needs of the coastal manager, the engineer and the geomorphologist are different. Those tasked with responsibilities for a coastline seek clear guidance on where the shoreline will be in the future; those who observe its behaviour need to be aware of the complexities and to communicate the extent to which they are uncertain about the future. Models will always be imperfect and deficient in their representation of the rare high magnitude events to which our coastal communities are highly vulnerable, as tragically demonstrated by the Sumatran tsunami in 2004, Hurricane Katrina in 2005 and Cyclone Nargis in 2008. However, morphodynamic modelling has made significant progress since the focus on coastal process studies began after World War II. Such models provide an additional tool that can add to the collective geomorphological experience to assist in the more prudent management of our coasts in future.

References

Anderson, R.S., Densmore, A.L. and Ellis, M.A. (1999) The generation and degradation of marine terraces. *Basin Research*, Vol. 11, Issue 1, pp. 7–19.

Baker, V.R. (1994) Geomorphological understanding of floods. *Geomorphology*, Vol. 10, pp. 139–156.

Bankes, S. (1993) Exploratory modeling for policy analysis. *Operations Research*, Vol. 41, pp. 435–449.

Batty, M. and Torrens, P.M. (2001) *Modeling complexity: the limits to prediction*. Centre for Advanced Spatial Analysis, Working Paper Series, Paper 36.

Beven, K. (2002) Towards a coherent philosophy for modelling the environment. *Proceedings of the Royal Society of London* (Series A), Vol. 458, 2465–2484.

Bird, E.C.F. (1985) *Coastline Changes*, Wiley and Sons, New York.

Bray, M.J. and Hooke, J.M. (1997) Prediction of coastal cliff erosion with accelerating sea-level rise. *Journal of Coastal Research*, Vol. 13, pp. 453–467.

Brimicombe, A. (2003) *GIS, Environmental Modelling and Engineering*, Taylor & Francis, London.

Brøker-Hedegaard, I., Deigaard, R. and Fredsøe, J. (1991) Onshore/offshore sediment transport and morphological modelling of coastal profiles, *Proceedings Coastal Sediments '91*, ASCE, pp. 643–657.

Bruun, P. (1962) Sea-level rise as a cause of shore erosion. *American Society of Civil Engineering Proceedings, Journal of Waterways and Harbors Division*, Vol. 88, pp. 117–130.

Carpenter, S.R. (2003) The need for fast-and-frugal models. In Canham, C.D., Cole, J.J. and Lauenroth, W.K. (eds) *Models in Ecosystem Science*, Princeton University Press, Princeton, NJ, pp. 455–460.

Chamberlin, T.C. (1897) The method of multiple working hypotheses. *Journal of Geology*, Vol. 5, pp. 837–848.

Chapman, D.M., Geary, M., Roy, P.S. and Thom, B.G. (1982) *Coastal Evolution and Coastal Erosion in New South Wales*, Coastal Council of New South Wales, Sydney.

Clark, J.S., Carpenter, S.R., Barber, M., Collins, S., Dobson, A., Foley, J.A., Lodge, D.M., Pascual, M., Pielke, R., Jr, Pizer, W., Pringle, C., Reid, W.V., Rose, K.A., Sala, O., Schlesinger, W.H., Wall, D.H. and Wear, D. (2001) Ecological forecasts: an emerging imperative. *Science*, Vol. 293, pp. 657–660.

Cooper, J.A.G. and Pilkey, O.A. (2004) Alternatives to the mathematical modeling of beaches. *Journal of Coastal Research*, Vol. 20, pp. 641–644.

Cooper, J.A.G. and Pilkey, O.A. (2007) Rejoinder to: Cowell, P.J. and Thom, B.G., 2006. Reply to: Pilkey, O.H. and Cooper, A.G., 2006. Discussion of: Cowell *et al.*, 2006. Management of Uncertainty in Predicting Climate-Change Impacts on Beaches. *Journal of Coastal Research*, Vol. 22, Issue 1, pp. 232–245; *Journal of Coastal Research*, Vol. 22, Issue, 6, pp. 1577–1579; *Journal of Coastal Research*, Vol, 22, Issue 6, pp. 1580–1584; *Journal of Coastal Research*, Vol. 23, pp. 277–280.

Cooper, N.J., Hooke, J.M. and Bray, M.J. (2001) Predicting coastal evolution using a sediment budget approach: a case study from southern England. *Ocean & Coastal Management*, 44, pp. 711–728.

Cornaglia, P. (1889) Delle Spiaggie. Academia Nazionale dei Lincei, Att. Cl. Sci. Fis., Mat. e Nat. Mem., Vol. 5, pp. 284–304.

Cowell, P.J., Roy, P.S. and Jones, R.A. (1995) Simulation of large-scale coastal change using a morphological behaviour model. *Marine Geology*, 126, pp. 45–61.

Cowell, P.J., Thom, B.G., Jones, R.A., Everts, C.H. and Simanovic, D. (2006) Management of uncertainty in predicting climate-change impacts on beaches. *Journal of Coastal Research*, Vol. 22, pp. 232–245.

Dalrymple, R.W., Zaitlin, B.A. and Boyd, R. (1992) Estuarine facies models: conceptual basis and stratigraphic implications. *Journal of Sedimentary Petrology*, Vol. 62, pp. 1130–1146.

Dawson, R.J., Dickson, M.E., Nicholls, R.J., Hall, J.W., Walkden, M.J.A., Stansby, P., Mokrech, M., Richards, J., Zhou, J., Milligan, J., Jordon, A., Pearson, S.G., Rees, J., Bates, P.D., Koukoulas, S. and Watkinson, A. (2009) Integrated analysis of risks of coastal flooding and cliff erosion under scenarios of long term change. *Climatic Change*, Vol. 95, pp. 249–288.

de Vriend, H.J., Zyserman, J., Nicholson, J., Roelvink, J.A., Péchon P. and Southgate, N.H. (1993) Medium-term 2DH coastal area modelling. *Coastal Engineering*, Vol. 21, pp. 193–224.

Dickson, M.E., Walkden, M.J.A. and Hall, J.W. (2007) Systemic impacts of climate change on an eroding coastal region over the 21st century. *Climatic Change*, Vol. 84, pp. 141–166.

Dubois, R.N. (2002) How does a barrier shoreface respond to a sea-level rise? *Journal of Coastal Research*, Vol 18, pp. III–V.

EUROSION (2004) Living with coastal erosion in Europe: sediment and space for sustainability, European Commission, Directorate General Environment.

French, P.W. (1997) *Coastal and Estuarine Management*, Routledge, London.

Goodwin, I.D., Stables, M.A. and Olley, J.M. (2006) Wave climate, sand budget and shoreline alignment evolution of the Iluka–Woody Bay sand barrier, northern New South Wales, Australia, since 3000 yr BP. *Marine Geology*, Vol. 226, pp. 127–144.

Hall, J.W., Lee, E.M. and Meadowcroft, I.C. (2000) Risk-based benefit assessment of coastal cliff protection. *Proceedings of the Institute of Civil Engineers: Water and Maritime Engineering*, Vol. 142, Issue Sept., pp. 127–139.

Harris, P.T. and Heap, A.D. (2003) Environmental management of clastic coastal depositional environments: inferences from an Australian geomorphic database. *Ocean and Coastal Management*, Vol. 46, pp. 457–478.

Harris, P.T., Heap, A.D., Bryce, S.M., Porter-Smith, R., Ryan, D.A. and Heggie, D.T. (2002) Classification of Australian clastic coastal depositional environments based upon a quantitative analysis of wave, tidal, and river power. *Journal of Sedimentary Research*, Vol. 72, pp. 858–870.

Ku, T.-L. and Kern, J.P. (1974) Uranium-series age of the Upper Pleistocene Nestor Terrace, San Diego, California. *Geological Society of America Bulletin*, Vol. 85, Issue 11, pp. 1713–1716.

Lippman, T.C. and Holman, R.A. (1990) The spatial and temporal variability of sand bar morphology. *Journal of Geophysical Research*, Vol. 95, Issue 11575–11590.

McLean, R.F. and Shen, J.-S. (2006) From foreshore to foredune: foredune development over the last 30 years at Moruya Beach, New South Wales, Australia. *Journal of Coastal Research*, Vol. 22, pp. 28–36.

Murray, A.B. (2003) Contrasting the goals, strategies, and predictions associated with simplified numerical models and detailed simulations. In Iverson, R.M. and Wilcock, P. (eds) *Prediction in Geomorphology*, AGU Geophysical Monograph, pp. 151–165.

Nicholls, R.J. and Mimura, N. (1998) Regional issues raised by sea-level rise and their policy implications. *Climate Research*, Vol. 11, pp. 5–18.

Nicholls, R.J. and Stive, M.J.F. (2004) Society and sea level rise requires modelling. *Science Magazine*, E-Letters June.

Oreskes, N. (2003) The role of quantitative models in science. In Canham, C., Cole, J., Lauenroth, W. (eds), Models in Ecosystem Science. Princeton, NJ: Princeton University Press, pp. 13–32.

Oreskes, N., Shrader-Frechette, K. and Belitz, K. (1994) Verification, validation, and confirmation of numerical models in the earth sciences. *Science*, Vol. 263, pp. 641–646.

Perry, G.L.W. (2009) Modelling and simulation. In Castree, N., Demeritt, D., Liverman, D. and Rhoads, B. (eds) *A Companion to Environmental Geography*, John Wiley and Sons, Chichester, pp. 336–357.

Pethick, J. (2001) Coastal management and sea-level rise. *Catena*, Vol. 42, pp. 307–322.

Pilkey, O.A. and Cooper, A.G. (2004) Society and sea level rise. *Science*, Vol. 303, pp. 1781–1782.

Pilkey, O.H. and Cooper, J.A.G. (2006) Discussion of Cowell *et al*, 2006, Management of uncertainty in predicting climate-change impacts on beaches. *Journal of Coastal Research*, Vol. 22, pp. 232–245.

Pillans, B. (1983) Upper Quaternary marine terrace chronology and deformation, South Taranaki, New Zealand. *Geology*, Vol. 11, Issue 5, pp. 292–297.

Ranasinghe, R., McLoughlin, R., Short, A.D. and Symonds, G. (2004) The Southern Oscillation Index, wave climate, and beach rotation. *Marine Geology*, Vol. 204, pp. 273–287.

Roy, P.S. (1984) New South Wales estuaries: their origin and evolution. In Thom, B.G. (ed.) *Coastal Geomorphology in Australia*, Academic Press, Sydney, pp. 99–121.

Roy, P.S., Thom, B.G. and Wright, L.D. (1980) Holocene sequences on an embayed high-energy coast: an evolutionary model. *Sedimentary Geology*, Vol. 16, pp. 1–9.

Roy, P.S., Cowell, P.J., Ferland, M.A. and Thom, B.G. (1994) Wave-dominated coasts. In Carter, R.W.G. and Woodroffe, C.D. (eds) *Coastal Evolution: Late Quaternary Shoreline Morphodynamics*, Cambridge University Press, Cambridge, pp. 121–186.

Roy, P.S., Williams, R.J., Jones, A.R., Yassini, I., Gibbs, P.J., Coates, B., West, R.J., Scanes, P.R., Hudson, J.P. and Nichol, S. (2001) Structure and function of south-east Australian estuaries. *Estuarine Coastal and Shelf Science*, Vol. 53, pp. 351–384.

Short, A.D. (ed.) (1999) *Handbook of Beach and Shoreface Morphodynamics*, Wiley, Chichester.

Short, A.D. (2006) Australian beach systems-nature and distribution. *Journal of Coastal Research*, Vol. 22, pp. 11–27.

Stive, M.J.F. (2004) How important is global warming for coastal erosion? *Climatic Change*, Vol. 64, pp. 27–39.

Stive, M.J.F. and Battjes, J.A. (1984) A model for offshore sediment transport. *Proceedings of the 19th Coastal Engineering Conference*, ASCE, pp. 1420–1436.

Sunamura, T. (1992) *Geomorphology of Rocky Coasts*, John Wiley & Sons, Chichester.

Thieler, E.R., Pilkey, O.H., Young, R.S., Bush, D.M. and Chai, F. (2000) The use of mathematical models to predict beach behavior for US coastal engineering: a critical review. *Journal of Coastal Research*, Vol. 16, pp. 48–70.

Thom, B.G. (1984) Transgressive and regressive stratigraphies of coastal sand barriers in eastern Australia. *Marine Geology*, Vol. 56, pp. 137–158.

Thom, B.G. and Cowell, P.J. (2005) Coastal changes, gradual. In Schwartz, M.L. (ed.) *Encyclopedia of Coastal Science*, Springer, Dordrecht, pp. 251–253.

Thom, B.G. and Roy, P.S. (1988) Sea-level rise and climate: lessons from the Holocene. In Pearman, G.I. (ed.) *Greenhouse: Planning for Climatic Change*, CSIRO, Melbourne, pp. 177–188.

Thom, B.G. and Hall, W. (1991) Behaviour of beach profiles during accretion and erosion dominated phases. *Earth Surface Processes and Landforms*, Vol. 16, pp. 113–127.

Trenhaile, A.S. (1987) *The Geomorphology of Rocky Coasts*, Oxford University Press, Oxford.

Trenhaile, A.S. (2000) Modeling the development of wave-cut shore platforms. *Marine Geology*, Vol. 166, pp. 163–178.

Trenhaile, A.S. (2001) Modeling the effect of late quaternary interglacial sea levels on wave-cut shore platforms. *Marine Geology*, Vol. 172, pp. 205–223.

Trenhaile, A.S., Alberti, A.P., Cortizas, A.M., Casais, M.C. and Chao, R.B. (1999) Rock coast inheritance: an example from Galicia, northwestern Spain. *Earth Surface Processes and Landforms*, Vol. 24, pp. 605–621.

Walkden, M.J.A. and Dickson, M.E. (2008) Equilibrium erosion of soft rock shores with a shallow or absent beach under increased sea level rise. *Marine Geology*, Vol. 251, pp. 75–84.

Walkden, M.J.A. and Hall, J.W. (2005) A predictive mesoscale model of the erosion and profile development of soft rock shores. *Coastal Engineering*, Vol. 52, pp. 535–563.

Woodroffe, C.D., Mulrennan, M.E. and Chappell, J. (1993) Estuarine infill and coastal progradation, southern van Diemen Gulf, northern Australia. *Sedimentary Geology*, Vol. 83, pp. 257–275.

Wright, L.D. and Short, A.D. (1984) Morphodynamic variability of surf zones and beaches: a synthesis. *Marine Geology*, Vol. 56, pp. 93–118.

Wright, L.D. and Thom, B.G. (1977) Coastal depositional landforms: a morphodynamic approach. *Progress in Physical Geography*, Vol. 1, pp. 412–459.

Zhang, K., Douglas, B.C. and Leatherman, S.P. (2004) Global warming and coastal erosion. *Climatic Change*, Vol. 64, pp. 41–58.

8

Modelling the coastal system

Chris Lakhan
Department of Earth and Environmental Sciences, University of Windsor, Canada

Computer simulation, statistical time series, and GIS-based models were presented for understanding and predicting the dynamics at work in the coastal system. Model results highlighted the influence of temporal stochastic processes on advance and retreat of the coastline at different spatial scales.

8.1   Introduction

The large-scale coastal system, with its numerous interacting subsystems, is one of the most complex and challenging systems to model. While significant progress has been made to model and understand the complex interactions of the various individual interdependent entities or processes (for example, waves, winds, tides, currents, sediments, nearshore circulation) which influence the behaviour of the coastal system substantial research, nevertheless, remains to be done on providing better insights on the multidimensional nonlinear processes operating at different spatial and temporal scales in the coastal system. To understand and predict the complexities of the coastal system researchers have employed various modelling approaches because 'models facilitate considerable more enlightenment on the relationships between process scales and scales of coastal behaviour and are instrumental to unravelling the complexities and the interactions of nonlinear hydrodynamic processes' (Lakhan, 2004, p. 658). The edited book by Lakhan (2003) presented reviews on the advances in the modelling of waves, currents, circulatory flows, sediment transport, beaches, shorelines, tidal basins, shore platforms, coastal water quality and coastal ecology. Moreover, comprehensive accounts on the development and application of various modelling approaches for understanding and predicting morphological changes and coastal evolution could be found in Lakhan (2004). In addition, the book by Hearn (2008) discussed the use of both analytical and numerical models to explain the dynamics of estuaries, bays and lagoons.

The increase in the use of mathematical and probabilistic models and computer-based simulation models could be attributed to the contention that models help to elucidate both the linear and nonlinear aspects of the processes governing the dynamic coastal system at various spatial and temporal scales. For instance, a simulation model not only permits controlled experimentation but also facilitates time compression whereby knowledge of one or more processes could be obtained in minutes which would take years to obtain equivalent information from the actual coastal system. Given the potential utility of models to provide insights into a phenomenon not yet described or understood this chapter focused on three types of modelling approaches which have applicability for not only understanding changes in the morphological states of the coastal system, but also for predicting the spatial and temporal positions of the coastline. The first approach described a computer simulation model with stochastic properties to simulate erosion and accretion and associated coastal changes. This was followed by time series modelling of coastal data to understand and predict the nature of the stochastic processes operating in the coastal environment. The third modelling approach demonstrated the application of a geographical information systems (GIS)-based model to predict future coastline positions. The Guyana coast was used to verify the model results because the coast could be characterised as one of the most dynamic coastlines in the world.

8.2   Computer simulation model

With the realisation that coastal accretion and erosion and associated coastline positional changes, unpredictable in magnitude and duration, cannot be satisfactorily studied with small-scale experimental studies and time-limited empirical investigations it was, therefore, worthwhile to formulate a simulation model with stochastic properties to facilitate prediction of the dynamic changes occurring in the coastal system. Details on the simulation design process for coastal models were presented by Lakhan (1989, 2005) who mentioned that a model with a justifiable level of abstraction could be developed by considering the various simulation design stages. Abstractness, considered as a measure of the level of repression of detail, is normally introduced into a

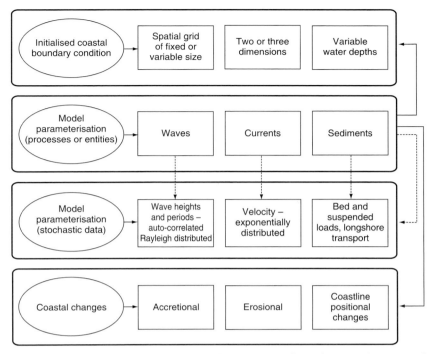

Fig. 8.1 Conceptual framework for modelling approach used to simulate coastal changes

simulation model because it is almost impossible to consider all of the details of the large number of poorly understood nonlinear processes that interact with the wide variety of micro and macro morphological states in the coastal system (Lakhan, 2004). To formulate a model that neither oversimplifies to the point where the model becomes trivial nor carries so much detail that the model becomes meaningless the notions of either Occam's razor (see Checkland, 1981) or Bonini's paradox (see Dutton and Starbuck, 1971) must be considered. Since both notions advocated the development of parsimonious models a conceptual model was formulated (see Fig. 8.1) to incorporate only the essential processes of the coastal system. Nearshore waves, currents and changes in the amount of sediments would not only effectuate changes to the initialised nearshore slope and bathymetry but also initiate erosional and accretional sequences. The coastline would shift position based on the amount of material gained or lost from the coastline. The driving forces influencing change in the model would

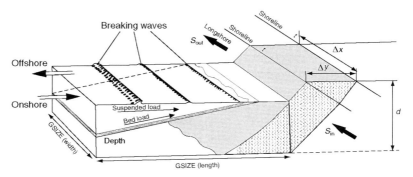

Fig. 8.2 Schematic framework for representation of coastal system (adapted from Lakhan, 1986)

vary stochastically in order to imitate the behaviour of real world processes.

8.2.1 Model parameterisation

Representation of the coastal system
To realistically compute the wave and current characteristics, breaker index, wave steepness, bed load, suspended load, and longshore transport at each iteration the coastal system was modelled with a set of spatially connected grids, extending from deep water to a straight coastline. In the simulation program, the coastal system was expressed by a combination of shore-parallel and shore-perpendicular grids. A schematic view of this system could be illustrated (Fig. 8.2).

Simulating wave characteristics
Since ocean waves have stochastic properties, and could have Rayleigh distributed heights and periods, the model generated autocorrelated Rayleigh distributed heights and periods (see Lakhan, 1981). On each iteration, which represented one-twelfth of a tidal cycle or approximately 70 minutes, a deep water wave height and period were generated and allowed to propagate along the initialised slope. On each iteration, the wave characteristics (height, length, celerity, horizontal and vertical particle velocities, mass drift, breaker index, wave steepness, etc.) were computed at each grid point with equations governing both linear and nonlinear wave theories. Lakhan's (1989) wave simulation program was

extended to integrate Stokes and Cnoidal wave theories in a nonlinear refraction model. The extended model provided wave heights and wave direction at specified grid nodes.

Calculation of bed load, suspended load and longshore transport
Although several recent studies (for example, Drake and Calantoni, 2001; Kamphuis, 2002; Hoefel and Elgar, 2003; Nielsen, 2006; Silva et al., 2006; Bayram et al., 2007; van Rijn, 2007a, 2007b; Tang et al., 2009) have expanded our knowledge of sediment transport in the coastal zone yet there are very few equations which could be used in simulation models to compute the amount of bed load and suspended load in the coastal zone. Hence, for this simulation bed load and suspended load were computed with the equations used by Lakhan and LaValle (1992).

To simulate longshore sediment transport rate, Kamphuis' (2002) formula was used because the formula included wave period, beach slope and grain size. The formula in the model for longshore sediment transport could be expressed as:

$$Q_{1st,m} = 2.27 H_{s,b}^2 T_p^{1.5} m_b^{0.75} D_{50}^{-0.25} \sin^{0.6}(2\theta_b) \tag{1}$$

in which $Q_{1st,m}$ is the transport rate of immersed mass per unit time, T_p is the peak wave period, m_b is the beach slope near the breaking, i.e. the slope over one or two wavelengths seaward of the breaker line, and D_{50} is the median grain size. The immersed weight is related to the volumetric rate as $Q_{1st,m} = (\rho_s - \rho)(1 - a)Q_{1st}$, where ρ is the density of water, ρ_s is the density of sand, and a is the porosity index ($\cong 0.4$).

8.2.2   Model execution and results
To trace the movement of the calculated bed and suspended loads and longshore transport, the coastal nearshore environment was modelled with a set of spatially connected grids, extending from deep water to the shore. One thousand grids were used to represent the nearshore, with each grid having a length of 20 m and a width of 1 m. For each of the grids, wave and sediment characteristics were calculated for 10 000 iterations, representing approximately 486 days.

Since the movement of sediments caused changes in the depth of the nearshore environment through erosion and deposition, the model assumed that each of the grids representing the nearshore was separated from the next by a so-called 'gate' 1 metre wide. The total amount of material that moved through the gate was modelled on the premise that from any grid i the equivalent amount of material will be removed. If i_s(suspended load) $+ i_b$(bed load) > 0, the net movement was from i to $i + 1$. If $i_s + i_b < 0$, the net movement was from $i + 1$ to i. When $i_s + i_b > 0$ direction was shoreward, and when <0 direction was offshore. By utilising these procedures the eventual change of the nearshore bed could be examined. For both i_s and i_b, the resulting change in depth equalled the volume of the material removed/deposited divided by the area of the grid size. The longshore transport rate was traced in a similar manner.

After 10 000 iterations (approximately 486 days) the model revealed that when a flat bed was affected by waves with randomly generated heights and periods, the bed changed from its initialised state through a sequence of transitory erosional and accretional states. The results demonstrated that, over time, persistently low and highly auto-correlated wave steepness values created an aggradational state while strong autocorrelation for waves with high steepness values produced a degradational state. When waves with high steepness values occurred in conjunction with strong currents $(>1\,\mathrm{m \cdot s^{-1}})$ distinctive erosion occurred on the majority of grid cells parallel to the shore. Erosion also occurred when strongly autocorrelated high steepness (i.e. >0.075) waves broke at different locations in the nearshore area.

As demonstrated in previous modelling efforts by Lakhan and Jopling (1987) this simulation also established that variations in wave steepness could be associated with not only the magnitude of the onshore/offshore movement of bed and suspended loads but also provided an indication of variations in wave velocity components, and breaker positions in the nearshore zone. When waves with an average steepness of 0.03 broke, the velocity components of the wave together with the volume of the material transported were highest at and slightly seaward at the break-point positions. Although wave breaking could be associated with a reduction in the bulk of the transported load, it should be pointed out that when waves broke the suspended load exceeded the amount of transported bed load. An analysis of the amounts of bed load and suspended load for the 1000 grids demonstrated that at least ten times more suspended load than bed load existed in the nearshore zone. Much of the material moving through the grids was in the form of suspended load. Evidently, areas which eroded along the coast were associated with grids with the highest suspended load. In addition to suspended load, the model results also implied that the longshore transport and current flows played a dominant role in changing the

190

temporal sediment fluxes in all shore-parallel grid cells. Hence, coastline positional changes could be associated with temporal differentials in sediment flows in the coastal system.

8.3   Time series modelling

8.3.1   *Types of time series models*

Time series models for many environmental and geophysical processes are allowing researchers to obtain invaluable information on the deterministic and stochastic processes operating in the natural system. Lakhan (2005) emphasised that time series modelling of the many natural phenomena occurring in the coastal environment, exhibiting random or probabilistic characteristics, is essential for understanding not only the operating processes but also for many coastal applications. Several types of models could be obtained from a stationary time series of coastal data, beginning with the general category of simple linear models, including the autoregressive (AR) models, the integrated (I) models, and the moving average (MA) models. The AR and MA types of models were combined into the mixed autoregressive moving average model (ARMA) (Lakhan, 2005).

Box and Jenkins (1970, 1976) extended the ARMA models to include certain types of nonstationary series, and proposed an entire class of models, called autoregressive integrated moving average (ARIMA) models. Other models presented by Box and Jenkins include the transfer function noise (TFN) models, and the seasonal autoregressive integrated moving average (SARIMA) models. The autoregressive fractionally integrated moving average (ARFIMA) model was introduced by Granger and Joyeux (1980). Further advances in time series modelling occurred with the development of nonlinear time series models, initially with bilinear models and threshold autoregressive and regime switching models that introduced nonlinearities into the usual autoregressive models (Lai and Wong, 2006). An explanatory account of a wide range of nonlinear time series models was presented by Tong (1990).

8.3.2   *Model selection*

Given the wide diversity of time series models, care must be taken on deciding whether linear models or nonlinear models should be selected for describing the dynamics of a coastal time series. In an attempt to demonstrate how to fit and select the most appropriate model for an empirical coastal time series, this chapter placed emphasis on the use

191

of Box–Jenkins modelling procedures to fit a model to a time series on coastal advance and retreat data. Nonlinear models, because of difficulties in interpretation, were considered to be beyond the scope of this chapter.

8.3.3 Time series of coastal advance and retreat data

The data analysed and modelled were acquired from the Government of Guyana records on foreshore data collected on an annual basis. The dataset consisted of the elevation levels for two (45GD and 50GD) contour positions. Since 1941 these contour data were collected from survey profile lines along various sections of the Guyana coast. After examining the entire dataset, the time series of measurements from 1941 to 1987 were selected. In this dataset measurements were obtained from 86 profile sections measured approximately 300 m apart along the Guyana coast. Several studies (Lakhan, 1994; Lakhan and Pepper, 1997; Lakhan *et al.*, 2003) provided accounts on the nature of Guyana's coastal system.

Data representation for model fitting

The coastal advance and retreat data were represented in an Excel spreadsheet as:

T_1 (1941): P1, P2, P3, P4...P86

T_2 (1942): P1, P2, P3, P4...P86

$\vdots$

T_{47} (1987): P1, P2, P3, P4...P86

where T_1 is the first time period at 1941 and T_{47} is the last time period at 1987. For each time period the data were from 86 profiles stretching from P1 to P86.

8.3.4 Box–Jenkins modelling procedures

The Box–Jenkins model construction procedures of identification, estimation and diagnostic checks were considered before fitting any statistically valid model to the time series. Here it is worthwhile to emphasise that in fitting a model to a dataset there should be: (a) no systematic change or trend in the mean; (b) no systematic change in the variance; (c) no deterministic periodic variations; and (d) the autocorrelation function must be dependent on the lag interval and not the starting point of the series (Chatfield, 1996).

With the use of Statistica (Statsoft Inc., 1999) software, the mean and the variance of the data were examined. The data were then detrended by generating standardised values for all profiles and for all years. After detrending, the data were then used to fit various models, including (a) an autoregressive (AR) model, (b) a moving average (MA) model, (c) a space-time autoregressive moving average (STARMA) model, and (d) a generalised space-time autoregressive (STAR) model. Descriptions of these models are provided below.

Autoregressive (AR) model
The *Engineering Statistics Handbook* (NIST/SEMATECH, 2006) expressed the autoregressive (AR) model as:

$$X_t = \delta + \phi_1 X_{t-1} + \phi_2 X_{t-2} + \cdots + \phi_p X_{i-p} + A_t \tag{2}$$

where X_t is the time series, A_t is the white noise, and

$$\delta = \left(1 - \sum_{i=1}^{p} \phi_i\right)\mu$$

with μ denoting the process mean.

Moving average (MA) model
The moving average (MA) model could be stated as:

$$X_t = \mu + A_t - \theta_1 A_{t-1} - \theta_2 A_{t-2} - \cdots - \theta_q A_{t-q} \tag{3}$$

where, X_t is the time series, μ is the mean of the series, A_{t-1} are white noise, and $\theta_1, \ldots, \theta_q$ are the parameters of the model. The value of q is called the order of the MA model.

Space-time autoregressive moving average (STARMA) model
The Box–Jenkins ARMA model is a combination of the AR and MA models:

$$X_t = \delta + \phi_1 X_{t-1} + \phi_2 X_{t-2} + \cdots + \phi_p X_{t-p}$$
$$+ A_t - \theta_1 A_{t-1} - \theta_2 A_{t-2} - \cdots - \theta_q A_{t-q} \tag{4}$$

where the terms in the equation have the same meaning as given for the AR and MA model.

Cressie (1993) provided details on how ARMA (Box–Jenkins) models could be generalised to include spatial location. These include the space-time autoregressive (STAR) models and space-time auto-regressive moving average (STARMA) models. The STARMA model uses an observation $Z(s_i; t)$ taken at spatial location s_i and time t, and defines $Z(t) \equiv [Z(s_i; t), \ldots, Z(s_n; t)]'$. The STARMA model takes the form (Cressie, 1993, p. 449):

$$Z(t) = \sum_{k=0}^{p} \sum_{j=0}^{\lambda_k} \xi_{kj} W_{kj} Z(t - k) - \sum_{l=0}^{q} \sum_{j=0}^{\mu_l} \phi_{lj} V_{lj} \varepsilon(t - 1) + \varepsilon(t) \qquad (5)$$

where W_{kj} and V_{lj} are given weight matrices, λ_k is the extent of spatial lagging on the autoregressive component, μ_l is the extent of spatial lagging on the moving average component, the residuals are given by $\varepsilon(t) \equiv [\varepsilon(s_i, t), \ldots, \in (s_n; t)]'$ and ξ_{kj} is the autoregressive parameter to be estimated while ϕ_{lj} is the moving average parameter to be estimated.

Generalised space-time autoregressive (STAR) model
The STAR models used in this chapter took the form:

$$Y_{s,t} = \psi_{s-1,t} Y_{s-1,t} \pm \psi_{s,t-1} Y_{s,t-1} \pm \psi_{s-1,t-1} Y_{s-1,t-1} \pm \varepsilon \qquad (6)$$

where the ψ terms represented the estimated autoregressive parameters and ε indicating the error or residual term.

8.3.5   Model identification
The time series (1941–87) was first modelled to obtain the best fit model for the entire dataset. Sub-series of ten-year intervals (for example, 1977–87) were then modelled. The assumption in modelling the sub-series was premised on the notion that a short data sample could mimic the dynamics of the coastal system that produced the original time series being investigated. For each of the models the auto-correlation coefficients were plotted against the lag intervals on a graph called a correlogram, and the resulting function called the auto-correlation function (ACF). In addition, the partial autocorrelation coefficients were plotted for the same number of lag intervals on a partial correlogram depicting the partial autocorrelation function (PACF). Based on an examination of the ACF and the PACF a model could be fitted to the data (LaValle *et al.*, 2001).

8.3.6 Model selection

Initial examinations of the autocorrelation functions and correlograms helped to provide an assessment of the nature of the autoregressive processes. Figure 8.3 provides an example of one of the correlograms produced from the iterative model fitting process for the sub-series 1977–87. From this correlogram it could be observed that all the autocorrelations fall inside of the 5% confidence bands. Since the auto-correlation functions did not decay exponentially to near zero the claim could be made that the time series could not be portrayed by a first-order autoregressive model. Furthermore, this correlogram did not illustrate an autocorrelation function with a single major spike at lag one and no significant autocorrelation elsewhere. Hence, the decision could be made that a first-order moving average model could not be fitted to the data.

Given the unsatisfactory fit of the time series to autoregressive moving average models a provisional evaluation could be made that a space-time autoregressive (STAR) model was best suited to the data. Before a decision was made to accept a STAR model it was necessary to examine the residuals associated with the model that produced the correlogram listed in Fig. 8.3. The residuals from the model could be found in Table 8.1 which displayed the autocorrelation and the associated standard error, Box–Ljung Q statistics and probability. The standard error and probability were all within acceptable values.

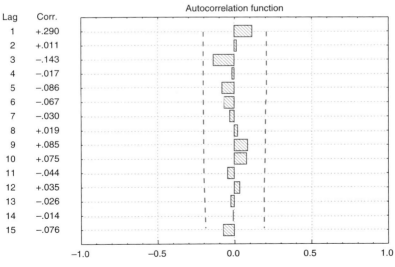

Fig. 8.3 *Correlogram of coastal advance and retreat sub-series, 1977–87*

Table 8.1 Residuals from the time-series model

Observed lag	Autocorrelation	Standard error: SE	Box-Ljung: Q	Probability: p
1	+0.290	0.1060	1.08	0.2995
2	+0.011	0.1054	1.09	0.5809
3	−0.143	0.1047	2.96	0.3977
4	−0.017	0.1041	2.99	0.5601
5	−0.086	0.1035	3.67	0.5972
6	−0.067	0.1028	4.10	0.6625
7	−0.030	0.1022	4.19	0.7579
8	+0.019	0.1015	4.22	0.8364
9	+0.085	0.1009	4.94	0.8399
10	+0.075	0.1002	5.49	0.8558
11	−0.044	0.0995	5.69	0.8930
12	+0.035	0.0989	5.82	0.9250
13	−0.026	0.0982	5.89	0.9500
14	−0.014	0.0975	5.91	0.9687
15	−0.076	0.0969	6.52	0.9695

Moreover, no significant autocorrelation existed in the pattern of residuals from the model as displayed by the non-significant Box–Ljung Q values. Q is distributed as χ^2 with degrees of freedom equal to the total number of lags minus the number of parameters and their associated probability values (any probability greater than 0.05 is considered non-significant). Given the distribution of the autocorrelation coefficients, and the clear indication that the residuals from the model did not have any significant autocorrelation effects then the STAR model could be selected with confidence.

8.3.7 Significance of model results

With the STAR model selected as the best fitting model for the coastal advance and retreat time series data, the suggestion could be made that temporal variations in accretion and erosion along the Guyana coast were indicative of a spatial autoregressive process. Cyclical patterns in erosional and depositional states occurred along the coastline. In effect the coastline responded to a combination of cyclical spatial and temporal processes which contributed to the spatial instabilities and positional shifts of the coast. Evidently, the statistically significant feedback within the time series reflected the influence of the periodic movements of the mudbanks along the coast. These mudbanks discussed by Lakhan *et al.* (2006) have a significant influence on where and when the coast accretes or erodes.

8.4   GIS-based modelling

In addition to time series modelling for understanding the temporal behaviour and dynamics of coastal processes, it is also worthwhile to develop GIS-based models for predicting changes occurring in the coastal system at varying temporal and spatial scales. The development and benefits of GIS-based modelling approaches for coastal investigations were described by Green and King (2003). Several recent studies (for example, Hennecke *et al.*, 2004; Snow and Snow, 2005; Wheeler *et al.*, 2008) have also focused on GIS-based modelling approaches to investigate changes and impacts in the coastal environment. This section of the chapter, therefore, focussed on demonstrating the development and use of a GIS-based model to predict coastal erosion and accretion and associated positional changes of the coastline. The same data used for the time series modelling of accretional and erosional changes along the Guyana coast, together with supplementary data, were analysed and modelled in a GIS environment. Figure 8.4 outlines the sequence of steps on how the acquired data were used to predict coastline positional changes for a length of Guyana's coast. As discussed briefly below each step required the application of GIS principles (see Lakhan, 1996) and specialised GIS functions.

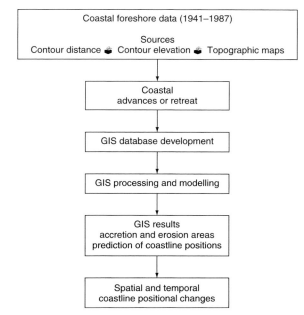

Fig. 8.4 Outline of GIS-based modelling approach

197

8.4.1 GIS database development

In ArcGIS 9.0 (ESRI, 2004), and ArcView GIS 3.3 (ESRI, 2002) used in this study, the locational coordinates were represented as x and y values. The survey profiles had permanent x-values or longitudinal coordinates. The y-values or latitude coordinates were the contour positions. The coordinate values for the 86 survey profiles were stored in a d-base file. The data file with the x and y values were then used in ArcView to create point and line themes. Here it should be noted that the coastlines for 1964 and 1986 were digitised as line themes. The digitised line themes for the two coastlines were compiled as ArcView shapefiles. The shoreline vectors were then converted to a UTM projection, with Zone 21N for Guyana. With the d-base file stored in ArcView point shapefiles were created representing transect points and nodes of a shoreline baseline. The baseline point shapefile was subsequently converted to a baseline line shapefile comprising three segments. Vertices (i.e. nodes) were then placed on the baseline segments at intervals associated with the locations of the 86 survey sections. The point shapefile was then edited to create a line shapefile. Figure 8.5 illustrates the

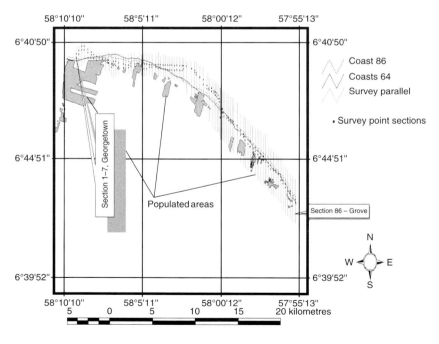

Fig. 8.5 Survey section parallels for the 86 sections with 1964 and 1986 coastlines

survey parallels which were positioned along the survey sections, and the digitised 1964 and 1986 coastlines.

8.4.2   GIS processing and modelling

Following GIS-based data preparation, long-term rates of shoreline change were generated in ArcGIS 9.0 with the Digital Shoreline Analysis System (DSAS), version 3.2 (Thieler *et al.*, 2005). DSAS files created in DSAS, version 2.0 (Thieler *et al.*, 2003) for ArcView 3.3 were imported for use in DSAS version 3.2. In brief, DSAS was used to compute rate of change statistics from multiple historic shoreline positions stored in the GIS. Essentially, the DSAS facilitated the shoreline change calculation process, providing both rate of change information and the statistical data necessary to establish the reliability of the calculated results (Thieler *et al.*, 2005). The rate of change methods incorporated in the DSAS are endpoint rate, weighted least squares regression, simple linear regression, and jackknife iterative regression techniques.

With the DSAS extension, the distance between the two coastlines (1964 and 1986) for each survey section (1–86) was derived. The rate of change per year for each survey section was calculated by using the total distance change value for each section, divided by the time period (i.e. 22 years) for the distance change to occur. With the assumption that the historical rate of coastline change provided the best estimate for predicting the future (Fenster *et al.*, 1993), it was decided to use the linear regression method for computing long-term rates of shoreline change. Figure 8.6 outlines the approach and application of the linear regression method as used in this research. For the prediction of future coastlines several conditions were necessary among them: (a) establishment of a pre-existing baseline coastline (i.e. 1964), (b) determination of the year(s) for prediction, (c) calculation of the total distance change for each survey section for the specified time period, and (d) estimating the trend in the coastline change data with a linear model to extrapolate future coastline positions. The linear trend was determined by fitting a least squares line to the coastline positions data (measurements based on the distance from the baseline) for all the survey sections. The linear curve fitted to the data yielded an intercept of 4.4 and a R^2-value of 0.582.

The intercept obtained in this estimation was used in the equation:

$$Y = mX + b \tag{7}$$

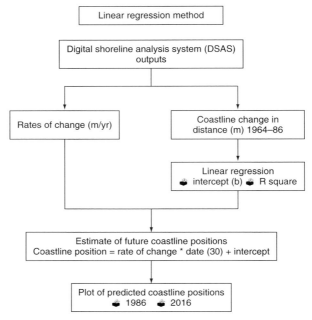

Fig. 8.6 Application of linear regression method procedures

or

$$\text{Coastline Position} = \text{Rate of Change} \times \text{Date} + \text{intercept} \qquad (8)$$

where Y denoted coastline movement (distance or position) or magnitude of change, m indicated the rate of coastline movement, X referred to the duration of time for coastline change, and b was the intercept. The intercept represented the trend component in the context of coastline movement.

The two base coastlines (1964 and 1986) were used to predict coastlines for different durations of time. After graphical outputs were obtained for the predicted coastlines, a buffer function in ArcMap GIS was utilised to spatially map the coastline positions using the magnitude change values obtained for each of the predicted coastlines.

8.4.3   GIS results

When the obtained magnitude change values for each of the predicted coastlines were used in the ArcMap GIS buffering process it was possible to produce maps to delineate the coastline positions in their real spatial

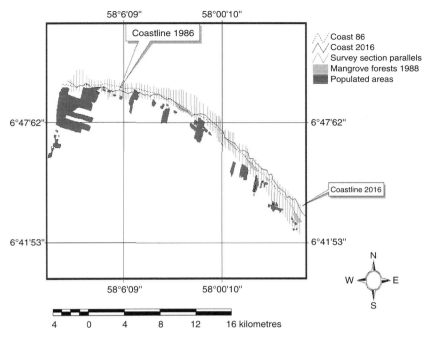

Fig. 8.7 Prediction of the 2016 coastline from the 1986 coastline

dimensions. Figure 8.7 is a spatial representation of the Demerara coastline in 2016.

An examination of Fig. 8.7 reveals that the width, configuration and positions of the Demerara coastline will change with time. The coast, at different spatial scales, and at different times will move landward or seaward. When the total number of sections experiencing accretional and erosional tendencies were counted and tabulated as a percentage of the total sections the results demonstrated that a total of 35 of the 86 section profiles will exhibit an erosional trend. The erosional pattern in the trend would be concentrated in the sections stretching from 6 to 46. Interestingly, sections 6 to 46 would correspond to a heavily populated area along the coast. Some areas along the coast would, however, display advance rather than retreat. A consistent pattern of accretion was modelled in the locality of Georgetown and its suburbs. Indications of spatial shifts in coastline positions would occur throughout the study area, but the overall trend would be more depositional than erosional.

The noticeable erosional and accretional trends of the predicted coastlines could be related to a combination of hydrodynamic processes,

201

not discussed here, which impact on the coast. Furthermore, the movement of mudbanks along the coast have a significant influence on the advance and retreat dynamics of the coast (Lakhan and Pepper, 1997). This would persist with time because the nonlinearities in the governing processes, in conjunction with sediment flows, would more than likely influence positional shifts of the coastline. Evidently, the GIS-based model would be able to predict spatial areas along the coast where changes will occur.

8.5   Conclusion

Different modelling approaches could provide substantial insights on dynamical processes operating in the coastal system, and the resultant spatio-temporal characteristics of coastal morphology. While computer simulation models are formulated with a certain level of abstraction they could, as demonstrated in this chapter, be parameterised with representative probability distributions to simulate the stochastic processes operating in the coastal system. The stochastic processes highlighted not only the transitory morphological states in the coastal system, but also indicated occurrences of persistence and periodicity in coastal behaviour. The simulated results could be considered as having high face validity because they matched pertinent empirical findings from the coast of Guyana.

Recognition of the deterministic and stochastic processes in the coastal system could be done by modelling empirical data with time series techniques. Evidently, along the Guyana coast and other coastal systems shifts in coastline positions could be linked to the influence of temporal stochastic processes operating at different spatial scales. The space-time model reflected that a coastline would likely experience shifts in erosional and depositional states varying in different magnitudes and durations through space and time.

The GIS-based modelling procedures proved to be beneficial in highlighting when and where there will be shifts in coastline positions. The positional shifts of the coastline could be associated with areas of coastal advance or coastal retreat. By using historical data to predict future coastline positions, the GIS-based modelling approach presented here would enable coastal managers to examine areas along the coast with different predicted magnitudes of erosion and accretion. These areas could then be visualised and analysed with 3D models in order to implement effective coastal protection strategies. Without doubt, the GIS-based and other modelling approaches introduced here should be considered as vital instruments by coastal resource managers and policy planners for the sustainable protection of the coast and its resources.

References

Bayram, A., Larson, M. and Hanson, H. (2007) A new formula for the total long-shore sediment transport rate. *Coastal Engineering*, Vol. 54, pp. 700–710.

Box, G.E.P. and Jenkins, G.M. (1970) *Time Series Analysis: Forecasting and Control*, Holden-Day, San Francisco, CA.

Box, G.E.P. and Jenkins, G.M. (1976) *Time Series Analysis Forecasting and Control*, 2nd ed., Holden-Day, San Francisco, CA.

Chatfield, C. (1996) *The Analysis of Time Series*, 5th ed., Chapman & Hall, New York.

Checkland, P. (1981) *Systems Thinking, Systems Practice*, John Wiley & Sons, New York.

Cressie, N.A.C. (1993) *Statistics for Spatial Data*, John Wiley Interscience, New York.

Drake, T.G. and Calantoni, J. (2001) Discrete-particle model for sheet flow sediment transport in the nearshore. *Journal of Geophysical Research*, Vol. 106, No. C9, pp. 19 859–19 868.

Dutton, J.M. and Starbuck W.H. (1971) *Computer Simulation of Human Behaviour*, Academic Press, Inc., New York.

ESRI (2002) *ArcView GIS 3.3*, Environmental Systems Research Institute, Redlands, CA.

ESRI (2004) *ArcGIS 9.0*, Environmental Systems Research Institute, Redlands, CA.

Fenster, M.S., Dolan, R. and Elder, J.F. (1993) A new method for predicting positions from historical data. *Journal of Coastal Research*, Vol. 9, No. 1, pp. 147–171.

Granger, C.W. and Joyeux, R. (1980) An introduction to long-memory time series models and fractional differencing. *Journal of Time Series Analysis*, Vol. 1, pp. 15–30.

Green, D.R. and King, S.D. (2003) Progress in geographical information systems and coastal modeling: an overview. In Lakhan, V.C. (ed.) *Advances in Coastal Modelling*, Elsevier Science Publishers, Amsterdam, pp. 553–580.

Hearn, C.J. (2008) *The Dynamics of Coastal Models*, Cambridge University Press, Cambridge.

Hennecke, W.G., Greve, C.A., Cowell, P.J. and Thom, B.G. (2004) GIS-based coastal behaviour modelling and simulation of potential land and property loss: implications of sea-level rise at Collaroy/Narrabeen Beach, Sydney (Australia). *Coastal Management*, Vol. 32, No. 4, pp. 449–470.

Hoefel, F. and Elgar, S. (2003) Wave-induced sediment transport and sandbar migration. *Science*, Vol. 299, No. 5614, pp. 1885–1887.

Kamphuis, J.W. (2002) Alongshore transport of sand. *Proceedings of the 28th International Conference on Coastal Engineering*, ASCE, pp. 2330–2345.

Lai, T.-L. and Wong, S.P.-S. (2006) Combining domain knowledge and statistical models in time series analysis. In Ho, H.-C., Ing, C.-K. and Lai, T.L. (eds) *Time Series and Related Topics*, IMS Lecture Notes – Monograph Series, Vol. 52, Beachwood, OH, pp. 193–209.

Lakhan, V.C. (1981) Parameterizing wave heights in simulation models with auto-correlated Rayleigh distributed variates. *Journal of the International Association of Mathematical Geology*, Vol. 13, No. 4, pp. 345–350.

Lakhan, V.C. (1986) Modelling and simulating the morphological variability of the coastal system, paper presented at the *International Congress on Applied Systems Research and Cybernetics*, Baden-Baden, Germany, 18 August.

Lakhan, V.C. (1989) Modeling and simulation of the coastal system. In Lakhan, V.C. and Trenhaile, A.S. (eds) *Applications in Coastal Modeling*, Elsevier Science Publishers, Amsterdam, pp. 17–42.

Lakhan, V.C. (1994) Planning and development experiences in the coastal zone of Guyana. *Ocean and Coastal Management*, Vol. 12, pp. 1–18.

Lakhan, V.C. (1996) *Introductory Geographical Information Systems*, Summit Press, Etobicoke, CN.

Lakhan, V.C. (ed.) (2003) *Advances in Coastal Modelling*, Elsevier Science Publishers, Amsterdam.

Lakhan, V.C. (2004) Perspectives on special issue papers on coastal morpho-dynamic modelling. *Coastal Engineering*, Vol. 51, pp. 657–660.

Lakhan, V.C. (2005) Time series analysis, in Schwartz, M. (ed.) *Encyclopedia of Coastal Science*, Kluwer Academic Publishers, pp. 1231–1236.

Lakhan, V.C. and Jopling, A.V. (1987) Simulating the effects of random waves on concave-shaped nearshore profiles. *Geografiska Annaler*, Vol. 69 A, No. 2, pp. 251–269.

Lakhan, V.C. and LaValle, P.D. (1992) Simulating the movement of bed and suspended loads in the coastal environment. *Environmental Software*, Vol. 7, pp. 165–173.

Lakhan, V.C. and Pepper, D. (1997) Relationship between concavity and convexity of a coast and erosion and accretion patterns, *Journal of Coastal Research*, Vol. 13, No. 1, pp. 226–232.

Lakhan, V.C., Ahmad, S.R. and Parizanganeh, A. (2006) Investigating shifting mudbanks along a coast subject to cycles of accretion and erosion. In Tubielewicz, A. (ed.) *Coastal Environment, Processes and Evolution*, EURO-COAST, Littoral 2006, Gdansk, Poland.

Lakhan, V.C., Cabana, K. and LaValle, P.D. (2003) Relationship between grain size and heavy metals in sediments from beaches along the coast of Guyana. *Journal of Coastal Research*, Vol. 19, No. 3, pp. 600–608.

LaValle, P.D., Lakhan, V.C. and Trenhaile, A.S. (2001) Space–time series modelling of beach and shoreline data. *Environmental Modelling & Software*, Vol. 16, pp. 299–307.

Nielsen, P. (2006) Sheet flow sediment transport under waves with acceleration skewness and boundary layer streaming. *Coastal Engineering*, Vol. 53, pp. 749–758.

NIST/SEMATECH (2006) *NIST/SEMATECH E-handbook of Statistical Methods, 6.4 Introduction to Time Series Analysis*, National Institute of Standards and Technology, US. Online at: http://www.itl.nist.gov/div898/handbook/pmc/section4/pmc4.htm

Silva, P.A., Temperville, A. and Santos, F.S. (2006) Sand transport under combined current and wave conditions: a semi-unsteady, practical model. *Coastal Engineering*, Vol. 53, pp. 897–913.

Snow, M.M. and Snow, R.K. (2005) GIS modeling and simulation of sea level rise scenarios. In Hamza, M.H. (ed.) *Proceedings of the Fourth Modelling and Simulation Conference IASTED*, International Association of Science and Technology for Development, Acta Press, Calgary, Canada.

Statsoft Inc. (1999) STATISTICA (data analysis software system), version 5.5, Tulsa, OK.

Tang, H.S., Keen, T.R. and Khanbilvardi, R. (2009) A model-coupling framework for nearshore waves, currents, sediment transport, and seabed morphology. *Communications in Nonlinear Science and Numerical Simulation*, Vol. 14, pp. 2935–2947.

Thieler, E.R., Himmelstoss, E.A., Zichichi, J.L. and Miller, T.L. (2005) *Digital Shoreline Analysis System (DSAS) Version 3.0: An ArcGIS© Extension for Calculating Shoreline Change*, Open-File Report 2005-1304, US Geological Survey (USGS), Washington, DC.

Thieler, E.R., Martin, D. and Ergul, A. (2003) *The Digital Shoreline Analysis System, Version 2.0: Shoreline Change Measurement Software Extension for ArcView*, Open-File Report 03-07, US Geological Survey (USGS), Washington, DC.

Tong, H. (1990) *Non-linear Time Series: A Dynamical System Approach*, Clarendon Press, Oxford.

van Rijn, L.C. (2007a) Unified view of sediment transport by currents and waves. I: initiation of motion, bed roughness, and bed-load transport. *Journal of Hydraulic Engineering*, Vol. 133, No. 6, pp. 649–667.

van Rijn, L.C. (2007b) Unified view of sediment transport by currents and waves. II: suspended transport. *Journal of Hydraulic Engineering*, Vol. 133, No. 6, pp. 668–689.

Wheeler, P.J., Coller, M.L.F., Kunapo, J., Peterson, J.A. and McMahon, M. (2008) Facilitating coastal zone inundation awareness using GIS-based scenario modelling and multimedia visualization. *Queensland spatial conference 2008: global warning: what's happening in paradise?* Gold Coast, Queensland, Australia, pp. 17–19.

9

Coastal and marine spatial data infrastructure

R. Longhorn
Director, EC Projects Office, Info-Dynamics Research Associates Ltd, UK

The definition and composition of spatial data infrastructure (SDI) differ widely across the globe. While many of the technical, data-oriented aspects of an SDI are similar between land and coastal geographies, important differences exist regarding other coastal/marine SDI (CSDI) components, such as priority data themes and the need to integrate disparate datasets, governance of information assets, the nature and composition of stakeholder groups, legislation and regulation, and trans-border issues. Yet access to informed use of multiple datasets is key to efficient coastal zone management.

9.1   Introduction

Effective management of the coastal zone and allied marine resources requires the ability to discover and use multiple datasets, often created by different departments and disciplines, for different purposes, in different formats and with different access and use/re-use policies. Resolving these differences is one of the main drivers for creating spatial data infrastructure (SDI)[i] at national, regional (trans-national) and global levels. Definitions for the term 'spatial data infrastructure' vary across countries and regions, and across disciplines and sectors even within a single nation.[ii] With more than 100 SDI initiatives in progress across the globe (Crompvoets *et al.*, 2004), this complicates direct comparison of the success or failure of any single initiative. NSDI initiatives tend to address geospatial information infrastructure needs with a terrestrial, land-based focus, often ignoring the specific needs for a joined-up, land–sea coastal and marine information environment. Thus, few nations have engaged in developing specific coastal SDI

(CSDI)[iii] components within their national SDI (NSDI) programmes. Before looking at some of those initiatives, we ask what is special about a 'coastal' SDI.

9.2   Why coastal SDI?

The coastal zone is a difficult area to manage due to overlapping physical geography and hydrography (offshore, near shore, shoreline, inshore), multiple legal jurisdictions and legal mandates covering similar zones, differing remits of government agencies working in the same zones, competing needs of stakeholders (often with diverse data policies) and temporal issues (tides and seasons). Thus, conflict resolution in this complex piece of real-estate called the 'coast' is one of the justifications for giving special attention to the coast within NSDI initiatives. The original impetus for the few national CSDI initiatives that do exist was the need for better management of coastal/marine environments, with regard to pollution control, flooding, marine resource management (near-shore and off-shore), coastal urban development, water management, etc. More recently, concerns over a range of climate change issues that impact on the coastal zone and marine environment, and for which these environments (especially oceanic) may affect climate change, have added new impetus to the need for harmonised, joined-up information in the coastal and marine realms.

Governments have failed to deliver integrated coastal information for several reasons. Historically, the coast was viewed as a strategic line of defence, not as a strategic component of environmental or economic policy, a viewpoint that is changing, but gradually. The coast is no longer viewed as the place where you defend the nation, where land meets the sea, from which an enemy might arrive, but rather as a source of multiple income streams to enrich a national economy – and the lives of citizens who use coastal areas in many ways. Most importantly, while the coast is the land–sea interface, it does not have its own 'management' agency. It is 'owned' partly by everyone and totally by no one. Hydrographic survey offices looked after the marine aspects of 'coastal' information, concentrating mainly on nautical navigation requirements. National mapping or cadastre agencies were responsible for diverse types of landward geospatial datasets, often in isolation from their hydrographic counterparts. Geological surveys were typically involved with subsurface geographies, becoming involved in offshore or near-shore geology in special cases, e.g. mineral exploration. Finally, integrating 'coastal' information is a complex and

207

costly enterprise, as evidenced by the fact that no totally integrated, fully harmonised, land–sea datasets exist today. Even in the UK, where this is being attempted by a privatised arm of the national hydrographic survey office, the work is done mainly on a commissioned basis, one piece of coastline at a time, based on specific client demand.

Although advances in geospatial data interoperability initiatives can help alleviate certain technical data sharing barriers, they have no impact on the more serious and far less easily resolved political and jurisdictional barriers inherent in government departmental infrastructures, hierarchies, and the resulting silos of expertise and authority, globally. This is where the non-technical components of an SDI definition come into play, e.g. data policies, intellectual property rights, government cost recovery regimes, governance and custodianship of important national datasets, capacity building to help adapt to new technologies (geoweb technologies, mashups, etc.) and organisational issues.

Governance issues are especially difficult to resolve easily, partly due to the inherent nature of the coast as an area that is typically in a state of flux, physically, and where there is little consistency across nations as to who is 'in charge' of the coast, if anyone. What should be the relatively simple act of acquiring an up-to-date dataset of physical characteristics of a section of coastline typically requires contact with at least a national mapping agency and hydrographic survey office, plus perhaps the geological survey. From these agencies, three quite types of data (themes) will be offered, typically at scales that do not match, quality that is inconsistent (e.g. certain data types being updated much more frequently that others), and data access and sharing policies that may not be harmonised.

It is the hope of those who work in the coastal zone, regardless of how that 'zone' is defined, that by including in national SDIs the important types of data relevant to coastal research and management, at least some of these complexities and barriers will be removed. What progress towards that ultimate goal has been achieved in those few countries that have tried to address the information infrastructure needs of coastal and marine communities so far? The next two sections of this chapter look at one of the earlier national CSDI initiatives, in the US, to see how it has developed over the years, and at a fledgling CSDI, in the UK, to give an impression of the level of detail and involvement in national SDI initiatives required of the coastal and marine stakeholder communities. Note that significant work in coastal SDI strategy, specification and development has also been accomplished in Canada, within their national SDI programme, GeoConnections (Poulin and Gillespie, 2001).

9.3   Coastal SDI in the US

A legally mandated NSDI initiative began in the US in April 1994 with
a Presidential Executive Order (Clinton, 1994) that addressed creation,
harmonisation and promulgation of technical standards by which all
federal geospatial information could be recorded. This task fell to the
Federal Geographic Data Committee (FGDC), created in 1990, with
metadata high on its list of priorities, so that existing spatial data
resources could be identified, accessed and used. Responsibilities for
NSDI implementation for all federal agencies in the US was set out in
the revised OMB Circular A-16 in 2002 (OMB, 2002). Legal aspects
of data access, sharing, use and re-use were less of an impediment in
the USA than has been the case in many other jurisdictions, mainly
because of existence of the US Freedom of Information Act which
places most government generated data in the public domain, i.e. without
any intellectual property rights protection. Progress on implementing the
US NSDI has been slower than expected. What many fail to realise – or
remember – is that the provisions of the Executive Order apply only to
federal data, not to data at other levels of government (state, county,
locality), nor do the freedom of information provisions apply automatically to other than federal data. Data themes in the US NSDI
with particular relevance to coastal stakeholders are shown in Box 9.1.

OMB Circular A-16, as revised 19 August 2002, also states that
(OMB, 2002):

> The components of the NSDI are data themes, metadata, the
> National Spatial Data Clearinghouse, standards, and partnerships ...
> (this) Circular requires the development, maintenance, and dis-
> semination of a standard core set of digital spatial information for
> the Nation that will serve as a foundation for users of geographic
> information.
>
>   Spatial data is a national capital asset. The NSDI facilitates
> efficient collection, sharing, and dissemination of spatial data
> among all levels of government institutions, as well as the public
> and private sectors, to address issues affecting the Nation's
> physical, economic, and social well-being. A coordinated approach
> for developing spatial data standards that apply to collecting,
> maintaining, distributing, using, and preservation of data will
> improve the quality of federal spatial data and reduce the cost of
> derivative products created by federal and non-federal users.
> Applications using spatial data that adhere to FGDC standards
> enable cost effective public and private policy development,

Box 9.1 US NSDI *data themes relevant to coastal/marine communities*

Baseline (maritime) – the line from which maritime zones and limits are measured.

Cadastral (offshore) – the land management system used on the outer continental shelf, extending from the baseline to the extent of US jurisdiction.

Climate – data describing the spatial and temporal characteristics of the Earth's atmosphere/hydrosphere/land surface system, both model-generated and observed (either in situ or remotely sensed) environmental information.

Elevation bathymetric – bathymetric data for inland and inter-coastal waterways is highly accurate bathymetric sounding information collected to ensure that federal navigation channels are maintained to their authorised depths. Bathymetric survey activities support the Nation's critical nautical charting programme. This data are also used to create electronic navigational charts. The bathymetric sounding data support the elevation layer of the geospatial data framework.

Federal land ownership status – land ownership status includes the establishment and maintenance of a system for the storage and dissemination of information describing all title, estate or interest of the federal government in a parcel of real and mineral property.

Flood hazards – the National Flood Insurance Program has prepared flood hazard data for approximately 18 000 communities.

Hydrography – includes surface water features such as lakes, ponds, streams and rivers, canals, oceans and coastlines. Each hydrography feature is assigned a permanent feature identification code (Environmental Protection Agency Reach Code) and may also be identified by a feature name. Spatial positions of features are encoded as centrelines and polygons. Also encoded is network connectivity and direction of flow.

Marine boundaries – depict offshore waters and sea beds over which the US has sovereignty and jurisdiction.

Offshore minerals – minerals occurring in submerged lands, such as oil, gas, sulphur, gold, sand and gravel, and manganese.

Outer Continental Shelf submerged lands – lands covered by water at any stage of the tide, as distinguished from tidelands, which are attached to the mainland or an island and cover and uncover with the tide. Tidelands presuppose a high-water line as the upper boundary; whereas submerged lands do not.

Shoreline – the intersection of the land with the water surface. The shoreline shown on NOAA (National Oceanic and Atmospheric Administration) charts represents the line of contact between the land and a selected water elevation. In areas affected by tidal fluctuations, this line of contact is the mean high water line.

Transportation (marine) – the Navigation Channel Framework consists of highly accurate dimensions for every federal navigation channel maintained by US Army Corps of Engineers. The Navigation Framework provides the basis for the marine transportation theme of the geospatial data framework.

Watershed boundaries – encodes hydrologic, watershed boundaries into topographically defined sets of drainage areas, organised in a nested hierarchy by size, and based on a standard hydrologic unit coding system.

Wetlands – provides the classification, location, and extent of wetlands and deepwater habitats, with no attempt to define the proprietary limits or jurisdictional wetland boundaries of any federal, state, or local agencies.

management, and operations.... Implementation of this Circular is essential to help federal agencies eliminate duplication, avoid redundant expenditures, reduce resources spent on unfunded mandates, accelerate the development of electronic government to meet the needs and expectations of citizens and agency programmatic mandates, and improve the efficiency and effectiveness of public management.

An early driver for the US coastal SDI initiative was to identify, and provide access to, the basic reference data needed to achieve goals for national programmes such as the Clean Water Action Plan – Coastal Research and Monitoring Strategy, which represented 'the first effort to integrate coastal monitoring and research activities on a national scale to provide thorough, cross-cutting assessments of the health of the nation's coastal resources' (CRMSW, 2000). Goals in the strategy included:

- improving monitoring programs for integration at national level
- integrating interagency research efforts
- conducting national and regional coastal assessments, and
- improving data management.

Later reports from the USA (Pew Oceans Commission, 2003; US Commission on Ocean Policy, 2004; Joint Oceans Commission Initiative,[iv] 2009a, 2009b) describe the strong coupling that exists between terrestrial, coastal and oceanic environments, for which harmonised information is needed in order to properly manage the physical environment as a whole, across multiple disciplines. These reviews continue to highlight the need for better integration of land and marine datasets. The US Commission on Ocean Policy mid-term report in 2002 found a tight connection between inland systems for development and agriculture to areas traditionally designated as coastal. 'The coastal zone is not a narrow band. It's the whole country' (US Commission on Ocean Policy, 2002). A 2004 report of the US National Research Council's Committee on National Needs for Coastal Mapping and Charting identified 11 recommendations regarding the requirement for, and benefits from, implementing a geospatial framework in the USA for the coastal zone (National Research Council, 2004).

The US CSDI, now embedded within the wider NSDI initiative, is led by the Coastal Services Centre (CSC) of the National Oceanic and Atmospheric Administration (NOAA). CSC participates in nine of the 13 FGDC Subcommittees, seven of the 11 FGDC Working Groups, and chairs the FGDC Marine and Coastal Spatial Data Subcommittee, the Geodetic Control Subcommittee, and co-chairs the Marine Boundary Working Group. The Marine and Coastal Spatial Data Subcommittee came into existence in 1996 with the mission to develop and promote the marine and coastal components of the NSDI so that 'current and accurate geospatial coastal and ocean data will be readily available to contribute locally, nationally, and globally to economic growth, environmental quality and stability, and social progress' (NOAA, 2007). The vision for the marine and coastal NSDI is that current and accurate geospatial coastal and ocean data will be readily available to contribute locally, nationally and globally to economic growth, environmental quality and stability, and social progress. The subcommittee, through its member agencies and the FGDC, is working to develop strategic partnerships, relevant standards, and to provide outreach that will enhance access to and utility of coastal and ocean framework data.

The original coastal SDI vision promulgated in 2001 by CSC was based on four goals relating to the NSDI (NOAA, 2001). These were:

- The coastal management community should understand and embrace the vision, concepts and benefits of the NSDI.
- Spatial coastal and marine framework data should be readily available to the coastal management community.
- Technologies to facilitate discovery, collection, description, access and preservation of spatial data should be widely available to the coastal management community.
- NOAA should help develop and implement spatial data applications to meet the needs of the coastal and marine communities.

The main elements of the NSDI that NOAA/CSC promote in regard to marine and coastal SDI are bathymetry, shoreline identification and marine cadastre, although other data types are obviously of interest, e.g. coastal imagery, marine navigation, tidal benchmarks and habitats. Marine cadastre standards are developed by the FGDC Marine Boundary Working Group (MBWG), co-chaired by NOAA-CSC and the Department of the Interior's Minerals Management Service (MMS). The MBWG was formed in 2001 to address issues relating to the legal and technical aspects of marine boundaries, with the goal to alleviate cross-agency problems concerning marine boundaries, plus provide outreach, standards development, partnerships, and other data development critical to the NSDI. A major product of the MBWG work to date is the FGDC's Shoreline Metadata Profile (FGDC, 2001).

Further standards under development include the National Shoreline Data Content Standard (FGDC, 2007), the Coastal and Marine Ecological Classification Standard (FGDC, 2008) and the Wetlands Mapping Standards (FGDC, 2009).

9.4   Coastal SDI developments in the UK

UK CSDI development began under the Inter-Agency Committee for Science and Technology (IACMST), which was replaced in 2008 by the MSCC – Marine Science Coordination Committee. Access to important UK sources of marine environmental data is by way of multiple MSCC member organisations and the UK Marine Environmental Data Action Group (MEDAG). A separate, but complementary activity, the Marine Data and Information Partnership (MDIP), provides a coordinating framework for managing marine data and information to facilitate improved management of the seas around the UK. Yet both of these programmes focus more on off-shore or near-shore data resources, as opposed to truly harmonised coastal datasets. Many UK agencies with marine information interests belong to both MEDAG and MDIP, presenting a slightly confusing picture as to what actually comprises a UK coastal/marine SDI. This is further complicated by including of marine and coastal data layers in the UK's Digital National Framework initiative, which purports to offer 'an industry standard for integrating and sharing business and geographic information from multiple sources' (DNF, 2008).

The UK Hydrographic Office sponsored a seminar investigating development of a UK Marine Geospatial Data Infrastructure (MGDI) in July 2003, following the success of the Integrated Coastal Zone Mapping pilot project (ICZMap) that aimed to 'create the first ever unified digital base map combining both onshore and offshore features' (Ordnance Survey, 2001). UKHO felt that an MGDI was needed to overcome various information barriers existing in the UK in regard to marine data, including disparate, incomplete and inconsistent data; lack of metadata (information about data); ad hoc dissemination methods; disparate data policies; and no 'joining up' of existing data resources.

Some coastal zone stakeholders expressed concern that the UK MGDI should encompass more than traditional hydrographic office charting and bathymetric data linked to land-based topographic data from the mapping agency. The UK MGDI should provide an electronic based service for geographic and geo-referenced thematic data underpinned by framework data from authoritative sources, assuring quality. The MGDI should provide a 'thematic hub with information about water depths, currents, tides, channel widths, seabed texture, sediment characteristics, temperature, wrecks, pipelines, cables, seabed obstructions, fish stocks, coastal terrestrial data, etc.; allow people to make better decisions (such as planning and protecting vital resources); (and) allow extraction of data from diverse sources, blend it and come up with original perspectives and innovative solutions' (Pepper, 2003).

Benefits from implementing a UK MGDI are seen as: better connection of the public sector and commercial sector by way of geospatial technology; bringing together expertise and technology to stimulate development of new applications and services; providing better metadata permitting easier discovery of existing data resources and linking to these resources; promoting data exchange and trading under various business models and supporting the Digital National Framework for all geospatial information in the UK. The MGDI architecture would encompass coastal management data, historical data, estates data, hydrographic data, marine protected areas and habitats, fisheries data, oceanographic data, geological and seismic data plus topographic data.

The suggested way forward to develop a UK MGDI includes: auditing current data holdings; identifying data capture requirements; defining the different roles of various types of coastal/marine data stakeholders; establishing and publicising metadata hub (catalogues); creating a formal Marine Geospatial Data Working Group that would interact with other agencies creating the UK's national SDI; creating 'centres of excellence' in use of marine/coastal geospatial data and services; establishing transparent data exchange and trading mechanisms and appropriate dissemination methodologies. It has been recognised from the outset that the commercial sector must be involved from the beginning of the initiative. Currently, government funding routes are being explored.

9.5 European regional coastal and marine SDI developments

In Europe, coastal zone management is seen as a key function of the Integrated Maritime Policy for Europe and the European Union (European Commission, 2007a) and the Marine Spatial Planning instrument within that policy. Access to harmonised marine and coastal information also figures largely in development of the EU's Shared Environmental Information System (SEIS) (European Commission, 2008). Both these initiatives claim dependency on continued development of the INSPIRE European SDI (European Commission, 2007b) to create the level of harmonisation needed to be able to discover, access and integrate disparate datasets that cross borders, cross disciplines and cover multiple data themes. The INSPIRE Directive goes much further than all but the most advanced national SDI implementation plans, in setting legal requirements that apply to spatial data sets (any data with a location attribute) at all levels of government, not just federal data, as in the USA. It also defines and promulgates very specific technical specifications for metadata, data and services, to current international standards set by the International Standards Organisation (ISO) and the Open Geospatial Consortium, Inc. (OGC).

215

Because the European Union's INSPIRE Directive to create a pan-European SDI is the only regional initiative that legally requires sovereign states (the 27 EU member states) to implement a wide range of SDI components, it is worth looking more closely at it in regard to how coastal SDI, as a separate theme, is catered for in its implementation – or not, as the case may be. INSPIRE defines 34 data themes spread over three 'Annexes' which determine the priority (timetable) within which the Directive's various rules and regulations must be brought into affect for each theme. Some themes are quite broadly defined, such as 'Area management/restriction/regulation zones and reporting units', which includes coastal zone management along with waste dumps, noise restriction zones, etc.

This legal Directive provides for 'implementing rules', which are also legally enforceable in all EU member states, developed by experts with agreement of a regulatory committee containing appointed representatives from all the states. These rules cover metadata standards and content, data harmonisation and interoperability specifications for all themes, various types of services (including performance criteria), data access and sharing principles, and monitoring performance of the SDI, its cost and impact. It is important that members of the different coastal and marine stakeholder communities be involved in creating the implementing rules, otherwise special characteristics of this otherwise generic SDI that are important for coastal SDI needs may be overlooked. This is equally true for national SDI initiatives, yet only a very few of the NSDIs now under development appear to have any special input from the coastal/ marine community.

Of the 34 data themes covered by the INSPIRE Directive, Boxes 9.2 and 9.3 indicate the 22 themes considered to be most applicable to the coastal and marine communities either directly or indirectly. The data specifications for the 34 INSPIRE data themes are being developed by Thematic Working Groups (TWGs), comprising thematic experts, working under guidance of the European Commission's Directorate General Joint Research Centre in Ispra, Italy (see: http://inspire.jrc.ec. europa.eu). It is important to note that, unlike other regional and even many national SDI initiatives, the components of the pan-European SDI are legally mandated by the European Union institutions. Thus, European Union member states must enact legislation and/or regulations implementing the specifications and standards developed within INSPIRE, according to a set timetable – one that currently stretches to 2019.

Box 9.2 INSPIRE data themes of direct relevance to coastal information needs

Annex I

Hydrography – hydrographic elements, including marine areas and all other water bodies and items related to them, including river basins and sub-basins.

Protected sites – area designated or managed within a framework of international, Community and Member States' legislation to achieve specific conservation objectives.

Annex II

Elevation – digital elevation models for land, ice and ocean surface. Includes terrestrial elevation, bathymetry and shoreline.

Annex III

Area management/restriction/regulation zones and reporting units – areas managed, regulated or used for reporting at international, European, national, regional and local levels. Includes dumping sites, restricted areas around drinking water sources, nitrate-vulnerable zones, regulated fairways at sea or large inland waters, areas for the dumping of waste, noise restriction zones, prospecting and mining permit areas, river basin districts, relevant reporting units and coastal zone management areas.

Agricultural and aquaculture facilities – farming equipment and production facilities (including irrigation systems, greenhouses and stables).

Environmental monitoring facilities – location and operation of environmental monitoring facilities includes observation and measurement of emissions, of the state of environmental media and of other ecosystem parameters (biodiversity, ecological conditions of vegetation, etc.) by or on behalf of public authorities.

Natural risk zones – vulnerable areas characterised according to natural hazards (all atmospheric, hydrologic, seismic, volcanic and wildfire phenomena that, because of their location, severity and frequency, have the potential to seriously affect society), e.g. floods, landslides and subsidence, avalanches, forest fires, earthquakes, volcanic eruptions.

Oceanographic geographical features – physical conditions of oceans (currents, salinity, wave heights, etc.).

Sea regions – physical conditions of seas and saline water bodies divided into regions and sub-regions with common characteristics.

Energy resources – energy resources including hydrocarbons, hydropower, bio-energy, solar, wind, etc., where relevant including depth/height information on the extent of the resource.

Mineral resources – mineral resources including metal ores, industrial minerals, etc., where relevant, including depth/height information on the extent of the resource.

Box 9.3 INSPIRE data themes of indirect relevance to coastal information needs

Annex I

Coordinate reference systems – systems for uniquely referencing spatial information in space as a set of coordinates (x, y, z) and/or latitude and longitude and height, based on a geodetic horizontal and vertical datum.

Geographical grid systems – harmonised multi-resolution grid with a common point of origin and standardised location and size of grid cells.

Annex II

Land cover – physical and biological cover of the Earth's surface including artificial surfaces, agricultural areas, forests, (semi-) natural areas, wetlands, water bodies.

Geology – geology characterised according to composition and structure, including bedrock, aquifers and geomorphology.

Annex III

Land use – territory characterised according to its current and future planned functional dimension or socio-economic purpose (e.g. residential, industrial, commercial, agricultural, forestry, recreational).

Human health and safety – geographical distribution of dominance of pathologies (allergies, cancers, respiratory diseases, etc.), information indicating the effect on health (biomarkers, decline of fertility, epidemics) or well-being of humans (fatigue, stress, etc.) linked directly (air pollution, chemicals, depletion of the ozone layer, noise, etc.) or indirectly (food, genetically modified organisms, etc.) to the quality of the environment.

Utility and governmental services – includes utility facilities such as sewage, waste management, energy supply and water supply, administrative and social governmental services such as public administrations, civil protection sites, schools and hospitals.

Production and industrial facilities – industrial production sites, including installations covered by Council Directive 96/61/EC of 24 September 1996 concerning integrated pollution prevention and control and water abstraction facilities, mining, storage sites.

Bio-geographical regions – areas of relatively homogeneous ecological conditions with common characteristics.

Habitats and biotopes – geographical areas characterised by specific ecological conditions, processes, structure, and (life support) functions that physically support the organisms that live there. Includes terrestrial and aquatic areas distinguished by geographical, abiotic and biotic features, whether entirely natural or semi-natural.

Species distribution – geographical distribution of occurrence of animal and plant species aggregated by grid, region, administrative unit or other analytical unit.

In many cases, the type of input and advice needed from the coastal community, directed to the various data specification TWGs, relates to ensuring that coastal information needs are not forgotten, for example in setting boundaries – in three dimensions and even in time – regarding aquaculture facilities, risk zones, location of offshore energy platforms or mineral extraction sources, etc. Hydrography, elevation (bathymetry and shoreline) and area management zones (including CZM) are the most obvious data themes where direct involvement of a coastal information expert on the relevant TWG would be useful.

While the themes in Box 9.3 do not appear to have direct relation to coastal information needs, the data to be harmonised within these themes relate to events, activities or features that do also affect or occur in the coastal zone and where any peculiarities relating to the physical nature of the coastal zone needs properly to be taken into account.

9.6   Global marine SDI initiatives

A prototype global oceanographic SDI exists in the form of agreed data collection, formatting, exchange and policy standards and guidelines from the Intergovernmental Oceanographic Commission (IOC) of UNESCO, by way of its Committee on International Oceanographic Data and Information Exchange (IODE) (Longhorn, 2002). While the data interchange collaboration work of IOC's IODE programme has been ongoing for several decades, specification of equivalent coastal SDIs at national level began much more recently. Marine SDI developments within the hydrographic community also received new impetus with formation of the International Hydrographic Organisation's Marine Spatial Data Infrastructure Working Group (http://www.iho-ohi.net/english/committees-wg/hssc/msdiwg.html) in May 2007, which held its inaugural meeting in February 2008 (Osborne and Pepper, 2008; IHO, 2008). The IHO is also developing a new Geospatial Standard for Hydrographic Data (S-100), which will 'support a greater variety of hydrographic-related digital data sources, products, and customers. This includes imagery and gridded data, and new applications that go beyond the scope of traditional hydrography (for example, high-density bathymetry, seafloor classification, marine GIS, etc.). It will also support the use of web-based services for acquiring, processing, analysing, accessing, and presenting data' (IHB, 2008).

9.7   Lessons learned and future trends in coastal/marine SDI development

The current global preoccupation with the impact of climate change, especially on coastal communities threatened with flooding and storm surges due to forecast sea level rise, should generate new interest – and impetus – in addressing coastal and marine SDI implementation issues more fully than in the past. However, the complex nature of coastal regions, where land and sea meet not only physically but also jurisdictionally, environmentally and culturally, creates practical barriers to more rapid development of CSDI components.

Today, CSDI development typically occurs under the umbrella of national SDI initiatives, albeit driven by a separate coastal/marine stakeholder group, e.g. in the US, Canada, Australia, etc. Former independent approaches, such as in the UK, where their MGDI initiative began life in the absence of an agreed national SDI strategy, are now being absorbed into national SDI programmes, in this case a marine component for the Digital National Framework (DNF, 2008). This trend is likely to continue in the future, especially as nascent national SDI initiatives gain momentum and have established coastal/marine SDI examples from existing initiatives on which to reflect and gain experience.

In most NSDI initiatives, there is evidence that only the more obvious data needs are being considered, e.g. shoreline, hydrography/bathymetry and cadastre or boundaries are included in the basic framework or reference data themes. Other important elements, such as marine habitat and nautical navigation, do not fit well within these primarily land-focused NSDI specifications. Efficient planning for, and monitoring and management of, coastal and marine environments – physical, cultural, and economic – take on greater importance, due partly to climate change impacts already mentioned, but also because of the current trend for general population movements to coastal regions.

We should not forget that data issues are only one aspect of SDI definition and implementation strategy. Institutional, organisational, jurisdictional, policy and interoperability issues also figure high on the agenda. Awareness and political will are required to tackle these non-technical barriers.

We see in the example of the pan-European SDI (INSPIRE) that coastal/marine geospatial data are accommodated within the many data themes to be covered by this trans-national Directive, yet there is no specific focus on 'coastal SDI' issues as such, e.g. multi-jurisdictional issues. Development of what is to become a widely implemented, mandated, standardised regional (multi-national) SDI took more than 12 years to reach the stage of the INSPIRE Directive. Adoption of the legal Directive took another two years and full implementation is scheduled to run through 2019, although many experts already expect that this date will also be pushed further into the future. This simply highlights that an SDI is more akin to a process than a thing that one can simply call into being – and a process that evolves over time, as technology and information culture itself changes with time.

The UK CSDI initiative initially addressed concerns from the UK Department for Environment, Food and Rural Affairs (DEFRA)

Marine Stewardship Report (DEFRA, 2002) which includes an environmental policy goal of 'clean, healthy, safe, productive and biologically diverse oceans and seas'. The pan-European INSPIRE initiative received its earliest legal mandate from the EU institutions as a direct result of the EU Water Framework Directive (European Commission, 2000). As fresh-water management and scarcity become ever more serious problems at global level, we can expect many more nations to underpin their fledgling CSDI/MGDI initiatives with political support and funding directly related to this critical issue.

Defining marine boundaries remains a difficult task, not only in the physical sense, but also in the jurisdictional (legal) sense. Take, for example, the definition of the coastal 'boundary' as used in the Intergovernmental Oceanographic Commission's original Coastal Ocean Observations Panel scoping statement (IOC, 2002): 'Although the emphasis will be on coastal ecosystems (e.g. estuaries, bays, sounds, fjords, open waters of the continental shelf), boundaries should be determined by the problems being addressed and the products that are to be produced.' This indicates that new ways of thinking about coastal information may be needed in the future, i.e. focusing more on its uses and purposes rather than on its format or delivery mechanisms.

Notes

i   The term 'spatial data infrastructure' in common use today supersedes prior terminology, such as 'geographic information infrastructure' and 'geospatial data infrastructure', even though the latter term is sometimes used today in regard to specific national coastal/marine SDI initiatives, e.g. in the UK and Canada.

ii The European Union's INSPIRE Directive for establishing a regional, multi-national SDI across Europe defines 'infrastructure for spatial information' as '... metadata, spatial data sets and spatial data services; network services and technologies; agreements on sharing, access and use; and coordination and monitoring mechanisms, processes and procedures...'. This encompasses the main components contained in most SDI definitions (European Commission, 2007b).

iii In some nations, the term marine geospatial data infrastructure (MGDI) is used versus CSDI. We will continue to use the single abbreviation CSDI throughout the text, rather than the more cumbersome CSDI/MGDI.

iv The Joint Ocean Commission Initiative (JOCI) [http://www.jointoceancommission.org] combines the activities of the former US government Commission on Ocean Policy (whose remit expired in December 2004) [http://www.oceancommission.gov] and the Pew Oceans Commission.

References

Clinton, W. (1994) Executive Order 12906, April 13, 1994, *Federal Register*, Vol. 59, No. 720, pp. 1771–17674.

CRMSW (2000) *Clean Water Action Plan: Coastal Research and Monitoring Strategy.* Coastal Research and Monitoring Strategy Workgroup. September 2000. Online at: http://water.usgs.gov/owq/cleanwater/coastalresearch/index.html

Crompvoets, J., Rajabifard, A., Bregt, A. and Williamson, I. (2004) Assessing the worldwide developments of national spatial data clearinghouses. *International Journal of GIS*, Vol. 18, pp. 1–25.

DEFRA (2002) *Marine Stewardship Report – Safeguarding Our Seas: A Strategy for the Conservation and Sustainable Development of our Marine Environment.* Department for Environment, Food & Rural Affairs, London. Online at: http://www.defra.gov.uk/marine/pdf/environment/marine_stewardship.pdf

DNF (2008) *The Digital National Framework.* For further information, see online at: http://www.dnf.org/Pages/home/default.asp

European Commission (2000) Directive 2000/60/EC of the European Parliament and of the Council of 23 October 2000 establishing a framework for Community action in the field of water policy. *Official Journal of the European Communities*, Vol. 2000, L327/1.

European Commission (2007a) *An Integrated Maritime Policy for the European Union.* Office for Official Publications, Luxembourg. Online at: http://ec.europa.eu/maritimeaffairs/policy_documents_en.html

European Commission (2007b) Directive 2007/2/EC of the European Parliament and the Council of 14 March 2007 establishing an Infrastructure for Spatial Information in the European Community (INSPIRE). *Official Journal of the European Communities*, Vol. 2007, L108/1. Online at: http://eur-lex.europa.eu/LexUriServ/LexUriServ.do?uri=OJ:L:2007:108:0001:0014:EN:PDF

European Commission (2008) *Communication from the Commission to the Council, the European Parliament, the European Economic and Social Committee and the Committee for the Regions – Towards a Shared Environmental Information System (SEIS)*, COM(2008) 46 final, Brussels, 1.2.2008. Office of Official Publications, Luxembourg. Online at: http://eur-lex.europa.eu/LexUriServ/LexUriServ.do?uri=COM:2008:0046:FIN:EN:PDF

FGDC (2001) *Shoreline Metadata Profile of the Content Standards for Digital Geospatial Metadata,* Marine and Coastal Spatial Data Subcommittee of the Federal Geographic Data Committee, Reston, VA, FGDC-STD-001.2-2001. Online at: http://www.csc.noaa.gov/metadata/sprofile.pdf

FGDC (2007) *National Shoreline Data Content Standard,* Federal Geographic Data Committee, Reston, VA. Online at: http://www.fgdc.gov/standards/projects/FGDC-standards-projects/shoreline-data-content/200701_ShorelineDataContentStandard.doc

FGDC (2008) *Coastal and Marine Ecological Classification Standard.* Federal Geographic Data Committee, Reston, VA. Online at: http://www.fgdc.gov/standards/projects/FGDC-standards-projects/cmecs-folder/FGDC%20Classification%20Proposal%20Final.doc

FGDC (2009) *Final Draft Wetlands Mapping Standard,* FGDC Wetlands Subcommittee, Federal Geographic Data Committee, Reston, VA. Online at:

http://www.fgdc.gov/standards/projects/FGDC-standards-projects/wetlands-mapping/FinalDraft_FGDC_WetlandsMappingStandard_2009-01.pdf

IHB (2008) *IHO Geospatial Standard for Hydrographic Data, Version 0.0.0 – January 2008.* International Hydrographic Bureau, Monaco, Special Publication No. 100. Online at: http://www.iho.int/COMMITTEES/CHRIS/TSMAD/S-100-Feb08.zip. Accessed 21/04/2009.

IHO (2008) *Marine Spatial Data Infrastructure Working Group (MSDIWG) Terms of Reference*, International Hydrographic Organization, IHB, Monaco. Online at: http://www.iho.shom.fr/COMMITTEES/CHRIS/MSDIWG/MSDIWG-TOR.pdf

IOC (2002) *Coastal Ocean Observations Panel: Scope of COOP*, Intergovernmental Oceanographic Commission, UNESCO, Paris.

Joint Oceans Commission Initiative (2009a) *Changing Oceans, Changing World: Ocean Priorities for the Obama Administration and Congress*, Meridian Institute, Washington, DC. Online at: http://www.jointoceancommission.org/resource-center/1-Reports/2009-04-07_JOCI_Changing_Oceans,_Changing_ World.pdf

Joint Oceans Commission Initiative (2009b) *One Coast, One Future: Securing the Health of West Coast Ecosystems and Economies*, Meridian Institute, Washington, DC. Online at: http://www.jointoceancommission.org/resource-center/1-Reports/2009-01-15_One_Coast_One_Future.pdf

Longhorn, R. (2002) Global Spatial Data sharing frameworks: the case of the Inter-governmental Oceanographic Commission (IOC). *Proceedings of GSDI-6*, Budapest, Hungary, 16–19 September. Online at: http://www.gsdidocs.org/gsdiconf/GSDI-6/Stream1/Wednesday_11hr/Roger_Longhorn/longhorn_gsdi6_paper.pdf.

National Research Council (2004) *A Geospatial Framework for the Coastal Zone: National Needs for Coastal Mapping and Charting*, National Academies Press, Washington, DC. Online at: http://www.nap.edu/openbook.php?isbn=0309091764

NOAA (2001) *Coastal NSDI*, National Oceanic and Atmospheric Agency, Coastal Services Center, Charleston, SC.

NOAA (2007) *FGDC 2007 – 2008 Work Plan – Marine and Coastal Spatial Data Subcommittee*, National Oceanic and Atmospheric Agency, Charleston, SC. Online at: http://www.csc.noaa.gov/mcsd/2007_2008_workplan_fgdc.pdf

OMB (2009) *Circular No. A–16 Revised, August 19, 2002*, Office of Management and Budget, Washington, DC. Online at: http://www.whitehouse.gov/omb/circulars/a016/a016_rev.html

Ordnance Survey (2001) *ISB Project 195 – ICZMap Project Manager's Project Completion Report.* Ordnance Survey, Southampton. Online at: http://www.seazone.com/files/finalreport.pdf

Osborne, M. and Pepper, J. (2008) Marine SDI and the International Hydro-graphic Community. *IHO/CHRIS Marine Spatial Data Infrastructure Working Group (MSDIWG) Meeting*, IHB, Monaco, 4–5 February. Online at: http://www.iho-ohi.net/mtg_docs/com_wg/MSDIWG/MSDIWG1/MSDIWG1-3A_Marine_SDI_Paper_for_IHO_271106.pdf

Pepper, J. (2003) 'Unlocking the treasure!' – towards a marine geospatial data infrastructure. *Proceedings of the Marine Geospatial Data Industry Seminar*, UKHO, 1–2 July. UK Hydrographic Office: Taunton.

Pew Oceans Commission (2003) *America's Living Oceans: Charting a Course for Sea Change. A Report to the Nation*, Pew Oceans Commission, Arlington, VA, May. Online at http://www.pewtrusts.org/uploadedFiles/wwwpewtrustsorg/ Reports/Protecting_ocean_life/env_pew_oceans_final_report.pdf.

Poulin, M. and Gillespie, R. (2001) MGDI: information infrastructure for the maritime community. 14th CHRIS Meeting, Shanghai, China, 15–17 August. Online at: http://www.iho.shom.fr/COMMITTEES/CHRIS/CHRIS/CHRIS14/ CHRIS-14-5B.pdf

US Commission on Ocean Policy (2002) *Developing a National Ocean Policy: Mid-term Report*, September, Washington, DC. Online at: http://oceancommission.gov/ documents/midterm_report/midterm_report.html

US Commission on Ocean Policy (2004) *An Ocean Blueprint for the 21st Century: Final Report*, Washington, DC. Online at: http://oceancommission.gov/documents/ full_color_rpt/000_ocean_full_report.pdf

Web references

US coastal SDI links

Coastal Services Center, NOAA – http://www.csc.noaa.gov
FGDC Marine and Coastal Spatial Data Subcommittee –
    http://www.csc.noaa.gov/mcsd/
FGDC Marine Boundary Working Group – http://www.csc.noaa.gov/mbwg/
Joint Oceans Commission Initiative – http://www.jointoceancommission.org
US Commission on Ocean Policy – http://oceancommission.gov

UK coastal SDI links

UK Digital National Framework – http://www.dnf.org
UK Marine Science Coordination Committee (IACMST/MSCC) –
    http://www.marine.gov.uk/
UK Marine Data and Information Partnership (MDIP) –
    http://www.oceannet.org/mdip/index.html
UK Marine Environmental Data Action Group (MEDAG) –
    http://www.oceannet.org/medag/index.html

10

Integrated coastal zone management progress and sustainability indicators

Alan H. Pickaver
Coast & Marine Union (EUCC), The Netherlands

Two sets of linked indicators are needed to determine whether ICZM is having a positive effect on sustainability *viz.* indicators which measure any changes in sustainability, and indicators which determine the progress being made in management implementation. This chapter explores the history and development of these indicators.

10.1 Introduction

Although ICZM, as opposed to straightforward sectoral management, has been widely recognised as an effective process for incorporating conservation and sustainable use of marine and coastal biodiversity aspects into the planning process, it is still not being widely implemented. This is partly due to the difficulty of implementing an integrated approach of the various involved coastal stakeholders when policies and implementing departments are themselves still operating from different departments and sub-departments at authority level. However, another reason is that the supposed added value of ICZM to standard sectoral management has still not been proven. It has still not been shown that ICZM is actually integrating management with policy nor that any ICZM which is doing so is actually benefiting the coastal resources and/or the associated social and economic well-being of our coastal societies.

Although the former problem is a matter for national, regional and local government (re-)organisation, the latter problem could conceivably be solved with the development of an indicator which could measure the progress of ICZM at governance level and couple it to sustainability indicators. In fact, the apparent failure of ICZM in many efforts worldwide in ensuring environmental health of coastal ecosystems while obtaining benefits from coastal development makes the development and monitoring of appropriate indicators a necessity to track ICZM both in terms of process and outcomes. It becomes vital that, in order to be able to demonstrate any benefits being accrued at the coast by ICZM, a series of sound monitoring and evaluation techniques using appropriate indicators is conducted.

An indicator provides a simplified view of a more complex phenomenon, or provides insights about a trend or event that cannot be directly observed. Thus, indicators both quantify and simplify information. They can also improve communication. There is no single 'perfect' indicator or set of indicators; rather indicators must be tailored to their expected use. Good indicators must be useful to their intended audience, be it the general public, policy makers, financial backers or the EC. Also indicators must provide meaningful, readily understandable information that is directly related to the goals of a project or specific policy. A good set of indicators will be the smallest relevant set of indicators, and may aggregate sets of indicators into indices. Good indicators will also be theoretically well-founded and will be supported by reliable and valid data. They are a tool that helps make clear assessments of, and comparisons between, management measures through time. They also can be used to simplify the description of the extent to which the objectives for the management programmes are being achieved.

With ICZM, therefore, it is necessary to have two indicators or sets of indicators. One of them needs to be able to determine whether, and how well, ICZM is being put into practice as a management process and the second one needs to be able to determine the effect that such management is having on the coastal environment. Only when this is done will it be possible to link well-implemented ICZM with 'success' in the recovery and sustained health of coastal resources as well as in the 'improvement' of the socio-economic conditions of coastal communities.

10.2   A short history of ICZM indicators

To date, most work on indicators has been done in formulating economic and social policy making. In coastal-related issues, indicators have been increasingly used to monitor certain aspects of environmental quality, e.g. the use of nitrate and phosphate loadings for eutrophication. These indicators are all related to measuring the state of the coast, i.e. the results obtained as a result of any type of management measures and decisions that have been taken (e.g. EEA, 2006a). They have no specific reference to ICZM. Indeed, coastal environmental monitoring has been taking place for decades, long before ICZM methodology came to the fore.

Several attempts have been made in the US and Europe to develop an indicator that can measure the degree of implementation during the cyclical progression of ICZM itself. These policy-relevant indicators have commonly tried to answer a number of criteria which are necessary for them to be useful in decision-making processes (OECD, 2003). In fact, despite the 30 or more year history of ICZM, there are few examples of strategies, plans or management practices from which to incorporate ideas of a progress indicator (Burbridge, 1997). The biggest constraints still seem to be the low level of awareness of the implicit value of coastal systems and the shortage of personnel trained to plan for, and manage, an integrated, sustainable use of resources generated by coastal ecosystems.

There has been a difference of emphasis, with the US developing methodologies largely to assess individual ICZM projects and Europe attempting to design an indicator that can measure the implementation of the overall progression of ICZM in a country. This has meant that a very different approach has been taken.

Within Europe, Burbridge (1997) has put forward a simple, generic framework for assessing ICZM initiatives which attempts to equate three factors *viz.* equity, economics and the environment. While the model has value in showing the various interrelationships between the three factors, it is suggested that it best be used to address individual ICZM initiatives. Another attempt was made using ICZM data from selected European countries (van Elburg-Velinova *et al.*, 1999). This study compared three criteria, horizontal and vertical integration and public participation, in 181 regions of 14 countries. These three indicators should show progress in ICZM in coastal regions per country since the further establishment of ICZM per region should show developments in all these directions. The results were mapped as regional coastal areas (defined as administrative bodies with principal responsibility for spatial and environmental planning) categorised according to whether ICZM was fully or partially established, whether it was in progress or whether there had been little or no progress. The preliminary conclusion was that some progress had been made in ICZM but that it had only been fully established in a few regions. The results were also biased, both positively and negatively, with those countries which have few regional, coastal communities e.g. Belgium (2), Netherlands

(5) against those that had more, e.g. UK (49). Of course, any regions that had made progress in areas of ICZM, other than those studied, would show up negatively in the analysis. The study was able to draw some conclusions concerning the state of implementation of ICZM and the classification used in the study proved to have operational value. The need for a proper, quantitative, methodology in order to compare ICZM development within a country, over a period of time and between countries was recognised.

Henoque (2003) also recognised that there was still a need to develop innovative approaches for measuring the status of an ICZM programme. He favoured the development of seven different indices with a value between 0 and 3 to measure individual case studies. Although they gave good information regarding the strengths and weaknesses of available ICZM tools in local situations, potentially leading to the development of a Good Practice Guide, they still fell short of meaning-fully evaluating ICZM progression as a policy tool.

Although the US has a much longer experience with ICZM, only recently have attempts been made in that country to develop a progress indicator. One of the most promising methodologies has been that described by Olsen (2003). He has developed a self-assessment question-naire which reflects the ICZM approach within a wider socio-economic and government (local, regional, national) setting. His concept provides a means for sorting coastal management initiatives that highlight the experience, capacity, scale and scope of the outcomes that are desired. The most important aspect of Olsen's idea, at least for the development of a more pragmatic model (Olsen *et al.*, 1999), was the recognition that the many actions that have to be undertaken to advance a coastal management initiative have to be organised around the ICZM policy cycle. This model stresses that successive initiatives link the steps within a management cycle. Nonetheless, the Olsen model which measures progress through a series of 'Orders of Outcomes' has still failed to reach mainstream policy-makers or form the basis for national and international ICZM decision making.

A breakthrough came with the publication in 2004 of the model developed by the current author (Pickaver *et al.*, 2004). For the first time, a methodology was used which was wholly pragmatic in its application. This new, model indicator set recognises that the ICZM management cycle can be broken down into a series of discrete, ranked actions. These Actions, 31 in total, show what is needed, using a straight-forward, step-wise set of questions which can show passage from a situation where no ICZM is being used to one where it is being fully implemented.

The Actions are grouped into a series of four, discrete, ordered but continuous phases (see Table. 10.1). The Actions are not completely exhaustive but are comprehensive enough to allow progress in ICZM to be measured. A comparative analysis can then be conducted by an assessment using semi-quantitative criteria. Billé (2007) stated that this indicator was a significant step forward and the model has gained currency in Europe and, as we shall see in the next section, is now the favoured model for measuring implementation by all EU coastal states.

10.3   The EU context

The growing concerns about the environmentally, socio-economically and culturally deteriorating state of the European coast have prompted the European Commission and Member States, since 1996, to introduce a range of measures to halt the trend. It is the intention that these will lead to a sustainable development of the whole European coast in the future.

The first of these was the Commission's ICZM Demonstration Programme to ascertain best practice in addressing coastal issues. This three-year programme (European Commission, 1996) included 35 individual projects and six thematic studies on important aspects which need to be addressed in any ICZM programme, embracing the Baltic Sea, North Sea. Atlantic seaboard and the Mediterranean Sea, was launched in 1996. It was a joint programme of the three Directorates General: Environment, Regional Development and Fisheries. Its aim was to test cooperation models for integrated management of the coastal zones and to stimulate a broad debate amongst the various stakeholders involved in coastal planning, management or use of the coastal zones. It was also to provide the technical results necessary to foster dialogue between the European Institutions and coastal stakeholders.

Based upon the results of this programme, the European Commission subsequently produced two important documents on the subject of Integrated Coastal Zone Management. The first of these was a Strategy for Europe (Commission of the European Communities, 2002a) concerning the implementation of ICZM throughout the EU coastal states. This 38 point strategy consists of a series of concrete actions building upon existing instruments, programmes and resources, and is a flexible, evolving instrument, designed to cope with the specific needs of the different regions and conditions. It reiterates the need for a strategic approach to the management of the coastal zone which is underpinned by a number of important principles such as the eco-system approach, the precautionary principle and adaptive management. One of the activities (no. 27) importantly calls for the improvement of data provisions and use of this data to produce indicator-based assessment reports.

The second document was a Recommendation (Commission of the European Communities, 2002b) which was called for as the first point of the strategy. This recommendation, adopted by Council and Parliament on 30 May 2002 although not legally binding, is now being implemented by all member states. This means that all EU (and acceding) countries are committed to ensuring that ICZM will be executed. Member States have, therefore, undertaken a national stocktake which analysed which major actors, laws and institutions influence the management of their national coastal zone (Rupprecht, 2006). Many have also, based upon the results of the stocktake, developed a national strategy for the implementation of ICZM. Such a strategy must include *i.a.* adequate systems for collecting and providing information in appropriate and compatible formats to decision makers at national, regional and local levels to facilitate integrated management.

The first (and so far, only) high level Forum on Community Strategies for ICZM was subsequently held in La Vila Joiosa (Spain) in 2002. It called, among other things, upon the Member States to promote the general use of existing comparable indicators for sustainable development and to develop indicators, on a national basis, to provide standardised descriptions of the status of the coast and possible impacts of human indicators as well as of *the progress made towards ICZM in Europe*. It further recommended that a Group of Experts be created with the object to support the implementation of the EC Recommendation. Such a group was drawn up and held its first meeting in October 2002 in Brussels. One of the decisions of the Group of Experts was to create a working group to deal with indicators and data (called WG-ID) under the leadership of the European Topic Centre Terrestrial Environment. The mandate of WG-ID was to advise the Expert Group on ways in which an indicator-based assessment could be taken forward and to prepare a report on coastal and ICZM indicators and data for the subsequent meeting of the Group of Experts to be held in June 2003.

At its first meeting, held in Barcelona on 7 February 2003, the WG-ID began an exchange of views concerning the types of indicators that are useful for monitoring progress in ICZM implementation. It recommended the use of comparable indicators to assess both the status of the coast and the degree to which an integrated system of coastal management is being implemented around the European littoral. A subsequent meeting set the objective to build a common set of indicators to ensure comparability of reporting at European, regional (regional seas), national and sub-national levels. This was highly significant because, for the first time, the development of a progress indicator had been driven by a political process rather than come through the scientific ranks. It was, therefore, highly likely that any reasonable progress indicator developed would be subsequently taken very seriously by politicians and policy makers alike.

The current author was delegated the challenging task of trying to produce an indicator set which could be used pragmatically to measure the degree of implementation of ICZM in the EU Member States.

10.4   An indicator to measure progress of implementation

An indicator set which shows the level of progress being made in the implementation of ICZM has been successfully formulated (Pickaver *et al.*, 2004). It takes the thinking of the complex, ICZM management cycle towards much more simplified comparative analysis by evaluating the progress using qualitative and semi-quantitative criteria. Thus, it recognises that the ICZM cycle can be broken down into a series of discrete, ranked actions. These actions, now 31 in total, are not completely exhaustive but are comprehensive enough to allow progress in ICZM to be measured (Table. 10.1). They show what is needed, using a straightforward, step-wise methodology, to pass from a situation where no ICZM is being used to one where it is being fully implemented, by being grouped into a series of four, discrete, ordered and continuous phases. These phases are:

- Phase I: Planning and management are taking place in the coastal zone. Such activities may still be non-integrated (often sectoral) but they can can lay the basis for the introduction of ICZM. It contains five discrete actions.
- Phase II: A framework exists for taking ICZM forward. It contains seven discrete actions.
- Phase III: Most aspects of an ICZM approach to planning and managing the coast are in place and functioning reasonably well. This holds that important aspects of ICZM such as vertical and horizontal integration of administrative and planning bodies exist within an ICZM programme. It embodies the essence of ICZM and is, therefore, the largest group with 12 representative actions.
- Phase IV: An efficient, adaptive and integrative process is embedded at all levels of governance and is delivering greater

Table 10.1 *An indicator for measuring progress in the implementation of ICZM in Greece*

Phase	Action	Description	National		Regional		Local	
			2000	2006	2000	2006	2000	2006
Aspects of coastal planning and management are in place	1	Decisions about planning and managing the coast are governed by general legal instruments	Yes	Yes	Yes	Yes	Yes	Yes
	2	Sectoral stakeholders meet on an ad-hoc basis to discuss specific coastal and marine issues	Yes	Yes	Yes	Yes	DK	Yes
	3	There are spatial development plans which include the coastal zone but do not treat it as a distinct and separate entity	Yes	Yes	Yes	Yes	Yes	Yes
	4	Aspects of the coastal zone, including marine areas, are regularly monitored	Yes	Yes	Yes	Yes	Yes	Yes
	5	Planning on the coast includes the statutory protection of natural areas	Yes	Yes	Yes	Yes	No	No
A framework exists for taking ICZM forward	6	Existing instruments are being adapted and combined to deal with coastal planning and management issues	Yes	Yes	Yes	Yes	DK	DK
	7	Adequate funding is usually available for undertaking actions on the coast	No	No	No	No	No	No
	8	A stocktake of the coast (identifying who does what, where and how) has been carried out	No	Yes	No	No	No	No
	9	There is a formal mechanism whereby stakeholders meet regularly to discuss a range of coastal and marine issues	No	Yes	No	Yes	No	No
	10	Ad hoc actions on the coast are being carried out that include recognisable elements of ICZM	No	Yes	No	Yes	No	Yes

Table 10.1 Continued

Phase	Action	Description	National		Regional		Local	
			2000	2006	2000	2006	2000	2006
	11	A sustainable development strategy which includes specific references to coasts and seas is in place	No	Yes	No	No	No	No
	12	Guidelines have been produced by national, regional or local governments which advise planning authorities on appropriate uses of the coastal zone	Yes	Yes	No	Yes	No	No
Most aspects of an ICZM approach to planning and managing the coast are in place and functioning reasonably well	13	All relevant parties concerned in the ICZM decision-making process have been identified and are involved	No	Yes	DK	DK	No	No
	14	A report on the state of the coast has been written with the intention of repeating the exercise every five or ten years	Yes	Yes	No	No	No	No
	15	There is a statutory coastal zone management plan	No	No	No	No	No	No
	16	Strategic environmental assessments are used commonly to examine policies, strategies and plans for the coastal zone	No	Yes	DK	DK	No	No
	17	A non-statutory coastal zone management strategy has been drawn up and an action plan is being implemented	Yes	Yes	Yes	Yes	No	No
	18	There are open channels of communication between those responsible for the coast at all levels of government	No	Yes	DK	DK	DK	DK
	19	Each administrative level has at least one member of staff whose sole responsibility is ICZM	No	No	No	No	No	No
	20	Statutory development plans span the interface between land and sea	No	Yes	No	Yes	No	No

No.	Statement								
21	Spatial planning of sea areas is required by law	No	No	No	No	No	No	No	No
22	A properly staffed and properly funded partnership of coastal and marine stakeholders is in place	No	No	No	No	No	No	No	No
23	ICZM partnerships are consulted routinely about proposals to do with the coastal zone	No	No	No	No	No	No	No	No
24	Adequate mechanisms are in place to allow coastal communities to take a participative role in ICZM decisions	No	No	No	No	No	No	No	No
25	*An efficient, adaptive and integrative process is embedded at all levels of governance and is delivering greater sustainable use of the coast* — There is strong, constant and effective political support for the ICZM process	DK	DK	DK	DK	Yes	DK	Yes	Yes
26	There is routine (rather than occasional) cooperation across coastal and marine boundaries	Yes	Yes	Yes	Yes	No	Yes	No	No
27	A comprehensive set of coastal and marine indicators is being used to assess progress towards a more sustainable situation	No	No	No	No	Yes	No	Yes	Yes
28	A long-term financial commitment is in place for the implementation of ICZM	DK	DK	DK	DK	DK	DK	DK	DK
29	End users have access to as much information of sufficient quality as they need to make timely, coherent and well-crafted decisions	No	No	DK	No	Yes	No	Yes	No
30	Mechanisms for reviewing and evaluating progress in implementing ICZM are embedded in governance	No	DK	No	No	No	No	No	No
31	Monitoring shows a demonstrable trend towards a more sustainable use of coastal and marine resources	DK	DK	No	DK	Yes	No	Yes	No

sustainability of the coast. It contains a further seven discrete actions.

The new model indicator set described was accepted by the second EU Group of Experts meeting, held in Brussels in April 2004 (Expert Group, 2004). This originally published Indicator (Pickaver *et al.*, 2004) had 26 actions grouped into five phases. It has been slightly modified following some preliminary testing of the indicator in Europe conducted principally by ICZM practitioners at all administrative levels in Spain, France and in the southern North Sea region (including coastal planners and managers from Belgium, France, the UK and Holland). The tests helped to clarify the comprehensibility of the language used in the table and led to a refinement in the description of some of the actions or, in a few cases, to move the action from one phase to another (EEA, 2006a). The revised progress indicator of 31 Actions divided into four phases with 5, 7, 12, 7 action levels respectively, in total 31 (see Table 10.1) was adopted by the Fifth Meeting of the EU ICZM Group of Experts in September 2005 with a recommendation that it now be used to measure the progress of ICZM in Member States (Expert Group, 2005).

Table 10.1 shows a typical response, in this case from the government of Greece (Ministry of the Environment, Physical Planning and Public Works, 2006) which demonstrates the sorts of conclusions that can be drawn and underline the added value of the methodology. Against each action a simple 'yes' or 'no' or 'don't know' has been entered for three governance levels: national, regional and local. However, because it is important to identify a trend through time, a layer of complexity can be added at each level by initially asking respondents to consider the action in two time periods, for the year 2000 and the year 2006. When the indicator is in regular use, of course, only the present time will need to be considered.

The table should be understood both vertically and horizontally. Vertical use will show how far along the ICZM cycle implementation has been effected. The horizontal dimension reveals the degree of integration between the three governance levels. In this case, Greece is managing its coast at all three levels of governance (Phase 1) but, significantly, it is of note that more appears to be being done at national level with respect to having a framework for, and actually implementing aspects of ICZM, than at local level. It is also clear that there are more yes values at all levels in 2006 than was perceived to have been the case in 2000 showing that there is some progressive trend already taking place. These results are similar to those produced in the EEA report

(2006a) in which a series of tests were conducted in Spain, Germany, Italy, France, Poland and Lithuania for the WG-ID as well as results published by Shipman and Stojanovic (2007) who conducted a survey in England, Wales, Scotland and Northern Ireland in the UK.

It is likely that progress in implementing ICZM will be as uneven as Table 10.1 suggests. Actions need not necessarily take place in sequence, especially within any given phase. Indeed, it would be surprising if they did. Adapting legal instruments to deal with coastal issues (action 6), for example, appear to be easier to achieve than a comprehensive funding programme (action 7). Again, regular cross-border co-operation (action 19) can precede a formal state of the coast report (action 14). Authorities, states and regions will respond differently to varying pressures. Some will seize an opportunity such as an oil spill or a planning application to construct an offshore wind farm, and help push ICZM along; others will take a more procedural approach. The nature of ICZM suggests there will not be blocks of 'yes' responses followed by blocks of 'no' responses but that the table will be more of a patchwork. However, as implementation progresses then progressively more 'yes' answers should be seen.

Practical experience suggests that during the first time period or cycle, pioneering authorities or regions might reach well into phase 3 of ICZM implementation but leave a number of 'no' responses in phases 1 and 2. During the second phase, they might complete those actions without going on to phase 4. Each turn of the management wheel will see an increasing number of 'yes' responses. Those actions answered positively in previous cycles are likely to be of a greater complexity, richness and impact as each cycle passes. A persistence of 'no' responses will suggest a blockage in the system or a problem which will need to be resolved.

Interestingly, the method of testing does not appear to affect the results obtained. There can be no doubt that discussing the progress indicator in a workshop setting is the most effective way of determining the outcome. However, it is the most costly both in terms of people's time and travel budgets. The work can just as effectively be done by email, one-on-one discussions or telephone. In the Greek case above, the information was collected on the basis of bilateral contacts between colleagues from different competent authorities, since there was no possibility to organise a meeting of stakeholders for technical reasons. However, given the fact that legislation and physical planning are to a very great extent decided at a central/governmental level, it was felt that there was no risk to miss important information that would change the replies of the matrix on the current situation simply because no such meeting had been convened. Telephone and email surveys, as well as meetings, were used in the EEA study (EEA, 2006a).

What has become clear from these tests is that any given person responsible for (aspects of) ICZM will complete the table differently according to their own perspective. Even people working in the same organisation would often differ with their colleagues in assessing whether a particular action is, or is not, being implemented. Therefore, it is important that the assessment be conducted by a group of responsible persons. Furthermore, it is apparent from the testing that local practitioners have restricted information about what, if anything, is happening at regional or national level, and vice versa. However, under the work-shop setting relevant persons from different departments responsible for ICZM sat together and discussed the action points. Eventually, even with different perspectives, a common consensus answer was reached for each of the points by the authority representatives. Although this is time-consuming initially, those who have experienced the training will themselves be able to act as trainers in any subsequent assessments.

The actions identified in the progress indicator provide a simplified 'road-map' for a complex, dynamic and adaptive process. The advantages of this progress indicator over any others that have so far been published are that:

- it allows the trend in the progress of implementation in any one country to be compared over a time period
- it allows a comparison between countries to be determined
- it will determine if the levels of governance are in synchrony with each other (the horizontal aspect)
- it identifies a problem area that needs attention (the vertical aspect)
- it is easy to complete and the use of colour coding (yes = green, no = red, don't know = yellow) gives an at-a-glance judgement. Although the results can only be considered semi-quantitative at best, there is normally real agreement (or disagreement) about the actions under discussion
- it is visually versatile in terms of displaying the results. Apart from the results shown in Table 10.1, it can also be visualised to compare the progress in ICZM for different geographical, administrative entities within a country by laying the results directly side-by-side (the NE, NW and South). The pooled results from all the respondents in a country or region with respect to the 31 action

levels can also be shown. Finally, it is not necessary to tabulate all the action levels individually but show the pooled results after grouping of all the actions within each phase to give a clear representation of the overall progress in ICZM with respect to each of the four phases (Pickaver, 2008).

Furthermore, there has been a consistent feeling that the process, itself, of completing the questionnaire in a workshop setting is of enormous benefit in bringing together different, but relevant, stakeholders to discuss the ICZM process. Persons dealing with ICZM on a daily basis are not often given the opportunity to discuss ICZM issues with persons from other departments or fields of work.

The work that has been conducted has, nonetheless, identified some difficulties where further work is desirable. A series of one day workshops was organised in Wales, northeast England, northwest England, Belgium and northwest France, and were conducted in English, French or Dutch (Flemish) accordingly, using translations where appropriate. The participants were coastal and marine practitioners from different administrations, organisations, agencies and interest groups who were asked to complete the table together. They represented national, regional and/or local interests. Between five and 25 persons were involved in each test (Pickaver, 2008).

There was general agreement that the binary scale was not sensitive enough and there should be some sort of semi-quantitative breakdown e.g. replacing the yes/no/undecided, for example, with a scale of 0–5. In fact, the original methodology of the progress indicator deliberately chose for a binary response in order to commit people to answering as definitively as possible. It was felt that most respondents would be reluctant to say either yes or no if given a middle-of-the-road choice. However, the participants felt that the current choice of replies offered only an inadequate response since it did not allow the multi-dimensional realities of ICZM to be fully expressed.

There can be sensitivity to the publication of the answers. Even within the confines of the closed workshops, one of the regions tested above only did so provided that the results would not be made available outside the group. Some participants were reluctant to have their answers published even if they, themselves, remained anonymous. This has to do with the competance of the participant and to their placement in the hierarchy of the Authority they are representing and who has the 'right' to complete the indicator in what may be considered unofficial situations.

Concern was also expressed that a comprehensive testing of coastal Member States would eventually lead to the publication of 'League Tables' which would show some countries in a bad light, even if this was not the objective. There were also some, rather country-specific concerns, e.g. in the case of France, the national, regional and local administrative boundaries are not really applicable.

Finally, there are still some concerns about the language used in some of the questions. These relate to comprehension of some of the language with respect to enabling an adequate translation of the terms in other European languages. However, it was also felt that some of the questions were open to interpretation in the English language.

These concerns will need to be addressed as experience in monitoring ICZM progress is developed using this progress indicator. It is to be anticipated the progress indicator will, itself, become an integral part of the ICZM process. Nevertheless, in the longer term, it will give the potential to allow mapping of coastal areas nationally, and even throughout Europe, in terms of the progress being achieved in implementing ICZM. To date, it has been completed officially by eight of the EU's coastal states.

This indicator will not, by itself, be able to show if ICZM has been successful in reversing the decline in Europe's coastal regions. In order to ensure that ICZM is actually leading to the sustainable use of coastal resources it will also be necessary to concurrently measure whether there has been any improvement in the sustainable use of the coast. Only then can it be stated with any degree of certainty that enhanced implementation of ICZM is leading towards local, regional and national sustainability.

10.5 Indicators of sustainability

There is a great number of indicators that are being used today but they are all predominantly state-of-the-coast indicators rather than sustainability indicators (e.g. EEA, 2006b; Belfiore *et al.*, 2005; OECD, 2003; van Buuren *et al.*, 2002). The European Commission has attempted to select a group which could be applied around the Union's coastline. A set of 27 so-called sustainability indicators was drawn up and tested by the Interreg project DEDUCE. Unfortunately, these indicators too reflect a state-of-the-coast rather than a true evaluation of sustainability. As a result, these indicators have still not been accepted by the Commission because it is felt there are too many for routine use and there are not uniformly applicable around Europe's coastline.

State-of-the-coast indicators, of which there are hundreds if not thousands, often rely upon regular, scientific monitoring and quantitative measurements with the results stored in, and compared with, others in a database. In many cases, data taken in one country are not comparable with that taken in another. Nonetheless, they have been measured at the coast for decades but none of them really give any information about sustainability, perhaps because sustainability cannot be measured quantitatively. Sustainability means different things to different people/ stakeholders. There is no definable element or elements at the coast where you can say, 'this is sustainability and this isn't'. It therefore follows that nothing you measure at the coast, even if you measure everything, can ever tell you whether you have reached sustainability. In other words, we are measuring the wrong parameters if we want information about sustainability. Because sustainability is itself qualitative you can only ever measure it using qualititative data/reasoning. The quantitative approach has probably been favoured to date because it is often the most attractive option to those tasked with demonstrating or measuring progress in sustainability.

As a consequence, using the same type of methodology that was applied to the development of the ICZM progress indicator, so we have been applying similar methodologies to the development of indicators that can truly measure sustainability (see Table 10.2). This has led to the initial recognition of 20 sustainability criteria which have been developed, tested and accepted, in all regions of Europe from Denmark and Poland to Spain, Portugal and Greece at selected, local authority level. These are the QualityCoast criteria which were developed, initially through an Interreg project called Coastal Practice Network (Pickaver and Salman, 2008). They were elaborated with the Gothenburg and Lisbon Agendas in mind, since the aim was to formulate a management programme which, when implemented, would lead to the sustainable use of European coastal services by its communities. They laid out *what* was required for local/regional municipalities to implement a sustainable and integrated, cross-cutting management approach. Perhaps, most importantly, policy makers and implementers were involved in their development: a true bottom-up approach with policy-makers both defining their needs and determining how those needs can be best satisfied.

These criteria appeal to policy makers and policy implementers at local and regional Authority level because they don't need expensive and routine monitoring equipment, standardisation of data collection or, most significantly, specialist, scientific interpretation. They also

Table 10.2 QualityCoast sustainability criteria in three categories: Nature, Environment and Socio-economic criteria

Category	Nature
QC 1	*Natural values*
Definition	Presence of internationally important species and habitats that occur in the local destination
QC 2	*Nature information*
Definition	Information sources and facilities that promote interaction with the local natural environment and are located within and/or near natural areas of interest
QC 3	*Contact with nature*
Definition	Appropriate level of accessibility of natural areas for low pressure recreational access
QC 4	*Green policies*
Definition	The extent to which natural values are protected through integrated, sectoral or cross-sectoral policies and management schemes
QC 5	*Open landscapes*
Definition	Presence of open landscapes and existing trends in land use and land cover patterns
QC 6	*Availability of quiet places*
Definition	Presence of areas where visitors can escape from traffic, crowds and noise

Category	Environment
QC 7	*Tourism pressure*
Definition	The number of visitors in relation to the number of local inhabitants and length of stay associated with their visit
QC 8	*Business involvement*
Definition	The extent to which the local business community is involved in efforts for environment and sustainable development, incl. the nr. of accommodation providers achieving an officially recognised eco-label
QC 9	*Bathing water quality*
Definition	Extent of fulfilling the requirements regarding bathing water quality in the water bodies of the area under scope, in accordance with Directive 76-160-CEE
QC 10	*Water management*
Definition	Efficient use of water, especially regarding drinking water quality, water supply and its provenance (external dependence) and reuse of depurated water
QC 11	*Sustainable transportation*
Definition	The availability and stimulation of sustainable transport modes
QC 12	*Waste and recycling*
Definition	Existence of structures for recycling and waste collection in place in the area
QC 13	*Climate change response*
Definition	Policy aimed at reducing greenhouse gasses and accommodating to climate change

Table 10.2 Continued

Category	Nature
QC 14	*Cultural heritage*
Definition	Presence and level of protection of elements that are connected to the origins and history of the destination. That though belonging to the cultural heritage of the community are no longer active
QC 15	*Cultural landscapes*
Definition	Presence of valuable landscapes that are man-made or man formed
QC 16	*Local identity*
Definition	Presence and attention for a distinct physical and/or social atmosphere that is considered typical for the destination. Activities and elements linked to the tradition but that are kept alive and integrated into the present time
QC 17	*Leisure and recreation*
Definition	Availability of leisure and recreation activities and facilities within the destination, with specific attention to those related with tradition
QC 18	*Community participation*
Definition	Local initiatives to promote community participation and stakeholder involvement in management and decision making
QC 19	*Tourist satisfaction*
Definition	The appreciation level of tourists and inhabitants regarding the destination
QC 20	*Safety*
Definition	Presence of a safe, healthy and secure environment and of preventive measures

have many other advantages over currently used state-of-the-coast indicators. They are truly pan-European and they don't have any regional focus. In testing the criteria, it was recognised that the methodology was cost-effective and resource-light. The message was easy to communicate, digest and, perhaps most importantly, attractive to those who needed to be engaged – service providers and local authorities. There was no pretence – it provided information, and in doing so highlighted gaps, challenges, etc. – and set an agenda for further discussion.

These 20 sustainability criteria have been subsequently tested on a Dutch municipality, Noordwijk, and each criterion was rated on a score of 1 to 5 according to how well it was judged they were doing in each. The results are shown in Fig. 10.1. Clearly, if this exercise is repeated in the future, it will be possible to gain some measurement as to how much further they have progressed towards sustainability. So far 12 other coastal towns and islands have completed a Quality-Coast pilot. It has proven to be an effective programme to promote sustainability at the local level, because communities are interested to

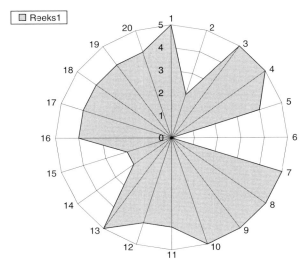

Fig. 10.1 *Data from a Dutch municipality, Noordwijk, which tested the 20 sustainability criteria and was scored 1–5 for each criterion*

use the results in their external marketing, thus firmly incorporating aspects of sustainability in their community policies.

In order to ensure that ICZM is actually leading to the sustainable use of coastal resources it will be necessary to concurrently measure whether there has been any improvement in sustainability while ICZM policies have been implemented. Together, the ICZM progress indicator set alongside these new indicators of sustainable development, will also be a test of the hypothesis underpinning current EU ICZM policy – that ICZM is a prerequisite for a more sustainable coast. Only then can it be stated with any degree of certainty that enhanced implementation of ICZM is leading towards local, regional and national sustainability.

10.6   Future developments for indicators of ICZM
With respect to the progress indicator, it will be increasingly important to further refine the action levels and, preferably, to expand the possible responses. Under the EU's Sixth Framework Programme called ENCORA (http://www.encore.eu) one of the cornerstones of ICZM *viz.* public participation has been analysed in more detail. This is covered in the Progress Indicator by Action 13 in Phase 3 'All relevant

parties concerned in the ICZM decision-making process have been identified and are involved'.

In order to come to grips with the notion of stakeholder participation in an ICZM decision-making situation, use was made of a classical social science publication (Arnstein, 1969), which recognised eight steps in a participation ladder starting from no participation at all through to 'total democracy'. In order to make these steps applicable to an ICZM decision-making process, one of the eight steps was dropped and all of them re-worded along the following lines.

- Level 1: all decisions are taken by governmental or regulatory bodies with no input at all by stakeholders.
- Level 2: stakeholders are placed on committees or advisory boards for the main purpose of gaining their support; they have no advisory capacity and certainly cannot take decisions.
- Level 3: stakeholders are simply informed but there is no channel for feedback; the information flow is one-way. It does lead to access of information and therefore awareness-raising.
- Level 4: the stakeholders are consulted, i.e. their opinions are asked. However, there are no other means of participation and although the opinions of those asked are generally taken into account there is no guarantee that they will be taken into consideration when decisions are taken.
- Level 5: the stakeholders have a truly advisory role. However, again, there is no certainly that the advice will be followed when a decision is taken.
- Level 6: there is real negotiation between the stakeholders and the decision makers; there is shared planning and decision-making responsibilities.
- Level 7: stakeholders have decision making delegated to them by the public officials resulting in the stakeholders achieving dominant decision-making authority. Stakeholders may hold veto power on decisions.

In order to see whether this breakdown could produce any meaningful results, it was circulated to 187 ICZM professionals from a variety of backgrounds, including scientific, national authorities (including national research institutes), regional authorities, local authorities, consultancy agencies and NGOs. Of these, 38 were returned from Belgium, Cyprus, Denmark, France, Germany, Greece, Ireland, Italy, the Netherlands, Poland, Portugal, Spain, Sweden and the UK (Table 10.3).

Table 10.3 The perceived level of public participation in a number of EU Member States

Country	Perceived level
Sweden	4–6
Netherlands	4–5
Portugal	4–5
Italy	4
Germany	3–5
United Kingdom	3–5
Poland	3–4
Cyprus	2–4
Belgium	2–4
Ireland	2–4
Spain	2–3
France	1–4
Greece	1–2

These results do show, even in such a small sample, that it is possible to differentiate between different levels of participation. The full range of the results covers six of the seven levels. Also, for the most part, the range of responses within any given country is not dissimilar. That differences of opinion exist is to be expected, since there is no absolute type of participation in any country and different persons will have different interpretations of what constitutes the different levels of participation. It is also likely that within an ICZM initiative or programme different levels of participation will be used at different stages in the process. Nonetheless, when grouped as above, it is clear that there is a real difference is the participatory approach within these countries with Greece perceived to have a very different type of stakeholder participation than, say, Sweden.

In Europe, participation generally is most often perceived as occurring at Level 4 with 11 of the 13 countries so identified by the respondents. This mechanism of participation is generally seen as attitude surveys, neighbourhood meetings and public hearings. While a valid step towards full participation, consultation alone means that there is no guarantee that stakeholder concerns and ideas will be taken into account. It is important to recognise that consultation is not full participation although many states argue otherwise.

Only in some cases, does full participation in ICZM decision making exist, usually in the form of partnerships. These are especially common in the UK. In a partnership, the power is shared by 'negotiation between public and stakeholders'. Planning and decision-making tasks are carried out through bodies like 'joint policy boards', 'planning committees' and other instruments that might enforce such a partnership. They work best with an organised power base in the region or community where meetings can be held, finances can be taken care of and where the group can do business with the decision makers. The key to effective partnership is good organisation and planning, although they often lead a precarious existence because funding is not guaranteed and they rely on voluntary stakeholder inputs.

The overall result indicates that the UK and Sweden are thought to have a high degree of public participation in ICZM. Legal instrumentation makes public participation mandatory for coastal projects, EU directives have been implemented, there are information campaigns for the general public, with both organised stakeholders and the general public being involved. In contrast, Greece has minimal legal instrumentation for public participation, other than EU directives, and there is a large gap between legal instrumentation and practice. Generally, the public is not informed and only minimally involved. Consultation is often not taking place and the wishes of the public are not taken into consideration. The majority of states are somewhere in between these two groups.

However the desire of participation is interpreted, it would again appear, that with further refinement, the current progress indicator has the potential to delineate different types of participation that can be agglomerated under Action 13 to sub-divide it into sub-levels 13a–13g. It is now the intention to take the other levels to see if any of them can be meaningfully sub-divided.

With respect to the sustainability indicators, there is still a great deal of work to be done, particularly at a political level, to choose a group of indicators which can work in all the regions of EU and which truly measure sustainability. It is disappointing that eight meetings of the EU ICZM Group of Experts, spanning seven years, has still not brought consensus as to which sustainability indicators should be applied. If, indeed, the actual premise for using quantitatively-based indicators is not correct then the work being conducted on the semi-qualitative ones will be eagerly anticipated. Focus now may switch to the Barcelona Convention, which passed an ICZM Protocol in 2008, and has the mandate to define *i.a.* indicators of the development of economic activities to ensure sustainable use of coastal zones and reduce pressures that exceed their carrying capacity.

10.7   Conclusion

So far, the results collated from around coastal, EU Europe using the progress indicator show that Phase 1 is showing good evolution. This phase of aspects of coastal planning and management being in place is completed in practically all the countries, even though a sectoral approach is still pre-dominant. In Phase 2 where a framework for ICZM is in existence, Actions 7 and 11 (adequate funding and the development of a strategy) present the greatest problems. However, in general, other actions are being implemented which, although still largely sectoral, now has a greater tendency towards integration. It is this phase which has shown most progress in the last few years. Some countries have even begun clearly to work in the direction of integration, e.g. France and Belgium. But the trend is positive for all countries. With respect to Phases 3 and 4, relating to having an ICZM planning and management approach in place and functioning well as well as having an efficient, adaptive and integrative process embedded in all levels of governance, some progress has been made but it is largely *ad hoc*, i.e. no trends are present in the EU and, in reality, very little improvement has been made. Any improvements have been largely determined by priorities set by each country. Quite clearly, further progress in ICZM needs to be seen in these two action levels in particular. Although these results will come as no surprise to those working in ICZM in the EU, the progress indicator now provides the means by which such conclusions can be drawn and a methodology for determining whether progress in implementation really is being achieved.

Measuring the progress of the implementation of the ICZM cycle alone will not necessarily be indicative of how successful ICZM is in reversing the decline in Europe's coastal regions. In order to ensure that the ICZM cycle is actually leading to the sustainable use of coastal resources it will also be necessary to use, concomitantly, sustainability indicators. Only then, with any degree of certainty can it be stated that enhanced implementation of ICZM is leading towards sustainability locally, regionally and nationally. The use of two indicator sets – one measuring progress on implementing ICZM and one measuring sustainable development of the coastal zone – is inextricably linked and should be seen as part of the ICZM cycle. Certainly, it can be expected that as more work is done on using ICZM as a programmatic approach to coastal management, work will also continue to define, and refine, the progress indicator itself. Used together, the progress indicator and sustainability indicators can give an indication of the degree to which the implementation of ICZM is correlated with a more sustainable coast. That is, decisions using an integrated approach should see a positive improvement in the state of the coast with concomitant progress towards sustainable development and increased or *status quo* biodiversity values. The indicators measuring sustainable development will in turn feedback to give policymakers an indication of the need for further action in ICZM.

References

1st European ICZM High Level Forum on Community Strategies for Integrated Coastal Zone Management (2002) La Vila Joiosa, Alicante, Spain.

Arnstein, S.R. (1969) A ladder of citizen participation. *Journal of the American Institute of Planners*, Vol. 35, No. 4, 216–224.

Belfiore, S., Barbière, J., Bowen, R., Cicin-Sain, B., Ehler, C., Mageau, C., McDougall, D. and Siron. R. (2005) *A Handbook for Measuring the Progress and Outcomes of Integrated Coastal and Ocean Management*. IOC manuals and guides 46, IOC, Paris.

Billé, R. (2007) A dual-level framework for evaluating integrated coastal management beyond labels. *Ocean and Coastal Management*, Vol. 50, pp. 796–807.

Burbridge, P. (1997) A generic framework for measuring success in integrated coastal management. *Ocean & Coastal Management*, Vol. 37, pp. 175–189.

Commission of the European Communities (2002a) Communication from the Commission to the Council and the European Parliament on integrated coastal zone management: a strategy for Europe. Brussels COM 547 final.

Commission of the European Communities (2002b) Council Recommendation of the European Parliament and of the Council of 30 May, concerning the implementation of integrated coastal zone management in Europe, Brussels L 148/24.

EEA (2006a) Report on the use of the ICZM indicators from the WG–ID: a contribution to the ICZM evaluation, European Environmental Agency.

EEA (2006b) The changing faces of Europe's coastal areas. European Environmental Agency Report 6/2006.

European Commission (1996) Demonstration Programme on Integrated Management of Coastal Zones. Document XI/102/96.

Expert Group ICZM Recommendation (2004) Minutes of the 3rd Meeting; 22 April, Brussels. Online at: http://ec.europa.eu/environment/iczm/pdf/minutes_22_04_04.pdf

Expert Group ICZM Recommendation (2005) Minutes of the 5th Meeting; 22 September 2005, Brussels. Online at: http://ec.europa.eu/environment/iczm/pdf/minutes_22_04_04.pdf

Henocque, Y. (2003) Development of process indicators for coastal zone management in France. *Ocean & Coastal Management*, Vol. 46, pp. 363–379.

Ministry of the Environment, Physical Planning and Public Works (2006) Report of Greece.

OECD (2003) OECD Environmental Indicators: Development, measurement and use, pp. 1–37, OECD Publications. Available from http://www.oecd.org/env/

OECD (2003) OECD Environmental Indicators Development, Measurement and Use.

Olsen, S. (2003) Frameworks and indicators for assessing progress in integrated coastal management initiatives. *Ocean & Coastal Management*, Vol. 46, pp. 347–361.

Olsen, S.B., Lowry, K. and Tobey, L. (1999) A manual for assessing progress in coastal management. *Coastal Management Report* 1999; No. 2211, University of Rhode Island.

Pickaver, A. (2008) Further testing of the approved EU indicator to measure the progress in the implementation of integrated coastal zone management in Europe. *Proceedings of the International Symposium on Integrated Coastal Zone Management*, 10–14 June 2007, Arendal, Norway. Dahl. E., Moksness. E. and Støttrup, J. (eds) Blackwell Publishing, Oxford.

Pickaver, A.H. and Salman, A.H.P. (2008) EU policies and ICZM implementation in Europe: measuring sustainability at the coast. *Proceedings of the 9th international conference*, Littoral 2008 A Changing Coast: Challenge for the Environmental Policies, Venice.

Pickaver, A.H., Gilbert, C. and Breton, F. (2004) An indicator set to measure the progress in the implementation of integrated coastal zone management in Europe. *Ocean & Coastal Management*, Vol. 47, pp. 449–462.

Protocol on Integrated Coastal Zone Management in the Mediterranean (2008) pp. 1–89. Online at: http://www.unepmap.org

Rupprecht (2006) *Evaluation of Integrated Coastal Zone Management (ICZM) in Europe*, Rupprecht Consult, Koln, Germany.

Shipman. B. and Stojanovic, T. (2007) Facts, fictions, and failures of integrated coastal zone management in Europe. *Coastal Management*, Vol. 35, pp. 375–398.

van Buuren, J., Smit, T., Poot, G., van Elteren, A. and Kamp, O. (2002) *Testing of Indicators for the Marine and Coastal Environment in Europe*, European Environment Agency, Copenhagen.

van Elburg-Velinova. D., Perez Valverde, C. and Salman, A.H.P.M. (1999) *Progress of ICZM Development in European Countries: A Pilot Study*, EUCC – The Coastal Union.

11

Developing a practical method to estimate water-carrying capacity for surf schools in north Cornwall, southwest England

David R. Green, * *Margaret Carlisle* * and *James Ortiz*†
* *Centre for Marine and Coastal Zone Management (CMCZM), Department of Geography and Environment, University of Aberdeen, Scotland, UK;*
† *North Cornwall District Council (NCDC), Bodmin, UK*

This chapter presents a brief overview of a simple, practical, objective and repeatable generic method for applying the concept of carrying capacity (CC) to estimate surf school numbers for surfing beaches in North Cornwall, in Southwest England, UK. The study considers three possible ways to calculate the maximum number of people who can occupy the water area next to a beach under different environmental conditions. The first of these uses the physical footprint of a surfer and an associated comfort zone, equated to a safety factor. The second uses a range of density values (persons/ha) derived from review of research in other similar activities. The third uses a single density value in combination with a local conditions factor (LCF) derived from the experiential knowledge of the Royal National Lifeboat Institution (RNLI) beach lifeguards. Ultimately the outcome of this study is to help justify the implementation of a surf school licensing scheme and byelaw to assist in the control of the numbers in surf school classes. The study is set within the wider context of beach and coastal management as a component of integrated coastal zone management (ICZM).

11.1   Introduction
As a leisure and recreational water activity surfing has become increasingly popular over the last ten years in the UK (Fig. 11.1), particularly

Fig. 11.1 Surfing at Polzeath Beach, North Cornwall, UK

on the 11 beaches of the north coast of Cornwall in the Southwest of England. The physical space available for surfing at any beach and associated water area is, however, limited. There is, therefore, the potential for overcrowding which may compromise individual and public safety. As a result there is additional pressure on the Royal National Lifeboat Institution (RNLI) beach lifeguard service, which is responsible for beach and water safety on UK beaches, and on North Cornwall District Council (NCDC), which is responsible for managing beach access and environmental quality. RNLI beach lifeguards can use a flagging system (black/white and yellow/orange) to limit the physical accessibility of parts of the beach or water, but other than blanket closure (through the red flag) of a beach, it is extremely difficult for RNLI beach lifeguards on the ground to control the numbers of the general public in the water.

Surf schools, however, have large numbers of participants (usually inexperienced) at any one time, are more easily identifiable, and have long-term working relationships with the beach lifeguards. It is therefore easier to manage water safety by controlling the number of participants in a surf school and the number of surf schools able to safely operate.

The aim of this chapter is to examine the potential for using the concept of water carrying capacity (WCC) as the basis to develop a simple and practical method for calculating the number of surfers who can comfortably and safely be accommodated in surf school lessons within the water area adjacent to any given beach. A generic method of calculation is proposed that can be applied to any beach with practical adjustments to accommodate local knowledge. The ultimate goal of this research is to help justify the setting of future surf school quotas in an objective, transparent, accountable and iterative licensing scheme and byelaw to be implemented by NCDC.

252

11.2   Methods

A literature review into the concept and practice of carrying capacity, particularly with regard to beach and water activities, was undertaken, with special emphasis on sourcing 'grey literature' research studies and guidelines for managers and operators.

RNLI personnel were informally interviewed several times throughout the research period, in order to obtain their initial assessments on water safety, based on their expertise and experiential knowledge, as well as their subsequent feedback on the numbers generated. Informal visits and discussions were also held with a number of the surf schools located or based at one beach, Polzeath, with the aim of obtaining their views on defining the carrying capacity of the water area for surf school operation. Additionally, a number of email communications were also carried out with surf schools from around the world.

A geographical information system (GIS) was used to calculate the necessary physical parameters, namely the surfer usable water areas at low and high tides, for each beach.

11.3   Review of carrying capacity

The concept of carrying capacity (CC) is not new and has attracted considerable attention as an objective approach to recreational management from as far back as the mid-1930s, becoming especially popular in the 1960s and 1970s. Calculation of the CC is simple, providing a straightforward limit, usually defined in units of either persons/hectare or m^2/person, to protect users from possible overcrowding that may ultimately cause physical deterioration of the site, limit freedom of movement and lead to safety issues. However, the use of the CC concept is not without its critics, who frequently cite reasons such as the difficulty of generating a meaningful number for use in practice. Rather than being a single, static number, which should be used for guidance only, it has been suggested that CC should be a 'broader concept' (Buckley, 2002a, 2002b): a range of values for each site that change over time, based on continual monitoring and revision, recognising different impacts and management systems.

A search of the available literature revealed only a small number of studies on CC as applied to surfing. Most are by Buckley (2002a, 2002b), who focuses on problems of crowding, quotas and management with the aid of permits. DSE (2005) developed a method for estimating beach and water carrying capacity for surf schools in Australia. There is much literature on carrying capacity for various other sports and recreational activities. However, some activities are bound by the rules of the game, e.g. tennis; or are relatively static, and are therefore less comparable with surfing. Other activities, however, are similar to surfing in that: (a) they involve a lot of movement over a large area and in one or more different directions, or; (b) they involve the use of specialised equipment, the use of which may necessitate far more 'operational space', and therefore involve risk and safety issues to others. These activities include sailing (Graves, 2003), skiing (Von Allmen, 2005; Manning, 1985, 1986; South East Canada Resort Planners, 1996; Hogg, 1997, 2000) and beach activity in general (Florida Department of Environmental Protection, nd). In the context of this paper, however, it is notable how few of the studies cited above provide any evidence of the development of a practical approach to the implementation of the CC concept for recreational and leisure activities.

11.4   One approach to the problem: from individual to area

Recreational activities, like many other human activities, are spatial in nature, and a water carrying capacity (WCC) can be calculated based upon the initial definition of *physical footprint* of the individual surfer. Knowing the area needed by each individual then allows for the calculation of the carrying capacity of an area. This approach is used for many other applications, including: the number of car parking spaces on a piece of land, and the number of boats that can fit into a marina; the number of skiers or snowboarders on a ski slope (South East Canada Resort Planners, 1996); and the number of boat moorings that can fit within an open water area (Graves, 2003). The problem under consideration is basically a spatial one as it involves human use of space (a regular or irregular geometric area), the occupation of that space by a number of individuals with their own spatial dimensions and requirements, and their spatial distribution and pattern, zones and areas that will all change over time.

The physical footprint can be defined as a circle, using measurements of the width of the individual plus equipment as the radius of that circle. The calculation takes into account the dimensions of the specialised equipment and whether the person is upright or horizontal; thereby defining the maximum operational space required by the activity. For surfing, calculation of the physical footprint radius is a composite of the height of the person, the length of the surfboard and the length of the safety leash. Although the individual may normally be within the physical dimensions of the surf board when riding it standing up,

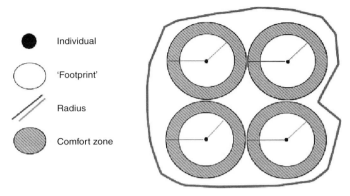

Fig. 11.2 Physical footprint (PF) and comfort zone (CZ)

or lying down, this will not always be the case, e.g. when the person falls off the board and is potentially lying and holding on to the board with the leash. For surfing there are different types of surf board with different lengths ranging from 1 to 3 m or more. Assuming a board length of 2 m, a leash of 2 m and a height of 2 m, the composite value or total length is 6 m. This defines the diameter of a circle. Half of this value (3 m) defines the radius of the circle, and πr^2 a circular footprint of approximately $28\,\text{m}^2$ (or $30\,\text{m}^2$).

However, as with any dynamic activity, movement in one or more directions can potentially lead to collisions. As such, the operational space defined by the footprint therefore needs to be extended to minimise the risk of collisions. To do this requires the addition of a safety buffer, referred to here as a *comfort zone*, to the physical footprint to increase the operational area needed for an individual. In so doing this will reduce the numbers physically able to use an area of water (Fig. 11.2).

This safety buffer can easily be adjusted: A larger operational area equates to greater safety because of reduced likelihood of collisions and can be used as the means to control numbers on the basis of skill level, i.e. a larger comfort zone for a beginner, leading to a larger overall footprint (physical footprint plus comfort zone) for safety, and therefore fewer numbers in the water, thus reducing the risk of a collision.

Calculations in the previous section of this paper suggest an individual footprint of approximately $30\,\text{m}^2$. This would give a user density of 333 persons per hectare. All stakeholders interviewed agreed that this value would be far too high. Therefore, adjustment is

Table 11.1 Linking footprint and comfort zones to carrying capacity density

CC footprint + comfort zone	$120\,m^2$ $(30\,m^2 +$ $30\,m^2 \times 3)$	$180\,m^2$ $(30\,m^2 +$ $30\,m^2 \times 5)$	$270\,m^2$ $(30\,m^2 +$ $30\,m^2 \times 8)$	$420\,m^2$ $(30\,m^2 +$ $30\,m^2 \times 13)$	$660\,m^2$ $(30\,m^2 +$ $30\,m^2 \times 21)$
Resulting CC density persons/ha	83	56	37	24	15

needed to reduce the density. While there are few studies giving carrying capacity estimates for water areas, there have been many estimating carrying capacity for beaches when the tide is out, and a good working maximum is 80 persons/ha (crowded beach). (Florida Department of Environmental Protection, nd). This value is in line with some ski user data (a comparable mobile sports activity) (Manning, 1985, 1986; South East Canada Resort Planners, 1996; Hogg, 1997, 2000), and was an acceptable maximum to all stakeholders interviewed. The detailed skiing study of the South East Canada Resort Planners (1996), which collated data from several other studies (e.g. Von Allmen, 2005) suggests a lower limit of ten persons/ha for the most extreme conditions (in the case of skiing, powder slopes over 60%). The same studies portray the progression from maximum to minimum density values as a set of non-linear curves, of varying degrees on non-linearity. Calculation of the comfort zones defined in terms of multiples of the physical footprint of $30\,m^2$, with these multiples following part of a Fibonacci sequence, gives as shown in Table 11.1.

The resulting density values follow a gentle non-linear curve, similar to those found by observation in the skiing studies summarised by South East Canada Resort Planners (1996), and with very similar upper and lower limits. The use of footprints and comfort zones may also be useful for other recreational activities where there is not much data on which to base upper and lower limits.

However, as regards this project to define surfing carrying capacity, incorporating non-linearity into what is meant to be a straightforward tool for everyday use is somewhat over-complex, and so a near-linear scale between 80 and 10 is chosen (Table 11.2). The carrying capacity density can be linked to other variables. Under certain conditions a life-guard would seek to reduce the numbers in the water, based upon environmental conditions such as weather conditions, sea state and visibility. Additionally, surf schools themselves would seek to reduce

Table 11.2 Linking carrying capacity to other safety variables

CC density persons/ha	80	60	40	20	10
Weather	Excellent	Very good	Good	Fair	Poor
Sea state	Very Low (calm)	Low (small swell/waves)	Moderate	High (large swell/waves)	Very high
Skill and expertise	Excellent	Very good	Good	Fair	Poor
Visibility	Excellent	Very good	Good	Fair	Poor

the numbers in the water based upon the need for individuals with less experience, fewer skills, less expertise and less confidence to have more space within the total area so as to reduce the risk of collision, accidents and injury. These variables can be incorporated into the calculations as shown in Table 11.2.

Each variable selected as representative of affecting safety is also chosen to be a factor that can be assessed visually at ground level by a lifeguard. For different on the ground assessments by a lifeguard for each safety factor one could then adjust the numbers: excellent weather gives a score of 80; moderate sea state, 40; poor skills, 10; excellent visibility, 80. The average of these four values is 52 persons/ha, and under this approach this can be taken as being the optimum CC density for these conditions. It is possible to add in more variables and these can be used/not used according to environmental conditions.

11.5   A second approach: incorporating local knowledge

As a practical guideline, Table 11.2 is an acceptable starting point. However, another major concern is one of practicality in the context of implementation of such an approach at the beach. While the CC (density – person/ha) numbers in Table 11.2 can easily be adjusted on the basis of the variables such as weather, sea state, skill and visibility, the hour-by-hour, day-to-day practicality of such flexibility in numbers at that level of detail is not really operationally feasible, particularly in the summer season on a crowded beach.

A different approach uses only one CC value and applies local RNLI expertise and experiential knowledge by way of the use of a local conditions factor (LCF). This is illustrated in Table 11.3. In this technique, the CC value chosen is the agreed maximum value of 80 persons/ha. Each beach was then assigned a local conditions factor, a cumulative assessment by the beach lifeguards on the safety of each beach on a

Table 11.3 Recommended capacity for surf school students per beach

Beach	Low tide					High tide				
	Surfer usable water area low tide: ha	Number of surfers at low tide	Local Conditions Factor (LCF)	LCF converted to % of students in total	Surf school students at low tide	Surfer usable water area high tide: ha	Number of surfers at high tide	Local conditions factor (LCF) as for low tide	LCF converted to % of students in total as for Low tide	Surf school students at high tide
	Maximum water carrying capacity: 80 person/ha					Maximum water carrying capacity as for low tide: 80 person/ha				
Porthcothan	0.30	24	3	25%	6	0.08	6			2
Trevarnon	0.09	0	3	25%	0	0.41	33			8
Constantine	0.20	16	3	25%	4	1.69	135			34
Booby's	1.69	135	3	25%	34	0.00	0			0
Harlyn	2.23	178	1	75%	134	0.69	55			41
Trevone	0.10	8	0	0%	0	0.23	18			0
Polzeath	1.89	151	1	75%	113	0.54	43			32
Widemouth	1.38	110	2	50%	55	1.77	142			71
Summerleaze & Middle Beach	1.14	91	1	75%	69	0.56	45			34
Crooklets	0.25	20	2	50%	10	0.01	1			1

scale of 0 to 3. This assessment incorporated local knowledge of the physical conditions and practical experience of lifeguarding at each beach; and as such it incorporates the four environmental variables of Table 11.2 into a single, average, value. A factor of 0 meant no surfing at all. A factor of 1 was assigned to a relatively safe, easy beach such as Polzeath, which can accommodate a larger proportion of learner surfers. Such a beach can accommodate 75% groups to 25% individual surfers. A factor of 2 represents a medium safety beach with 50% groups to 50% individuals, and a factor of 3 represents a dangerous beach (such as Constantine or Treyarnon), which can only accommodate a small proportion, 25%, of learners in groups relative to 75% of more experienced individuals.

11.6   Combining carrying capacity with area estimates

A geographical information system (GIS) was used to calculate the surfer usable water areas at low and high tides, for each beach (Table 11.3). Initial, approximate, GIS calculations had arrived at fairly large water areas (Carlisle and Green, 2008), but this process was heavily revised by further input from stakeholders. As a result the surfer usable water areas are comparatively small within the total water area, for several reasons. Only the surf zone itself is of interest to surfers, and this is a narrow band within the total water area. The length of this band is the waterline, and the width is approximately 50 m. Additionally, areas with rocks, cables, currents, river and sewage outlets are unsafe for surfing, and were therefore eliminated from the calculations via use of buffer zones. Third, some parts of the water area are zoned for other users (e.g. jet-skis). Finally, although most beaches in open bays have longer, and therefore larger, surf zones at low tide than high tide (e.g. Polzeath), four beaches (Treyarnon, Contantine, Trevone and Widemouth) have larger surf zones at high tide than low, due to local characteristics such as increased surf when a specific sand bar is covered by high tide.

   These area estimates can be combined with either of the two carrying capacity techniques described above. Table 11.2 illustrates the simplest combination, which is with the local conditions factor. The resulting values are a simple range of the number of surf school students allowed on each beach; at Polzeath, for example, the range is from 32 to 113 students. In effect there is only one straightforward variable that the beach lifeguards need to continually assess, and that is the state of the tide. This clearly demonstrates the main advantage of the LCF approach, namely its ease of use. It should be noted, however, that it is less sensitive to environmental variables than the first two techniques.

These numbers can be usefully compared with the people counts obtained from use of panoramic digital photography. At Polzeath, a count made on one day of a sunny bank holiday weekend, at what appears to be a peak time, gives a figure of 465 people in the water. Comparison with Table 11.2 indicates a desired maximum number of surfers of 151 for this beach's water area. Even if many of the people counted were not themselves surfers, they would most probably be in the surfer usable water area. The excess of 300 people over the calculated water carrying capacity indicates the scale of the safety problem faced by the RNLI lifeguards.

11.7   Conclusions

The outcomes of this study are three practical water carrying capacity (WCC) approaches to determine a safe range of surf school student numbers for different beaches and tidal conditions. In theory the numbers can also easily be adjusted to provide a flexible response to several different environmental conditions. In practice, however, the problem is limited by translation into hour-by-hour operational beach management, leading to the conclusion that the simplest technique, the LCF, is the most appropriate. To conclude, this research will hopefully establish a framework for decision-making and a basis for regulatory action to help ensure water areas are used in a safe way that helps to minimise accidents and injury, while also enhancing the user experience, possibly also helping to overcome perceptions of overcrowding and contributing to beach management. As noted by Da Silva (2002, p. 190):

> The limitations encountered do not place the validity of (such) studies in doubt, as they are evidently of great importance for beach management and thus should be used in a flexible way, fully adapted to the existing specific site conditions.

Acknowledgements

North Cornwall District Council (NCDC) for the research funding and their time, and Steve Instance, John Broad and Bobby Renaud, all of the RNLI for their help, patience and valuable discussions and input to this work.

References

Buckley, R.C. (2002a) Surf tourism and sustainable development in Indo-Pacific Islands. I. The industry and the islands. *Journal of Sustainable Tourism*, Vol. 10, pp. 405–424.

Buckley R.C. (2002b) Surf tourism and sustainable development in Indo-Pacific Islands. II. Recreational capacity management and case study. *Journal of Sustainable Tourism*, Vol. 10, pp. 425–442.

Carlisle, M.A. and Green, D.R. (2008) A Template for Human Impacts Evaluation, University of Aberdeen. Available at: http://www.abdn.ac.uk/cmczm/about.htm & COREPOINT February 2008.

Da Silva, C.P. (2002) Beach carrying capacity assessment. How important is it? *Journal of Coastal Research*, Special Issue 36, pp. 190–197.

DSE (2005) Licensing of surf schools in Victoria: standard procedures for land managers. Unpublished.

Florida Department of Environmental Protection (nd) *Visitor Carrying Capacity Guidelines Appendix I – Recreation Facility Design Guidelines*, Florida Department of Environmental Protection: Division of Recreation and Parks.

Graves, S.C. (2003) Marina Mooring Optimization 15066j System Optimization and Analysis. Professor Stephen C. Graves, Summer 2003, available at: http://www.uspowerboating.com/swinging_radius.htm, http://www.jubileeyc.net/moorings.htm)

Hogg, D. (1997) Perisher Blue Ski Resort Ski Slope Capacity Model. Perisher Blue Internal Working Paper, June.

Hogg, D. (2000) Calculation of slope capacity. Perisher Blue Internal Working Paper, January.

Manning, R.E. (1985) Crowding norms in backcountry settings: a review and synthesis. *Journal of Leisure Research*, Vol. 17, pp. 75–89.

Manning, R.E. (1986) *Studies in Outdoor Recreation: Search and Research for Satisfaction*, Oregon State University Press, Corvallis, OR.

South East Canada Resort Planners (1996) *Guidelines to Alpine Ski Area Development in British Columbia: Prepared for Ministry of Environment, Lands and Parks SE Canada*, The Resort Planners Whistler, BC, June.

Von Allmen, B. (2005) How to Measure Trail Capacity. Unpublished Paper. Online at: http://www.alpentech.net

12

Vulnerability assessment

Pamela A. Abuodha and Colin D. Woodroffe
GeoQuest Research Centre, School of Earth and Environmental Sciences,
University of Wollongong, Australia

Vulnerability assessment aims at assisting policymakers in adequately responding to the challenges of climate change by investigating how projected changes in the Earth's climate may affect natural systems and human activities. Natural coastal systems appear particularly threatened by the impacts of climate change, both in terms of exposure and susceptibility. Where socio-economic systems are at risk there is a need for adaptation. This chapter traces the lineage of methods used to assess the vulnerability of coasts to climate change. Early approaches, such as the Bruun rule, have been criticised for their simplicity, but they continue to underpin efforts to model coastal response. There have been several global-scale vulnerability assessments triggered by a 'common methodology' that was proposed by the Intergovernmental Panel on Climate Change (IPCC). Alternative regional-scale approaches have focused on segmenting a linear representation of the shoreline. Examples of this are the coastal vulnerability index applied on many of the US coasts and geomorphic stability mapping applied on the Tasmanian coast. However, few of these methods adequately incorporate social or cultural aspects of coastal systems. Information incorporating social and cultural aspects of coastal systems is important to help assess the magnitude and threat of climate change and thus motivate the broader community to take an appropriate level of action. It is important that each assessment is undertaken at the relevant spatial and temporal scales, because the results are often appropriate only at those scales.

12.1   Introduction

A significant body of scientific evidence clearly indicates that climate change is a serious and urgent issue (Stern, 2007). Coastal systems are

Coastal zone management
978-0-7277-3641-1

increasingly threatened by potential impacts as a result of climate change, and the most widespread risks foreshadowed for coasts are accelerated coastal erosion, increased inundation of low-lying areas, and saline intrusion into coastal waterways and water tables (Nicholls *et al.*, 2007). Although recent assessments by the Intergovernmental Panel on Climate Change (IPCC) have identified a series of other climate change drivers that will impact the coast, such as possible increases to sea-surface temperatures, greater variability in the patterns of rainfall and runoff, altered wind patterns, possible changes to wave climate, changes to the frequency and intensity of storms, and ocean acidification, sea-level rise remains the single most widespread and pressing concern, with the impacts likely to become most apparent in association with extreme weather events (floods, droughts and cyclones) posing additional threats to human infrastructure and settlements. These variations in climate will make the assessment of the extent to which the climate is changing much harder. It is therefore of great importance to develop tools that can be used to assess coastal vulnerability. This chapter reviews the chronological development, application and evaluation of coastal zone vulnerability assessment tools with the objective of developing appropriate adaptation strategies and improved forecasting skills.

12.2   Coastal vulnerability

The IPCC was established by the United Nations Environmental Programme (UNEP) and the World Meteorological Organisation (WMO) in 1988 to assess the scientific, technical and socio-economic information relevant for the understanding of human induced climate change, its potential impacts and options for mitigation and adaptation. The IPCC and its coastal zone management subgroup (CZMS) have been at the forefront in developing global methods for coastal vulnerability assessment in order to examine the impact of human-induced climatic change on coastal systems. In the IPCC third assessment report (TAR), vulnerability is defined as the degree to which a system is susceptible to, or unable to cope with, adverse effects of climate change, including climate variability and extremes. This concept of vulnerability embraces: (1) the physical and socio-economic susceptibility to global climate change; and (2) the ability to cope with these consequences (i.e. susceptible countries or areas may not be vulnerable). Vulnerability is a function of the character, magnitude, and rate of climate variation to which a system is exposed in relation to its sensitivity, and its adaptive capacity (IPCC, 2001).

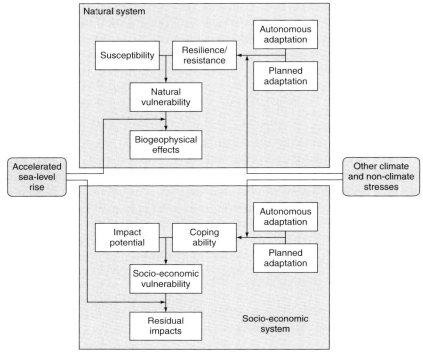

Fig. 12.1 A conceptual framework for coastal vulnerability assessment (after Klein and Nicholls, 1999), used in UNEP and other approaches for vulnerability assessment to sea-level rise

Many assessments of coastal vulnerability have found it useful to adopt the framework summarised in Fig. 12.1, distinguishing between natural system vulnerability and socio-economic vulnerability to climate change, but emphasising their interrelatedness and interdependence (Klein and Nicholls, 1999).

A coastal system's natural vulnerability to the effects of accelerated sea-level rise (ASLR) is a function of its natural susceptibility, its resistance and its resilience. Certain geomorphic settings are more vulnerable than others, for example, deltas, small islands and, most particularly, low-lying coral atolls are especially vulnerable (Bijlsma *et al.*, 1996). Natural susceptibility is the coastal system's potential to be affected by ASLR. This is largely independent of human influences. Resistance is the ability of the system to avoid perturbation in the first place, a seawall or a cliff is resistant, whereas resilience is the ability for the system to return to its original state after being perturbed and the speed at which this occurs. Resilience and resistance are different aspects of the system's stability in the face of possible perturbation. These can be strongly dependent on human influences. Autonomous adaptation is the coastal system's spontaneous and natural adaptive response to ASLR, a function of its resilience and resistance (Fig. 12.1). Human influences may be disruptive (e.g. over-exploitation of an ecosystem), and can increase the coastal system's natural vulnerability to ASLR. Planned adaptation includes measures taken to enhance the systems natural resilience and resistance (e.g. create buffer zones).

Assessment of vulnerability needs to start with an understanding of the natural system and its biophysical response to climate change (in particular sea-level rise). Important concepts include the system's susceptibility (exposure, or potential of the system to be affected by hazards), and its sensitivity, the responsiveness or its natural capacity to cope. Coastal landforms and ecosystems may also show resistance or resilience in terms of other aspects of the coastal management process, such as social, cultural, or institutional resilience (Kay and Hay, 1993). Adaptive capacity describes how this ability to cope may be increased either through natural (autonomous) adaptation or through planned adaptation. Even with planned adaptation, residual risks remain, as tragically demonstrated when coastal defences around New Orleans failed under the impact of Hurricane Katrina in 2005.

In this chapter, 'climate change' follows the IPCC definition and refers to any change in climate over time, whether due to natural variability or as a result of human activity (IPCC, 2007), and impact assessment refers to investigations designed to evaluate the effects of future changes in climate on human activities and the natural environment (Feenstra *et al.*, 1998). This differs from a definition used by the United Nations Framework Convention on climate change (UNFCCC). UNFCCC Article 1.2 states that climate change means 'a change of climate which is attributed directly or indirectly to human activity that alters the composition of the global atmosphere and which is in addition to natural climate variability observed over comparable time periods' (UNFCCC, 1992). The UNFCCC developed from the United Nations conference on environment and development (UNCED), which was held in Rio de Janeiro, Brazil, in June 1992.

The UNFCCC underpinned the Global Environment Facility (GEF), established in 1991, which helps developing countries fund projects and programs that protect the global environment and promotes sustainable livelihoods in local communities. GEF is the United Nations Development Program (UNDP) component of a UNDP–UNEP–World Bank initiative with a project portfolio operating in 112 developing countries. In 2004, the UNFCCC compiled a useful compendium on methods and tools to evaluate impacts of vulnerability and adaptation to climate change, adopting a summary table format to assess the techniques (UNFCCC, 2004).

The vulnerability of coastal landforms to the physical and socio-economic impacts of coastal hazards can be broadly-defined at three scales, international, national and local scales. The international or global scale of vulnerability tends to focus on national indicators; for example, to group less developed countries or compare progress in human development among countries with similar economic conditions. It may be the first stage to indicate which broad global regions may require further assessments. The national or regional scale of vulnerability assessments contribute to setting development priorities and monitoring progress. Sectoral or local assessments provide more details and targets for strategic development plans, generally focusing on particularly vulnerable sites within a region. This scale involves identifying regional variations in the energies driving coastal changes (such as wave energy, tidal range, vertical land movement). Finally, the local or community scale of vulnerability assessment helps to identify vulnerable groups or site-specific areas and the coping strategies implemented. This often employs participatory methods. Participatory research is defined as a process of practical learning by the community as well as the scientists leading a vulnerability assessment project. Participation promotes interaction between scientists of different disciplines as well as between team and local community. The approach challenges the way knowledge is produced and disseminated by dominant educational institutions.

12.3 Sea level rise and shoreline retreat

One of the first attempts to develop a conceptual model of the way that a shoreline might respond to sea-level rise was by Per Bruun, a coastal engineer, who proposed the so-called Bruun rule, based on an equilibrium beach profile (Bruun, 1954). This describes an average profile shape maintained by the shoreface, related to sediment size and wave climate, with slight seasonal and wave-related fluctuations using a characteristic parabolic equilibrium beach shape given by equation 1 below:

$$h = Ax^m \tag{1}$$

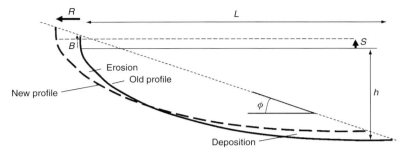

Fig. 12.2 The Bruun rule of shoreline erosion, showing the parameters defined in eqn 2, and the erosion of the beach and deposition in the nearshore anticipated as a consequence of sea-level rise

where h is still-water depth; x is horizontal distance from the shoreline; A is a dimensional parameter related to sediment characteristics and m is an exponent, often around $\frac{2}{3}$.

Bruun (1962) expanded on this theory to predict the response of a beach profile to rising sea level. The Bruun rule basically states that as sea level rises, the shoreline retreats uniformly so as to maintain a constant equilibrium profile (Fig. 12.2). Sand is moved from the upper part of the beach profile to accumulate on the lower part of the profile.

The Bruun rule has been widely adopted to provide a forecast of how shorelines may respond to sea-level rise based on conservation of mass of sediment. It is expressed as shown in equation 2 below:

$$R = S(L/(B + h)) = (S)1/\tan\phi \qquad (2)$$

where, in a typical equilibrium nearshore profile, L is the length of the profile, ϕ is the profile slope angle, B is the berm height and h is the depth at the base of the profile beyond which significant sediment exchange with the offshore does not occur (the closure depth). For a sea-level rise of the amount S, the profile will shift landward by the amount R according to the Bruun rule equation (Bruun, 1988; Fig. 12.2). The rate of shoreline retreat is a function of the slope of the shoreface, but as this lies within a narrow range of values it is often simplified further to indicate that shoreline erosion rate is approximately 100 times the rate of sea-level rise (Bruun, 1988).

The Bruun rule is based on a series of assumptions, particularly that: (1) the nearshore system is closed: no sediment is lost landward of the dunes nor seaward of a depth on the shoreface called the closure depth; (2) the profile maintains its shape in the long term, despite the presence

267

of any seasonal/storm fluctuations; and, (3) shoreline change is 2D, expressed by the profile, and is not influenced by 3D factors such as variably bathymetry or alongshore transport gradients (Bruun, 1988).

The simplicity of these assumptions has led to widespread criticism of the Bruun rule. Pilkey *et al.* (1993) argue that: (1) the Bruun rule ignores the action of alongshore currents; (2) shorefaces are not closed systems in the cross-shore direction; (3) underlying geology plays a major role in the shoreface profile; and (4) not all profiles assume the concave shape described by Bruun.

The SCOR Working Group 89 (1991) identified a number of limitations to the Bruun rule and Cooper and Pilkey (2004) criticise it on the basis of the restrictive assumptions it makes, the omission of important variables and the erroneous relationships that are inferred. These three factors are further discussed below with examples. The key assumption is that there is a closed material balance for the profile, i.e. there can be no net gain or loss of sediment from the profile from any other source including longshore transport. The concept of the 'closure depth', also called the 'sediment fence', is based on the assumption that sediment transport on the shoreface only occurs by way of the interaction of wave orbitals and sand on the sea floor; it has proved particularly controversial and is a gross oversimplification (Pilkey *et al.*, 2000; Cooper and Pilkey, 2004). The Bruun rule is unsuitable for use in highly complex sedimentary environments such as where there are spatial and temporal variations in sediment supply, wave conditions and coastal retreat rates, or geological control on profile shape (Cooper and Pilkey, 2004).

The Bruun rule implies that erosion of the shoreline due to sea-level rise is a function of the average slope of the shoreface, which is typically the steepest part of the nearshore profile. However, no evidence from field studies has been presented to demonstrate that shoreface steepness bears any relationship to shoreline retreat rates (Cooper and Pilkey, 2004). It has now been shown that many other parameters, i.e. wave energy, storm frequency and sediment supply, determine the shape of the shoreface (Cooper and Pilkey, 2004).

Although the Bruun rule has been found to have many limitations, it continues to be widely applied due to the simplicity of the model for describing a very complex environment (Davidson-Arnott, 2005). There is also a number of other reasons for its longevity, including: (1) the appeal of a simple and easy to use analytical model; (2) its relatively inexpensive application thus allowing rapid assessment of large areas of the coast; (3) positive advocacy by many coastal engineers;

and (4) the simple numerical expression of the model (Cooper and Pilkey, 2004). Furthermore, modifications to the Bruun rule have been incorporated into several other computational techniques for assessing shoreline response, including the Shoreline Translation Model (Cowell *et al.*, 2006; STM considered in greater detail by Dickson, Cowell and Woodroffe, Chapter 7 of this volume) and the coastal impact module of the SimCLIM system software (CLIMsystems, 2007).

The Coastal Impact Module (CIM) of SimCLIM is a computer-based tool that can simulate the behaviour of the shoreline in response to particular scenarios of sea-level change. The tool is stochastically driven to produce projections, rather than predictions. The shoreline is presumed to move towards adopting an equilibrium profile as in the basic Bruun rule (CLIMsystems, 2007); however, two important limitations of the Bruun rule have been addressed. First, a stochastic storm-cut can be generated, and second, a time lag can be input to represent the gradual adjustment towards equilibrium. SimCLIM is designed to support decision making and climate proofing in a wide range of situations where climate and climate change pose risk and uncertainty. The key aim of the coastal impact module (CIM) is to simulate the range of Bruun-type responses that a shoreline may show in response to sea-level change and scenarios of storm occurrence. Although it addresses several of the concerns about the Bruun rule, these approaches address shore profiles and are not tools that are designed to yield specific geographical information about the pattern of shoreline response, simplifying much of the complexity of shoreline behaviour.

12.4   Global-scale vulnerability assessment

In September 1991, the IPCC CZMS published 'The seven steps for the assessment of the vulnerability of coastal areas to sea-level rise – a common methodology' (IPCC CZMS, 1992, Section 3, p. 11). A second revision was released in 1992 in *Global Climate Change and the Rising Challenge of the Sea*, accompanied by techniques to inventorise and delineate areas vulnerable to sea-level rise (IPCC CZMS, 1992). The objectives of the common methodology were to provide a framework to: (1) identify and assess physical, ecological, and socio-economic vulnerabilities to accelerated sea-level rise and other coastal impacts of global climate change; (2) understand how development and other socio-economic factors affect vulnerability; (3) clarify how possible responses can mitigate vulnerability and assess their residual effects; and (4) evaluate a country's capacity for implementing a response within a broad coastal zone management framework (IPCC CZMS, 1992; IPCC, 1994). Studies using the common methodology were meant to serve as preparatory assessments, identifying priority regions and priority sectors and providing an initial screening of possible adaptation measures.

The seven steps of the common methodology are outlined in Table 12.1. In assessing vulnerability to sea-level rise, the common methodology considers the potential impacts on population, on economic, ecological and social assets, and on agricultural production. The scenarios to be considered were the high (1 m) and low (0.3 m) scenarios of the IPCC sea-level rise projections developed in 1990. The common methodology includes three scenario variables: global climate change factors, local development factors, and response options. It considers national or local development by extrapolating 30 years from the present situation. The common methodology focused on monetary valuations of vulnerable areas so that a cost–benefit analysis could be applied to assess the best response option (IPCC CZMS, 1992). The generally accepted range of options at that time included: (1) protection of the coast by defence works; (2) accommodation of changes; (3) retreating from vulnerable areas; or (4) doing nothing (IPCC CZMS, 1992; Harvey and Woodroffe, 2008).

The common methodology had the advantage of providing a simple to follow, step-by-step methodology for assessing coastal vulnerability to sea-level rise and no other methodology has been applied as widely and evaluated as thoroughly as the common methodology (e.g. Kay *et al.*, 1996). During the 1990s, a series of vulnerability assessment studies was initiated throughout the world, especially within specific country studies programmes (IPCC CZMS, 1992; IPCC, 1994). Results from these studies were presented at the Eastern hemisphere workshop in Tsukuba, prior to the World Coasts Conference in 1993 (McLean and Mimura, 1993).

While the common methodology and related methods generated large amounts of data, they have also been criticised. Many studies that used the common methodology encountered inadequate data necessary for impact and adaptation assessment (Klein and Nicholls, 1999). Further criticism arose because the economic-based assessment technique was inconsistent with planning approaches or failed to include social and cultural factors. The method uses monetary valuations to estimate a coastal nation's vulnerability to future sea-level rise, employing a cost–benefit test to assess the preferred response option to remediate future coastal impacts. In addition to minor operational shortcomings, more fundamental methodological concerns

Table 12.1 *The seven-step common methodology and other methodologies developed to remedy it (modified from Harvey et al., 1999)*

	IPCC CZMS (1992)	Kay and Waterman (1993)	Harvey et al. (1999)
Definition of study areas			
Delineation of case study area	Stage 1		Stage 1
Spatial scale			Stage 2
Temporal scale			
Focus on physical and biological conditions		Stage 1	
Incorporation of current human-induced hazards and climatic change hazards			Stage 2
Data collection			
Inventory of study area	Stage 2		
Characteristics biophysical			Stage 3
Socio-economic and cultural and heritage			Stage 4
Analysis of vulnerable and resilient components including socio-economic and cultural systems		Stage 2	
Analysis of links between and within systems and connected areas		Stage 3	
Inventory of study sites selected from study area- biophysical, socio-economic, cultural and heritage			Stage 5
Identification of relevant development factors	Stage 3		
Identification of relevant legislation			Stage 6
Assessment			
Assess physical changes and natural system responses	Stage 4		
Assessment of vulnerability profile and interpretation of results	Stage 6		
Assessment of vulnerability in qualitative and quantitative terms			Stage 7
Responses			
Formulate response strategies–cost/benefit analysis	Stage 5		
Formulation of management strategies with regard to government policies		Stage 4	
Identify future needs and develop a plan of action	Stage 7		
Setting of priorities for management – current and long term			Stage 8

with the common methodology have included: the applicability of economic-based assessment in the case of primarily subsistence economies in the Asia-Pacific region; inadequacy as a tool for coastal managers to formulate sea-level rise impact assessment policies; lack

271

of time dependency and the narrow geographic definition of the coastal zone (Kay and Waterman, 1993; Kay *et al.*, 1996). The common methodology was considered to be particularly inappropriate for small islands in the South Pacific due to their subsistence-based economies and lack of the most basic data among other factors. As a result, an alternative approach to vulnerability assessment was developed specifically for these islands (Yamada *et al.*, 1995).

Nevertheless, the common methodology provided the basis on which a series of subsequent global assessments of vulnerability has been based. These include, among others, the South Pacific Islands Methodology (SPIM) (Yamada *et al.*, 1995), the IPCC technical guidelines (Carter *et al.*, 1994), US Country Studies (Beniof *et al.*, 1996) and the UNEP Guidelines (Burton *et al.*, 1998). The first global vulnerability assessment (GVA), using the common methodology, was conducted by WLI Delft Hydraulics under the auspices of the Netherlands Ministry of Transport, Public Works and Water Management/National Institute of Coast and Sea (Hoozemans *et al.*, 1993). The GVA was limited to four elements of the coastal zone and accompanying impacts: (1) population at risk (i.e. the number of people subject to regular flooding) on a global scale; (2) wetlands at loss (i.e. the ecologically valuable coastal wetland area under a serious threat of loss) on a global scale, (3) rice production at change (i.e. the changes in coastal rice yields due to less favourable conditions due to accelerated sea-level rise) in South, South-East and East Asia; and (4) protection cost updates of the estimates in the 1990 IPCC CZMS report (Baarse, 1995; Hoozeman *et al.*, 1993). The report and the datasets that were generated have underpinned a series of the subsequent developments, such as DIVA, described in Section 12.5, and, although the GVA did not develop an explicit spatial model, several approaches using a linear segmentation of the shoreline have arisen (Nicholls and Hoozemans, 2005).

A major project on synthesis and upscaling of sea-level rise vulnerability assessment studies (SURVAS) also developed out of the common methodology. The SURVAS project undertook a range of activities including: (1) reviewing the potential impacts of human-induced sea-level rise at the national and sub-national scale; (2) using this understanding to improve regional and global perspectives on sea-level rise and associated impacts; and (3) considering the next steps for this type of assessment. Products from SURVAS include a standard vulnerability data set that has been made available on the SURVAS web site (http://www.survas.mdx.ac.uk/). The SURVAS project has also fed directly into the DINAS-COAST project (http://www.pik-potsdam.de/~richardk/

272

dinas-coast/) which developed a state-of-the-art modelling tool, called dynamic interactive vulnerability assessment (DIVA), for national, regional and global vulnerability assessment of coastal areas.

The common methodology approach has underpinned several subsequent vulnerability assessment procedures, including the study by Harvey *et al.* (1999; Table 12.1). As a result of criticisms of the common methodology described earlier in this section, an alternative methodology was proposed by Kay and Waterman (1993), which had four key stages (Table 12.1). Stage 1 focused on the physical and biological conditions of the study area and delineated those areas of potential future sea-level coastal hazard. Stage 2 considered susceptibility to stress, shock and damage caused by climate change while recognising that susceptibility is conditioned by the resilience of the natural coastal system. Stage 3 focused on the linkages within the system and between connected systems and stage 4 considered the interaction of the systems and the range of policy options that would be determined by government policies and plans (Harvey and Woodroffe, 2008).

A South Australian study undertaken by Harvey *et al.* (1999) followed the Kay and Waterman methodology but encountered methodological problems. While the Common Methodology may have been an attempt to produce a comparable quantitative assessment, the Kay and Waterman methodology gave no guidance for ranking management and response option priorities (Table 12.1). Harvey *et al.* (1999) therefore expanded the South Australian vulnerability studies to a broader range of coastal environments (bio-physical and socio-economic) in an attempt to provide and test a more appropriate methodology for coastal vulnerability assessment.

The Harvey *et al.* (1999) methodology comprises eight stages which are described below and are compared with various stages in both the common methodology and the Kay and Waterman methodologies (Table 12.1). To overcome the lack of spatial and temporal scales defined by Kay and Waterman (1993), the first two stages of the Harvey *et al.* (1999) methodology define the spatial scale of the study area using bio-physical and socio-economic boundaries (Stage 1) and the temporal scale incorporating current human-induced hazards and potential climate change hazards (Stage 2). The Harvey *et al.* (1999) methodology then collects data on the relevant bio-physical characteristics of the study area (Stage 3) and socio-economic, cultural and heritage characteristics of the study area (Stage 4), followed by a reiteration of steps 1 to 4 for selected study sites (Stage 5). Once Stages 1–5 are completed, the relevant legislation, jurisdictions, plans and policies

273

are identified for the study area (Stage 6). It is then possible to assess coastal vulnerability in both qualitative and quantitative terms from the various techniques (Stage 7). Finally, the revised methodology sets priorities for management and long-term objectives according to identified problems (Stage 8, Harvey and Woodroffe, 2008, p. 72).

12.5   Shoreline segmentation

There is a number of methods of vulnerability assessment that adopt geographic information systems (GIS), automated mapping software, based on spatial information and associated databases in which attributes can be captured, stored, analysed, displayed (e.g. maps) and visualised. A commonly adopted GIS data model for these vulnerability assessments is a linear segmentation of the shoreline. The DINAS-Coast method and the DIVA tool developed by the consortium will be described first, because it was derived from the GVA, and other more regional techniques using this methodology will be described subsequently.

The European project, DINAS-Coast (dynamic and interactive assessment of national, regional and global vulnerability of coastal zones to climate change and sea-level rise) has developed the DIVA tool to help policymakers interpret and evaluate coastal vulnerability. The DIVA tool enables analysis of a range of mitigation and adaptation scenarios. It comprises a global database of natural system and socio-economic factors (expanded from GVA), relevant scenarios, a set of impact-adaptation algorithms and a customised graphical-user interface. Factors that are considered include erosion, flooding, salinisation and wetland loss. DIVA enables users to produce quantitative data on a range of coastal vulnerability indicators for user-selected climatic and socio-economic scenarios and adaptation policies, for future sea-level rise. Figure 12.3 shows shoreline segmentation of the UK coast using the DIVA tool and an example of mapping at administrative unit level. Segmentation of the world's coastline was performed on the basis of a series of physical, administrative and socio-economic criteria (Vafeidis *et al.*, 2008; McFadden *et al.*, 2007).

An innovative approach to developing a coastal vulnerability assessment for the US was undertaken by Gornitz and Kanciruk (1989). They considered inundation, flooding and susceptibility to erosion. It was proposed by Gornitz (1991) that the index, termed the coastal vulnerability index (CVI), might be applied worldwide, although its application was only demonstrated for the US in her study. Table 12.3 shows the matrix for determining the CVI involving seven physical variables;

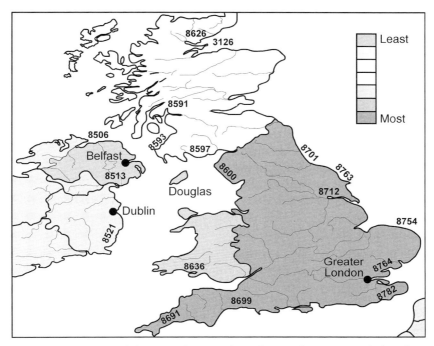

Fig. 12.3 A sample of the type of output derived using the DIVA tool (based on the DINAS Coast database). The attribute mapped for the UK is the area of coastal floodplain; to the left at the scale of individual shoreline segments (selected segments are numbered, note that the shoreline of the Wash shows extensive plains) and to the left aggregated to the level of administrative units

(a) relief, (b) rock type, (c) landform, (d) vertical movement, (e) shoreline displacement, (f) tidal range and (g) wave height. This method yields a semi-quantitative value that can be equated directly with particular physical effects, highlighting areas where sea-level rise may have the greatest impact. The CVI is a dimensionless index, obtained by manipulating scores of 1 to 5 attributed to each of the seven variables, shown in Table 12.2, using eqn 3 outlined below to aggregate them:

$$CVI = \sqrt{\frac{a \times b \times c \times d \times e \times f \times g}{7}} \qquad (3)$$

where, a = relief, b = rock type, c = landform, d = vertical movement, e = shoreline displacement, f = tide range and g = wave height. On the basis of this index, coasts can be grouped into three categories: low, moderate and high vulnerability. A high value might be expected for a region of low relief, unconsolidated sediments, with barrier islands,

275

Table 12.2 Matrix for determination of coastal vulnerability index (CVI) (source: Gornitz and Kanciruk, 1989)

Category	Very low	Low	Moderate	High	Very high
Variable	1	2	3	4	5
(a) Relief: m	≥30.1	20.1–30.0	10.1–20.0	5.1–10.0	0–5.0
(b) Rock type (relative resistance to erosion)	Plutonic volcanic (lava) High-medium-grade metamorphic	Low-grade metamorphic sandstone and conglomerate (well cemented)	Most sedimentary rocks	Coarse and/or poorly-sorted unconsolidated sediments	Fine unconsolidated sediments Volcanic ash
(c) Landform	Rocky, cliffed coasts	Medium cliffs, indented coasts	Low cliffs, salt marsh, coral reefs, mangrove	Beaches (pebbles), estuary, lagoon	Barrier and bay beaches, mudflats, deltas
(d) Vertical movement (RSL change): mm/yr	≤−1.1 Land rising	−1.0–0.99	1.0–2.0 Within range of eustatic rise	2.1–4.0 Land sinking	≥4.1
(e) Shoreline displacement: m/yr	≥+2.1 accretion	1.0–2.0	−1.0–+1.0 stable	−1.1–−2.0	≤−2.1 Erosion
(f) Tidal range: m (mean)	≥0.99 Microtidal	1.0–1.9	2.0–4.0 Mesotidal	4.1–6.0	≥6.1 Macrotidal
(g) Wave height: m (max)	0–2.9	3.0–4.9	5.0–5.9	6.0–6.9	≥7.0

Table 12.3 Summary of coastal vulnerability indices described in this chapter, their geographical application and the variables needed to implement them

Index	Geographical application	Variables considered	Reference
Coastal vulnerability index (CVI)	USA	Relief, rock type, landform, vertical movement, shoreline displacement, tidal range, wave height	Gornitz and Kanciruk (1989), Gornitz (1991), Gornitz *et al.* (1991)
Coastal vulnerability index (CVI)	USA	Historic shoreline erosion rates, geomorphology, relative rates of sea-level rise, coastal slope, wave height, tidal range	Thieler (2000) and numerous other USGS reports
Social vulnerability index (SoVI)	USA	Principal components analysis of Census-derived social data	Boruff *et al.* (2005)
Coastal social vulnerability score (CSoVI)	USA	Combination of CVI and SoVI	Boruff *et al.* (2005)
Sensitivity index (SI)	Canada	Relief, sea-level trend, geology, coastal landform, shoreline displacement, wave energy, tidal range	Shaw *et al.* (1998)
Risk matrix	South Africa	Location, infrastructure (economic value), hazard	Hughes and Brundrit (1992)
Sustainable capacity index (SCI)	South Pacific	Vulnerability and resilience of natural, cultural, institutional, infrastructural, economic and human factors	Kay and Hay (1993) Yamada *et al.* (1995)

high tidal range, high wave energy levels and rapid relative sea-level rise (Table 12.2). A low value would be expected for a coast with high relief, a rocky shore with resistant non-eroding bedrock, falling sea level, low tidal range and low wave energy (Table 12.2). The vulnerability index method of classifying coasts accommodates not just sea level but also the potential of other factors that render the coast more or less vulnerable to change.

A potential limitation of the Gornitz CVI is that, in its present form, it does not include demographic or economic factors in evaluating the susceptibility of a given area to sea-level rise. The CVI is best applied at a regional scale to a section of a coast where there is much variation in risk. The method yields numerical data which cannot be directly equated with particular physical effects; it does not measure rate of retreat, or volume of erosion. Nor does it capture storm surge or sediment transport; Gornitz recognised that the CVI could be improved if it had a term related to storm frequency, and if it included a term related to population at risk (Gornitz *et al.*, 1991).

Since the initial development of the CVI by Gornitz and Kanciruk in 1989, many coastal vulnerability approaches have been derived as summarised in Table 12.3. A coastal vulnerability index, similar to that proposed by Gornitz, has been used to evaluate many shorelines around the US by the United States Geological Survey (USGS) (Thieler, 2000), involving a series of specific reports for different areas, along the Atlantic, Pacific, and Gulf of Mexico coasts (Hammar-Klose and Thieler, 2001; Hammar-Klose *et al.*, 2003; Pendleton *et al.*, 2004). This approach uses relative contributions of six variables: tidal range contributing to inundation hazards, wave height linked to inundation hazard, coastal slope (susceptibility to inundation and rate of shoreline retreat), historic shoreline erosion rates, geomorphology (relative erodibility) and historic relative rates of sea-level rise (eustatic and hydroisostatic) (Hammar-Klose and Thieler, 2001; Thieler *et al.*, 2002; Hammar-Klose *et al.*, 2003; Table 12.3) but does not include a human component. The CVI is derived to show relative vulnerability; it combines the coastal system's susceptibility to change with its natural ability to adapt to changing environmental conditions, yielding a relative measure of the system's natural vulnerability to the effects of sea-level rise. The purpose of CVI calculation is to assess the impacts of a rise in relative sea-level. Figure 12.4 shows relative coastal vulnerability for the Assateague Island National Seashore (ASIS) in Maryland and Virginia, east coast, USA (Pendleton *et al.*, 2004). To create a regionally comparable index, the USGS then re-ranked CVI on an ordinal scale from 1 to 5 (Thieler and Hammar-Klose, 1999, 2000a, 2000b). The re-ranked CVI was used in analysis to test for regional differences in physical vulnerability.

The Gornitz and Kanciruk approach has also given rise to a sensitivity index (SI) that has been applied in Canada to assess coastal sensitivity to sea-level rise (Table 12.3). In this case it was assessed for the entire Canadian coastline using 2899 maps at a scale of 1:50 000 and the index was scaled using a 1–5 scaling developed for Canadian coastal types, with final ranking as low, moderate or high. A shortcoming was that numerous areas of high sensitivity were overlooked at this scale (Shaw *et al.*, 1998; Table 12.2).

A different approach, although also adopting segmentation of a shoreline, has been developed in Australia by Sharples (2004). It was

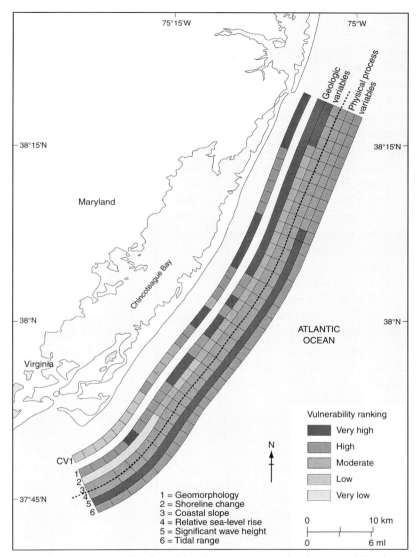

Fig. 12.4 Relative coastal vulnerability for Assateague Island National Seashore in the eastern USA. The tinted bars are separated into the geologic variables (1–3) and physical process variables (4–6). The innermost colour bar is the relative coastal vulnerability index (CVI). The very high vulnerability shoreline is located in low overwashed areas where rates of shoreline erosion are highest. The low vulnerability shoreline is located at the southernmost end of Assateague in Virginia near the Chincoteague Inlet, where shoreline accretion rates are high (source: Pendleton et al., 2004: USGS Open File Report 2004-1020: http://pubs.usgs.gov/of/2004/1020/images/pdf/asis.pdf)

279

applied initially in Tasmania, but has subsequently been upgraded for application to the coast of the mainland also. In his 2004 study, updated and extended in 2006, Sharples examined both the vulnerability to inundation and the physical stability of the shoreline and, hence, its potential for erosion (Sharples, 2006). The inundation component is carried out by assessing topography on the basis of available digital elevation models (DEM) in comparison to the highest water levels anticipated by a consideration of the geographical pattern of extreme water levels around the Tasmanian coast.

It takes a pragmatic approach referred to as 'first pass' which identifies and maps Tasmanian shoreline landform types that are potentially vulnerable to sea-level rise, including sandy beaches, slump- and rock-fall-prone shores and several other classes of soft shores. Also termed indicative mapping, it was intended as the first stage in a hierarchical sequence of assessments. The second stage, also referred to as regional assessment, would involve identifying regional variations in the energies driving coastal changes (such as wave energy), and a final level of detail would be achieved by site-specific or local studies which model all relevant variables at specific locations identified as potentially sensitive by the preceding stages of assessment (Harvey and Woodroffe, 2008, p. 77).

The shoreline geomorphic mapping involves segmenting a shoreline and assigning multiple attributes to the segments describing the coastal landforms; these descriptive landform attributes can subsequently be used to define sensitivity classes by identifying shoreline segments having combinations of attributes corresponding to different types of sensitive shore. The principal attributes used in the first stage of mapping comprised separate fields for upper intertidal, lower intertidal and backshore landforms (Fig. 12.5). In addition, an attribute called profile was used to give a qualitative indication of the average slope of the hinterland, and a bedrock attribute described the geology of the shore. Vulnerability classes were derived from these attributes. For example, attributes for upper intertidal, backshore and profile were used to differentiate beaches backed by low depositional plains from those backed by hard bedrock; the former being more vulnerable. In the case of Tasmania, many shorelines are rocky, and the classification includes categories characterising the rocky shores in terms of their perceived sensitivity (Harvey and Woodroffe, 2008, p. 78). Figure 12.5 shows an example of Tasmanian shoreline geomorphic mapping indicating the level of detail and type of geomorphic attributes.

The shoreline geomorphic mapping has several advantages compared to traditional polygon mapping. A key advantage of the model

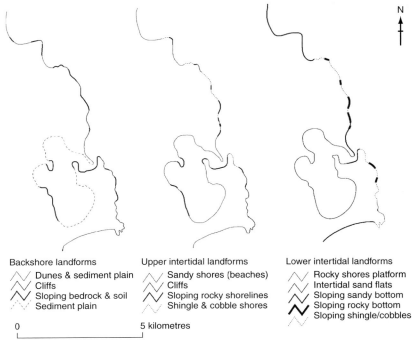

N

Backshore landforms
⋀⋁ Dunes & sediment plain
⋀⋁ Cliffs
⋀⋁ Sloping bedrock & soil
⋰⋰ Sediment plain

Upper intertidal landforms
⋀⋁ Sandy shores (beaches)
⋀⋁ Cliffs
⋀⋁ Sloping rocky shorelines
⋰⋰ Shingle & cobble shores

Lower intertidal landforms
⋀⋁ Rocky shores platform
⋀⋁ Intertidal sand flats
⋀⋁ Sloping sandy bottom
⋀⋁ Sloping rocky bottom
⋰⋰ Sloping shingle/cobbles

0   5 kilometres

Fig. 12.5 Example of the Tasmanian shoreline geomorphic mapping, indicating the level of detail and variation in backshore, upper intertidal and lower intertidal landform attributes (based on mapping of Bellerive Beach area, Hobart, adapted from Sharples, 2006)

is its ability to capture a very wide range of information for a coastal zone at different levels of detail depending on available data. It also allows many types of data analysis to be undertaken efficiently, and can utilise a hierarchical system where insufficient data are available to adequately describe landform characteristics. The line map format enables the creation of a complete coastal map faster than would be possible for polygon mapping, and it can be queried easily for a wide range of purposes.

12.6   Socio-economic systems

Why study social vulnerability? There are two main reasons why the scientific community is presently addressing the issue of the consequences of climate change. First, information regarding the scale of the problem is required in order to assess the magnitude of the threat and thus motivate the broader community to take an appropriate level of action. This is, perhaps, the primary driving force behind the work of the IPCC. Second, information regarding potential consequences is needed to identify effective means of promoting remedial action to limit impacts. The indices described above in Section 12.5 suffer from the shortcoming that they only incorporate physical variables and do not incorporate risk as it affects socio-economic aspects of the coast, such as settlements, infrastructure or cultural assets.

An index applied in South Africa was a modification of Gornitz's CVI (Hughes and Brundrit, 1992). In this case the index needed modification because of the shortage of data on shore displacement (ongoing shoreline change) and vertical land movements. Added, however, was an element that assessed economic value in terms of infrastructure, so that the index included location, infrastructure at risk and hazard (Table 12.3). The greatest hazards overall for the South African coast involve extreme storm and flood events and the most vulnerable infrastructure is that of private housing. This initial attempt to extend the CVI has not been followed up in this form.

An alternative approach to incorporate social data on people at risk, and the most detailed social vulnerability analysis so far is a synthesis undertaken for the US coast by Boruff *et al.* (2005) (Table 12.3). The social vulnerability index (SoVI) uses socio-economic variables on a coastal county basis in a principal components analysis (PCA) to produce the overall coastal social vulnerability score (CSoVI). Boruff *et al.* (2005) took issue with the CVI conceptualisation of vulnerability as only an exposure measure and developed a method for combining physical exposure factors with socio-economic indicators that, in tandem, more accurately reflect the vulnerability of a specific coastal county to erosion hazards. The place vulnerability index (PVI) provides a comparative metric of vulnerability applied at a coastal county scale.

The results of applying the CSoVI and the PVI indicate that place vulnerability along the coast is highly variable and influenced by a range of social, economic, and physical indicators. Not only can one compare different places, but one can also separate the scores to see whether physical or social factors or both tend to be more influential in producing the vulnerability of each county to coastal hazards. Regionally, Gulf Coast vulnerability is more of a product of social characteristics rather than physical attributes. The opposite is true of Pacific and Atlantic coastal counties, where physical characteristics are more influential in determining erosion-hazard vulnerability.

It is clear that overall vulnerability needs to involve social, economic, built-environment, and physical characteristics, but methods for combining these components are not widely used at present by coastal scientists and policymakers, rendering hazard assessments incomplete and mitigation plans untenable for many places. There needs to be greater use of social data in assessing vulnerability. Although not developed for examining climate change specifically, the community vulnerability assessment tool (CVAT), developed by the Coastal Services Centre of National Oceanographic and Atmospheric Administration (NOAA) supports the linking of environmental, social and economic data in the coastal zone. The CVAT is a static geographic information system (GIS) map overlay procedure that enables a relative risk or vulnerability analysis of coastal communities to a series of existing threats. The CVAT procedure comprises seven steps: (1) hazard identification and prioritisation; (2) hazard analysis; (3) critical facilities analysis; (4) societal analysis; (5) economic analysis; (6) environmental analysis; and (7) mitigation opportunities (NOAA Coastal Services Centre, 1999; Flax *et al.*, 2002). This GIS-based approach could be used to map vulnerability of the coast to a series of hazards including those related to climate change and may foreshadow a more encompassing approach to vulnerability assessment.

12.7 Future directions for vulnerability assessment

A range of different approaches has been adopted to assess vulnerability of the coast to climate change, primarily involving anticipated sea-level rise. Several general points emerge concerning vulnerability assessment of coastal zones. First, the coastal zone does not behave homogeneously, and techniques need to focus on the geographical variability of response. Second, any tool needs to integrate several different kinds of information, preferably encompassing both physical and social variables. Third, the definition and quantification of vulnerability should not be associated with subjective elements, but needs to be undertaken in a way that different observers working on different parts of the coast can derive similar values or indices. Finally, the results should provide meaningful data suitable for proper coastal zone planning and management. Perhaps the greatest challenge is for semi-quantitative tools to adequately accommodate natural and social systems (Szlafsztein and Sterr, 2007), and to be effective at different scales both geographically and over short to long-term perspectives (Ness *et al.*, 2007).

The purpose of vulnerability assessment is to provide decision makers with an evaluation of global to local integrated nature–society systems in short- and long-term perspectives in order to assist them to determine which actions should or should not be taken in an attempt to make society sustainable. Vulnerability assessment needs to be designed for the scale of enquiry that is required by the user. A major conclusion is that it is not appropriate to generalise vulnerability from one scale to another, say, from the local up to the regional scale. Vulnerability indices produce relative rankings in terms of vulnerability but do not provide quantitative measures (land lost, etc.). While there has been a recent proliferation of tools for vulnerability assessment and adaptation planning, there has been limited research on lessons learned from their application.

Each of the various tools and approaches that have been reviewed here concentrate on sea-level rise as the most significant consequence of climate change. Most studies identify coastal erosion as a prominent impact, although in many cases this is an *a priori* premise through adoption of the Bruun rule that assumes that if the sea rises the shore retreats, without necessarily considering field setting. The next most common impact foreshadowed is increased flooding, both from river inundation of low-lying coastal plains, and increased storm surge levels. Few other climate impacts are examined for coastal areas.

Conducting a global-scale assessment of vulnerability to sea-level rise requires a wide range of physical, ecological, and socio-economic data and information on the world's coasts. The non-linearity of processes within the coastal system, particularly in the context of interaction of energy, sediment, and spatial scale produce a complex physical environment. The coast is not a single linear entity but a more complex zone of interactions within which a wide range of processes and activity occur. It is essential that the data underpinning vulnerability assessment is in a form that allows a simple, yet realistic representation of the coastal system (McFadden *et al.*, 2007). Segmentation of the shoreline enables data capture along open coasts, and provides a mapping visualisation of relative vulnerability.

The approaches described in this chapter are primarily concerned with identifying the factors which shape vulnerability and trends rather than any measure of the state of vulnerability itself. Factors, and the trends they exhibit, can be compared and contrasted across a wider area but we do not consider that they can be meaningfully combined (although some factors and trends may be national, regional or global in scale).

DINAS-COAST is a regional to global database. GVA analysis did not allow the effective characterisation of the physical and socio-economic processes that drive vulnerability at the global scale. One of the issues that needs to be considered is the metrics that are used to measure vulnerability. Metrics are required, first to assess the exposure to climate change, and secondly to consider the impact. Global sea-level rise scenarios (and preferably 'local' sea-level rise scenarios) and elevation data are a prerequisite for most assessments.

The more complex issue of metrics that adequately assess impact and that can appropriately incorporate adaptation poses still further challenges. The most widely adopted approach has been to calculate the costs of coastal protection. Coastal defences are already widespread in Europe and the assets at risk justify hard engineering solutions (and increasingly soft engineering, such as beach nourishment). A summary of various indices described in this chapter is shown in Table 12.3.

A contradiction is emerging in the development of vulnerability assessment tools. On the one hand there is the demand for approaches that have more specific assessment performance, that are more case- and site-specific. At the same time there exists the demand for tools that are broader and accessible to a wide user group for differing case circumstances. There is also the need for more standardised tools that give more transparent results. Can future assessment tool development meet the challenges of allowing for better assessment tool guidelines and data availability and for succinct analyses on a more diverse range? Like the many facets of the concept of vulnerability itself, proper tool development can only happen when all parameters are considered simultaneously (Ness *et al.*, 2007).

12.8 Conclusion

Climate change vulnerability assessment aims at assisting policymakers in adequately responding to the challenge of climate change by investigating how projected changes in the Earth's climate may affect natural systems and human activities. Generally, studies consider exposure or susceptibility of natural coastal systems, the effect on socio-economic systems ('impact assessment'), and/or how human actions may reduce adverse effects of climate change on those systems or activities ('adaptation assessment', a measure of adaptive capacity). The framework for a climate change vulnerability assessment depends on the system under consideration, stressors, responses (effects), and actions (adaptation). It is important that each assessment is undertaken at the relevant spatial and temporal scales, and the results are often appropriate only at those scales.

Several approaches to coastal vulnerability assessment have been trialled and are reviewed in this chapter. Those that build directly on the common methodology, such as SURVAS and the DINAS-Coast and DIVA are intended for use at a global scale and rarely function as effectively at regional or local scale. Several of these approaches are based on the Bruun rule with a range of modifications incorporated depending on assumptions about, for example, the physical processes that are actively occurring. Others, such as CVAT used by NOAA in the US, adopt a more human-focused approach.

Metrics that have been adopted to describe impact include, land area lost, people displaced, ecosystem losses or change, economic value lost, human infrastructure lost, cultural or heritage losses, adaptation costs, changes in extreme event frequency, and rates of accelerated erosion. The data to establish these parameters are even more difficult to obtain and often presupposes a biophysical response that is itself uncertain. Approaches adopted have used administrative boundaries, for example the social vulnerability study of the US coast ranks coastal counties based on CVI and CSoVI (Boruff *et al.*, 2005).

The tools presented in this chapter are more or less limited to a particular geographic region or to the effects of specific processes such as erosion or sea-level rise. Diversity of resources, economies and societies means that no one approach to vulnerability assessment fits every need. However, vulnerability research, if it is to contribute to wider debates on resilience and adaptation, faces significant challenges: in measurement, in handling perceptions of risk, and in governance (Adger, 2006). The challenges for human dimensions research include those of measuring vulnerability within a robust conceptual framework, addressing perceptions of vulnerability and risk, and of governance. All these challenges are common to the domains of vulnerability, adaptation and resilience. They relate to both social resilience and the resilience of the ecosystems on which human well-being ultimately depends.

References

Adger, N.W. (2006) Vulnerability. *Global Environmental Change*, Vol. 16, pp. 268–281.

Baares, G. (1995) Development of an Operational Tool for Global Vulnerability Assessment (GVA)-Update of the Number of People at Risk Due to Sea Level Rise and Increased Flooding Probability. *CZM Centre Publication No. 3, Ministry of Transport, Public Works and Water Management*, The Hague, The Netherlands, 17.

Beniof, R., Guil, S. and Lee, J. (1996) *Vulnerability and Adaptation Assessment: An International Handbook*, Kluwer, Dordrecht.

Bijlsma, L., Ehler, C.N., Klein, R.J.T., Kulshrestha, S.M., McLean, R.F., Mimura, N., Nicholls, R.J., Nurse, L.A., Perez Nieto, H., Stakhiv, E.Z., Turner, R.K.

and Warrick, R.A. (1996) Coastal zones and small islands. In Watson, R.T., Zinyowera, M.C. and Moss, R.H. (eds) *Impacts, Adaptations and Mitigation of Climate Change: Scientific-Technical Analyses, The Second Assessment Report of the Intergovernmental Panel on Climate Change, Working Group II*, Cambridge University Press, Cambridge, pp. 289–324.

Boruff, B.J., Emrich, C. and Cutter, S.L. (2005) Erosion hazard vulnerability of US coastal counties. *Journal of Coastal Research*, Vol. 21, pp. 932–943.

Bruun, P. (1954) *Coast erosion and the development of beach profiles*. US Army Beach Erosion Board Technical Memorandum Beach Erosion Board. Corps of Engineers, Washington, DC, 44, 82.

Bruun, P. (1962) Sea-level rise as a cause of shore erosion. *Journal of Waterways and Harbors Division American Society Civil Engineering*, Vol. 88, pp. 117–130.

Bruun, P. (1988) The Bruun rule of erosion by sea level rise: a discussion of large-scale two- and three-dimensional usages. *Journal of Coastal Research*, Vol. 4, pp. 627–648.

Burton, I., Smith, J.B. and Lenhart, S. (1998) Adaptation to climate change: theory and assessment. In Feenstra, J.F., Burton, I., Smith, J.B. and Tol, R.S.J. (eds) *Handbook on Methods for Climate Change Impact Assessment and Adaptation Strategies*, Institute for Environmental Studies, Vrije University, Amsterdam; UNEP Headquarters, Atmosphere Unit, Nairobi.

Carter, T.R., Parry, M.L., Nishioka, S. and Harasawa, H. (1994) Technical Guidelines for Assessing Climate Change Impacts and Adaptation. Report of Working Group II of the Intergovernmental Panel on Climate Change. University College London, London, and Centre for Global Environmental Research, Tskuba, Japan.

CLIMsystems (2007) *User Guide for SimCLIM Version 2*. In Warrick, R. (ed.) 2.0 ed. Hamilton.

Cooper, J.A.G. and Pilkey, O.H. (2004) Sea-level rise and shoreline retreat: time to abandon the Bruun rule. *Global and Planetary Change*, Vol. 43, pp. 157–171.

Cowell, P.J., Thom, B.G., Jones, R.A., Everts, C.H. and Simanovic, D. (2006) Management of uncertainty in predicting climate-change impacts on beaches. *Journal of Coastal Research*, Vol. 22, pp. 232–245.

Davidson-Arnott, R.G.D. (2005) Conceptual model of the effects of sea level rise on sandy coasts. *Journal of Coastal Research*, Vol. 21, pp. 1166–1172.

Feenstra, J., Burton, I., Smith, J. and Tol, R. (eds) (1998) *United Nations Environment Programme*, Nairobi, and Institute for Environmental Studies, Vrije Universiteit, Amsterdam (Version 2.0).

Flax, L.K., Jackson, R.W. and Stein, D.N. (2002) Community vulnerability assessment tool methodology. *Natural Hazards Review*, Vol. 3, pp. 163–176.

Gornitz, V. (1991) Global coastal hazards from future sea level rise. *Palaeogeography, Palaeoclimatology and Palaeoecology*, Vol. 89, pp. 379–398.

Gornitz, V. and Kanciruk, P. (1989) Assessment of global coastal hazards from sea-level rise. *Proceedings of the 6th Symposium on Coastal and Ocean Management*, ASCE, 11–14 July, Charleston, SC.

Gornitz, V.M., White, T.W. and Cushman, R.M. (1991) Vulnerability of the US to future sea-level rise. Coastal Zone '91, *Proceedings of the 7th Symposium on Coastal and Ocean Management*, American Society of Civil Engineers, pp. 1345–1359.

Hammar-Klose, E.S. and Thieler, E.R. (2001) Coastal vulnerability to sea-level rise: a preliminary database for the US Atlantic, Pacific, and Gulf of Mexico coasts. *US Geological Survey* 68.

Hammar-Klose, E.S., Pendleton, E.A., Thieler, E.R. and Williams, S.J. (2003) Coastal vulnerability assessment of Cape Cod National Seashore to sea-level rise. *US Geological Survey* 2002–233.

Harvey, N., Clouston, B. and Carvalho, P. (1999) Improving coastal vulnerability assessment methodologies for integrated coastal zone management: an approach from South Australia. *Australian Geographical Studies*, Vol. 37, pp. 50–69.

Harvey, N. and Woodroffe, C.D. (2008) Australian approaches to coastal vulnerability assessment. *Sustainability Science*, Vol. 3, pp. 67–87.

Hoozemans, F.M.J., Marchand, M. and Pennekamp, H.A. (1993) *Sea Level Rise: A Global Vulnerability Assessment-Vulnerability Assessments for Population, Coastal Wetlands and Rice Production on a Global Scale*, Delft Hydraulics and Rijkswaterstaat, Delft and The Hague, The Netherlands. 2nd revised ed.

Hughes, P. and Brundrit, G.B. (1992) An index to assess South Africa's vulnerability to sea-level rise. *South African Journal of Science*, Vol. 88, pp. 308–311.

IPCC (1994) Preparing to meet the coastal challenges of the 21st century. *Conference Report. World Coast Conference 1993, 1–5 November*. Noorwijk, the Netherlands, Ministry of Transport, Public Works and Water Management, The Hague, the Netherlands.

IPCC (2001) *Climate Change 2001: Impacts, Adaptation and Vulnerability. Summary for Policymakers*, Cambridge University Press, Cambridge.

IPCC (2007) *Climate Change 2007: The Physcial Science Basis. Summary for Policymakers*, Cambridge University Press, Cambridge.

IPCC CZMS (1992) Global Climate Change and the Rising Challenge of the Sea. Report of the Coastal Zone Management Subgroup (CZMS), Response Strategies Working Group of the Intergovernmental Panel on Climate Change, Ministry of Transport, Public Works and Water Management-Tidal Waters Division, the Netherlands.

Kay, R.C. and Hay, J.E. (1993) A decision support approach to coastal vulnerability and resilience assessment: a toll for integrated coastal zone management. In McLean, R.F. and Mimura, N. (eds) *Vulnerability Assessment to Sea Level Rise and Coastal Zone Management: Proceedings of the Eastern Hemisphere workshop*, Department of Environment Sport and Territories, Tsukuba, pp. 213–225.

Kay, R.C. and Waterman, P. (1993) Review of the applicability of the 'common methodology for assessment of vulnerability to sea-level rise' to the Australian coastal zone. In McLean, R.F. and Mimura, N. (eds) *Vulnerability Assessment to Sea Level Rise and Coastal Zone Management: Proceedings of the Eastern Hemisphere Workshop*, Department of Environment Sport and Territories, Tsukuba, pp. 237–248.

Kay, R.C., Eliot, I., Caton, B., Morvell, G. and Waterman, P. (1996) A review of the Intergovernmental Panel on Climate Change's Common Methodology for assessing the vulnerability of coastal areas to sea-level rise. *Coastal Management*, Vol. 24, pp. 165–188.

Klein, R.J.T. and Nicholls, R.J. (1999) Assessment of coastal vulnerability to climate change. *Ambio*, Vol. 28, pp. 182–187.

McFadden, L., Nicholls, R.J., Vafeidis, A. and Tol, R.S.J. (2007) A methodology for modeling coastal space for global assessment. *Journal of Coastal Research*, Vol. 23, pp. 911–920.

McLean, R. and Mimura, N. (eds) (1993) Vulnerability assessment to sea-level rise and coastal zone management, *Proceedings of the IPCC Eastern Hemisphere Workshop*, Tsukuba, Japan, Department of Environment, Sport and Territories, Canberra.

Ness, B., Urbel-Piirsalua, E., Anderbergd, S. and Olssona, L. (2007) Categorising tools for sustainability assessment. *Ecological Economics*, Vol. 60, pp. 498–508.

Nicholls, R.J. and Hoozemans, F.M.J. (2005) Global vulnerability analysis. In Schwartz, M. (ed.) *Encyclopaedia of Coastal Science*, Kluwer Academic Publishers, Dordrecht, the Netherlands, pp. 486–491.

Nicholls, R.J., Wong, P.P., Burkett, V.R., Codignotto, J.O., Hay, J.E., McLean, R.F., Ragoonaden, S. and Woodroffe, C.D. (2007) Coastal systems and low-lying areas. In Parry, M.L., Canziani, O.F., Palutikof, J.P., Van Der Linden, P.J. and Hanson, C.E. (eds) *Climate Change 2007: Impacts, Adaptation and Vulnerability*, Contribution of Working Group II to the Fourth Assessment Report of the Intergovernmental Panel on Climate Change, Cambridge University Press, Cambridge, pp. 315–356.

NOAA Coastal Services Center (1999) Community vulnerability assessment tool – New Hanover County–North Carolina. National Oceanic and Atmospheric Administration, Coastal Service Center. NOAA/CSC/ 99044-CD, Charleston.

Pendleton, E.A., Williams, S.J. and Thieler, E.R. (2004) Coastal vulnerability assessment of Assateague Island National Seashore (ASIS) to sea-level rise. USGS Open File Report 2004-1020. Online at: http://pubs.usgs.gov/of/ 2004/1020/images/pdf/asis.pdf

Pilkey, O.H., Young, R.S., Bush, D.M., Sallenger, A.H., Jr, Morton, R., Fletcher, C., Thieler, E.R., Howd, P. and Galvin, C. (2000) Comment on 'Sea-level rise shown to drive coastal erosion', by Stephen Leatherman, Keqi Zhang and Bruce C. Douglas. *EOS Trans. America*, 81, p. 436.

Pilkey, O.H., Young, R.S., Riggs, S.R., Smith, A.W.S., Wu, H. and Pilkey, W.D. (1993) The concept of shoreface profile of equilibrium: a critical review. *Journal of Coastal Research*, Vol. 9, pp. 255–278.

SCOR Working Group 89 (1991) The response of beaches to sea-level changes: a review of predictive models. *Journal of Coastal Research*, Vol. 7, pp. 895–921.

Sharples, C. (2004) *Indicative Mapping of Tasmanian Coastal Vulnerability to Climate Change and Sea Level Rise: Explanatory Report*, 1st edn, Tasmania, Department of Primary Industries, Water and Environment.

Sharples, C. (2006) *Indicative Mapping of Tasmanian Coastal Vulnerability to Climate Change and Sea-level Rise Tasmania*, 2nd edn, Consultant Report to Department of Primary Industries and Water.

Shaw, J., Taylor, R.B., Forbes, D.L., Ruz, M.-H. and Solomon, S. (1998) Sensitivity of the coasts of Canada to sea-level rise. *Bulletin of the Geological Survey of Canada*, Vol. 505, pp. 1–79.

Stern, N.H. (2007) *The Economics of Climate Change: The Stern Review*, Cambridge University Press, Cambridge.

Szlafsztein, C. and Sterr, H. (2007) A GIS-based vulnerability assessment of coastal natural hazards, state of Pará, Brazil. *Journal of Coastal Conservation*, Vol. 11, pp. 53–66.

Thieler, E.R. (2000) National Assessment of Coastal Vulnerability to Future Sea-Level Rise. *US Geological Survey*. USGS Fact Sheet FS-076-00.

Thieler, E.R. and Hammar-Klose, E.S. (1999) National Assessment of Coastal Vulnerability to Sea-level Rise, US Atlantic Coast: *US Geological Survey*. Open-File Report 99-593.

Thieler, E.R. and Hammar-Klose, E.S. (2000a) National assessment of coastal vulnerability to sea-level rise, US Gulf of Mexico Coast: *US Geological Survey*. Open-File Report 00-179.

Thieler, E.R. and Hammar-Klose, E.S. (2000b) National Assessment of Coastal Vulnerability to Sea-level Rise: Preliminary Results for the US Pacific Coast. Woods Hole, MA: *US Geological Survey* (USGS). Open File Report 00-178.

Thieler, E.R., Williams, S.J. and Beavers, R. (2002) Vulnerability of US National Parks to Sea-level Rise and Coastal Change. USGS 095-02.

UNFCCC (1992) United Nations Framework Convention on Climate Change. Convention Text. IUCC. Geneva. Online at: http://unfccc.int/essential_background/convention/background/items/1349.php

UNFCCC (2004) Compendium on Methods and Tools to Evaluate Impacts of Vulnerability and Adaptation To Climate Change, *UNFCCC*. 155.

Vafeidis, A.T., Nicholls, R.J., McFadden, L., Tol, R.S.J., Hinkel, J., Spencer, T., Grashoff, P.S., Boot, G. and Klein, R.J.T. (2008) A new global coastal database for impact and vulnerability analysis to sea-level rise. *Journal of Coastal Research*, Vol. 24, Issue 4, pp. 917–924.

Yamada, K., Nunn, P.D., Mimura, N., Machida, S. and Yamamoto, M. (1995) Methodology for the assessment of vulnerability of South Pacific island countries to sea-level rise and climate change. *Journal of Global Environmental Engineering*, Vol. 1, pp. 101–125.

13

Marine and coastal education in a virtual environment: the potential of the virtual fieldtrip

David R. Green
Centre for Marine and Coastal Zone Management (CMCZM), Department of Geography and Environment, University of Aberdeen, Scotland, UK

This chapter considers the virtual coastal environment as a potential educational information and fieldtrip resource. It begins by examining some of the innovative ways now available to access and visualise a wide range of data and information for studying coastal environments. These range from using simple data and image viewers, to online GIS-based maps and images, including Google Earth, NASA's World Wind, and Microsoft's Virtual Earth. Online access to visualisation tools for handling geospatial data and information characterising the Ythan Estuary, an offshore windfarm, and a waterfront regeneration project in Aberdeen, Scotland, UK, are briefly discussed as examples to illustrate the chapter. Building upon project work undertaken at the University of Aberdeen, to facilitate wider access to coastal data and information resources, the chapter also considers using Google Earth as the basis for constructing virtual fieldtrips to introduce under-graduate and postgraduate students to coastal fieldwork in both an educational and training environment.

13.1   Introduction

There are now many different commercially available software applications and software utilities available to construct virtual coastal environments and virtual fieldtrips (see Chapter 15 by Carlisle and Green). Data and information from numerous different sources can now easily be acquired and input to freely available and distributed software (e.g. viewers) to display digital terrain models (DTMs), present temporal animations, create model scenarios, and to generate fly-throughs of coastal zone and marine areas with the aid of products such as Google Earth (GE) and more recently Google Ocean (GO). Already there are many different examples of online coastal information systems available. A couple of good examples are the Digital Coast (formerly the Ocean Planning and Information System: OPIS – http://www.csc.noaa.gov/opis/) and OzCoast – the Australian Online Coastal Information system (http://www.ozcoasts.org.au/). Both provide access to a vast resource of data and information about different coastal environments for educational and research purposes. Use of these software tools also provides an exciting way for students to examine and interact with coastal landscapes using maps and images linked to documents, video clips and audio, all of which provide the potential for a unique educational and training resource. Furthermore, combinations of the software and utilities available also provide opportunities to develop online information resources, such as map and image archives, online GIS, decision support systems (DSSs), and even virtual fieldtrips. The software may also be used by students to construct their own information system or virtual fieldtrip which can subsequently be shared and used as the basis for class or seminar presentations.

This chapter considers the virtual coastal environment as a potentially valuable educational, training, and fieldtrip information resource. It begins by examining some of the innovative ways now available to access and visualise a wide range of data and information for coastal environments. Particular consideration is given to the potential role of online digital datasets, freely available viewers to explore images and maps, map and image-based information systems including Google Earth, NASA's World Wind, and Microsoft's Virtual Earth. Finally, the chapter is illustrated with some Scottish examples: the Ythan Estuary, Nigg Bay and Aberdeen Bay. These have all been developed to provide online access to data and information for education, training and research, and ultimately for creating online virtual fieldtrips and coursework environments for modules in the Marine and Coastal Resource Management (MRCM) Degree Programme (http://www.abdn.ac.uk/mcrm) at the University of Aberdeen in Scotland, UK.

13.2   Digital datasets

Access to digital geographical data and information has greatly improved in recent years, largely with the aid of internet-based catalogues and archives. While not all datasets are freely available, many are now much more affordable, and an increasing number of digital map and image archives are becoming widely available across the internet. Subscribing academic institutions in the UK, for example, have access to Ordnance Survey (OS) digital map data (vector, raster and DEM datasets) which is free for educational and research purposes by way of Edina Digimap (http://www.edina.ac.uk). More recently access has also been provided to Seazone Solution's marine data, e.g. Hydrospatial (http://www.seazone.com/index.php). Access to Landsat, SPOT, LIDAR and ERS data and imagery is free by way of LandMap (http://www.landmap.ac.uk). Additional boundary datasets may be acquired through UKBorders (http://edina.ac.uk/ukborders/), the MAGIC (Coastal and Marine Resource Atlas – http://www.magic.gov.uk/DataDoc/datadoc.asp), Natural England (NE) (http://www.english-nature.org.uk/pubs/gis/gis_register.asp), Scottish Natural Heritage (SNH) (http://gateway.snh.gov.uk/pls/htmldb_ddtdb1/f?p=188:1:5207488318992642052), and NESBReC (http://www.nesbrec.org.uk/). Limited access to Lidar and CASI imagery for the UK coastline is also available from the Environment Agency (EA) (http://www.environment-agency.gov.uk). There are also a number of good resources for map and image datasets originating in the US, many of which cover the UK, e.g. ASTER (http://asterweb.jpl.nasa.gov/). Other digital maps and imagery can be purchased through online archives or image catalogues (e.g. SPOT (http://www.spotimage.fr/). High quality digital aerial imagery can also be obtained from sources such as Bluesky (http://www.bluesky-world.com/).

With the growth in popularity of GIS and Google Earth (GE), more datasets are being provided in the GML (Geographic Markup Language) and KML (Keyhole Markup Language) formats. For example, data are provided in both the GML and KML formats by Scottish Natural Heritage (SNH) as an alternative to the ESRI.shp (Shape) format. The Maritime Coastguard Agency (MCA) in the UK also provides some small hydrographic chart datasets in the Shape and KML formats for public use (http://www.mcga.gov.uk/c4mca/mcga07-home/shipsandcargoes/mcga-shipsregsandguidance/mcga-dqs-hmp_hydrography/civil_hydrography_ programme_results.htm). The MCA website also provides access to some data from the Joint Nature Conservation Committee (JNCC) and CEFAS (http://www.mcga.gov.uk/c4mca/mcga07-home/shipsandcargoes/mcga-shipsregsandguidance/mcga-dqs-hmp-hydrography/ds-data_sharing.htm). Many KML datasets are also available at the JustMagic Google Ocean website – http://www.justmagic.com/GM-GE.html.

While many of the free datasets are by no means temporally or spatially ideal (few free data sources seem to provide current datasets) they are nevertheless potentially very useful when it comes to examining coastal environments in an educational or training context.

13.3   Viewers

There is a number of freely available image and map viewers for displaying remotely sensed data and GIS map (vector) data. Similar in concept to Adobe Acrobat Reader for viewing PDF (Portable Document Format) files, such viewers provide a simple interface to one or more different file formats to allow for the display of image files (e.g. .tif and geotiff or .jpeg) commonly used for distributing and sharing scanned aerial photographs or satellite images. A good example is the Leica Erdas Imagine Viewer (Viewfinder 2.1: http://gi.leica-geosystems. com/LGISub2z288x0.aspx) that provides a means to view Erdas Imagine (.img) format files without the need for access to the Imagine software suite. Likewise, GIS map data can be viewed using free software viewers such as TatukGIS (http://www.tatukgis.com) Viewer (1.7.1), ESRI's MapExplorer (UK), and ESRI's ArcExplorer (USA) (http:// www.esri.com/software/arcexplorer/explorer.html). Besides 2D map and image viewers other freely available software, e.g. USGS dlg32Pro (http://mcmcweb.er.usgs.gov/drc/dlgv32pro/) provide the opportunity to display 3D files such as Digital Terrain Models (DTMs). A special version of Global Mapper, this viewer allows for the draping of multiple files onto a surface, complete with simple navigational aids (pan, zoom, rotation). Others such as 3DEM can be used to generate fly-throughs and short video, e.g. .avi capture files (http://www.visualizationsoftware. com/3dem.html). Most viewers, however, only provide basic navigational functionality and have little in the way of analytical tools. Nevertheless, they are all relatively easy to use, can read (and often write) multiple file types, and also facilitate access to map and image files providing sufficient functionality to make them useful as a means to display, explore, integrate, measure and visualise geospatial data for a coastal environment.

13.4   Google Earth/Ocean, NASA World Wind and MS Virtual Earth

Using a downloadable virtual globe, Google Earth (http://earth.google. com/) provides a spatial viewer and a user control panel for displaying

Fig. 13.1 The Aberdeen waterfront viewed in Google Earth

map, image and DEM data for the Globe. Users can simply enter a place-name and Google Earth will *fly* you to the selected destination. Zoom and Pan controls allow the user to navigate the location and to zoom into the level of detail provided for that location. A coordinate grid and various different map themes can also be added to the view. The scene displayed in Google Earth can also be tilted forwards and back-wards to provide a 3D view of the terrain, and the user can then fly over the terrain. An example is shown in Fig. 13.1. Additionally, users can pinpoint and save destinations so as to be able to retrieve them quickly at a later date.

As a freely accessible global visualisation tool, Google Earth (GE) provides a good opportunity to examine any coastal area in the World. The main advantage of Google Earth is that it is freely available – in its most basic form – and is relatively quick to download and become familiar with. This provides a good basis for the development of virtual fieldtrips. However, the detail at any location is currently limited by the availability of high resolution imagery in GE for that particular area. This can of course be enhanced by overlaying other higher resolution sources of imagery for the location if available. Another possibility is that the standard GE view can be enhanced relatively easily using freely available software such as Google Sketchup (http://www.microsoft.com/virtualearth/), MapWindow (http://www. mapwindow.org/) and Shape2Earth (http://shape2earth.com) to add ESRI Shape files and 3D objects, such as buildings, providing additional locality-specific information. People with KML scripting skills can also make use of animations within Google Earth, e.g. coastal flooding due to sea-level rise (e.g. http://freegeographytools.com/2007/high-resolution-sea-level-rise-flooding-animations-in-google-earth). There are many possibilities to enhance the potential of Google Earth through the Google Earth Blogs and support sites (e.g. http://www.gearthblog.com/; http://www.ogleearth.com/).

Other similar global viewing products such as NASA's World Wind (http://worldwind.arc.nasa.gov/) and Microsoft's Virtual Earth (http://www.microsoft.com/virtualearth/) further illustrate the growing popularity and potential of these interfaces to geographical data and information. Most recently, Google Earth has been added to in the form of Google Ocean (http://www.justmagic.com/GM-GE.html) extending the 3D visualisation capability to beneath the waves. At a recent NOAA Coastal Geotools conference in Myrtle Beach, South Carolina, USA, Giencke and Miller (2009) revealed how Google Earth 5 is currently being developed to extend the capabilities to visualise both terrestrial and ocean datasets.

13.5 Virtual fieldtrips

Virtual fieldtrips have become increasingly popular in educational establishments in recent years for a number of reasons. With declining funds, larger student numbers, and rising costs of travel, virtual fieldtrips offer a *common-sense* alternative, with the potential to offer students a rich resource of information to explore a locality or remote places but without the associated costs. Other advantages include no scheduling problems; no need to rely on suitable weather; the opportunity for students to at their own pace; no safety problems or hazards; and potentially access to a combination of expert and current information; all of which can easily be shared. Even where traditional access to the field is still possible, virtual fieldtrips can provide a valuable complementary online resource for a field study area, one which, with the aid of computer technology, offers a student the possibility to visualise and interact with a destination, perhaps prior to visiting the study area. Ranging from examples that are simply a combination of documents and images linked by a path and using different software utilities, or Microsoft PPT slideshows, to more specialised examples, generated with the aid of specialist authoring software, virtual fieldtrips can comprise simple exercises or a combination of maps, digital terrain models, animations, models, imagery, and video.

13.6   YthanView Project

At the University of Aberdeen in Scotland, UK, the Ythan Estuary, 14 km north of Aberdeen, and the adjoining sand dune system, the Sands of Forvie National Nature Reserve (NNR) managed by Scottish Natural Heritage (SNH), have long been an area for education, field-work and academic research. General studies about the geography of the area have been complemented by those on hydrography, sediment, bird habitat, ecology and macro-algal weedmats providing a wealth of data and information resource (e.g. Green, 1995; Green and King, 2005). In recent years, this has been added to by work undertaken at the Macaulay Institute (http://www.mluri.ac.uk) in Aberdeen, the Formartine Partnership, and the Scottish Environment Protection Agency (SEPA) (http://www.sepa.org.uk/) among many others.

The YthanView Project (Fig. 13.2) is an ongoing research project designed to provide improved access to geospatial datasets for the Ythan Estuary and surrounding area (in particular the Sands of Forvie National Nature Reserve (NNR)) in northeast Scotland, UK for educators, researchers and students at the University of Aberdeen. The project originated, in part, with the educational and research work currently undertaken by the Centre for Marine and Coastal Zone

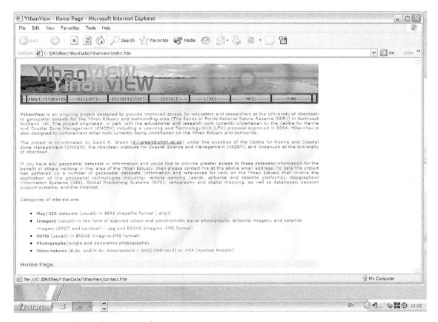

Fig. 13.2 The YthanView homepage

Management (CMCZM – http://www.abdn.ac.uk/cmczm) including a project with the University of Aberdeen Learning and Technology Unit (LTU) in 2004, and most recently with a research programme currently being undertaken within the Aberdeen Institute for Coastal Science and Management (AICSM – http://www.abdn.ac.uk/aicsm). YthanView was also designed to complement other work currently being undertaken on the Ythan Estuary and its surrounds by other researchers within the University, e.g. OceanLab (http://ww.abdn.ac.uk/oceanlab), and some of the research interests of the East Grampian Coastal Partnership (http://www.egcp.org.uk).

The project work is coordinated by the Centre for Marine and Coastal Zone Management (CMCZM) in the University of Aberdeen (http://www.abdn.ac.uk/cmczm). To date, the project has gathered together a number of geospatial datasets, information and references for work on the Ythan Estuary that involve the application of the geospatial technologies, including: remote sensing (aerial, airborne and satellite platforms), geographical information systems (GIS), global positioning systems (GPS), mobile data collection (GPS, mobile phones, digital photography and video, PDAs, and GIS (Pocket GIS: http://www.posres.co.uk)), cartography and digital mapping, as well as databases, decision support systems, and the Internet. These form the basis of the resources to be made available to staff and students. Initially stored on an internally accessible network drive, these datasets and documents will subsequently be provided as a searchable online catalogue and database with online map and image access using map and image server technology, as well as password protected access to the datasets where only internal access is permitted. Current developments to the project include extending YthanView to include a virtual fieldtrip for the Ythan Estuary together with some Virtual Reality (VR) simulations in the context of coastal zone management scenarios. This element of the project formed some of the input to the COREPOINT project (http://corepoint.ucc.ie/) –as discussed in Chapter 15 by Carlisle and Green – and the idea is currently being continued within the IMCORE project (http://imcore.eu) (see later in this chapter) with the aim of developing a coastal atlas.

13.7   Visualisation

As part of the YthanView Project, some additional work was carried out to investigate how a variety of geospatial (image and map) datasets could be brought together using 'off-the-shelf' information technology

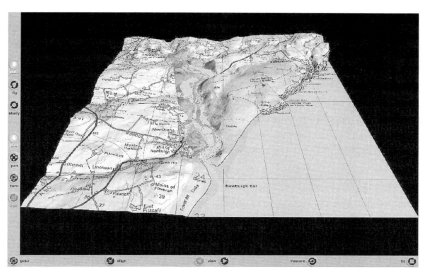

Fig. 13.3a An interactive hypermedia animation with several forms of interactivity generated with Erdas Imagine 8.5 using the ParallelGraphics Cortona® VRML Client used to view VRML model. An Ordnance Survey (OS) GRID Digital Elevation Model (DEM) at a scale of 1:50000 (exaggeration 2; level of details 4%) was overlaid with Ordnance Survey raster map data at a scale of 1:50 000; an aerial colour photographic mosaic, and a polygon cover (.shp) for 1989 macroalgal weedmat cover

tools to facilitate visualisation of the Ythan Estuary and surrounding environment as the basis to provide a simple virtual fieldtrip (Green and Bojar, 2005a, 2005b). Using available datasets and a wide range of commercially available off-the-shelf software products, visualisations were produced for the Ythan Estuary and the Sands of Forvie. Software used included Erdas Imagine 8.5, ArcView 3.3, Bryce 5, Global Mapper, and Microsoft Internet Explorer, using a number of different plugins for 3D, video and animation. Only a small selection of examples generated is shown here in Figs 13.3a–c.

Figure 13.3a shows an interactive hypermedia animation with several forms of interactivity generated with Erdas Imagine 8.5 using the ParallelGraphics Cortona® VRML Client used to view VRML model. An Ordnance Survey (OS) GRID Digital Elevation Model (DEM) at a scale of 1:50 000 (exaggeration 2; level of details 4%) was overlaid with Ordnance Survey (OS) raster map data at a scale of 1:50 000; an aerial colour photographic mosaic, and a polygon cover (.shp) for 1989 macroalgal weedmat cover. It was saved in VRML (Virtual Reality

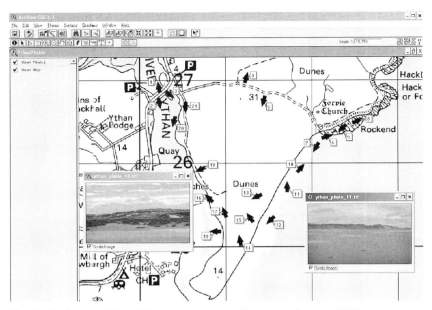

Fig.13.3b An ArcView 3.3. project using Ordnance Survey (OS) raster map data at a scale of 1:50 000 with hotlinks to 21 ground-truth colour photographs at 1280 × 960 pixels resolution saved in a TIFF format and hot-linked into a series of photographic arrays showing the direction in which the photograph was taken

Modelling Language) in Erdas Imagine 8.5. This application has potential for the analysis of weedmat distribution and land-use/land-cover analysis dependent upon surface relief. The second example, Fig. 13.3b, is an ArcView 3.3 project using Ordnance Survey (OS) raster map data at a scale of 1:50 000 with hotlinks to 21 ground-truth colour photographs at 1280 × 960 pixels resolution saved in a TIFF format and hot linked into a series of photographic arrays showing the direction in which the photograph was taken. Potential applications include a visual presentation of tourist attractions in the context of sustainable coastal tourism. Figure 13.3c, the third example, is a video clip (11.4 Mb filesize, with a duration of 25 seconds, comprising 375 frames, at 15 frames per second, using the DivX High Definition Profile, at a resolution of 768 × 512) generated by the Bryce 5 software. The imagery contained in the video was created using a combination of Erdas Imagine 8.5 and Virtual GIS, VRML 1.0, and Corel Photo Paint 9. This is an example of cast-based, process animation, using motion and trajectory with some elements of thematic animations (comparing

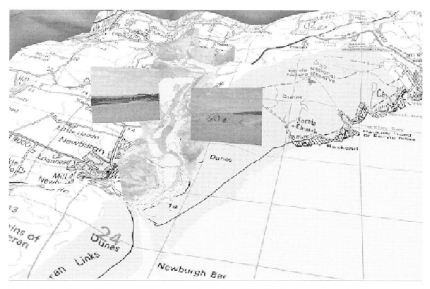

Fig. 13.3c The third example, is a video clip (11.4 Mb filesize, with a duration of 25 seconds, comprising 375 frames, at 15 frames per second, using the DivX High Definition Profile, at a resolution of 768 × 512) generated by the Bryce 5 software

distribution) and aerial animations (fly-through), and a non-temporal animation with elements from animation with successive build-up (displaying themes in sequences) and the animation with changing representation (a simulated fly-through).

13.8   Recent developments

A number of recent project developments, designed to progress this work, include the incorporation of the geospatial datasets into a virtual fieldtrip using the University of Aberdeen Learning and Technology Unit's (LTU) in-house Virtual Fieldtrip application. The geospatial database of data and information accumulated will be used as the basis to generate a Virtual Fieldtrip for the Ythan Estuary. Combining maps and images and 2D and 3D viewing capabilities with opportunities to mine the data from the surface down through the water column and into the estuarine sediments will be developed for selected sites. Access to multi-temporal video imagery from an in-situ sediment video camera system developed at OceanLab by Solan (2005) is used to allow students to examine benthic organisms living in the estuary within a

Fig. 13.4 Google Earth screenshot of Sands of Forvie/Ythan Estuary – showing heather with moss placemark. Note also the image embedded within the placemark description on aerial photographic mosaic and Ordnance Survey (OS) overlay backdrop

virtual laboratory. As an extension to this work, Green *et al.* (2007) also explored the development of a virtual fieldtrip for the Ythan Estuary with the aid of the more familiar and easy to use Google Earth (GE) software (Fig. 13.4).

Subsequently the use of Google Earth has been extended to a number of other coastal visualisation scenarios including a planning proposal for an offshore windfarm in Aberdeen Bay (Fig. 13.5), and a waterfront regeneration project in Nigg Bay (Fig. 13.6), the latter being part of an exercise to explore the use of a simple form of Public Participation GIS (PPGIS) in a local community for the redevelopment of an area in south Aberdeen. This involved using Google Earth with a number of community groups of different ages as a visualisation tool to fly through the area, as well as to explore a number of different scenarios for locating a marine and coastal resource centre, a boat slip, and the placement of environmental screening and landscaping to improve the coastal landscape. In addition, a number of virtual reality scenarios are to be developed to examine some coastal management scenarios in the context of the impacts of climate change and coastal adaptation as part of an Interreg Project, IMCORE (http://imcore.eu).

Fig. 13.5 An offshore windfarm siting proposal for Aberdeen Bay using Google Earth – combining ArcView.shp files for the spatial location of the wind turbines, MapWindow, Shape2Earth, and wind turbines constructed in Google Sketchup

13.9   Raising awareness and education

Several years ago Green (2006) proposed the development of an integrated geospatial framework as the basis for the Marine and Coastal Resource Management (MCRM) degree programme offered at the University of Aberdeen in Scotland, UK. The rationale behind this proposal was the growing use of databases, modeling, the Internet, remote sensing, and mobile GIS for the collection, storage, processing, analysis, display, and visualisation of marine and coastal data in the workplace.

In the last ten years, nearly all commercial, governmental and academic organisations have begun to utilise one or more of these technologies (e.g. GIS, remote sensing, cartography, digital mapping, GPS and the internet) as part of their work for routine day-to-day monitoring, mapping and

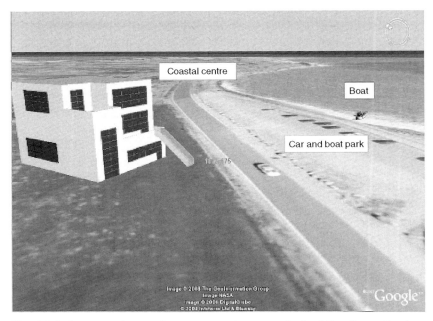

Fig. 13.6 A proposed waterfront regeneration scenario for Nigg Bay, Aberdeen using Google Earth and Google Sketchup

modelling of the coastal environment: the coastal zone, terrestrial, and marine environments, and in the wider context of Integrated Coastal Zone Management (ICZM). Numerous different examples can be found in the literature, ranging from tracking of cetaceans; seal habitat monitoring and mapping using remotely sensed data and GIS; sediment budget process models; oil spill monitoring and contingency plans; ship tracking; coastal zone management; online data and information archives; and Decision Support Systems (DSSs). Used on their own or in combination these technologies provide a powerful suite of tools to monitor, map and model the coastal and marine environment at a wide variety of different spatial and temporal scales.

Given the widespread use of these different technologies by agencies and organisations around the world it is therefore important for students to be: (a) made aware of and have an appreciation of the technologies currently available; (b) educated in the theory and practice of these technologies; (c) knowledgeable about the breadth of applications; and (d) able, where possible, to make practical use of these technologies. At the University of Aberdeen, students are now presented with a broad overview of the use of geospatial technologies in marine and coastal studies at Level 1. This is built upon at Level 2 with a compulsory course in monitoring and mapping the environment, and later at Levels 3 and 4 through the availability of more advanced options covering GIS, remote sensing, and cartographic visualisation, which allows the student to gain a more in-depth appreciation of the subject matter. In addition, all MCRM Programme modules should now be able to provide examples of some of the different ways in which such technologies can be applied to a particular area of study. Provision of a core module in the geospatial technologies helps to prepare students for the many potential applications they will encounter. Furthermore, a knowledge and understanding of such technologies also provides a useful set of tools for a student to use in a dissertation or thesis, as well as a set of transferable skills that can be useful for employment once they graduate. While they may not become proficient in the use of all these different technologies awareness, knowledge and understanding of the way in which they can be used is very beneficial in the context of their future education, training and employment.

Practical use of some of these technologies, set within a virtual field-trip context, also provides one way to help raise awareness and to educate the student about the role such technologies can play in the study of coastal and marine environments including the provision of access to data and information in databases, image analysis, integration within GIS, analysis, visualisation, and communication with a wider audience, including the public, the coastal stakeholder, and coastal communities. This is becoming of increasing importance as awareness and interest in the coastal and marine environment is growing almost daily with environmental issues such as climate change, sea-level rise, storm surges, and coastal flooding in the news.

13.10 Summary and conclusions

Providing students with the potential to access coastal environments with the aid of computer technology adds a very valuable dimension to their academic and vocational studies. Not only does it allow them to explore one or more environments at any time and at their leisure, without having direct access to the location, which may be remote, but it also facilitates the development of virtual fieldtrips with opportunities to interact by following a predefined guided tour or the freedom to roam. Depending upon the availability of the data and information for a location, as well as software and expertise, a fieldtrip can take the form of a simple diary or illustrated walk, an online visual tour, or a very rich and dynamic visual and interactive experience that incorporates fly-throughs, animations, hotlinks to other documents and image libraries. This provides the opportunity for students to compare environmental datasets, to become actively involved in practical field exercises, and to participate in the learning process by designing their own fieldwork investigations The concept of the virtual fieldwork interface developed at the University of Aberdeen will provide additional tools to assist in the construction of these virtual environments, and to utilise many of the existing software tools and utilities to enhance student appreciation of the coastal and marine landscape. Potentially this will also provide more students with the opportunity to visit more coastal environments, to access and integrate data for different coastal studies, as well as to raise awareness of the different ways in which geospatial data and information can be of use to study a coastal and marine environment.

References

Giencke, P. and Miller, S. (2009) Visualizing dynamic weather and ocean data in Google Earth 5. Paper presented in *Visualization: Mash-Ups session at Coastal GeoTools 2009*. NOAA. Myrtle Beach, South Carolina, USA. Available at: http://www.csc.noaa.gov/geotools/program.html

Green, D.R. (1995) Preserving a fragile environment: integrating technology to study the Ythan Estuary. *Mapping Awareness*, Vol. 9, 3 April, pp. 28–30.

Green, D.R. (2007) Promoting the development of a geospatial technology framework for a Marine and Coastal Resource Management Degree Programme: An Example from the University of Aberdeen, Scotland, UK. In: Woodroffe, C.D., Bruce, E., Puotinen, M. and Furness, R.A. (eds) *GIS for the Coastal Zone: A Selection of Papers from CoastGIS 2006*. University of Wollongong, 13–16 July 2006. Wollongong Papers on Maritime Policy No. 16. pp. 25–36.

Green, D.R. and Bojar, K. (2005a) 'YthanView' – visualizing an estuary and virtual fieldwork at the Ythan Estuary, Scotland, UK. *Proceedings of CoastGIS 2005 Symposium and Exhibition in Aberdeen*, Scotland, 21–23 July.

Green, D.R. and Bojar, K. (2005b) 'YthanView" – visualizing an estuary and virtual fieldwork at the Ythan Estuary, Scotland, UK. *Proceedings of ICC 2005 Conference in A Coruña*, Spain, 9–16 July.

Green, D.R. and King, S.D. (2005) Applying geospatial technologies to weed mat monitoring and mapping: the Ythan Estuary, NE Scotland. *Zeitschrift fur Geomorphologie*, Special Issue, Vol. 141, pp. 197–212.

Green. D.R., Carlisle, M. and Mouatt, J. (2007) Constructing a local coastal GIS, virtual field-trips, and virtual reality simulations using Google Earth (GE). In: *Proceedings of CoastGIS07: 8th International Symposium on GIS and Computer Mapping for Coastal Zone Management*, 8–10 October, Santander, Spain. Vol. 1: SDI, Policy Implementation, Web Services, Open Source, and Posters, pp. 224–234.

Solan, M. (2005) Personnal communication.

14

The role of voluntary coastal partnerships in ICZM

John McKenna and J. Andrew G. Cooper
Centre for Coastal and Marine Research, School of Environmental Sciences,
University of Ulster, Coleraine, UK

In Europe, and particularly in the UK, the absence of formal statutory bodies to undertake *integrated* coastal zone management (ICZM) has stimulated the formation of voluntary coastal partnerships. The partnerships are typically participatory and consensus driven. Their commitment to inclusivity and trust gives them particular strengths in identifying stakeholders and getting them to talk with each other. The partnerships have an excellent track record in identifying management issues, and teasing out areas of common interest and conflict.

However, the partnerships have always faced substantial problems. They lie outside the statutory system and therefore they lack executive authority. Their emphasis on participation and, in particular, consensus creates inefficiency and non-optimum compromise outcomes. They face chronic financial problems, and therefore their survival cannot be guaranteed. They have also been criticised as non-representative and non-accountable.

Recent developments in both Europe and the UK suggest that a statutory basis for coastal management may be on the horizon. If so, there would be no logical reason for the continuance of the partnerships, because statutory organisations have huge advantages as management agencies, for example in authority and access to human, financial and infrastructural resources. Voluntary coastal partnerships can be regarded as an evolutionary 'pioneer' stage in the management of the coast because ultimately they will make themselves redundant by successfully persuading government of the need for statutory ICZM.

Coastal zone management
978-0-7277-3641-1

14.1   Introduction

It is widely accepted that traditional sectoral coastal management has failed to prevent coastal degradation, for example Spain provides many notorious case studies, (Suárez de Vivero and Rodríguez Mateos, 2005) In response to this perceived failure of sectoral management, a trans-sectoral model of integrated coastal zone management (ICZM) evolved over the last 20 years. This model is typically voluntary and partnership-based, and lies outside existing statutory structures which are sectoral in nature. The latter are viewed negatively because, by definition, sectoral governance cannot deliver effective integration of management. During the last decade, the voluntary partnership model of ICZM has been enthusiastically promoted by the European Union as a process with great potential for resolving coastal issues and enabling sustainable development. Its development has been stimulated further by a European Recommendation (European Parliament and Council, 2002) which was itself based on lessons learned from the projects in the EC Demonstration Programme on ICZM, 1997–2000 (European Commission, 1997a, 1999b, 1999c).

Even before the significant involvement of the European Union, the partnership management concept had taken off in the UK, where in the absence of formal statutory bodies to undertake ICZM, since the early 1990s (and in some cases earlier) local coastal partnerships were established as voluntary mechanisms to coordinate the activities of coastal interests such as those associated with ownership, administration, statutory control of specific activities, economic activity, or voluntary interest. Partnership-based initiatives in ICZM are usually driven by perceived difficulties in existing approaches, or where no satisfactory statutory framework exists that can adequately deal with the perceived problems. There is a recognition that current or traditional approaches are not working, leading inevitably to a downward spiral of degradation. Among the reasons for this failure are: the limitations of sectoral management which does not (or cannot) take a holistic approach; the scarcity of resources (personnel, financial, skills) which can be countered only by pooling and co-operation; the shortcomings and inefficiencies of statutory bodies in their efforts to manage the coast; gaps and loopholes in statutory powers which allow damaging activities to take place; difficulty in enforcement particularly where management is sectoral; and cultural differences which might demand flexibility and a variety of approaches. The motivation to intervene is, therefore, a need to do something to 'rescue' a deteriorating situation, or to maintain an existing one.

Some coastal partnerships are established in response to a specific set of circumstances, usually a perceived problem or threat, but many are established opportunistically to take advantage of funding opportunities. Various individuals may play the pioneer role, but probably most often the initial impetus comes from an interested officer in a local authority, or a conservation-orientated member of an NGO or other interest group. Subsequently, other stakeholders join the partnership for a range of reasons from active commitment to the integration ideal in coastal management, to pragmatic self-interest, and, in some cases, purely for public relations reasons.

14.2   Definition of partnership

ICZM partnerships are defined by the nature of their membership, their voluntary status and their distinctive working methods. DEFRA (2006) defines coastal partnerships as consortia of coastal stakeholders that 'broadly aim to achieve a more integrated approach to coastal issues by facilitating co-operation between different organisations, raising awareness of local issues, collecting and distributing information, and discussing issues of local concern' (DEFRA, 2006).

In describing rural partnerships (forums) Scott (1998) states:

> ... a new and more sophisticated phase in organizational structures has emerged with a move from traditional sectoral positions of conflict to grouping of organisations with common interests using negotiation, networking, accommodation and bargaining as principal tools ... Such forums or groupings, therefore, may be defined as umbrella organisations in pursuit of informed discussion and debate involving a cross section of legitimate interests... Commonly, most forums revolve around the need to promote a neglected or wider concern. They all have at their heart information production, transmission and debating functions, with the objective of informing and influencing their membership and sometimes a wider audience.

As in the Scott (1998) reference above, the word 'forum' is frequently used as an acronym for partnership, e.g. the Forth Estuary Forum, the Dorset Coast Forum and the Solent Forum. However, to avoid confusion, we have chosen not to use forum in this sense, because the term is also used to describe one specific organisational element of some partnerships, *viz.* a regular roundtable meeting of all the stakeholders.

To be described as a *partnership*, an organisation must have the structural characteristics typical of partnership working (see below), and its membership must be multi-sectoral. Therefore, statutory or voluntary organisations, with essentially sectoral remits focusing on particular aspects of the coastal resource or its use, for example conservation, water-based recreation or aquaculture, cannot be described as ICZM partnerships. Even where the focus of a voluntary organisation is less sectoral and more general, the partnership label cannot be accurately applied if it has a conventional hierarchical power and administrative structure. Thus, land-owning NGOs such as the National Trust, direct action bodies such as the British Trust for Conservation Volunteers (BTCV), and 'support and network' organisations such as the European Union for Coastal Conservation (EUCC), and CoastNET are not partnerships.

The term 'coastal forum' is also widely used to describe a national or regional scale grouping of invited coastal stakeholders who meet occasionally under government auspices to discuss ICZM-relevant matters. These bodies are top-down in that they are established by and sponsored by statutory government agencies, usually by the lead Environmental Department. In practice, they are quasi-statutory in that, while there is no statutory duty on government to establish such a body or follow its advice, the logic of its existence and its very close links with the sponsoring department mean that at minimum it has the status of a preferred advisory body. Top-down coastal fora tend to be much better resourced and more stable than the bottom-up voluntary partnerships, because they have access to government resources both financial and infrastructural, e.g. government will provide secretariat and meeting rooms, and perhaps fund a project officer, publications, etc. The scale of discussion is national or regional, not site-specific, although case studies will be used to illustrate issues. It could be argued that these larger-scale fora should be described as partnerships because they satisfy the basic criteria of being voluntary, multisectoral and participatory. This view may have some validity, but unlike the true partnerships the high-level fora are essentially advisory bodies that have little, if any, capacity for independent management action, although they may be able to make representations directly with other government departments by way of their sponsor department if they identify important issues or problems. Since implementation is the preserve of the sponsoring department and other statutory bodies, these regional/national level fora often focus on public outreach and dissemination objectives. Examples are the recently established Northern Ireland Coastal Forum and the Scottish Coastal Forum.

310

14.3   Coastal partnerships: characteristics

The partnerships are typically:

- bottom-up
- voluntary
- inclusive
- participatory (stakeholder driven)
- consensus-driven
- often forum-based
- experimental
- site-based rather than regional
- self-policing
- funded short-term by a combination of internal and external donors
- staffed by short-term contract workers
- governed by a sustainability ethos, often with a conservation emphasis.

A typical vision statement for a partnership is that of the Forth Estuary Forum (1999): 'through partnership achieve a consensus Strategy for the management of the Forth that identifies measures needed for a "proper balance" between securing future economic prosperity and maintaining environmental quality . . .' (p. 17). The principle underpinning the partnership approach is that if local people 'take ownership' of the coastal resource it can be locally managed in an agreed way much more effectively than by top-down imposed management by a distant authority. Consequently, the principles of inclusivity and participation are fundamental to the partnerships. Anyone with a stake in the coast (stakeholders) is included in the decision-making process, and has a right to be heard and to contribute. Partnerships will include a wide range of coastal interests: private individuals, landowners, industry, tourism interests, commercial companies, conservation organisations and specific interest groups e.g. fishermen, boat owners, etc. Statutory bodies with coastal responsibilities also need to be included in the partnership if the aim of inclusivity is to be met.

The bottom-up, voluntary non-statutory IZM partnership contrasts with the imposed 'top-down' approach typical of statutory management. Rather than being ideologically driven by management, planning or even ICZM theory, the partnership concentrates on finding agreed concrete solutions to real coastal problems over a relatively limited coastal stretch. Solutions to problems are generated within the partnership by an iterative process of democratic discussion and experiment. Generalisation comes later, if at all. Within the partnerships disparate interests (stakeholders) meet, identify management issues and problems, collate and disseminate information, seek additional information, consult widely with other stakeholders, reach consensus, develop solutions, publicize findings, implement solutions, monitor outcomes, then review the process and if necessary adjust and adapt it. The partnership's agreed ground rules are formulated to ensure that, at least in theory, it is a community of equals, with no participant dominating the group. This is important where a member is a major landowner or a statutory body with potentially disproportionate influence or power relative to the other participants. In particular, it is important that the lead agency or major source of funding does not 'outweigh' other members. In many cases coastal partnerships find that they can gain significant advantages from employing the methodology and techniques of conflict resolution or consensus building. These skills can be 'bought in' from professional bodies.

Most partnerships have a Steering Committee chosen/elected from the general membership. There is usually a lead agency which hosts the project officer(s), and provides a basic secretariat and other facilities such as meeting rooms. However, some partnerships do not have any full-time staff and rely on the voluntary work of committed members. Inclusivity within partnerships is often realised through the establishment of a 'coastal forum'. (As noted above, the forum concept is often so central to the partnership concept that the word 'forum' is used as an acronym for 'partnership'.) The forum within an ICZM partnership is a roundtable discussion body in which the diverse range of individuals and groups that make up the partnership can meet and discuss issues in a plenary forum. The forum represents the broad base of the organisational pyramid, and consists of representatives of all stakeholder groups. The forum meets at regular intervals to discuss the activities of the partnership, for example the Solent Forum's internal forum meets twice a year, while the Sefton Coast Partnership has a forum that meets annually. However, not all ICZM partnerships have an element that can be described as a 'forum', for example the Medway Swale Estuary Partnership does not have a forum style group (Fletcher, 2007a).

Members of a partnership represent a wide range of interests, and join for a wide range of reasons. What a partnership can do and achieve reflects the interaction of its membership profile with the level and quality of human, financial and infrastructural resources available. The circumstances prevailing at the time of establishment, and the interests and motivations of the most committed groups and personalities, will greatly influence the precise direction taken by any given partnership. Many are 'green' in tone with a heavy orientation towards conservation issues, while others are somewhat more representative of a wider range of interests including industry. Even some of the latter have a strong conservation bias, for example the industry-funded and highly proactive INCA partnership in the Humber Estuary has an explicit conservation title and aims: 'Humber Industry Nature Conservation Association'.

Another important variable is the nature of the partnership's leadership. Initially, a coastal partnership may be primarily a 'talking shop' which seeks to develop trust and identify issues as essential first steps in achieving the eventual objective of integrating human activities in a sustainable way. However, Scott (1998) notes that, over time, some partnerships evolve from an initial information and debating vehicle to a more proactive and project-led role. These 'mature-phase' partnerships may undertake original research through specialised sub-groups, may publish a range of informative material, and may go on to develop comprehensive strategies or management plans.

Unlike statutory management approaches, non-statutory ICZM initiatives such as partnerships can adopt an experimental attitude in that they can test the suitability of various approaches. The projects in the EC Demonstration Programme on ICZM, 1997–2000 (European Commission, 1997a, 1999b, 1999c) were explicitly experimental in character. Funding for ICZM partnership may come from the constituent bodies, notably the lead agency, but external funding is usually essential. Such external support may be contributed by industry, government via statutory authorities, or the European Commission, e.g. most of the projects in the Demonstration Programme were funded by the European Commission's financial instruments, LIFE and TERRA.

Through its commitment to inclusivity and its democratic structure, the non-statutory partnership approach hopes to achieve a moral authority that substitutes for the legal authority of a statutory approach. Consequently, voluntary initiatives will be self-policing, as management decisions have been reached by consensus among all the players in the coastal zone. There is, however, a grey area between statutory and non-statutory ICZM where a statutory organisation participates as a stakeholder in a consensus-driven partnership, but where the agreed outcomes, such as management plans, can be given 'teeth' by the legal powers of the statutory participant. This was the situation in the Bantry Bay Charter partnership where the statutory participant, the Department of Marine and Natural Resources (DMNR), had the power to implement recommendations on the seaward side of mean high water.

14.4   Discussion

14.4.1 Advantages

Partnerships have particular strengths in identifying stakeholders and getting then to talk with each other in a non-threatening environment. They also have an excellent track record in identifying management issues, and teasing out areas of common interest and conflict. Through social interaction, and with sympathetic and sensitive leadership, partnerships can create a sense of common purpose and solidarity. Their ability to generate trust gives the partnerships a decided advantage in accessing information held by disparate stakeholders, and partnerships can often build up an impressive and comprehensive database of the information necessary for management. Their community basis also bestows an advantage in terms of outreach, dissemination and publicity. The fact that management measures are consensually agreed may make it easier for a voluntary group to effectively police management measures, than it would be for a theoretically more powerful statutory authority. Breaches of agreed solutions are likely to be perceived as anti-community. The local basis and wide range of its membership means that the partnership does not face the problem of being perceived as an impersonal external authority with no emotional or other commitment to the area. The partnership's status as a consortium of interests allows it to act as a pressure group with few fears of being labelled single interest.

The central role of inclusivity and public participation in the partnerships is one of their greatest potential strengths. It is true that public consultation may also be part of the statutory process, but essentially management solutions are imposed from above and there is no real empowerment of the coastal stakeholders. Gaining public acceptance and respect for this type of autocratic and paternalistic coastal management can be an uphill battle. One of the risks is that solutions generated in one environment may be transferred to localities where circumstances are different, without any sensitivity being shown to local tradition or other cultural realities. An example might be the attempt to transfer the relatively regimented management regime of public beaches in California to beaches in rural Ireland.

Consensus is at the heart of the partnership model. Its great advantage is that it offers the possibility of achieving coherent, integrated management of a coastal environment through the voluntary participation and

314

agreement of all the stakeholders. These stakeholders will include those who own property, e.g. farmers, conservation NGOs and tourist interests, and also those who are involved in various coastal and marine activities such as commercial fishing and yachting. All these stakeholders have major interests which they regard as fundamental and, consequently, they will act to defend those interests against any perceived threat. Each stakeholder or owner makes personal decisions which are designed to further or maintain a personal or sectoral interest. The result of the conflict between competing interests may be a kind of management equilibrium or *status quo* that is essentially unsustainable because it does not consider the health of the coastal system as a whole, or the interests of other users. Stakeholders may even be aware of this problem, but they may regard any imposed management regime as a threat to their interests, and refuse to cooperate in its implementation. In contrast, in the partnership model management strategies are reached by consensus and nothing is imposed. For this reason the agreed management regime is likely to be sustainable and accepted.

Even in situations where agreement is simply not possible because interests are diametrically opposed, and a 'win-win' solution is not possible, the process of dialogue helps to create awareness of other viewpoints and to define the issues. Indeed, it can be argued that achieving the aim of getting disparate, and often competing, interests, to voluntarily enter a process of debate and discussion is in itself sufficient to justify the existence of the partnerships and represents their unique contribution to ICZM.

14.4.2 Disadvantages

Despite the expenditure of large sums of money by national governments and the European Community (for example on the 30 + projects in the EC ICZM Demonstration Programme) the voluntary partnership model of ICZM is patently failing in its aim of protecting the European coast. The environmental degradation of coasts is accelerating (European Environment Agency, 2006). Despite the well-intentioned efforts of those who support and work for the partnerships the voluntary, bottom-up participatory model of ICZM is seriously undermined as an effective instrument of integrated coastal management by a number of flaws: These include:

- lack of a statutory basis and therefore statutory authority
- lack of guiding legislation, government policy and direction
- preoccupation with participation, consultation and consensus

- insecure funding basis
- short-term staffing
- project-based focus
- problems of representativeness and accountability
- perceived conservation bias, i.e. the partnership is viewed as a hindrance to economic development, rather than as a means of achieving sustainable development.

The main problems faced by the partnerships lie in four areas:

- They lie outside the statutory system.
- Their emphasis on participation and consensus creates inefficiency.
- They lack recurrent funding and therefore guaranteed permanence.
- They may not be representative or accountable.

14.5   Problems related to non-statutory status

Legal authority at the coast is derived from either statutory mandate or property ownership. A coastal partnership *per se* has neither of these. This gives rise to the perception among some users of the coastal zone that the partnership is a voluntary organisation that 'lacks clout', and therefore can be ignored as a non-essential layer of consultation. Some important stakeholders can make a tactical decision to 'sit out' and refuse to participate. The partnership faces a continual battle to achieve or retain credibility. The internal relationships may be productive, but external relationships can be entirely dependent on personal factors (Fig. 14.1). For example, the partnership's relationship with a particular statutory body may be good simply because the partnership's project officer and an officer in the statutory body have a good personal understanding. Relationships with other bodies may be weak to virtually non-existent. Even if relationships are good, no statutory body would (or could) allow its policies or work programmes to be too heavily influenced by a non-statutory organisation. If the partnership's objectives coincide with those of the statutory authority those objectives may be met. If they do not, or have much lower priority, the partnership may find it very difficult to make progress.

In the absence of the legal powers deriving from property ownership or statutory mandate, partnership working methods are characterised by a search for the lesser 'authority' of consensus, which in turn demands a commitment to lengthy stakeholder participation exercises. However, it is important to emphasise that the partnerships do not embrace participation and consensus solely because they have no other option.

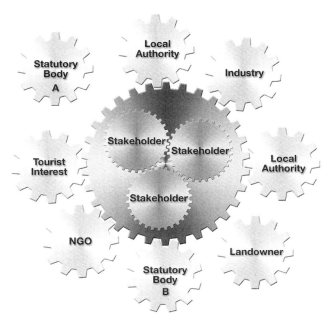

Fig. 14.1 Relationships between the members of a partnership (inner cogwheel) often show a high degree of interconnection. The relationships between the partnership and bodies external to it are, however, of variable quality. In the worst cases, there may be no connection whatever

Necessity may certainly be a factor, but the partnership model has a fundamental philosophical commitment to the participatory and consensus approach, and positively values it as the way to achieve the goal of agreed management (see below).

14.6 Problems arising from the participation and consensus imperatives

All ICZM partnerships operate within a contemporary management paradigm that attaches high value to public participation in decision-making. This is well illustrated by the inclusion of public participation as one of the eight principles of successful ICZM in the European Recommendation on ICZM (European Parliament and Council, 2002). The Recommendation expresses this as, 'involving all the parties concerned (economic and social partners, the organisations representing coastal zone residents, non-governmental organisations and the business sector) in the management process, for example by means of agreements and based on shared responsibility'.

317

Participatory planning, in turn, is part of a modern fashion of public 'empowerment', a management philosophy in which top-down, centralised prescriptive management is seen in a negative light, while bottom-up, decentralised participatory management is perceived positively. The philosophy of public participation is now so deeply embedded that, in the current climate, coastal management initiatives searching for funding must jump through the participation hoop set in front of them if they are to have any hope of success. Stakeholder participation is now an imperative to the extent that, in the coastal management literature, the emphasis is on how it should take place, not if (Edwards *et al.*, 1997; King, 2003; O'Riordan, 2005). It could be argued that participatory planning has resulted from the failures of the statutory equivalent – public consultation exercises in which statutory bodies ask for input but then go ahead and do what they initially wanted to do regardless. The perceived value of participation in ensuring accountability, local democracy and stakeholder 'buy-in' is now so well entrenched that Fletcher (2007c, p. 315) states that 'inclusive participatory coastal management is the prevailing coastal decision-making paradigm in much of the world'.

As a general principle, the participation of the public is desirable in developing management models that will affect them. However, there are two linked aspects of public participation as seen in ICZM partnerships that create huge difficulties and inefficiencies. These are, first, the level at which participation it takes place and, second, its obsession with consensus (McKenna and Cooper, 2006).

The first of these concerns definition of the 'lowest appropriate level' at which ICZM projects should operate. European Union countries already have national, regional and local democratic structures. However, the participation principle in ICZM is clearly based on the assumption that ever more local levels of consultation and agreement are necessary. (The emphasis placed on the subsidiarity principle by the EC may have greatly encouraged this focus on base-level participation.) This leads to a situation where established statutory fora comprising local elected representatives are relatively neglected, while project staff must spend huge amounts of time, energy and money organising and servicing local public meetings, stakeholder meetings, public surveys and follow-up consultation exercises. This reflects a widespread ICZM distrust of all existing organisations. This often leads to a situation where ICZM efforts become characterised by 'consultation paralysis', a condition where nothing can be done because yet someone else must be consulted or re-consulted.

This situation is made much worse when the only acceptable outcome of this lengthy and cumbersome participation iteration is consensus. Many statutory authorities, for example planning departments, routinely conduct laudably comprehensive consultation exercises, but at no stage does the authority relinquish its power to act in the absence of consensus. Indeed, there is no presumption that consensus will be achieved. In contrast, many ICZM projects are permeated by a 'nothing is agreed until all is agreed' philosophy. For example, the overall aim of the Bantry Bay Charter Project in Ireland, part of the EU Demonstration Programme in ICZM, was to 'develop a consensus-based integrated coastal zone management strategy for Bantry Bay' (Cummins *et al.*, 2004, p. 39).

It may be asked why the coastal management partnerships have become hooked on consensus outcomes. (Funding bodies almost invariably require stakeholder participation, but none demand consensus.) In practice, partnerships have little option because they operate within a self-imposed power vacuum. Since the typical partnership possesses neither the powers associated with ownership, nor those of statutory authority, consensus may be perceived as the only way to win the support of stakeholders. Having initially rejected the possibility that sectoral agencies could deliver ICZM, and having then committed themselves to participation as opposed to mere consultation, the partnerships lack the ability to take unilateral (indeed any) executive action. This remains the case even where powerful statutory bodies are represented on ICZM initiatives, because it has become customary in the prevailing ethos that they participate on equal terms with other stakeholders on a one person, one vote basis. This approach may be impressive as an exercise in local democracy, but in practical terms it is ill-advised, because power to act is effectively lost.

Those involved in participatory consensus-seeking exercises often concentrate on issues where agreement is most likely to be achieved, and avoid those that seem intractable. For this reason partnerships tend to accept past mistakes as baseline conditions, especially where dealing with a problem would also involve long-term strategic planning and substantial expenditure, for example the removal of inappropriate coastal defence structures. This issue is dealt with in a report on Scotland's local coastal management partnerships, which observes that, 'it may be considered that none of the partnerships has really been tested on the anvil of ICZM in the face of a large substantive coastal zone development issue' (Scottish Executive, 2002, p. 19). Under the heading, 'Maintaining Consensus – What Cost?', the report (p. 20) voices concerns that in their attempts to reach consensus, the partnerships have actively avoided conflict and controversial issues: '...by only dealing with those "motherhood and apple-pie" issues that everyone can easily sign-up to, the partnerships are not moving forward the cause of ICZM, as they are maintaining the status quo, and not challenging any stakeholders positions relating to the coast'. However, the report also points out that, in some cases, the non-statutory partnerships have been bypassed by developers who deal directly with the statutory bodies. It may be a defensible strategy for developers to treat the partnerships as an unnecessary extra layer of consultation. The perception may be that there is little point in consulting them since the statutory authorities must be dealt with in any case, either because they are the planning authority or because they are statutory consultees.

The search for consensus, or even just a high level of agreement, can lead to long delay, and management inertia. In these circumstances a participatory process acts as a brake on executive authority, and can work against the public interest rather than in its favour. Participation can lead to such a dilution of authority that it generates public disempowerment. This concept of participation as disempowerment may appear counter-intuitive, but the public is disadvantaged when those whose duty it is to protect its interest do not do so. The pursuit of consensus (in ICZM speak 'win-win' situations) has become a 'Holy Grail' whose devotees often will not face unpleasant facts, such that consensus demands compromise. A consensus position might represent a socially acceptable compromise, but not necessarily (or even often) one that is environmentally acceptable. The objective carrying capacity of a coastal environment in physical, ecological and human terms represents the bottom line in sustainability, not a 'political' consensus. In practice, some stakeholders will wish to negotiate a consensus position that favours their own interests. It is very much in their interest if statutory authorities feel inhibited from taking proactive steps while attempts to reach consensus through a participatory process are ongoing. Self-serving stakeholders have much more to fear from a powerful statutory body determined to protect the interests of the wider public, than a well-meaning but consensus-hamstrung voluntary initiative. The participatory approach is unwieldy and time consuming, and there is little accepted or standard methodology to guide it. Attempts to achieve agreement among so many varied interests can involve long tortuous negotiations and endless compromises. In the face of such a powerful motivating force as self-interest the imperative to achieve consensus among so many players may not produce an

320

optimum solution, but may produce instead the 'least non-acceptable' solution.

There is a viewpoint that one advantage of the current system is that the coastal partnerships can act as honest brokers applying pressure on erring local authorities or developers, perhaps even using 'naming and shaming' sanctions against them. Partnerships can sometimes be quietly effective pressure groups, but they rely so much on consensus that any stronger action is unlikely to be agreed. In any case a more aggressive strategy could rebound against the partnerships if they are subsequently frozen out of decision making.

Even if consensus is not explicitly sought, in a participation exercise the more powerful stakeholders often have a dominant influence with the lead management authority, which may have an agenda of its own (for example, to increase employment). All may have a say, but some receive a more sympathetic hearing than others. A property developer, or industry representative, can dominate participatory structures. Even Edwards *et al.* (1997, p. 162), strong advocates of bottom-up participatory approaches in the UK, concede that, 'one must also consider whether geographically-integrated long-term strategic management objectives would be likely to be achieved were management authority to be entirely devolved to local communities, especially considering the potential for local short-term priorities, particularly those of dominant user groups, to override other interests'.

The perceived need to have high levels of public participation can lead to intractable scale problems. As the spatial scale increases so does the number of stakeholders and the complexity of issues. Since most projects are short and have few full-time staff their best chance of achieving participation and consensus objectives is to focus the project on a relatively small spatial scale. The outcome is that the coast becomes an uncoordinated mishmash of relatively localised and sometimes overlapping (in both space and time) ICZM partnerships and projects of varying scale. It is ironic that a process that puts so much emphasis on 'joined-up' management sometimes does not have its own initiatives integrated with each other. This is largely a function of the transient project basis of so much ICZM work.

14.7 Problems arising from the financial insecurity of the partnerships

What the partnerships can achieve is limited by membership and resources. Existing sectoral management structures tie up recurrent government expenditure on coastal management (in the widest sense). ICZM partnerships are forced onto the funding fringes where they must rely on, and frequently compete for, external financial support. Such support is usually short term, rarely more than three years. For initiatives to survive longer, they must generate funding from other sources. The majority of partnerships are created explicitly to utilise the funding available. The typical ICZM partnership is a 'project' hosted by a local authority, funded for two–three years by a government or EU financial instrument, and run by a project officer employed on a contract basis for the time span of the project. In some cases the host organisation will directly fund the project officer's salary, but it is common for national statutory agencies with an environmental remit to provide the initial funding, for example English Nature in England and Wales. In the last decade the European Community has been the major financial support of many projects, funding them under various financial instruments such as LIFE, TERRA and INTERREG.

It is a commonly stated objective of ICZM partnerships that they will strive to continue beyond the period supported by start-up funding. In practice, however, the partnerships are characterised by chronic financial insecurity which threatens their work and even their survival (Scottish Executive, 2002, p. 18; McGlashan, 2002, 2003) and failure to secure additional external funding sometimes results in their collapse. For example, the Bantry Bay Charter initiative in County Cork, Ireland was originally funded by the LIFE Environment Programme of the EU as part of the Demonstration Project in ICZM, and subsequently by the local authority, Cork County Council. It collapsed following withdrawal of Council financial support in 2002. The partnerships exhibit a high degree of financial vulnerability and dependency because their own resources are so limited, for example the Cardigan Bay Partnership receives 80% of total income from grants and donations (Scott, 1998). Membership subscriptions may be the only significant internal source of income. However, in practice, there is a relatively low ceiling to the fees that a partnership can charge without haemorrhaging members, and in any case higher fees would unfairly disadvantage the less well-resourced stakeholders. Membership numbers tend to vary widely, and it is a major challenge to collect all subscriptions. The Forth Estuary Forum, established in 1993, is one of the best known and most highly regarded partnerships. In 2006 it had 81 members, but the total contributed in annual membership subscriptions was only £14 354, which did not even come close to paying the salary of one employee. In order to progress one of its initiatives it took the

322

Forum a year to source funding for the salary of the project officer. In the event it was funded from 11 sources, two of which provided two-thirds of the total.

Financial insecurity has a knock-on effect in preventing the partnerships acquiring any sense of permanence because they can offer only short-term contracts at relatively low salaries. They cannot afford to employ many staff. Again the Forth Estuary Forum provides an example. In 2006 the forum advertised for a forum manager. The salary offered was c. £22K with two years postgraduate experience. The contract was guaranteed until March 2008 with a possible extension. In contrast, in 2006 a first-year teacher in Scotland earned £19 878, rising in second year to £23 841 and after six years to £31 707. The teacher is likely to be on a permanent contract.

Partnerships with no paid employees rely heavily on the goodwill and enthusiasm, and perhaps funding, of particularly committed individuals and organisations among the membership. A lot of time and effort is expended on fund-raising and competing for grant aid. Staff are often obliged to spend a disproportionate amount of time seeking funding to maintain their own position. One study estimated that, on average, project officers spent half their time trying to raise funds (McGlashan, 2003, p. 394). Success often depends on securing funding for core activities, e.g. from European programmes such as INTERREG, and to secure this funding a partnership may have to buy in to working methods and objectives that are oblique to its central interests. In pursuit of financial security, the partnerships often rely heavily on grants for specific 'projects'. Staff then must focus on these grant-led programmes, and this dilutes other activities. One of the dangers of the project focus is that staff can get drawn into the very systems and structures that the partnership is trying to change. Partnerships operate so much within the confines of externally-funded time-limited projects that they become conditioned to the short-termism of the project ethos, and are defined by it. (Indeed the word 'project' is often used to define the entire initiative.) Funding and staffing insecurities deter the partnerships from undertaking longer-term strategic projects.

Partnerships are usually staffed by project officers, typically in their twenties or early thirties. Job insecurity is a dominant influence, and this often motivates staff to move away from contract employment to a permanent job (perhaps entirely outside the ICZM field), or to another contract at the start of its cycle. This means that, even if the project is eventually extended or a new project quickly follows, the original project officer has departed and a new employee must be

323

recruited. If a job opportunity presents itself, an employee may move before the end of his/her current contract. At best, staff turnover results in the loss of useful contacts and experience; at worst the loss of a project officer at a critical time in mid contract can greatly demoralise and damage the whole enterprise. By 2002 only one of the nine local coastal partnerships in Scotland had retained any of the same staff from start-up, and some had only employed their first project staff in 1999 (McGlashan, 2002, p. 5).

Short-term contracts mean that project officers rarely attain the seniority that would increase their effectiveness and influence within their host organisations. A contributory factor is that even where a project officer does remain through consecutive contracts there is no structured career progression, and the status and job title of the employee remains the same. If seconded project officers are promoted they often return immediately to new positions in mainstream employment. Project officers typically do not remain long enough to build up the network of personal friendships and professional relationships that form a potent part of the effectiveness of any worker. These are particularly important in the ICZM role, as the project officer is, by definition, trying to modify traditional attitudes and habits (for example, to encourage integration rather than sectoral work practices). Contract staff suffer from a general perception that they are employees of the project, rather than full employees of the host institution.

Young, temporary employees have little influence in large organisations in comparison to older, permanent and much more highly paid staff. It is lack of permanence and seniority, rather than youth, which are the more serious drawbacks. In discussing English Nature's review of its Estuaries Initiative Hayes (1999, p. 5) notes that 'the seniority of representation on steering and management groups was identified as a useful indicator of local commitment and support for projects; more successful projects tend to engage more senior representation'. There is little incentive to change attitudes and work practices at the behest of someone who is perceived as an inconsequential transient. The project is seen, quite correctly, as a temporary 'add-on' to normal institutional life, something that will disappear in the not too distant future. Indeed, in some authorities other employees are barely aware of the project's existence.

14.8   Issues of representativeness and accountability

Partnerships vary greatly in their operating culture, but major issues of legitimacy, representativeness, accountability and effectiveness have been largely unaddressed. For example, Fletcher (2007b) has pointed out that questions can be asked about the extent to which representatives in coastal partnerships really represent the views of their constituencies. Even where they do, their input is restricted by the demands of their own organisations. He points out that representatives are often poorly motivated, have limited accountability, and have a poor record of information dissemination. Few partnerships can claim that they are truly representative with all potential interests involved. In some cases some stakeholders are deliberately excluded, perhaps because it is anticipated that they will skew the debate, or prove troublesome, or just to keep numbers at a manageable level. In practice, most partnerships exhibit some degree of imbalance in their representation, certainly among the most active members. There tends to be a lack of grass-roots membership and an associated dominance of academia and formal agencies. Certain interests prevail while others are effectively disenfranchised. Criteria for membership vary among partnerships. Some have a virtually open-door policy – membership is open to anyone who feels that they have an interest in the issue. This extends to individual members of the public in the case of the Moray Firth Partnership.

Open-door membership strategies can give rise to the problems of managing a wide range of interests, leading to difficulties in articulating a single coherent view, for example when asked to comment on policy documents and management plans. In terms of their internal 'politics', it can be difficult for widely-based coastal partnerships to move beyond their constrained discussion and information dissemination functions to a more proactive stance where they speak with a clear unified voice on specific management issues. The general point here is that an exaggerated focus on public participation can weaken broad-based organisations like the coastal partnerships, and, make them less effective pressure groups. The constraints of participation and in particular, the search for consensus make it difficult to get agreement on anything other than generalities. This creates a perception that the coastal partnerships are lightweight, and lack a cutting edge. In contrast, well established players such as the National Trust, Friends of the Earth, World Wildlife Fund, and specific user groups such as sailing interests, may be more effective in exerting pressure on those with authority because they have a focused remit undiluted by the need for consensus among a plethora of interest groups. For example, in 2006 Friends of the Earth in Northern Ireland took the lead in the ultimately successful instigation of infraction proceedings against the Department of the Environment (DOENI) at the European Court of Justice over breach of European Wastewater Directives. The use by third-parties of legal procedures in this way may be one of the few effective ways for an NGO or voluntary body to influence or change government policy, but it would be very difficult for broadly-based bodies committed to partnership decision-making to get all stakeholders to agree on such a radical strategy. In fact, the application of such societal safeguards may be weakened if consensus is a requirement for pursuing them. (Note: recently it has become more difficult to take a third-party case because organisations have to prove that they have 'sufficient interest'. However, the Aarhus Convention should change this.)

Some partnerships exercise a tighter control on those who are invited to become members, for example they will make a judgment that only those with an obvious common interest will be invited. Limiting membership to bodies with a clear common interest makes it easier to address strategic and management issues with clear unified voices, but this may be at the expense of representing all interests and concerns. This leads into a fundamental debate about whether the partnership *process* or its *outcomes* should be the emphasis. Is it more important to have all legitimate interests involved (i.e. process dominant) or is it more important to produce a tangible and desirable outcome for each participant? In general, many partnerships have too few stakeholders from industry and business concerns (INCA is an exception). One reason for this, and a generic problem faced by voluntary ICZM groups, is the general misconception that coastal partnerships are essentially environmental groupings. While the partnerships are not always explicitly conservation-orientated, many of those most active in them are predominantly concerned about the negative effects of uncoordinated activities on coastal habitats and landscapes. Many leading members are strongly identified with the environmental movement, and may also play a dominant role in such organisations. This perception puts off leisure, business and local community groups. On this point it may be worth asking how many of the partnerships were established because their founders were principally concerned about over-development. There may be an element of truth in the charge that some partnerships are effectively coastal conservation NGOs acting as pressure groups to preserve the *status quo*, rather than advocating balanced development.

A linked problem is that a partnership's steering group or working parties can be dominated by members who are also significant figures in other organisations that are part of the establishment. The influence of dual or multiple membership can hinder a partnership's ability to bring about change in these other bodies. Indeed, other organisations and individuals may be able to manipulate a partnership to deliver their own agendas. The danger is that, perhaps unconsciously, the partnerships do not challenge the status quo because they are 'packed' with influential but instinctively conservative members who repress any suggestion of radical thought or action. In this way they simply reinforce existing viewpoints, and may alienate potential members who want real change. Partnerships must overcome this if they are to achieve the primary function of inclusiveness. A growing perception that they are impotent and cannot bring about real change 'because the same people are still in charge' may explain why partnerships typically report declining audiences and participation rates over time.

14.9   The statutory alternative to coastal partnerships

In comparing the statutory US and the current voluntary EU approaches to coastal management Humphrey *et al.* (2000) state that, 'we consider that a voluntary approach alone is unlikely to work at this stage' and, 'in terms of effectiveness, a framework Directive would be a better option for bringing about ICZM in Europe'.

Coastal partnerships are a fig leaf for government inaction (and European caution) in the area of integrated coastal zone management. Official lip service to their work and achievements cannot mask the fact that these voluntary 'bottom-up' approaches are unsustainable, and lack the authority and resources to deliver ICZM. Partnerships have too many fundamental weaknesses and legitimate doubts can be raised about their effectiveness in achieving their stated aim of sustainable development through integration of management (McKenna *et al.*, 2008). It is the great irony of ICZM that its core objective of sustainability of management is pursued by a movement itself characterised by non-sustainability.

Advocates of the partnership approach are traditionally dismissive of sectoral agencies because their focused remit discourages integration and holistic vision. In practice, this purist attitude becomes a self-fulfilling prophesy because it inevitably leads to the establishment of voluntary partnerships which try to do on meagre resources what government, both national and local, should be doing; effectively it lets them off the hook. It is true that the 'ideal' framework for ICZM, a dedicated statutory agency, does not currently exist anywhere in Europe; nevertheless the potentially most effective controls on coastal degradation are the government statutory functions of spatial planning, environmental protection and conservation designation. Even though their remit is sectoral, these statutory agencies have many advantages over partnerships, and the ICZM 'movement' should try to harness these strengths. There will be no significant improvement in the take-up of ICZM so long as it continues to function as a series of short-term projects run by voluntary, powerless, and under-funded partnerships. Hayes (1999, p. 5) points out that, in some estuaries, 'the voluntary authority of Project Officers was not sufficient to achieve integration of plans and projects'. In contrast, sectoral agencies (e.g. the Environment Agency in England and Wales) have a much greater potential to deliver effective management of the coast than the contemporary generation of voluntary ICZM initiatives, because they wield executive authority and have recurrent funding.

Integrated Coastal Zone Management (ICZM) needs a more professional approach than that offered by voluntary partnerships. It needs formal government recognition and endorsement to be credible, which means that the lead role in ICZM should be undertaken by statutory authorities. A sound statutory and legislative basis is an essential prerequisite for effective coastal management, and this cannot be delivered by a voluntary partnership. Without statutory recognition, authorities have other priorities and staff time is given preferentially to more pressing, i.e. statutory, concerns. Local authorities are local government in practice and action, not just administrators; legally they have a flexible remit to meet the needs of the community and they can 'do' ICZM if they can be persuaded to commit to it. Statutory bodies are *structurally* much better equipped to deliver ICZM (official status, power, funding, permanence). 'Turf wars' *within* (not *between*) authorities are the major constraint on integration. Their biggest weaknesses are lack of capacity and expertise, but these can be supplied by training. Statutory management does not rule out stakeholder participation and debate; most government departments, e.g. planning, now run very comprehensive public consultation programmes.

Within statutory bodies, time-limited projects, including those funded by the European Community and Government, could still be used to advance ICZM because funding opportunities should not be spurned, but the projects will be explicitly short term. Projects will end on a known date, and there will be no assumption or expectation that they will continue beyond that date. The project will be similar to a time-limited consultancy contract. It will make recommendations as to how issues can be resolved, but it will not be conceived as an implementation instrument. The project ethos is that it does the

328

detailed analytical work that senior management does not have the time (or remit) to do. When the project ends a report will be made to the appropriate authority. The senior officers armed with their statutory powers can now take up the issues that have been identified and clarified by the project. Indeed, projects run by voluntary partnerships could still play a role alongside a statutory authority. However, they should be seen as naturally ephemeral and when an issue is fully explored, they wind up. Such initiatives would not be conceived as permanent features of the coastal management landscape.

What matters is the sustainability of the ICZM process within competent authorities, not the long-term survival of an individual ICZM partnership. Partnerships (and the projects they are often synonymous with) are typically insecure and possibly ephemeral, but the process is the long-term organisational strategy of a stable, permanent organisation with recurrent funding. Sustainability of the ICZM process within a local authority is most likely to be achieved when all coastal management activities, including routine work and specific projects, are carried out by permanent employees who do not owe their jobs to short-term funding. Permanent staff work within a career structure characterised by job security, sequential experience building, and promotion. The involvement of permanent staff will develop their capacity to deal with coastal management issues, and there is the considerable benefit that senior staff will be involved. In contrast to contract employees, personnel with permanent jobs are unlikely to leave on end of 'project' funding, and their accumulated knowledge and experience is retained by the organisation. The existing knowledge of local authority practice held by an employee is a direct benefit in that this can enable insights into the practical means of achieving ICZM. The authority might still employ short-term contract employees, but their role is to support the permanent staff for the duration of a given project.

Coastal management actions undertaken in-house by a responsible statutory authority will have more status than those undertaken by partnerships because they are integral to the institution rather than 'add-ons', and because they are staffed by permanent employees. The authority may well plan its work programme as a series of discrete projects, but successive projects will be integrated with each other because there is a permanent cadre of knowledgeable employees who are following some kind of strategic ICZM plan. Indeed, even voluntary projects existing alongside in-house projects will be integrated because they report to the same authority.

Integrated coastal zone management capacity should be built in existing statutory authorities which should focus on developing the coastal management skills of employees currently in post. With its own in-house coastal management capacity, an authority can maintain independence and integrity. Coastal management initiatives run in-house by a statutory authority will be free of the characteristic partnership inefficiencies resulting from insecure contract employment, endless participation exercises and the consensus imperative. In-house projects informed by sound ICZM principles, but free from the drawbacks of the current partnership model, could lead to significant positive changes in the *modus operandi* of local authorities. Time-limited participatory projects would be used to gain information on conflicts and issues that transcend existing sectoral boundaries, but this information would be passed to the established statutory authorities for action.

At local government level, sectoral focus is a lesser problem. Integrated coastal zone management should explicitly target senior officers, i.e. top-down as well as bottom-up. Partnerships should work in support of statutory bodies. The ICZM *process* is more important than any given *project*. In most contexts, commitment to the broad principles of ICZM among a very small group of senior officials in national, regional and local authorities would do more to protect and advance a sustainable coast than a multitude of attempts to 'empower' thousands of local citizens by achieving an unattainable or unsustainable consensus. Those best placed to bring it about change, and quickly, are the powerful senior officers within these statutory authorities. It is unrealistic to expect that a coastal partnership founded on an uncertain basis of short-term funding and staffed by young temporary employees can bring about fundamental cultural change in coastal management philosophy and practice within a time scale even remotely appropriate to deal with coastal degradation. An in-house ICZM unit should be in a much stronger position as it will be an organic part of the host organisation, and will involve permanent staff, some of whom may be relatively senior. Time-limited coastal management projects should be primarily concerned with providing the information bank on which the senior officers of statutory bodies can act. Far more attention should be given to influencing these senior officials in an avowedly top-down ICZM strategy.

14.10 Coastal partnerships: the future

The European Union has not yet produced an ICZM Directive and, at first consideration, the outlook for ICZM 'with teeth' appears unpromising given the comment in the recent Communication (European Commission, 2007, p. 5) that, 'at this time a new specific legal instrument to promote ICZM is not foreseen'. Nevertheless, there are reasons to believe that future prospects for statutory ICZM in Europe are actually quite positive. Every recent EC and international environmental management initiative advocates integration, and there is a strong sense that statutory ICZM is on its way, even if there is no ICZM Directive. Among the vehicles that might carry this ICZM legislation are, at national level in the UK, the new Marine Bill, and at European level a number of new and proposed instruments including the Floods Directive, the Marine Strategy Directive, and the Maritime Policy. At international level the OSPAR Working Group, which includes the European Community, is also moving in the same direction.

Given that the drift of events appears to be towards a statutory basis for coastal management, there is an urgent need to reappraise the partnership concept which has been the dominant feature of the ICZM scene for most of the last two decades. Current coastal partnerships fill a vacuum. They exist because it is perceived that existing statutory management of the coast is inadequate, specifically that it is not integrated. If statutory management was significantly improved, especially in regards to integration, there would be no logical reason for the continuance of the partnerships, because statutory authorities have huge advantages as management instruments, for example in their permanent status, in holding real executive authority, and in their access to human, financial and infrastructural resources.

Many of the problems experienced by partnerships are directly linked to their efforts to attain financial security and permanence. The corollary is that many of these problems disappear when the partnerships are viewed as useful but temporary elements of the ICZM scene. It is simply unrealistic to expect that the EU or national governments will ever commit themselves to the long-term recurrent expenditure involved in keeping scores of local ICZM partnerships afloat indefinitely, and they will be even less likely to do so if a statutory model of coastal management is established. Sustainability of the voluntary partnerships and their individual projects is not a realistic or even desirable goal. In contrast, sustainability of the ICZM *process* should be the aim.

Partnerships are most successful when working to influence others rather than trying to implement change unilaterally. They are at their best when they are involving and informing individuals and groups about coastal issues, and they have been successful in raising the profile of coastal management, and in providing information to the public.

331

Arguably this is their unique contribution, because no other mechanisms existed to carry out these roles. They carried out the groundwork for other initiatives, including those initiated by statutory bodies, and they can take credit for that. It is possible that the more stable coastal partnerships could have a future by evolving into advisory bodies to statutory authorities. As such they could act as early-warning systems of impending or actual problems.

Voluntary coastal partnerships can be regarded as an evolutionary 'pioneer' stage in the management of the coast. Over the c. 20 years of their existence they have discovered both the areas where they are effective, and also their limits. Many areas of human activity now under statutory governance, such as aspects of social work, education, and conservation of the environment, were once the preserve of dedicated amateur enthusiasts and philanthropists. If coastal management also becomes a statutory activity it will not mean that the voluntary partnerships have failed. Rather it will mean that they have succeeded in making themselves redundant by successfully persuading government of the need for statutory integrated coastal management.

References

Cummins, V., O'Mahony, C. and Connolly, N. (2004) *Review of Integrated Coastal Zone Management and Principles of Best Practice*, The Heritage Council, Kilkenny.

DEFRA (2006) *Promoting an Integrated Approach to Management of the Coastal Zone (ICZM) in England*, HMSO, London.

Edwards, S.D., Jones, P.J.S and Howell, D.E. (1997) Participation in coastal zone management initiatives: a review and analysis of examples from the UK. *Ocean and Coastal Management*, Vol. 36, pp. 143–165.

European Commission (1997a) *Better Management of Coastal Resources: A European Programme for Integrated Coastal Zone Management*, Office for Official Publications of the European Communities, Luxembourg.

European Commission (1999b) *Lessons from the European Commission's Demonstration Programme on Integrated Coastal Zone Management (ICZM)*, Office for Official Publications of the European Communities, Luxembourg.

European Commission (1999c) *Towards a European Integrated Coastal Zone Management (ICZM) Strategy: General Principles and Policy Options*, Office for Official Publications of the European Communities, Luxembourg.

European Commission (2007) Communication from the Commission: Report to the European Parliament and the Council: An Evaluation of Integrated Coastal Zone Management (ICZM) in Europe.com(2007)308 final. Brussels, 7.06.2007, Office for Official Publications of the European Communities, Luxembourg.

European Environment Agency (2006) *The Continuous Degradation of Europe's Coasts Threatens European Living Standards* EEA Briefing 2006(3), (TH-AM-06-003-EN-C), Copenhagen.

European Parliament and Council (2002) *Recommendation of the European Parliament and of the Council of 30 May 2002 Concerning the Implementation of Integrated Coastal Zone Management in Europe* (2002/413/EC). Official Journal of European Union L148 06.06.2002

Fletcher, S. (2007a) Converting science to policy through stakeholder involvement: an analysis of the European Marine Strategy Directive. *Marine Pollution Bulletin*, Vol. 54, pp. 1881–1886.

Fletcher, S. (2007b) Representing stakeholder interests in partnership approaches to coastal management: experiences from the United Kingdom. *Ocean and Coastal Management*, Vol. 50, pp. 606–622.

Fletcher, S. (2007c) Influences on stakeholder representation in participatory coastal management programmes. *Ocean and Coastal Management*, Vol. 50, pp. 314–328.

Forth Estury Forum (1999) The Forth Integrated Management Strategy, Forth Estuary Forum, Edinburgh.

Hayes, G. (1999) Towards sustainable estuary management in England. *Coastnet*, Vol. 4, p. 5.

Humphrey, S., Burbridge, P. and Blatch, C. (2000) US lessons for coastal management in the European Union. *Marine Policy*, Vol. 24, pp. 275–286.

King, G. (2003) The role of participation in the European Demonstration Projects in ICZM. *Coastal Management*, Vol. 31, pp. 137–143.

McGlashan, D.J. (2002) Financing in UK local coastal for a. *Coastnet*, Vol. 6, p. 5.

McGlashan, D.J. (2003) Funding in integrated coastal zone management partnerships. *Marine Pollution Bulletin*, Vol. 46, pp. 393–396.

McKenna, J. and Cooper, J. Andrew G. (2006) Sacred Cows in Coastal Management: The need for a 'cheap and transitory' model. *Area*, Vol. 38, pp. 421–431.

McKenna, J., Cooper, J. Andrew G. and O'Hagan, Annemarie (2008) Managing by Principle: A critical analysis of the European principles of integrated coastal zone management (ICZM). *Marine Policy*, Vol. 32, pp. 941–955.

O'Riordan, T. (2005) Inclusive and community participation in the coastal zone: opportunities and dangers. In Vermaat, J.E., Bouwer, L., Turner, K. and Salomons, W. (eds) *Managing European Coasts: Past, Present and Future*, Environmental Science Monograph Series, Springer, Berlin, pp. 173–184.

Scott, A.J. (1998) The contribution of forums to rural sustainable development: a preliminary evaluation. *Journal of Environmental Management*, Vol. 54, pp. 291–303.

Scottish Executive (2002) *Assessment of the Effectiveness of Local Coastal Management Partnerships as a Delivery Mechanism for Integrated Coastal Zone Management*. Report to Scottish Executive Social Research, The Stationery Office, Edinburgh.

Stojanovic, T. and Barker, N. (2008) Improving governance through local coastal partnerships in the UK. *The Geographical Journal*, Vol. 174, Issue 4, pp. 344–360.

Suárez de Vivero, J.L. and Rodríguez Mateos, J.C. (2005) Coastal crisis: the failure of coastal management in the Spanish Mediterranean region. *Coastal Management*, Vol. 33, pp. 197–214.

Further reading

DEFRA/LGA Coastal SIG/Coastal Partnerships Working Group (2008). *The Financial Benefits of Working in Partnership at the Coast*. Final Report July 2008, ENTEC UK Ltd.

Fletcher, S., Beagley, E., Hewett, T., Williams, A. and McHugh, K. (2007) The Hamble Estuary Partnership and Solent Forum: duplication or integration? *Marine Policy*, Vol. 31, pp. 619–627.

Power, J., McKenna, J., MacLeod, M., Cooper, J.A.G. and Convie, G. (2000) Developing integrated participatory management strategies for Atlantic dune systems in County Donegal, Northwest Ireland. *Ambio*, Vol. 29, Issue 3, pp. 143–149.

15

The role of virtual reality (VR) in visualising the coast

Margaret Carlisle and David R. Green
Centre for Marine and Coastal Zone Management (CMCZM), Department of
Geography and Environment, University of Aberdeen, Scotland, UK

Virtual reality (VR) simulations, from simple panoramas and animations to fully realised 3D buildings and structures in a true 3D environment, are becoming increasingly widely used, both by individuals and by large organisations such as local authorities. Five VR techniques are examined, with regard to their strengths, weakness, constraints and opportunities for use as tools within coastal environmental management.

15.1   Introduction

Computer-based visualisation is rapidly becoming increasingly important in natural resource management including coastal management. An array of tools and techniques, such as virtual reality (VR), are now providing new ways of viewing, analysing, and interpreting data offering a visual perspective that was difficult, if not impossible, to obtain in the past (Thurmond *et al.*, 2005). Virtual reality is one area of interest to natural resource managers, as it provides tools to both illustrate and explore an environment and display environmental change (Mouatt, 2006).

This chapter explores some of the different ways that virtual reality can be used to provide access to environmental information as a means for exploration, interaction and participation in coastal management. In recent years a number of studies has considered how geospatial data for coastal environments can be integrated with the aid of geographical information system (GIS) software and the associated visualisation tools. The output from many of these can be considered as examples of virtual reality offering researchers, the public, coastal

Coastal zone management
978-0-7277-3641-1

managers and stakeholders the opportunity to explore areas that are difficult or remote to visit, to provide the basis for virtual fieldtrips, and to fly over and through terrain both above and below sea level. Today there exist a range of powerful tools that can be used to create virtual landscapes, from the simple to the complex, and the low cost to the high cost. This chapter explores some of the different ways that virtual reality can be used to provide access to environmental information as a means for exploration, interaction and participation in coastal management. The chapter is illustrated with a number of examples.

15.2   VR factors and their resource implications

Virtual reality is frequently used to describe a computer-generated environment or landscape that represents or is a model of reality. Over time, the capability to create more realistic visualisations of environments has improved considerably and today good quality computer representations of the real world can now be generated with the aid of standard desktop computers and low-cost off-the-shelf commercial software. There are four important factors in defining a product as virtual reality (VR):

1. Level of immersion – body suit, goggles and auditory stimulation being full immersion; looking at a computer screen being minimal immersion.
2. Level of graphic realism – high resolution photography, with panoramic 360° viewing, being full graphic realism; line structures being minimal graphic realism.
3. Level of interactivity – physically interacting with structures, etc. by way of a body suit being full interactivity; using a mouse to guide a flythrough with complete control over position, direction and angle of view being medium-high interactivity; using a mouse to guide a panoramic view (no control over position, but some over angle of view) or a time-series slider being medium-low interactivity; passively watching a flythrough or unfolding time-series being minimal interactivity.
4. Level of dynamism – a long (30 seconds or more), smooth flowing sequence with considerable change either over time or in space is a high level of dynamism; a short (5 seconds or less) sequence is medium dynamism; the absence of any change sequence (i.e. no movement) is minimal dynamism.

336

Several useful definitions of VR are also available online. The definitions supplied by IT professionals emphasise the factors of immersion and interactivity (e.g. http://www.unesco.org/education/educprog/lwf/doc/portfolio/definitions.htm). Definitions supplied by those outside the IT professional world emphasise the factors of graphic realism and dynamism (e.g. http://coe.sdsu.edu/eet/articles/vrk12/index.htm). Fully immersive VR (body suit and wrap-around helmet) is a highly specialised and, to date, extremely costly field, although the emergence of the Nintendo Wii may well be the first step in making it more accessible. Achieving high levels of graphic realism, interactivity and dynamism are usually less expensive, but they can still be costly in terms of the software needed and, more importantly, in terms of computing and personnel time. In particular, generating new graphically realistic textures for planned, but as yet non-existent, structures is often highly demanding of personnel/processing time, unless one has access to a library of textures.

The remaining discussion of resource use implications uses five examples of virtual reality simulations, ranging from the very simple to the very complex:

1. animated time-series
2. 360° panoramas
3. fully interactive VRMLs (3D scenes) created using GIS
4. adding imagery and shapefiles and creating 3D objects in Google Earth
5. landscape visualisation theatre.

Several of these examples are held on the University of Aberdeen CMCZM website at http://www.abdn.ac.uk/cmczm where they may be viewed 'in action'.

15.2.1 Example 1: simple animations

Graphic realism is perhaps the factor that can be most easily sacrificed when creating VR visualisations. If enough context is supplied (in terms of legends, written scene descriptions, etc.) a surprisingly basic image can be enough, the viewer's experience and imagination being relied upon to 'fill in the gaps'. This is, of course, the basis of successful cartography.

One useful example of a website that has practically zero graphic realism but which provides some degree of both dynamism and interactivity can be found at the UK Met Office http://www.metoffice.gov.uk/weather/uk/surface_pressure.html. This provides the European

Surface pressure forecast

These charts of surface pressure, from analysis (T+0) to the 84-hour forecast (T+84) are produced daily

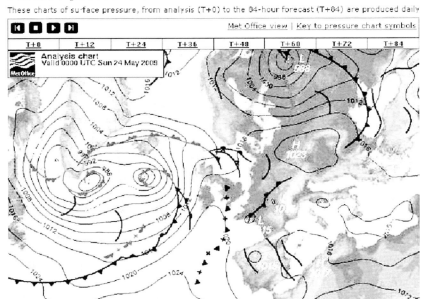

Fig. 15.1 Met Office surface pressure chart

surface pressure charts for eight time frames (from 0 to 84 hours ahead) (Fig. 15.1). The charts can either be selected using the mouse (hence the interactivity) or viewed as an animation (hence the dynamism), which gives a better idea of how the frontal systems are developing. No concession is made to graphic realism, however, as it is assumed that the viewer will have a basic understanding of isobar charts. These eight charts are produced daily, but, because of their simplicity, putting them up on the website every day is no doubt a short and simple task.

It is possible to produce a very simple animated area time series with any GIS software, by taking a 'brute force' approach and building the animation frame by frame. The example chosen here is the flooding that took place at Baleshare, North Uist, Western Isles in the UK in January 2005, where a large area of farmland was inundated by the sea, resulting in the loss of much livestock. The extent of the final flooded area is based on eye witness accounts, and the intermediate flood maps are based on interpretation of the terrain together with the eye witness accounts. Four screenshots from the final animation (constructed in ArcView then Apple Quicktime Pro) are shown in Fig. 15.2.

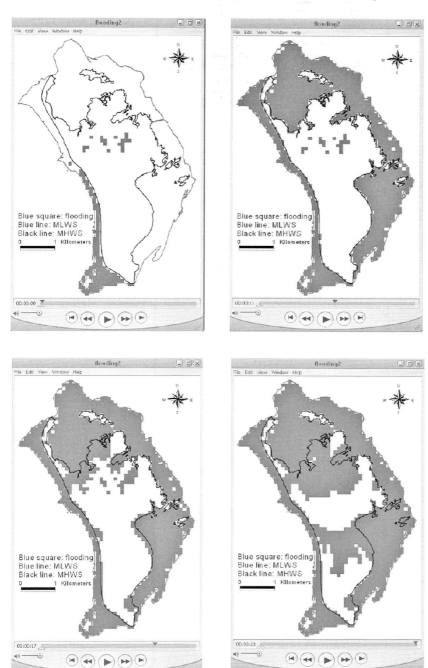

Fig. 15.2 Animation of Baleshare flood event

339

Fig. 15.3 Part of Ben Nevis panorama

Animations such as these can be viewed in standard media players such as Apple Quicktime (http://www.apple.com/quicktime/download/win.html), Realplayer (http://uk.real.com/player/), or Windows media player. These are set up to display a number of media, including movies and animations, which can be interpreted as VR in the sense that they are highly dynamic, and the use of a time-slider allows a small degree of interactivity. Again they can score highly on the level of graphic realism, depending on the original input. Additionally, almost all home computers will have one if not all of these three media players, and they are all free to download.

15.2.2 Example 2: 360° panoramas

Panoramic VR is the creation of a virtual reality by displaying a *panoramic* image mapped onto a virtual sphere. Panoramic VR is most notably different from traditional 3D implementations of VR by restricting the viewer or the object viewed to one point in space. As a result, the viewer cannot 'walk' around in a Panoramic VR space in the way that they might in a 3D environment. The benefit of this approach is that it is possible to produce photographic quality VR at very little cost.

Figure 15.3 shows a section of a panoramic VR of Ben Nevis and Carn Mor Dearg, taken from the CIC Hut (near Fort William, Highland, Scotland, UK). This section of the panorama was constructed with three standard-sized photographs in Panavue software (http://www.panavue.com/). The whole 360° panorama was constructed with 12 photographs, resulting in a Quicktime movie, nevisorama1.mov, which can be viewed interactively i.e. the person viewing can use the mouse to pan round the panorama, stopping at views of interest.

Figure 15.4 shows a more purely coastal panorama, in this case the estuary of the River Ythan (near Aberdeen, Scotland, UK). This illustrates that the restriction on the viewpoint of panoramic VR is more of a limitation for flat areas. It is therefore a technique best

Fig. 15.4 Part of Ythan panorama

suited to areas with a great deal of vertical interest i.e. mountainous or built-up areas.

15.2.3 Example 3: GIS and VRML

A geographical information system (GIS) is often defined as a collection of computer hardware, software and geographic data for capturing, managing, analysing, and displaying all forms of geographically refer-enced information. One example of GIS software, ESRI's ArcView 3.3, has the following functions, among others:

1. changing map projections
2. dissolving features based on an attribute
3. merging adjoining themes together
4. clipping one theme based on another
5. union of two themes (intersecting polygons and assigning attributes from both original themes)
6. creating buffers around selected features (a common tool in development planning)
7. finding the area or perimeter of a polygon, and the length of a line/ network
8. calculating statistics (histograms, etc.) for a theme
9. converting a vector dataset (polygons) to raster (cell grids) and vice versa
10. converting vector data (e.g. contour lines) to a 3D digital terrain model DTM and vice versa
11. deriving slope and aspect from a DTM
12. calculating hillshade and viewshed from a DTM
13. model building – applying the cell values of selected raster themes within a rule based algorithm in order to obtain a predictive distribution for a criterion of interest.

All of these functions are dependent on the relational links between the features on the map (known as a 'theme' in ArcView) and the data held in the database (the 'attribute table' in ArcView). All true GIS have this capability, although terms different to *theme* and *attribute table* may often be used. Some GIS, particularly those provided as freeware, have a fairly basic set of functions, these usually being categorised as 1–7 on the above list. ArcView 3.3 is considered to be a mid-range GIS in terms of both functionality and price. Top-end GIS such as ArcGIS have an extremely extensive set of functions and capabilities, and are priced accordingly.

The most obvious limitation of GIS software is cost. As a rough guide, the greater the functionality, the more expensive the software. For example, ESRI's ArcGIS (ArcView 9.1 plus 3D analyst) is several thousand dollars. However, for the purpose of creating simple themes with perhaps some very basic geo-processing functionality one of the many GIS freeware may be adequate. A more serious limitation, vis-à-vis producing *dynamic* and *interactive* graphics that can be considered as being VR, is accessibility. While the results of any GIS can be screen captured and put up on websites as still images, and increasing numbers of GIS software are being designed as webGIS (i.e. are being designed for simple investigation on the web – switching layers on and off, panning around the aerial view, etc.), it is not possible in most cases for the VR product of a GIS to be viewed directly on the web unless it has been converted to a format *in widespread use* (which cannot be said to be true for any GIS).

VRML stands for 'virtual reality markup language' and is currently the most used format for simple VR simulations, although the new standard X3D will eventually supersede it. This display software scores highly for the first two VR criteria of dynamism and interactivity, and can score highly for graphic realism, depending on the original input.

However, VRML cannot be said to be in widespread use, and it is a possibility that visitors to a website with VRML examples may not make the effort to download the necessary freeware in order to view it. It should also be noted that there is much variation in the performance of VRML players, due to the lack of standardisation of this format. Cortona and other free VRML players can be found at (http://cic.nist.gov/vrml/vbdetect.html).

ArcView 3.3 was used for the next example, as it has the ability to produce VRMLs from depth and altitude data. Figure 15.5 shows the ArcView shapefile for the bathymetry of the Golfe de Morbihan, Brittany, France.

A series of steps (detailed in Carlisle *et al.*, 2008 http://www.abdn.ac.uk/cmczm/about.htm) was undertaken, resulting in the generation

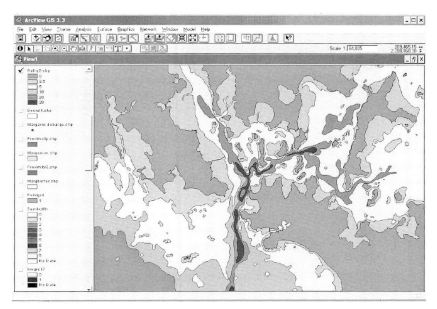

Fig. 15.5 Bathymetry shapefile of Golfe de Morbihan (© CEDEM/UBO/ IFREMER 2006)

of a 3D scene in VRML 2.0 which can be opened in a VRML player. In this instance, Cortona was found to be effective, and this is illustrated in Fig. 15.6. Once loaded into a VRML player, one can move around the 3D scene at will. Figure 15.6 shows a close-up of the deep water trench at the mouth of the Golfe de Morbihan. Obviously the depth has been deliberately exaggerated (note that this was done in ArcView), but it still demonstrates some of the visualisation power of even very simple 3D scenes.

Earlier work at Aberdeen (Green and Bojar, 2005) used a wide range of commercially available off-the shelf software products to visualise datasets for the Ythan Estuary and Sands of Forvie in Scotland, UK. This included the use of Erdas Imagine 8.5, ArcView 3.3, Bryce 5 and Microsoft Internet Explorer with a number of different plugins for 3D, video and animation. For example, an interactive hypermedia animation with several forms of interactivity generated with Erdas Imagine 8.5 using the ParallelGraphics Cortona® VRML Client was used to view a VRML model (Fig. 15.7a). Ordnance Survey (OS) GRID Digital Elevation Model (DEM) at a scale of 1:50 000 (exaggeration 2; level of details 4%) was overlaid with raster Ordnance Survey map data at a

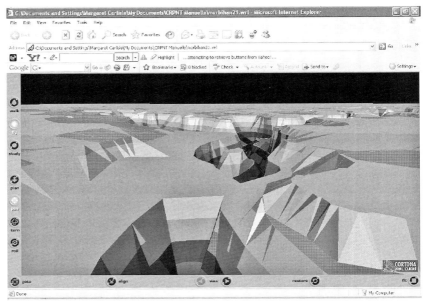

Fig. 15.6 3D scene of Golfe de Morbihan (© CEDEM/UBO/IFREMER 2006)

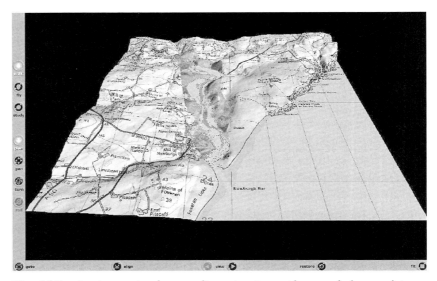

Fig. 15.7a An interactive hypermedia animation with several forms of inter-activity generated with Erdas Imagine 8.5 using the ParallelGraphics Cortona®
VRML

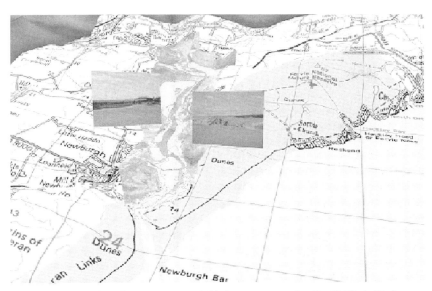

Fig. 15.7b A video clip comprising 375 frames using the DivX High Definition Profile, generated by the Bryce 5 software

scale of 1 : 50 000; an aerial colour photographic mosaic, and a polygon cover (.shp) for 1989 macroalgal weedmat cover. It was saved in VRML in Erdas Imagine 8.5. Another example created a video clip (11.4 Mb filesize, with a duration of 25 seconds, comprising 375 frames, at 15 frames per second, using the DivX High Definition Profile, at a resolution of 768×512) generated by the Bryce 5 software. The imagery contained in the video was created using a combination of Erdas Imagine 8.5 and Virtual GIS, VRML 1.0, and Corel Photo Paint 9 (Fig. 15.7b).

15.2.4 Example 4: Google Earth

Google Earth (GE) (http://earth.google.com/) is an internet interface that allows the user to 'browse' the Earth. It consists of a virtual globe with satellite imagery, maps and a global DTM (digital terrain model – also known as a DEM or digital elevation model). The low-cost of GE and its ease of use have made it immediately attractive to many people and as a result it has already become *standard* software on many home computers. It is not the only 'digital globe' – major competitors are Microsoft's Virtual Earth and NASA's World Wind – but it is the most well known.

345

One can move through the GE landscape using the navigation tools on the GE screens, allowing the user to pan, tilt or zoom in (move forward). One can record one's movements as a GE 'tour', which can be saved as a unit and made available for others to view.

Another GE function is the ability to download one's GPS data plus timestamps into GE and create from this a linear timeline – an interesting example is found at http://www.gearthblog.com/blog/archives/2005/09/tracking_a_whal.html, where a GPS tagged whale shark can be followed on its travels around the Indian Ocean. These timelines are equivalent to linear time series.

GE uses a streaming process to move from low resolution imagery and terrain (when looking at large areas of the globe) to high resolution imagery and terrain (when looking at an area of a few square kilometres). The satellite imagery covers the entire globe, and is of excellent quality, even for areas such as the Arctic. However, it should be noted that the satellite imagery is for visualisation purposes only and is not accessible for data analyses such as supervised classification (e.g. where the vegetation cover of the image can be determined through spectral analysis). The GE user guide does not specify the original resolution, (http://earth.google.com/userguide/v4/#getting_to_know) although in most locations it appears to be sub-metre.

The maps held on GE include roads, transportation (rail, etc.) and geographic features. Even more map themes are available by way of the Google Earth community. However, the most useful 'free data' from Google Earth are the terrain models. The benefit of this is that it saves a lot of time, energy and money, because:

- Obtaining digital national survey elevation data or pre-produced DTMs can be very expensive.
- Digitising elevation data from raster maps encounters copyright issues with the relevant national survey organisation, and is also very time consuming.
- Generating rough DTMs is very easy, but it becomes more time consuming if a higher quality product is desirable.

Having an accurate DTM for the coastline is an important prerequisite for the development of VR simulations for coastal areas. It is relevant, therefore, to examine the quality and accuracy of the GE DTM. As an example, a mountainous area was chosen in order to examine the quality of the GE DTM – Loch Hourn, Highland Region, Scotland, UK (Fig.15.8). When the DTM was originally examined in October 2006, there were several serious anomalies noted, including areas of

Fig. 15.8 Loch Hourn (Oct 2006)

sea with an altitude of 120 m. In the most fjord-like part of the loch, Inner Loch Hourn, the loch appeared to be tilted at an angle part way up the opposite hillside (Fig. 15.8). However, on 17 December 2006, GE installed an extensive upgrade of the DTM, and this resolved most of these problems. Further upgrades in the years since then have improved the DTM still further (Fig. 15.9). However, the DTM is still not perfect, as shown by Fig. 15.10 (Honopu (Hawaii) coastline), where part of the satellite imagery waves 'creep' up a rock outcrop.

Until recently the Google Earth DTM did not include bathymetry (Carlisle *et al.*, 2008 (http://www.abdn.ac.uk/cmczm/about.htm)), but since early 2009 this has been incorporated into the digital world as GoogleOcean. A sample view of a bathymetric feature, Honopu canyon off the islands of Hawaii, is shown in Fig. 15.11. However, it should be noted that there is, *as yet* (May 2009), no smooth linking of the two DTMs (altitude and bathymetry), and the two exist separately using the littoral (intertidal) area as a zero contoured buffer zone between them. This considerably lessens GE's usefulness to coastal managers. However, given the huge improvements in GE's DTM quality in just a few years (cf. Figures 15.8 and 15.9), it is to be hoped that this

347

Fig. 15.9 Loch Hourn (May 2009)

issue will soon be addressed. Another issue is that the bathymetry is based on US Navy data, and so is less extensive for non-US coastal regions. Again, this may be subject to improvement in the future.

A second limitation of GE is that it does not, as yet, support any analytical functionality approaching that of a GIS. Even GE's top-end product, GE Pro, does no more than allow one to measure the area of a polygon or the length of a line/network. This means that it is not possible, within GE itself, to undertake even the simplest geo-processing in order to add value to a map or dataset. Therefore, anybody with a wish to either produce their own data or to analyse existing datasets will need to have a GIS in *addition* to GE. Downloading GIS freeware would allow the use of basic GIS functionality, enabling simple data analyses to be undertaken prior to display in GE. There are several GIS freeware programs available at http://opensourcegis.org/ and at http://www.gislounge.com/ll/opensource.shtml.

It is possible for users to overlay their own information through the addition of geo-referenced images and GIS maps. Image file types that

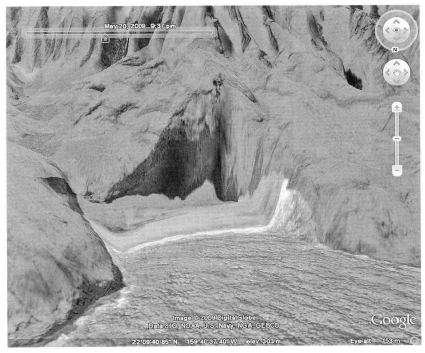

Fig. 15.10 Honopu: coastline (May 2009)

can be added directly to the standard free version of Google Earth are jpg, tiff, png and gif. GIS maps can be converted to kmls and opened directly in GE. Both images and shapefiles can be draped over the DTM once the 'terrain' layer is switched on. The GE *User's Guide* (http://earth.google.com/userguide/v4/) has detailed instructions on pasting images into GE in the desired location and the guide authored by Carlisle *et al.* (2008) (http://www.abdn.ac.uk/cmczm/about.htm) has detailed instructions on converting GIS maps (specifically ESRI shape-files) to Google Earth kmls.

Figure 15.12 illustrates a UK Ordnance Survey 1:50 000 tif cropped and draped over Elgol and the Southern Cuillin, Skye, Scotland. Figure 15.13 shows a converted shapefile for two of the most important biomes in the Western Isles, Scotland, the machair (black) and the vegetated dunes (white).

It is also possible to design and create 3D objects (e.g. houses, sea defences, etc.) for placement within Google Earth using Google SketchUp, which is freely available at http://sketchup.google.com/.

349

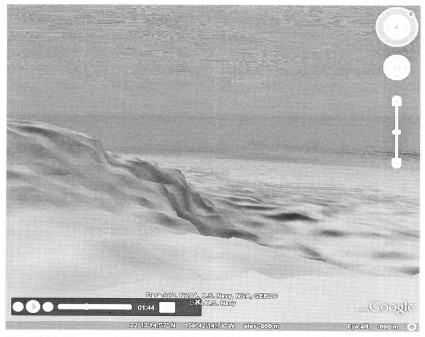

Fig. 15.11 Honopu: 600 m depth (May 2009)

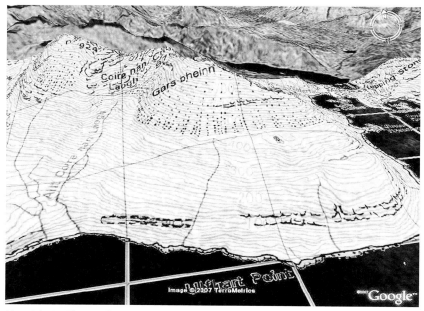

Fig. 15.12 Skye – drape over DTM

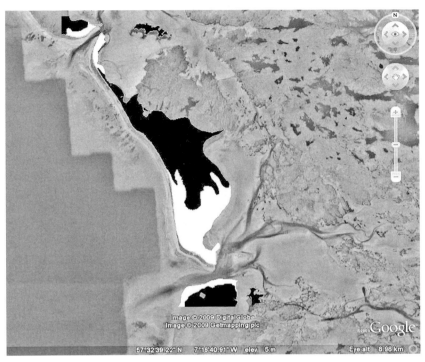

Fig. 15.13 Uist – shapefile biomes

Figure 15.14 shows a simple model, sitting on a draped map image in GE. Another example is the visualisation of a planning proposal for the Aberdeen Bay offshore windfarm in Aberdeen, Scotland, UK that combines the use of spatial datasets originating in ArcView (converted for GE use using MapWindow and Shape2Earth) and Sketchup (Fig. 15.15). These may also be used to create virtual fieldtrips to coastal areas if access to the field is limited by distance and travel time or cost.

15.2.5 Example 5: Landscape Visualisation Theatre

The most complex, and resource-expensive, example discussed here is the Macaulay Institute's mobile and static Landscape Visualisation Theatres (LV) (http://www.macaulay.ac.uk/landscapes/). The static version utilises a solid curved 160° screen, an array of three synchronised data projectors, several software packages and a suite of three PCs with an operator. The software used includes Vega-Prime 2.0, ArcScene, 3ds MAX, Octaga Professional, ERDAS IMAGINE VGIS, Visual Nature

Fig. 15.14 3D structure on top of Skye drape in GE

Fig. 15.15 Aberdeen offshore windfarm proposal in GE

Fig. 15.16 The Macaulay Institute Landscape Visualisation Theatre

Studio. Figure 15.16 illustrates the LV Theatre in action. As described on the Macaulay Institute website:

> Small groups have the opportunity to experience landscapes by moving around the virtual world – and they can even provide feedback by means of a voting handset. That way the public can be directly involved in the planning decisions that affect them. (http://www.macaulay.ac.uk/landscapes/)

There is also a mobile version, using similar hardware and software but based around a portable theatre and screen (http://www.macaulay. ac.uk/landscapes/technicaldetails.php). This facility is the first mobile unit of its kind in the UK, and as well as being used to engage with the public on issues of landscape change it can be used for scientific research specifically to improve understanding of the complex issues surrounding land use and rural societies, including those at the coast (http://www.macaulay.ac.uk/landscapes/).

As noted above, there are several software packages required to 'build' scenes for the LV Theatre, and there are also correspondingly high levels of expertise and personnel time required to do so. For the mobile LV Theatre there is also a high requirement for personnel time due to the complex set-up. During use of the LV Theatre, the movement through the VR landscape is controlled by an operator, who can respond to requests from viewers to 'travel' through the landscape in one direction or the other, and to add, move and remove objects in the view. Satellite imagery draping can be used for 'flat' parts of the landscape such as crop fields, but trees, bushes, buildings and other volumetric structures have to be built in to the landscape and as such have to be textured. The resulting graphic realism is high, but not of photographic quality. Where the LV Theatre scores most highly is in terms of its level of immersion, the wrap-around screen providing the viewer with a real sense of being part of the landscape.

15.3   Choosing a VR technique for future projects

Table 15.1 briefly illustrates the strengths and weaknesses of each of the VR options as discussed in the previous section. The 14 criteria in the left-hand column can be grouped as follows:

- accessibility (cheap, easy to use, in widespread use)
- DTM issues (free, bathymetric, littoral)
- VR quality (interactivity, dynamism, graphic realism, immersion)
- Functionality (2D analytical capability, 3D buildings capability, time series capability).

It is important, that anyone wishing to build a VR should first answer the following questions:

1. is there a specific VR output in mind, and;
2. is there a need to produce a simple VR using available data as easily as possible?

This can be achieved using the following steps and answering the following questions:

Question 1:
- Examine the list of criteria above (accessibility, DTM issues, etc.).
- Identify the most suitable VR approach for the proposed project.
- Compare with immediately available data and immediately available software.
- Identify further data and software requirements and associated costs. Will the necessary data be expensive, or are they held under stringent copyright conditions that preclude their use? Will

Table 15.1 Evaluation of different VR options

	Animation	Panoramic	GIS & VRML	Google Earth	Landscape Visualisation Theatre
Cheap	Yes	Yes	Depends on GIS software chosen	Yes	No – very expensive
Easy to use	Yes	Yes	No	Yes	No
In widespread use	Yes	Yes	No	Yes, and increasing	No
Free DTM	No	No	No	Yes	No
Bathymetric DTM	Potentially, yes	No	Potentially, yes	Yes (for some areas)	Potentially, yes
Littoral DTM	Potentially, yes	No	Potentially, yes	No	Potentially, yes
Interactivity	Low	Low to medium – depends on extent of field of view used	High	High	High, though not controlled by viewer
Dynamism	Low to medium – depends on number of frames used	Low	High	High	High
Graphic realism	Low	High to very high	Depends on quality of draped imagery – potentially, high	Generally high to very high	Medium
Immersion	Low	Low	Low	Low	High, though not controlled by viewer
Analytical functionality	No	No	Yes	No	Yes, in GIS prior to Theatre viewing
Wireframe buildings	Yes	Possible, but not easy	Yes	Yes	Yes
Textured buildings	Generally, no	No	Generally, no	Yes	Yes
Linear time lines	Yes	No	No	Yes	No
Area time series	Yes	No	No	No	No

the necessary software be expensive? Is there any existing expertise in the organisation in using it, if not will it be easy to learn?

- Sufficient resources (finance for buying software, staff time for learning how to use it) will need to be committed to the project.

Question 2: For this option the process is much easier. Simply assess:
- immediately available data and immediately available software
- if the area of study has a great deal of vertical interest (i.e. tall buildings or structures, or high mountains close by) and one already has, or can easily obtain, a set of digital photos for the area

then a panoramic VR is the obvious choice. If one already has GE downloaded, and has digital satellite/aerial/map imagery which can be draped over the GE DTM, then a GE tour can be chosen. If one has a good set of time-related GPS data, then a linear timeline in GE would be the most appropriate.

15.4　Conclusion

As described above, there are VR options to suit every combination of data availability, finance availability and technical expertise. The most resource-expensive of these is the Landscape Visualisation Theatre, but it could be a valuable tool for large organisations (e.g. local planning authorities) to use to promote public discussion and participation around high-profile issues (e.g. windfarm applications). Another approach would be to use Google Earth and Google SketchUp, the results of which could be put up on a website for members of the public to download and view at home, in their own time. The prime advantage of this second approach is its cheapness. A second advantage is the ability to reach a large number of people – the exponential growth in the popularity of Google Earth means that one of the major difficulties in previous use of VR for communication, namely, persuading viewers to download the necessary viewing software, is lessened, as more and more people choose to have GE on their home computers as a permanent download. Microsoft's Virtual Earth and NASA World Wind, the other two 'digital globes' on offer as freely available software, are also becoming increasingly popular. A third advantage of the 'digital globe' approach is that it is challengeable – the viewer can check that the structures are in the correct location and of the correct height, for example, rather than having to take this element on trust. However, as a 'digital globe' is viewed individually, it does not provide the forum for public discussion that the LV Theatre does.

Another advantage of the 'digital globe' approach is that an individual can easily create his/her own VR in response to those issues he/she is interested in, and so fosters a 'bottom-up' approach to coastal environmental communication, education and stakeholder interaction. GE and other 'digital globes' are not the only VR option for the individual or for organisations with few resources, however. Media players such as Apple Quicktime and RealPlayer are also becoming ubiquitous, and it has become increasingly easy to make animated movies using these. With the exponential increase in digital photography Panoramic VR software has also become increasingly widespread and popular, and is easy to display in one of the above mentioned popular media players. GIS is certainly less popular than any of these three low-cost tools (digital globes, media players and panoramic software), but because it is the only alternative that offers true geographical analytical capability it is steadily growing in use, particularly with the increased amount of GIS freeware available. The GIS-associated VR tool, VRML, produces excellent results in terms of true 3D VR. However, VRML viewers are highly variable in performance and are not in widespread use.

In conclusion, VR simulations, from simple panoramas and animations to fully realised 3D buildings and structures in a true 3D environment, will become increasingly common as a tool for exploration, interaction and participation in coastal management.

References

Carlisle, M.A., Green, D.R. and de la Fons, G. (2008) A *Template for Virtual Reality Simulations*, University of Aberdeen. Online at: http://www.abdn.ac.uk/cmczm/about.htm. and *COREPOINT* March 2008.

Green, D.R. and Bojar, K. (2005) 'YthanView' – Visualizing an Estuary and Virtual Fieldwork at the Ythan Estuary, Scotland, UK. Paper in the *Proceedings of ICC 2005 Conference in A Coruña*, Spain, 9–16 July.

Mouatt, J. (2006) The Google Earth Phenomenon: GIS, the Internet and the masses. MSs Thesis (Geospatial Information Systems), University of Aberdeen.

Thurmond, J.B., Drzewiecki, P.A. and Xu, X. (2005) Building simple multiscale visualizations of outcrop geology using virtual reality modelling language (VRML). *Computers & Geosciences*, Vol. 31, pp. 913–919.

Weblinks

http://cic.nist.gov/vrml/vbdetect.html
http://coe.sdsu.edu/eet/articles/vrk12/index.htm
http://earth.google.com/

http://earth.google.com/userguide/v4/#getting_to_know
http://opensourcegis org/
http://sketchup.google.com/
http://uk.real.com/player/
http://www.abdn.ac..ik/cmczm
http://www.apple.com/quicktime/download/win.html
http://www.gearthblog.com/blog/archives/2005/09/tracking_a_whal.html
http://www.gislounge.com/ll/opensource.shtml
http://www.metoffice.gov.uk/weather/uk/surface_pressure.html
http://www.panavue.com/
www.unesco.org/education/educprog/lwf/doc/portfolio/definitions.htm

Further reading

Brown, I.M. (1999) Developing a virtual reality user interface (VRUI) for information retrieval on the internet. *Transactions in GIS*, Vol. 3, pp. 207–220.

Brown, I., Jude, S.R., Koukoulas, S., Nicholls, R., Dickson, M. and Walkden, M. (2006) Dynamic simulation and visualization of coastal erosion. *Computers, Environment and Urban Systems*, Vol. 30, No. 6, pp. 840–860.

Butler, D. (2006) The web-wide world. *Nature,* Vol. 439, pp. 776–778.

Carver, S. (2001) Guest editorial: public participation using web-based GIS. *Environment and Planning B: Planning and Design*, Vol. 28, pp. 803–804.

Chang, Y.-S. and Park, H.-D. (2004) Development of a web-based geographic information system for the management of borehole and geological data. *Computers & Geosciences*, Vol. 30, pp. 887–897.

Chang, Y.-S. and Park, H.-D. (2006) XML web service-based development model for internet GIS applications. *International Journal of Geographical Information Science*, Vol. 20, Issue 4, pp. 371–399.

Chestnut, C. (2006) Creating a Virtual Earth plugin for NASA's World Wind (29/08/06), Via Virtual Earth. Online at: http://www.viavirtualearth.com/VVE/Articles/WorldWind.ashx.

Dunne, D. (2005) Development of a 3D web-enabled geodata visualization system with an associated neural network classification tool. MSc Thesis, National University of Ireland, Cork.

Dunne, D. and Sutton, G. (2006) 3D web-mapping: integrating marine data into NASA World Wind. *Hydro International*, Vol. 10, Issue 9, pp. 7–9.

Dunne, D. and Sutton, G. (2006) 3D web-mapping: integrating marine data into Google Earth. *Hydro International*, Vol. 10, Issue 7, pp. 27–29.

Huang, B. and Lin, H. (1999) GeoVR: a web-based tool for virtual reality presentation from 2D GIS data. *Computers & Geosciences*, Vol. 25, pp. 1167–1175.

Huang, B. and Lin, H. (2002) A Java/CGI approach to developing a geographic virtual reality toolkit on the internet. *Computers & Geoscience*, Vol. 28, pp. 13–19.

Huang, B., Jiang, B. and Li, H. (2001) An integration of GIS, virtual reality and the internet for visualization, analysis and exploration of spatial. *International Journal of Geographical Information Science*, Vol. 15, Issue 5, pp. 439–456.

Isenegger, D., Price B., Wu, Y., Fischlin, A., Frei, U., Weibel, R. and Allgower, B. (2005) IDOPLAS – A Software Architecture for Coupling Temporal Simulation Systems, VR, and GIS. *Journal of Photogrammetry & Remote Sensing*, Vol. 60, pp. 34–47.

Jude, S.R., Jones, A.P. and Andrews, J.E. (2001) Visualization for coastal zone management. In: Bartlett, D. and Smith, J. (eds) *GIS for Coastal Zone Management*, CRC Press, Boca Raton, FL.

Jude, S.R., Jones, A., Bateman, I.J. and Andrews, J.E. (2003) Developing techniques to visualise future coastal landscapes. In: Buhmann, E. and Ervin, S.M. (eds) *Trends in Landscape Modeling. Proceedings at Anhalt University of Applied Sciences*, Anhalt University, Germany.

Jude, S.R., Jones, A.P., Andrews, J.E. and Bateman, I.J. (2006) Visualization for participatory coastal zone management: a case study of the Norfolk coast, England. *Journal of Coastal Research*, Vol. 22, Issue 6, pp. 1527–1538.

Jude, S.R., Jones, A.P., Watkinson, A.R., Brown, I. and Gill, J.A. (2007) The development of a visualization methodology for integrated coastal management. *Coastal Management*, Vol. 35, pp. 525–544.

Kim, R. (2006) World Wind 1.3 (30/08/06), National Aeronautics and Space Administration. Online at: http://worldwind.arc.nasa.gov/index.html.

Smith, G.M., Spencer, T. and Moller, I. (2000) Visualization of coastal dynamics: Scolt Head Island, North Norfolk, England. *Estuarine, Coastal and Shelf Science*, Vol. 50, pp. 137–142.

Useful websites

http://ag.arizona.edu/agnet/icac/pans.html
http://ag.arizona.edu/agnet/icac/vrml/
http://astrowww.astro.indiana.edu/animations/
http://www.auridian.com/glossary/HTML/V.htm
http://bbs.keyhole.com/ubb/showthreaded.php/Cat/0/Number/345508/an/0/page/0
http://download.sketchup.com/sketchuphelp/gsu6_win/gsuwin.html
http://freeware.intrastar.net/vrml.htm
http://java.sun.com/products/java-media/3D/
http://reviews.cnet.com/4520-3513_7-6229928-1.html
http://sketchup.google.com/support/bin/answer.py?answer=36241&topic=9057
http://woodshole.er.usgs.gov/operations/modeling/
http://www.abdn.ac.uk/~clt011/PanoramicVR/
http://www.adobe.com/products/photoshop/index.html
http://www.anquet.co.uk/
http://www.cem.uvm.edu/util/html/definitions.php
http://www.christine-gis.com/
http://www.clarklabs.org/
http://www.crs4.it/Animate/
http://www.csanet.org/newsletter/spring02/nls0205.html
http://www.earthscienceagency.com/gis/
    ?gclid=CMSEx8bjyYsCFQUrlAodSEkRBQ
http://www.gearthblog.com/blog/archives/2005/09/tracking_a_whal.html

http://www.gearthblog.com/blog/archives/2006/04/ski_snowbird.html
http://www.graphics.stanford.edu/~tolis/toli/research/morph.html
http://www.gis.com/
http://www.grc.nasa.gov/WWW/MAELVRSTATION/media/ISS_animation/
    animation.html
http://www.intuition-eunetwork.net/
http://www.irfanview.com/
http://www.javacoffeebreak.com/tutorials/gettingstarted/index.html
http://www.kartografie.nl/pubs/geovisualization/5-2.html
http://www.lloydbailey.net/airspace.html
http://www.mapwindow.com/
http://www.modelpress.com/verml-software.htm
http://www.rockware.com/catalog/pages/arcview3x.html
http://www.saugus.net/Computer/Terms/Letter/V/
http://www.tatukgis.com/products/summary/products.aspx
http://www.teladesign.com/ma-thesis/glossary.htm
http://www-vrl.umich.edu/intro/index.html
http://www.xj3d.org
https://j3d-webstart.dev.ava.net/test/

16

The urban coastline and waterfront development

Paola Salmona
ICCOPS – Landscape, Natural and Cultural Heritage Observatory, Italy

The concept of urban coastline, frequently used in the field of coastal management, has no single, unique meaning, but, rather, it indicates a raft of meanings that will vary according to the particular context. In this paper, urban coastline is viewed as a combination of both natural and man-made features. Relationships between the natural environment and human activity and coastal uses have been analysed and represented by means of indicators, to point to what actually identifies the 'urban' qualities of a coastal area, and how this is reflected as waterfront. The Gulf of La Spezia (Italy) is used as a case study and its main features are analysed and represented with the support of GIS. This process has aided their interpretation in an integration-oriented view.

16.1   Introduction

Even if all integrated coastal area management (ICAM) interventions are based on general and common principles, it is necessary to fine-tune the way they are implemented, according to the different situations and the priorities they need to address.

In this paper urbanised coastal areas, due to the complexity of their natural, cultural and economic aspects, deserve particular attention. In this context, every phenomenon has greater emphasis as compared with the hinterland area. The relationships among coastal elements are tighter, the 'reaction time' is shorter and there are (at least proportionally) more human agents who feel the effects of their interactions and who could, and should, have a say in the matter. Moreover, in many cases, human action has modified some components of the coastal complex to the extent of jeopardising their identity. Based on these premises the task of a coastal manager is, in the present situation, to establish a balance among coastal components and to trigger a chain of processes in order to make it self-sustaining. In particular it is important to understand how the uses and activities of the coastal strip, both land and sea areas, are reflected and managed in the narrow contact area (Cicin-Sain and Knecht, 1998; Brachya *et al.*, 1994; Coccossis *et al.*, 1999).

In this chapter, some issues relating to the urban coastline will use the Gulf of La Spezia (Italy) as a case study. In particular, an ICAM-oriented outline of the area will be drawn, with the aim of supplying some methodological guidelines that may be transferable to other urbanised coastal areas.

16.2   Defining the urban coastline

It is not easy to find in the literature an exhaustive definition of the urban coastline, despite this being a frequently used term, even in generic and non-technical publications.

In coastal areas characterised by settlements (including large towns) that may be rather distant from each other, and separated by long stretches of almost uninhabited coastline, the urban coastline is generally defined as the tangible expression of the intrusion of man into the natural coastal environment (Australian Government website, 2006). As a consequence, it is often charged with negative connotations involving pollution, environmental degradation and lack of control – even if, occasionally, the cultural, social and economic values and the dynamism of such areas are acknowledged. Moreover, it is most often negatively compared to its counterpart, the 'non-urban coastline', which is seen as representing the natural, scenic, and, in general, positive aspects of a coastal area.

In more densely populated areas, such as the Mediterranean basin, where coastal settlements are fairly close to each other, the relationships between the natural environment and human communities are closer still. Ignoring some inaccessible coastal stretches, most coastlines have been modified over many centuries and to different extents by human intervention, and natural features coexist, in a more or less balanced way, with buildings and infrastructures so that the dichotomy between natural and artificial it is no longer sufficient to identify the boundary between urban and non-urban coastline. Coastal areas are perceived as being characterised by their high degree of complexity, with all its implications, both beneficial (high natural, economic and cultural value, concentration of productive activities, opportunities) and negative (overcrowding, environmental and social degradation, conflicting demands) (Benoit and Comeau, 2005).

From both visions it emerges that the urban coastline can be identified as a strip of land and sea, where the multiplicity of uses, activities, human agents and relationships characterising coastal urban areas take place, and it is apparent that in such a 'sensitive' area specific management actions are therefore necessary.

With this in mind, the first step is to analyse the coastal fabric, identifying, along the coast, the relationships either among the features typical of an urban area, or between these and the external environment, always keeping in mind the geographical and socio-economic context in which the work is carried out. For example, a coastal area considered as urbanised in the outskirts of a northern European town often suffers from a lower human impact than one considered as 'not urbanised' in the Mediterranean basin.

In the present paper, some aspects related to coastal area organisation will be considered, which can be used as indicators for pointing out and characterising the urban coastline.

16.3   Waterfront and urban coastline

One typical expression (one that represents the terrain) of the in many ways abstract concept of urban coastline is the waterfront, in the sense of the part of an urban area in direct contact with the water. The continuous process of change in the use of harbours or docks and the various industrial activities in coastal areas has led to the abandonment of large parts of many towns and, consequently, to the separation of two elements, the town and the sea. The problem of how to reconstruct a balance between these two important components has been discussed from the town planning and architectural points of view by several authors, and is becoming more and more topical, in particular with regard to the creation of public open spaces and the improvement of public access to the sea (UN Urban 21, 2000).

From an ICAM-oriented point of view, these two elements cannot be considered separately: in point of fact, all the uses that identify the urban coastline have to be organised as a totality to create the structures and forms that constitute the waterfront, so as to optimise the sustainability of the whole coastal complex, the usability of its resources, including those that are intangible and non-material or whose cost or value are difficult to ascertain (e.g. landscape, cultural heritage, etc.), and to mitigate the conflicting and declining situations that exist.

It is therefore necessary to meet the following two main needs:

- Identify the uses, factors and relationships characterising an urban area. In this regard it is important to specify the concept of coastal use. A good definition has been given by Vallega, namely 'the use of coastal resources to achieve a particular result' (Vallega, 2003a). Such a concept refers to all the interventions and operations made on a resource to achieve a certain output and implies that coastal use does not necessarily mean coastal economic activity.
- Define the extent of a coastal area that has to be identified as an urban coastline. In an integrated vision, a management intervention specific to a coastal area where the presence of human communities is the main feature, cannot refer only to a town waterfront or, more generally, to a littoral area extending along the front of a town, but it should include the coastal strip of the whole area that in some way accommodates urban features and activities. Therefore, particularly in densely populated areas, it is quite difficult to define the extent of the urban coastline, both inland and along the shoreline, because there are often transitional areas where some urban functions or aspects co-exist with others that typify non-urban areas and settlements. In fact, these transitional areas are peculiar because of:
  - the presence of the sea, which is a shared element and a very strongly unifying factor
  - the distribution of resources, and therefore of their uses, along directions defined by the morphology of the coastline
  - where relevant, the existence of non-accessible areas of coastline and the consequent restraints imposed by them
  - the high concentration of various functions, activities, cultural heritage, etc. in a very narrow land strip (Malta Environment and Planning Authority website, 2002).

16.4   The Gulf of La Spezia: a case study

The previous discussion opens questions that will be discussed throughout the development of a case study relating to the Gulf of La Spezia, in the eastern Liguria coast of Italy, that is particularly suitable for the purpose because:

- the area's morphology is characterised by rather clear natural boundaries
- many different land uses and activities are found in a relatively small area

- it is a dynamic area, where many waterfront transformations are foreseen or are already under way.

Moreover, since some studies have already been carried out on the area, much documentary material is available.

The Gulf of La Spezia, also called the 'Poets' Gulf' is a long and wide bay located at the eastern end of the Ligurian coast. It is oriented on a north-west/south-east axis and is surrounded by hills. Its westward end is the promontory of Portovenere, with the Palmaria, Tino and Tinetto islands, while eastwards it is delimited by the cape of Punta Bianca and the Magra river valley. The gulf is about 4.5 kilometres deep and 3.5 kilometres wide and is enclosed by outer walls, leaving only two channels open to allow the passage and harbouring of cargo and navy vessels. Administratively, the whole gulf is part of the province of La Spezia and is divided into the municipalities of La Spezia, Lerici, Portovenere and Ameglia.

The morphology of the gulf of La Spezia is characterised by a shallow slope that has favoured its settlement. At the centre of the gulf, in a relatively flat area, lies the town of La Spezia, with about 100 000 inhabitants. This developed around its arsenal, mainly as a consequence of the Napoleonic campaigns and, afterwards, as an industrial, military and commercial port. Presently a redesign of the waterfront is underway, which, as well as improving existing commercial functions, also envisages areas devoted to tourism, in particular to a yacht marina. The original military vocation of the area is still evident in the western part of the gulf, in the form of barracks, military exercise areas or areas forbidden to public because of military constraints, that, just recently, have started to be converted for non-military purposes (http://it.wikipedia.org/wiki/La_Spezia).

The easy accessibility of the eastern part of the gulf, above all to the municipality of Lerici, together with its high environmental and cultural values, has been attracting numerous tourists since the nineteenth century. First came the 'villas' of select noble or wealthy foreigners (among them some significant poets, for example, Lord Byron (hence the name 'Poets' Gulf'). Afterwards, at the beginning of the twentieth century, followed hotels and luxury guest-houses for the upper-middle classes. The consolidated role of the area as a centre for upper-class tourism, as well as a good balance between tourism and other traditional productive activities (above all, agriculture), has preserved it from the unregulated expansion that characterised and spoiled most Ligurian seaside towns during the 1960s–80s, in response to the ever-growing demands of mass tourism.

Portovenere, meanwhile, is characterised by elite tourism, which has almost completely replaced the more traditional activities of ship-building, fisheries and aquaculture, conserving the landscape and the aesthetic and environmental value of the area.

In order to make the features of the gulf more evident, a comparison area has been chosen westward of the gulf, which includes the so-called Cinque Terre. The Cinque Terre area, separated from the gulf by the promontory of Portovenere, is characterised by a high and rather abrupt coastline, with a few small, scattered settlements. Over the centuries, small agricultural plots have been made by terracing this very steep and almost inaccessible land, and this has at the same time created a unique and exceptionally valuable landscape. Since the 1970s, because of the unprofitability of traditional agriculture and the difficulty of using machines in order to exploit it, parts of the previously cultivated land have been abandoned and many inhabitants have left the area. At the same time, due to the valuable natural features of the area and its distinctive landscape, tourism has started to develop. Tourism has become increasingly relevant, and the growing demand for tourist accommodation and services has fostered the abandonment of agriculture in favour of more profitable and less demanding activities, triggering a process that threatens to jeopardise the area's character and features.

Fig. 16.1 The study area

Both the gulf and the Cinque Terre are characterised by their high environmental and cultural value and many controls have been implemented to protect and safeguard them. In 1997, UNESCO classified the area of Cinque Terre, Portovenere and the islands (Palmaria, Tino and Tinetto) in the register of World Heritage Sites; in 1999, the whole Cinque Terre area became a National Park, two Protected Marine Areas were created along the Cinque Terre and the Portovenere coast, and two Natural Regional Parks have been instituted in the promontory of Portovenere and in the area of Montemarcello and Magra river, in the municipality of Ameglia (http://www.provincia.sp.it) (see Fig. 16.1).

16.5   The use of indicators to point out relevant issues

A general methodological framework is provided by the principles and guidelines of integrated coastal area management. In this context, the first step required is to compare the study area with the criteria that most comply with specific management needs. Geo-morphological, ecological and human features have been considered and some boundaries have been suggested, in accordance with the following scheme (Vallega, 1999):

- main and secondary catchment basins
- altimetry
- ridges
- coastal ecosystems (natural and semi-natural)
- coastal settlements
- administrative boundaries
- maritime jurisdictional boundaries.

This part of the analysis is at the scale of 1 : 100 000 and has been set up mainly using shareware data, which have been downloaded from the internet and other readily available sources (see Appendix 16.1 for the data used).

In this phase, rather than looking for data accuracy, the objective is to create a general framework base, from which to determine which are the essential data for the continuation and deepening of the analysis process. Using this framework, only the required data need be requested from the owner agencies.

The extension of land delimited in such a way can be defined as the coastal area of the reference territory and the first factor to help identify the urban coastline. Nevertheless, in order to obtain a more complete outline, one that is also compliant with the concept of an urban coast-line as defined above, it is necessary to compare this coastal area with

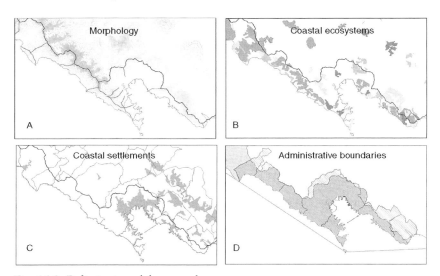

Fig. 16.2 Delimitation of the coastal area

the uses of the territory and the relationships between these uses (see Fig. 16.2).

Some guidelines for the identification and assessment of the most characteristic uses within the coastal complex have been given in specific literature. In particular, this work makes reference to the classification elaborated by UNEP in 1995 (Brachya *et al.*, 1994), which identifies and describes the most relevant fields of interaction between human communities and the coastal area, and to the scheme elaborated by Vallega in 2003, which proposes a model for the systematisation of present coastal uses in order to facilitate the setting-up of Integrated Coastal Area Management programmes and actions (Vallega, 2003b, 2003c).

UNEP identifies eight categories of coastal uses and points out the impact each one has upon the reference territory. Vallega, on the other hand, identifies coastal uses at a more detailed level and groups them according to four levels (see Table 16.1), focusing on the relationships among the different uses and the potentially conflicting or unbalanced outcomes. It can be said that UNEP proceed from the general to the detailed level, while Vallega adopts the opposite approach. Both approaches are sound but, to be practically useful, it is necessary to synthesise and compare those findings that are presented as abstract concepts and features that are too specific to create a comprehensible framework.

Table 16.1 *UNEP and Vallega classification*

UNEP classification		
Coastal uses		
Urbanisation		
Tourism		
Industry		
Energy production		
Fisheries and aquaculture		
Transports		
Forestry		
Agriculture		

Vallega classification		
Category	Sub-category	Use
Conservation	Natural heritage	Protected areas
		Fragile ecosystems
	Cultural heritage	Material heritage
Primary uses	Animal biological resources	Onshore
		Offshore
	Vegetal biological resources	Agriculture
		Natural areas
	Mining industry	Hydrocarbons
		Other materials
Secondary uses	Water	Surface and groundwater
	Energy production	Not renewable and renewable
	Industry	Any kind of industry
Tertiary uses	Settlements	Urban areas
	Transports	Land transports
		Maritime transports
	Harbours	Goods
		Passengers
		Services
	Cables and pipes	Fuel
		Water
		Submarine cables
	Tourism	Bathing
		Other activities
	Communication	Stations
	Defence	Defence restricted areas
	Waste disposal	Solid and liquid waste

It has therefore been decided to represent coastal uses by means of indicators, pointing out their location and the pattern of their diffusion, and, by reference to this, to delimit and characterise the urban coastline.

The use of indicators is a practice suggested in ICAM because it permits the synthesis of heterogeneous data, the 'standardisation' and

369

comparison of information about areas even if different, and can refer to different time-spans and then describe evolutionary processes. Specific local features are compared with official ICAM guidelines, in order to synthesise the available information and draft a general, management-oriented outline of the area.

Thirteen indicators were chosen, out of 61, drawn from the following lists of indicators, all specific to coastal evaluation and management (drafted by authoritative organisations):

- 34 priority indicators for the 'Mediterranean Strategy for Sustainable Development' Follow-up (Blue Plan, 2006).
- Interreg III Project DEDUCE – DÉveloppement DUrable des zones Côtières Européennes (Martì *et al.*, 2007).

The indicators proposed by the Blue Plan and by the DEDUCE project are somewhat similar in kind and imply results that are generally expressed by numbers, for example as a percentage. Analogous indicators were chosen from both sources in order to allow for a comparison and integration between the European and the Mediterranean approach to ICAM. Some of them might look rather banal and are likely to supply items of information already known; they have been included in the set to build up an outline of the area that is as complete as possible (see Table 16.2).

While detailed specifications are available to explain the methodology for the calculation of most indicators, others are described only by general indications and it has been necessary to interpret them in a way that is in consistence with the issues discussed. Moreover, when it has not been possible to stick to the specifications (i.e. for lack of data, presence of specific local features, etc.), some changes have been made, explaining the motivations.

To be meaningful, indicators should have terms of comparison, so it was decided to apply them to the whole coastal area identified above. Since some indicators are based on data only available at the municipal scale (i.e. population, tourist accommodation capacity, etc.), the municipality has been chosen as spatial reference unit and the data about each municipality have been compared.

The indicator set was built up in accordance with the following preference criteria:

- capability of drafting a general outline of coastal uses for their organisation
- ease of interpreting their results

- output of their application (i.e. qualitative assessment, score, per-cent, etc.)
- suggested reference area
- transferability, meaning the capability of application to other coastal areas
- capability of being calculated in terms of data, calculation processes, work time
- possibility of mapping the calculation results (i.e. thematic maps) in order to make their interpretation easier.

Some indicators reported, even if they would have supplied interesting pieces of information, were not selected because the data required to calculate them were not available, or not easily findable, or because the calculation methodology would have been too complicated or time consuming.

When possible, the selected indicators were localised and represented with the aid of a GIS (application used: Geomedia Professional 6.0 by Intergraph) using:

- surface aggregation and intersection
- mathematical operation on surfaces
- digitalisation on a raster base of specific elements
- creation of thematic maps
- storage as attributes or linked files of non-spatial information.

The results of the calculation of the indicators have been integrated with some basic information about the area, such as morphology, hydrology, vegetation, land use, the main transport infrastructures (as shown in Appendix 16.2).

16.6   Identification of fields of action

Subsequently, the selected indicators have been associated with the categories of coastal uses identified above. The classification proposed by UNEP is instinctive and has been used to roughly characterise the study area, but it does not give the correct weight to the natural and cultural features of a coastal area nor to how coastal uses interact, i.e. the relationships between industrial areas and aquaculture.

Therefore it was decided to organise and compare the indicators' results according to a draft scheme of Vallega's adapted to the study area because it allows a better representation of the complexity of the uses characterising the area and paves the way for the analysis of their relationships (see Table 16.3).

371

Table 16.2 *Selected indicators*

Fonte	General objective	Specific objective	Code	Indicator name
Blue Plan	Promote sustainable tourism	Diversify tourism by developing offers that enhance Mediterranean diversity (eco-tourism, cultural, urban and rural tourism)	TOU_P01	Share of 'non-seaside resort beds' vs. total number of beds
Blue Plan		Combat desertification and the loss of productive land by 2015; reduce by at least one-third the present rates of quality agricultural land losses due to erosion, salinisation, desertification, urban and other development and abandonment	AGR_P02	Loss of arable land
Blue Plan	Promote sustainable management of the sea and the coastal areas and take urgent action to put an end to the degradation of coastal zones	Promote balanced development and integrated management of the coastline. Push back urbanisation to prevent artificialisation of coasts. Avoid linear and continuous urbanisation	COA_P01	Share of artificialised coastline
Blue Plan		Halt or reduce substantially marine and coastal biodiversity loss by 2010. Bring at least 10% of the marine and coastal surface under some form of protection	COA_P04	Surface of protected coastal and marine areas
DEDUCE	To control as appropriate further development on undeveloped coast	Demand for property on the coast	1.1	Size and structure of the population living on the coast
DEDUCE			1.2	Value of residential property

DEDUCE		Area of built-up land	2.1	Percent of built-up land by distance from the coastline
DEDUCE		Pressure for coastal and marine recreation	5.1	Number of berths and moorings for recreational boating
DEDUCE	To protect, enhance and celebrate natural and cultural diversity	Land take by intensive agriculture	6.1	Proportion of agricultural land farmed intensively
DEDUCE		Amount of semi-natural habitat	7.1	Area of semi-natural habitat
DEDUCE		Area of land and sea protected by statutory designations	8.1	Area protected for nature conservation, landscape and heritage
DEDUCE	To ensure that beaches are clean and that coastal waters are unpolluted	Quality of bathing water	16.1	Percent of bathing water compliant with the European Bathing Water Directive
DEDUCE	To reduce social exclusion and promote social cohesion in coastal communities	Second and holiday homes	22.1	Ratio of first to second and holidays homes

Table 16.3 Indicators related with the use network

Conservation	Natural heritage	Protected areas	Surface of protected coastal and marine areas
		Fragile ecosystems	Area protected for nature conservation, landscape and heritage
	Cultural heritage	Material heritage	Area protected for nature conservation, landscape and heritage
Primary uses	Animal biological resources	Offshore	Accurate data not available
	Vegetal biological resources	Agriculture	Loss of arable land
			Proportion of agricultural land farmed intensively
		Natural areas	Area of semi-natural habitat
			Land use map
	Mining industry	Other materials	Land use map
Secondary uses	Water	Surface and groundwater	Hydrography map
	Energy production	Not renewable and renewable	Accurate data not available
	Industry	Any kind of industry	Land use map
Tertiary uses	Settlements	Urban areas	Size and structure of the population living on the coast
			Percent of built-up land by distance from the coastline
			Share of artificialised coastline
	Transports	Land transports	Transport infrastructures map
		Maritime transports	Accurate data not available
	Harbours	Goods	Land use map
		Passengers	Land use map
		Services	Land use map

Cables and pipes	Fuel	Accurate data not available
	Water	Accurate data not available
	Submarine cables	Accurate data not available
Tourism	Bathing	Percent of bathing water compliant with the European bathing water directive
	Other activities	Share of 'non-seaside resort beds' vs. total number of beds
		Number of berths and moorings for recreational boating
		Ratio of first to second and holidays homes
		Value of residential property
Defence	Defence restricted areas	Accurate data not available
Waste disposal	Solid and liquid waste	Land use map

Most reported indicators are expressed as a cluster of values (numbers, percentage, etc.) related to the different aspects of a specific phenomenon or that supply useful pieces of information to set it into an appropriate context, i.e. they help to interpret the values not in an absolute but in a relative way.

Industry is certainly a relevant aspect of the study area, just as for many other coastal areas, but in the lists used there are no specific indicators to represent this kind of use. Generally, industrial areas are akin to urban ones as regards space requirements and man-made changes to the coastline, and also with regard to ecological factors, which are not so relevant for this work, such as pollution. Related information, therefore, has not been calculated but the main industrial areas have simply been pointed out in the land use map.

The reference sources also propose several indicators related to transport, mainly with the objective of assessing sustainability, but they require data that are not usually available or that could only be obtained from a very time-consuming field survey. Thus, in this case also, it was decided to take into consideration only the location of the main transport infrastructures.

16.7   Relationship between natural and urbanised areas

At the base of any consideration, it is necessary to point out the importance of the substratum (aspects of the original morphology and the natural features of the area, as if there had been no urbanisation). Even where the natural features of the terrain have been heavily modified, what still remains should be taken into consideration as a shared element and the base for all subsequent transformations. In particular, if an urbanised area lies on different substrata it is interesting to analyse how they are reflected in its structure and development.

The first aspect to consider in defining the urban coastline is that part of the coastal area that is covered by artificial structures, both along the coastline, and towards the hinterland. Two indicators deal with this issue in complementary ways. The Blue Plan focuses attention on the length of artificialised coast compared with the total coast length ('share of artificial coastline', Blue Plan, 2006), while the specifications of the DEDUCE project refer to the variations of the built-up area in accordance with distance from the coastline ('area of built-up land', Martì *et al.*, 2007).

Both indicators have been calculated, bringing some modifications to the original specifications, in particular adjusting the proposed

376

delimitations to the features of the study area. The Blue Plan proposes to divide the coastline into uniform stretches called 'coastal segments'. If at least 30% of the surface of a rectangle, whose sides are the length of a coastal segment and a 200-metres-wide strip across the coastline, is artificial, then the coastal segment is defined as artificial. The coastline of the study area is very indented and mostly characterised by cliffs. It is therefore hard to identify uniform coastal segments and areas located 100 metres towards the hinterland are often quite elevated where they join the sea. Moreover, the regional data on coastal artificialisation refer to the state-owned strip, which has a variable width and which, due to the coastal morphology, is often narrower than 100 metres. As a consequence, the indicator has been referred to the whole state-owned strip, considering as coastal length the part of its perimeter washed by the sea.

Meanwhile, the DEDUCE specifications propose to calculate the ratio between the built-up area and the total surface of two strips 1 kilometre and 10 kilometres wide from the coastline. Such strips are of little meaning in an area characterised by a high coast and a ridge that separates two different hydrographic catchments close to the sea, so it has been decided to take as reference areas two strips of 300 metres (the distance indicated by Italian law 431/85 for landscape constraints in coastal and riverside areas) and 1 kilometre wide and the whole coastal area as above identified.

Within the gulf, from Portovenere to Lerici, almost all the coastline is now artificial: the harbour of La Spezia stretches along all the coast of the municipality, while the coast of the municipality of Portovenere and Lerici is characterised by facilities for tourism and aquaculture. As regards built-up areas, the strip 300 metres wide is consistent with the former indicator, with two exceptions: part of the Portovenere coast is protected by an artificialised cliff, but its hinterland is not built up; and in Lerici, a rather wide built-up area is located behind a natural beach. Within 1 kilometre from the coastline only the central part of the municipality of La Spezia is densely urbanised, while toward Lerici built-up areas alternate with open areas and toward Portovenere they are actually scattered. The coastline of the comparison area, in contrast, is mostly natural with the artificialised parts being constituted of small harbours and beach defence works. Settlements are small and are usually located within 300 metres of the coastline (see Fig. 16.3).

This synthesis is compared with open areas, either natural and semi-natural areas, or agricultural land. The former have been represented by

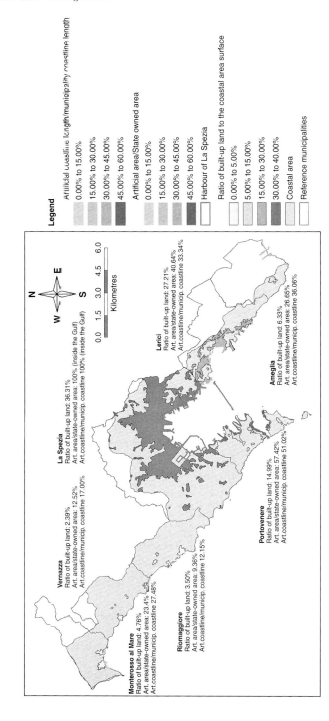

Legend

Artificial coastline length/municipality coastline length

- 0.00% to 15.00%
- 15.00% to 30.00%
- 30.00% to 45.00%
- 45.00% to 60.00%

Artificial area/State owned area

- 0.00% to 15.00%
- 15.00% to 30.00%
- 30.00% to 45.00%
- 45.00% to 60.00%

Harbour of La Spezia

Ratio of built-up land to the coastal area surface

- 0.00% to 5.00%
- 5.00% to 15.00%
- 15.00% to 30.00%
- 30.00% to 40.00%

Coastal area

Reference municipalities

Vernazza
Ratio of built-up land: 2.39%
Art. area/state-owned area: 12.52%
Art.coastline/municip. coastline 17.00%

La Spezia
Ratio of built-up land: 36.31%
Art. area/state-owned area: 100% (inside the Gulf)
Art.coastline/municip. coastline 100% (inside the Gulf)

Lerici
Ratio of built-up land: 27.21%
Art. area/state-owned area: 40.64%
Art.coastline/municip. coastline 33.34%

Ameglia
Ratio of built-up land: 6.33%
Art. area/state-owned area: 26.65%
Art.coastline/municip. coastline 36.06%

Monterosso al Mare
Ratio of built-up land: 4.76%
Art. area/state-owned area: 23.4%
Art.coastline/municip. coastline 27.48%

Riomaggiore
Ratio of built-up land: 3.50%
Art. area/state-owned area: 9.36%
Art.coastline/municip. coastline 12.15%

Portovenere
Ratio of built-up land: 14.99%
Art. area/state-owned area: 57.42%
Art.coastline/municip. coastline 51.02%

N
W — E
S

0.0 1.5 3.0 4.5 6.0
Kilometres

Fig. 16.3 Artificial coastline and built-up areas

the indicator 'Area of semi-natural habitat' (Martì *et al.*, 2007), while the agricultural context has been described combining the indicators 'Portion of agricultural land farmed intensively' (Martì *et al.*, 2007) and 'Loss of arable land' (Blue Plan, 2006). The indicators 'Portion of agricultural land farmed intensively' and 'Area of semi-natural habitat' have been calculated in accordance with the zoning used to assess built-up areas (within 300 metres, 1 kilometre and the whole coastal area), while the indicator 'Loss of arable land' has been used to refer just to municipalities and their coastal area.

The objective of the synthesis is to identify areas where agriculture is a predominant and ongoing activity, as well as those characterised by a high ecological integrity, in contrast with those where farmland plots coexist with abandoned farmland, highly fragmented semi-natural areas, and built-up areas. As a consequence of the morphology of the area, agriculture is profitable, or at least economically worthwhile, only if it is practised intensively, so highly fragmented farmland and areas farmed in an extensive way, characterised by fallow or woodlands, have been assumed as on the road to abandonment. The presence of already abandoned or shortly to be abandoned areas might recall two different transitional situations: on the one hand farmlands are abandoned because they are scarcely profitable, far from urban settlements, and demand tiring and time-consuming work; on the other hand the expansion of urbanised areas causes the progressive shrinking and fragmentation of neighbouring farmlands, so that they become unproductive and are soon abandoned. To assess the extension and location of the latter areas it is useful to understand the transition from an urbanised area to a rural or natural one.

In the study area, even if the amount of open area (farmland and natural or semi-natural areas) is rather large, a good part of it is characterised by such phenomena as abandonment, decay and fragmentation that might suggest a state of transition.

Three main cases can be identified in the study area:

- hinterland areas where formerly cultivated lands have begun a renaturalisation process
- hinterland outskirts of the town of La Spezia
- outskirts of the settlements in the Cinque Terre area, mostly within 1 kilometre of the coastline.

The first case is part of a wider phenomenon of land abandonment, in particular in hinterland rural areas. Many scattered settlements,

379

which by their nature involve tiring and unproductive agricultural activity, are abandoned and the inhabitants move to coastal towns or to other areas farther afield. Above all, in the past decades, this has caused a related expansion of urbanised areas and it remains a factor of human pressure on the coast.

The second case is more relevant for the identification of urbanised areas and it involves the morphology and the socio-economic features of the area. The western part of the municipality of La Spezia is characterised by steeply sloping land, making settlement for productive activities difficult and the building of residential estates expensive. In this area, the expansion of the town is actually restricted, therefore there is little competition to traditional activities and patterns and the urban coastline ends rather sharply, with a very narrow transition area.

Eastwards, toward the municipality of Lerici, the town meets an area where, due to its favourable morphology, agriculture is more productive and consolidated and in a relatively good balance with the other activities of the area, above all with tourism, and the high natural and cultural value of the area means that the conservation of the terrain and landscape is an investment. Again, the transition area is quite narrow.

By contrast, behind the centre of La Spezia the almost flat terrain, and the scarcity of particular environmental values that could justify the conservation of the area's integrity, have favoured the settlement of productive activities, paving the way for the fragmentation and abandonment of cultivated land and urban expansion.

The third case, the most widespread in the study area, characterises non-urban situations, where tourism is an emerging or predominant activity. Coastal cultivated areas are abandoned because agriculture brings less wealth than the development of tourism, which, generally, does not lead to the depopulation of those areas, but to a change in the socio-economic pattern that might foster the expansion of coastal settlements.

In conclusion, in the study area, the rather abrupt transition between urban and non-urban coastline, due to both natural and socio-economic constraints, has caused the saturation of the coastline and the movement towards the hinterland of new productive activities and residential settlements. Moreover, it is useful to point out that, even if between the municipalities of La Spezia and Lerici there are very few open coastal areas, the different organisation of uses makes them two absolutely distinct areas (see Fig. 16.4).

380

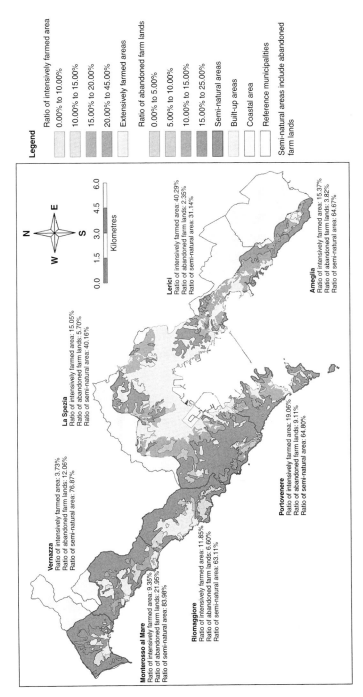

Fig. 16.4 Open areas

16.8 Protection of natural and cultural heritage

What has emerged so far is only partially confirmed by the information related to the percentage of protected area. The indicator 'area protected for nature conservation, landscape and heritage' (Martì *et al.*, 2007) identifies the part of the territory that is somehow subject to protection. Even if this factor is actually relevant to understanding coastal organisation, the results drawn from the study area are of little significance because almost all the analysed territory is subject to different kinds of constraints (i.e. landscape, hydro-geological, military, etc.) that supply little useful information about the organisation of coastal uses and that create a very complex frame of reference (i.e. overlapping of constraints, contradictions, etc.) that risks confusing the indicator objectives. The methodology proposed by the Blue Plan, 'Surface of protected coastal and marine areas' (Blue Plan, 2006), on the other hand, takes into consideration only those areas devoted to the conservation of the natural environment, specifically the Natural Parks and the Sites of Community Interest (SCIs), and allows a more comprehensible result for an outline of conservation measures to be drawn.

The situation of the study area is in any case rather complicated because all of the Ligurian coastal sea is included in the international protected area known as Sanctuary of Cetaceans, all of the coastal area west of the La Spezia Gulf is subject to conservation interventions (one National Park, one Regional Park, two Marine Protected Areas and, partially overlapping, some marine and land SCIs) extending to the town of Portovenere and to the hinterland western suburbs of La Spezia and another Regional Park and some SCIs, are located in the eastern part of the La Spezia gulf. The central part of the gulf, in the municipalities of Portovenere, La Spezia and Lerici, in contrast, is not subject to conservation interventions. In particular, it is interesting to observe that the protected area extends almost as far as the town of Portovenere, while, even if the area is environmentally valuable, it is a long way to the town of Lerici (see Fig. 16.5).

16.9 Factors of human pressure

Another relevant factor is the population of the area, taken into consideration by the indicator 'Size and structure of the population living on the coast' (Martì *et al.*, 2007), which describes the population evolution during the past 25 years and the human pressure on the coast in terms of persons per surface unit and coast length unit.

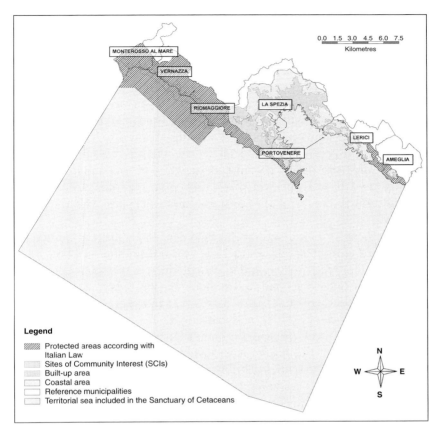

0.0 1.5 3.0 4.5 6.0 7.5
Kilometres

MONTEROSSO AL MARE

VERNAZZA

RIOMAGGIORE

LA SPEZIA

LERICI

PORTOVENERE

AMEGLIA

Legend

▨ Protected areas according with
Italian Law
░ Sites of Community Interest (SCIs)
▒ Built-up area
☐ Coastal area
☐ Reference municipalities
☐ Territorial sea included in the Sanctuary of Cetaceans

N
W ←✦→ E
S

Fig. 16.5 Protected areas

With the exception of Ameglia, where the population, after a decrease in the 1980s, is now growing again, all municipalities report a relevant decrease (up to −27.5%), mainly for ageing and consequent population balance deficit. It is important to underline that, even if the population is decreasing, the municipalities of Lerici and La Spezia report a high rate of immigration of people coming from outside the municipality, either from other municipalities or from abroad, while, obversely, in the other municipalities this rate is close to zero or slightly declining. This shows their role of reference within the study area.

Taking the year 2007 as a reference point, the population density in the municipalities facing the Gulf of La Spezia is higher than the province average, while that in the comparison area is markedly lower. A maximum is reported in the municipalities of La Spezia and

383

Lerici. Portovenere's population density is slightly lower, but the islands of Palmaria, Tino and Tinetto are almost uninhabited. The density of the municipality of Ameglia is similar to the average, but its main town is in the hinterland and its main productive activities are located around it, in the Magra river valley.

Finally, some relevant aspects related to tourism have been analysed. La Spezia's activities are mainly linked to its commercial and military port and to the industrial areas in its hinterland and tourism is merely a secondary aspect, due above all to the town's proximity to well-known tourist resorts. By contrast, its neighbouring municipalities are characterised by a high level of tourism that, exploiting the natural and cultural resources of the area, has almost replaced all the other activities.

The indicators considered for this field deal with tourist accommodation ('share of non-seaside resort beds vs. total number of beds', Blue Plan, 2006), property values and housing ('value of residential property' and 'ratio of first to second and holiday homes', Martì et al., 2007), recreational boating ('number of berths and moorings for recreational boating' Martì et al., 2007) and bathing ('percent of bathing water compliant with the European Bathing Water Directive', Martì et al., 2007). Comparing the results it is possible to draw an outline of the organisation and the spatial distribution of this activity.

Most of the tourist accommodation is located in the municipalities of Lerici, followed by Ameglia and La Spezia, and is restricted to relatively few, large-scale dedicated facilities (hotels, residential hostels, etc.). The opposite situation characterises the comparison area, where several small-scale tourist facilities (bed and breakfasts, guest houses, renting from private landlords, etc.) are able to supply only a limited number of beds. The municipality of Portovenere, finally, characterised by an elite tourism, offers extremely luxurious and prestigious accommodation for a very limited number of tourists. The ratio of beds and residents is extremely high in the Cinque Terre area, halved at Lerici and Ameglia and very low at La Spezia (see Fig. 16.6).

As regards the ratio of second and holiday homes as opposed to accommodation for full-time residents, it is correspondingly very low in the municipality of La Spezia but it increases according to the distance from the chief town. The ratio in Lerici and Portovenere is rather high, but more similar to that of La Spezia than for the Cinque Terre municipalities.

The indicator 'value of residential property' completes these data by supplying some information about the market and rent prices of the

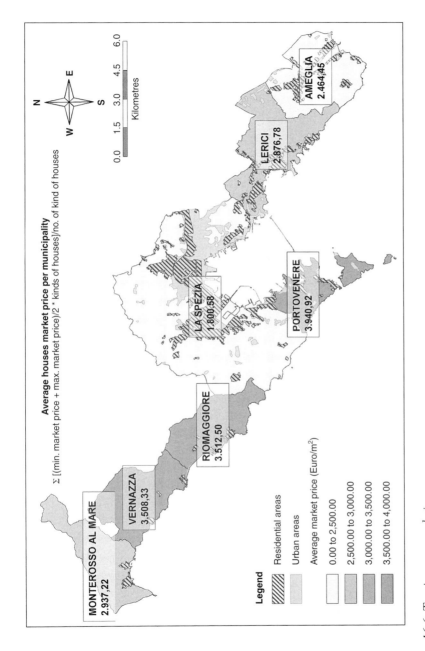

Fig. 16.6 Tourist accommodation

Table 16.4

	Indicator		Ameglia*	La Spezia	Lerici	Monterosso al Mare	Portovenere	Riomaggiore	Vernazza
Built up areas	Percent of built-up land by distance from the coastline	Ratio of built up land to the coastal area surface	6.33%	36.31%	27.21%	4.76%	14.99%	3.50%	2.39%
	Share of artificialised coastline	Artificial area/State owned area	26.65%	100% (a) 0% (b)	40.64%	23.34%	57.42%	9.36%	12.52%
	Share of artificialised coastline	Artificial coastline length/Municipality coastline length	36.06%	100% (a) 0% (b)	33.34%	27.48%	51.02%	12.15%	17. 00%
						See maps			
Open areas	Loss of arable land	Ratio of abandoned farm lands (coastal area)	3.82%	5.70%	2.35%	21.95%	9.11%	6.60%	12.06%
	Land take by intensive agriculture	Ratio of agricultural land farmed intensively to the coastal area surface	15.37	15.05	40.29	9.35	19.06	11.85	3.73
	Area of semi-natural habitat	Ratio of semi-natural area to the coastal area surface	64.67%	40.16%	31.14%	83.98%	64.80%	63.11%	76.87%
						See maps			
Protection of natural and cultural heritage	Surface of protected coastal and marine areas	Ratio of protected areas to coastal area				9.07% See map			
	Area protected for nature conservation, landscape and heritage				Little relevant at this scale (all the area is interested by different and overlapping constraints)				

Category	Description	Indicator							
Settlements	Size and structure of the population living on the coast	Resident people (2007)	4535	94192	10625	1579	3897	1735	1006
	Size and structure of the population living on the coast	Population density (2007, inhabitants/Km^2)	316.10	1826.52	662.87	140.23	518.60	168.83	81.68
	Size and structure of the population living on the coast	Density along the coast (2007, inhabitants/Km)	595.99	2333.49	682.87	354.70	140.92	192.00	135.89
Tourism	Share of "non-seaside resort beds" vs total number of beds	Beds per Municipality	1633	1529	2896	1268	503	965	594
	Share of "non-seaside resort beds" vs total number of beds	Beds per 100 residents	36.01	1.62	27.26	80.30	12.62	55.59	59.05
	Value of residential property	Average market value (€/m^2)	2464.45	1800.58	2876.78	2973.22	3940.92	3512.50	3508.33
	Value of residential property	Average rent (€/m^2 per month)	7.16	5.25	8.38	8.56	11.54	10.96	10.92
	Ratio of first to second and holidays homes	Ratio of second and holiday homes to total homes	48.21%	9.72%	34.53%	53.56%	26.71%	41.68%	46.69%
	Number of berths and moorings for recreational boating	Equivalent 12 metres moorings	1720	1311	223	15	825	0	25
	Number of berths and moorings for recreational boating	Moorings as counted in 2007	3041	1632	551	50	1354	0	82
	Percent of bathing water compliant with the European Bathing Water Directive	Ratio of bathing coast to total coast length (2007) (c)	92.77%	64.98% 0% (b)	100.00%	100.00%	49.06%	95.81%	100.00%

Cross-cutting indicator, little relevant to delimit urban coastline

387

different kinds of houses, and according to their location. The lowest values are found in the municipality of La Spezia, then in that of Ameglia, while the most expensive is Portovenere, followed by the Cinque Terre. It is peculiar that, in Lerici, even if this is a famous resort, residential property value is markedly lower, probably because the glamour of Portovenere and the low pressure of mass tourism on the Cinque Terre are the features in the area that are most highly valued. It is also interesting to note the relevance of the property's position compared with the central town area in determining prices, which vary accordingly, and also the way in which prices vary in accordance with the tourism vocation of the municipality. In La Spezia, residential property values gradually decrease outward from the town centre, but in the other municipalities, prices are almost halved just outside the historical settlements.

Facilities for yachting and recreational boating, described and quantified by the indicator 'number of berths and moorings for recreational boating', have proved to be a ubiquitous feature in the whole Gulf of La Spezia, while being almost absent in the Cinque Terre. Even if the indicator is useful to describe the features of the study area and to draft its coastal organisation, per se, it supplies little information relevant to defining the boundaries of the urban coastline.

Meanwhile, in relation to sea bathing, the results of the study show that, within the gulf, bathing is forbidden along all the coastline of the municipality of La Spezia and most of that of Portovenere (around the main town), because of its incompatibility with other coastal uses, specifically commercial port, industrial, and military activities and aquaculture. Even if this data does not provide relevant details about the water quality in this area, nevertheless it is meaningful as an indicator of its complexity.

In Table 16.4, for each indicator, some characteristic results have been synthesised and collated according to the thematic fields presented above. Each indicator reports a typical urban feature, according to the relevant scheme.

16.10 Synthesis of the results

The data related to each municipality have subsequently been compared with the above defined features and the three higher values have been singled out.

Of course, the data concerning the municipality of La Spezia are particularly consistent with the definitions of 'urban' as given above.

In general, all the indicators offer the same picture of a saturated urban coastline, characterised by a very high density of uses, uses which may overlap or even conflict. Natural boundaries, as well as different and stabilised organisational patterns, prevent expansion, forcing urban areas to expand towards peripheral ones.

These results are even more interesting as regards the neighbouring municipalities, Portovenere and Lerici, where they show the alternation of urban and non-urban features, which taken as a complex whole, characterise them and point out their peculiarity within the study area. It is interesting that, rather than transition areas, these appear to be 'autonomous' settlements, with their own identity defined by either natural/physical or, at least in part, socio-economic features. A synthesis map can help in identifying the boundaries, as well as the spots to which specific attention should be paid (see Fig. 16.7).

16.11   Conclusion

Throughout the case study, examples are presented of factors that characterise the complexity of the urban coastline. The use of indicators has the advantage that it can supply comparable outputs, both among the different parts of the study area, and among the different features of each part. Besides the results, this methodology creates the base for further and more specific analyses, pointing out some common points:

- The presence of the sea involves some constraints, but also many opportunities linked to a different perception and use of the area (i.e. the opportunity to move along straight lines, therefore a different way in which to assess distances). Moreover, access to the sea attracts many activities that make high demands on both the sea and the adjacent land, and which either modify the natural environment or adapt themselves to it.
- It is important to assess the continuity of functions and, where still perceivable, environments, both along the coast and toward the hinterland. The same uses might take place in extremely different areas, and vice versa.
- Often unbalanced situations (i.e. excessive concentration of a specific activity on the territory, high fragmentation of natural areas, etc.) are linked with socio-economic tension and risk triggering conflicts between uses and users
- The landscape is a result of the way of life and of the activities that take place in a territory and it evolves accordingly. Local

390

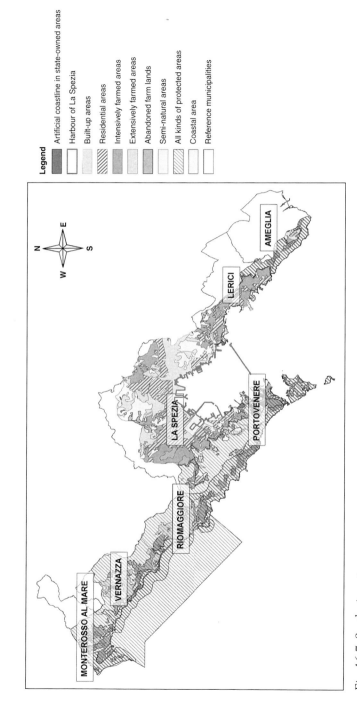

Legend

Artificial coastline in state-owned areas
Harbour of La Spezia
Built-up areas
Residential areas
Intensively farmed areas
Extensively farmed areas
Abandoned farm lands
Semi-natural areas
All kinds of protected areas
Coastal area
Reference municipalities

MONTEROSSO AL MARE

VERNAZZA

RIOMAGGIORE

LA SPEZIA

PORTOVENERE

LERICI

AMEGLIA

Fig. 16.7 Synthesis map

communities have the right to the enjoyment of quality landscapes independently of the particular kind of landscape they are (i.e. urban, natural, industrial, historic, etc.). Moreover it should not be forgotten that waterfront landscape has a double value: landscape landward and landscape seaward.

- The analysis of coastal features takes into consideration the local communities' role in managing their coastal area and specifically their waterfront – local communities should be important agents in planning and managing their territory, above all when many values and interests are concentrated on it. This seldom happens, either because the administrative processes are not so open to public participation, or, often, because people are not willing to commit themselves in work that may not lead to any immediate benefit and may expose them to criticisms and other nuisances.

As a synthesis, identifying those elements that characterise an urban coastline, besides accurately delimiting and describing an area that, within the context of ICAM, deserves particular attention, also supplies a comprehensive view of the issues and the human agents that are going to be implicated in a subsequent management intervention.

References

Benoit, G. and Comeau, A. (2005) A sustainable future for the Mediterranean. The Blue Plan's environment and development outlook, Earthscan, London.

Brachya, V., Juhasz, F., Pavasovic, A. and Trumbic, I. (1994) *Guidelines for Integrated Management of Coastal and Marine Areas with Special Reference to the Mediterranean Basin*, PAP/RAC (MAP-UNEP) Split (HR).

Blue Plan Regional Activity Centre (2006) Methodological Sheets of the 34 Priority Indicators for the 'Mediterranean Strategy for Sustainable Development', Sophia-Antipolis, France.

Cicin-Sain, B. and Knecht, R.W. (1998) *Integrated Coastal and Ocean Management: Concepts and Practices*, Island Press, Washington, DC.

Coccossis, H., Burt, T. and Van Der Weide, J. (1999) *Conceptual Framework and Planning Guidelines for Integrated Coastal Area and River Basin Management*, PAP/RAC (MAP-UNEP) Split (HR).

Martí, X., Lescrauwaet, A., Borg, M. and Valls, M. (2007) Indicators Guidelines. To Adopt an Indicators-based Approach to Evaluate Coastal Sustainable Development, DEDUCE Consortium, Department of the Environment and Housing, Government of Catalonia, Barcelona, Spain.

UN 'Urban 21: Global Conference on the Urban Future' (2000) *10 Principles for Sustainable Urban Waterfront Development*, Berlin, Germany.

Vallega, A. (1999) *Fundamentals of Integrated Coastal Management*, Kluwer Academic Publisher, Dordrecht, Netherlands.

Vallega, A. (2003a) Concetto di uso; Identificazione degli usi; in *Linee Guida per la Gestione Integrata Costiera*, ENEA Centro Ricerche Ambiente Marino, S. Teresa, La Spezia, Italy.

Vallega, A. (2003b) Identificazione degli usi, in *Linee Guida per la Gestione Integrata Costiera*, ENEA Centro Ricerche Ambiente Marino, S. Teresa, La Spezia, Italy.

Vallega, A. (2003c) Rete degli usi; in *Linee Guida per la Gestione Integrata Costiera*, ENEA Centro Ricerche Ambiente Marino, S. Teresa, La Spezia, Italy.

Further reading

Belfiore, S., Balgos, M., McLean, B., Galofre, J., Blaydes, M. and Tesch, D. (2003) A Reference Guide on the Use of Indicators for Integrated Coastal Management – ICAM Dossier 1, *IOC Manuals and Guides n. 45. ICAM Dossier,* 1 UNESCO, Paris.

Belfiore, S., Barbière, J., Bowen, R., Cicin-Sain, B., Ehler, C., Mageau, C., McDougall, D. and Siron, R. (2006) A Handbook for Measuring the Progress and Outcomes of Integrated Coastal and Ocean Management. *IOC Manuals and Guides, n. 46; ICAM Dossier,* 2 UNESCO, Paris.

Council of Europe (2000) European Landscape Convention, European Treaty Series – No. 176, Florence, Italy.

Ogrin, D. (2005) Mediterranean Landscapes – Contribution to a Better Management, A report commissioned by Priority Actions Programme, Split.

Prieur, M. and Ghezali, M. (2000) National Legislations and Proposals for the Guidelines Relating to Integrated Planning and Management of the Mediterranean Coastal Zones, PAP/RAC (MAP-UNEP), Split.

Sairinen, R. and Kumpulainen, S. (2006) Assessing social impacts in urban waterfront regeneration. *Environmental Impact Assessment Review*, Vol. 26, pp. 120–135.

Vogiatzakis, I.N., Griffiths, G.H., Cassar, L.F. and Morse, S. (2005) *Mediterranean Coastal Landscapes – Management Practices, Typology and Sustainability*, The University of Reading, Reading, UK.

Web references

Australian Government, Dept. of Environment, Water, Heritage and the Arts (2006) State of the Environment 2006 – Indicator: CO-30 Length and Area of Coastal and Estuarine Foreshore Altered for Human Purposes. Online at: http://www.environment.gov.au/soe/2006/publications/drs/indicator/142/index.html

http://www.wikipedia.il Golfo della Spezia

http://www.provincia.sp.it Provincia della Spezia

Malta Environment and Planning Authority (2002) Coastal Strategy Topic Paper – Final Draft (MT), http://www.mepa.org.mt/Planning/factbk/SubStudies/CoastalTP/CoastalTP_ExecSum.pdf

Appendix 16.1
Data sets used to delimit the coastal area

Data set	Source	Year	Scale	Notes
Lacoast LAnd cover changes in COASTal zones	Joint Research Centre, Ispra (IT)	1995	1:100 000	Vector coverage of the land use changes from 1975 to 1992 in a strip 10 km wide from the coastline
Corine Land Cover 2000 (COoRdination de l'INformation sur l'Environnement)	APAT (Agenzia per la Protezione dell'Ambiente e iservizi Tecnici)	2005	1:100 000	The original classification in three levels has been enlarged by the Italian Ministry of Environment up to five levels for semi-natural areas The map unit is 20ha
Protected areas (vector)	APAT (http://www.mais.sinanet.apat.it/cartanetms)	2005	1:25 000	Protected areas as defined by the Protected Areas Framework Law (L 394/91)
Sites of Community Interest (SCIs) and Specially Protected Areas (SPAs)	Regione Liguria	2000	1:25 000	Implementation at the Regional level of directions of the Nature 2000 net
Rivers and catchments	APAT (http://www.mais.sinanet.apat.it/cartanetms)		1:250 000 and 1:100 000	
Hydrogeologic complexes Extract from: Mouton J. *et al.*, 1982, 'Tema 1 – Acquiferi' (Issue 1, Aquifers), vol. 6 of the 'Atlante delle Risorse Idriche Sotterranee della Comunità Europea', (EC Atlas of Underground Water Resources) digitised by CNR-CNUCE (national Council for Research) in 1993	APAT (http://www.mais.sinanet.apat.it/cartanetms)		1:500 000	

Appendix 16.1 Continued

Data sets used to delimit the coastal area

Data set	Source	Year	Scale	Notes
Municipalities	Regione Liguria	2005	1 : 5000	
Census units (towns and hamlets)	ISTAT (Istituto nazionale di Statistica – National Statistics Institutes)	2001	1 : 5000	Only for coastal municipalities, updated to the 2001 population survey
Baselines – Territorial sea	ICCOPS dataset			Not official
Maritime districts	Portolano del Mediterraneo	2001	text indications	
Elevation	ICCOPS dataset		1 : 100 000	Curves every 100 m
Streets and motorways	ICCOPS dataset			Not official
Railways	ICCOPS dataset			Not official
Raster map	Istituto Geografico Militare		1 : 100 000	It has some problems in georeferring. It has been used just as general reference

Appendix 16.2
Data sets used to calculate the indicators

Data set	Source	Year	Scale	Notes
Regional Technical Map	Regione Liguria	1995	1:25 000	Raster
Regional Technical Map	Regione Liguria	2004	1:10 000	Raster, draft from the scale 1:5000 map
Municipal boundaries	Regione Liguria	2000	1:5000	
Land-use map	Regione Liguria	2000	1:25 000	Used layers: Land Use and Coverage Map (1:25 000) Artificial Terraces (1:25 000)
Sites of Community Interest (SCIs)	Regione Liguria	2005	1:10 000	
Specially Protected Areas (SPAs)	Regione Liguria	2000	1:25 000	
Tourist harbours in Liguria	Unioncamere Liguria	–	–	Data downloadable at: http://www.lig.camcom.it/index.php?screen=turismo&pag=portitur
14° General Italian Census of Population and Houses	ISTAT (Istituto nazionale di Statistica – National Statistics Institutes)	2001	–	Data sets about Municipalities and hamlets
8° General Italian Census of Industry and Services	ISTAT (Istituto nazionale di Statistica – National Statistics Institutes)	2001	–	Data sets about Municipalities and hamlets and Local Employment Systems
5° General Italian Census of Agriculture	ISTAT (Istituto nazionale di Statistica – National Statistics Institutes)	2000	–	Data sets about Municipalities
14° General Italian Census of Population and Houses – Census units	ISTAT (Istituto nazionale di Statistica – National Statistics Institutes)	2001	1:5000	Map of Census units in coastal Municipalities
Protected areas	APAT (downloaded from: http://www.mais.sinanet.apat.it/cartanetms)	2003	1:25 000	Protected areas as defined by the Protected Areas Framework Law (L 394/91)

17

Coastal hazards and risk

Michael Elliott, [*] *Anna Trono* [†] *and Nicholas D. Cutts* [*]
[*] *Institute of Estuarine & Coastal Studies, University of Hull, UK;*
[†] *Department of Arts and Heritage, University of Salento, Italy*

This chapter gives the background to and evidence for the causes and consequences of natural and anthropogenic hazards on the coast, including transitional waters, and links these to disasters (for society). It takes the view that hazard is the potential that there will be damage to the natural or human system and so it is the product of an event which could occur multiplied by the probability of it occurring. The degree of risk then relates to the amount of assets, natural or societal, which are likely to be affected. The review considers there to be 12 types of hazard for the natural system and for the social system and so it introduces the topic with definitions (and perceptions) of hazard, disaster and risk and then gives examples of the types of hazards and disasters and where they occur.

In presenting long- and short-term perspectives and large- and small-scale perspectives, the chapter shows that the hazards leading to disasters will include flooding, erosion and tsunamis among others, as well as the types of erosion (slumping (soft coasts) versus undercutting (cliff falls on hard coasts)). Using examples taken worldwide, this includes the impact of wetland creation and wetland loss on vulnerability and the way in which the problems have been exacerbated by building (and wetland vegetation clearance) on vulnerable coasts. Hence we emphasise the importance of considering hazard and risk on vulnerable and sensitive coasts.

The chapter mentions the tools for assessing and managing the impacts including the indicators for defining risk and hazard and mapping systems as examples. These will allow policy makers to determine the consequences for natural and human systems. In this, it is necessary to separate the locally-derived problems from the large-scale

Coastal zone management
978-0-7277-3641-1

effects (e.g. climate change, sea-level rise and isostatic rebound as unmanaged exogenic pressures whereby we respond to the consequences rather than the causes). However, it is also necessary to put the problems into context by assessing hazards and the conflicts between different users – ports, urban areas, habitat protection, tourism and so indicate the types of management responses. These can indicate the use of hard and soft engineering as solutions – beach nourishment, managed realignment, set back schemes and hard protection. The chapter ends with a discussion regarding coping with disaster and hazard and the task for the future (scenarios and forecasts) with the ability (or inability) of society to have policies for control of the problems and consequences.

17.1 Introduction

There are many hazards present in the coastal and coastal wetland areas, each of which have causes and consequences. *Hazard* is the cause compared to *risk* which is the probability of effect (likely consequences) leading to disaster (as the human consequences). The severity of the hazard is measured by the number of people affected or the value of the assets affected. The concept of disaster then represents the interplay between the social and the natural systems. Responses to hazards results from a perception of risk and the willingness to act depends on the perception and evidence, e.g. storm surge barriers as a response to the 1953 storm surge (see below). Natural risk can be defined as the damage expected from an actual or hypothetical scenario triggered by natural phenomena or events following natural events. Because of space constraints, this chapter can only present a wide-ranging albeit brief account of the topic of risk and hazard as related to the coastal zone but the reader is also directed to more detailed works such as the excellent text by Smith and Petley (2009).

Coastal hazards can perhaps be divided into those over which individuals or communities have some control, for example by agreeing not to inhabit vulnerable areas, and those where they have no control, for example tectonic failure or extreme landslip such as the postulated mega tsunami resulting from potential failure of Cumbre Vieja on La Palma. Such hazards then require to be tackled using technological, governance and economic approaches, for example whether we have the capacity in methods, laws and funding to modify and protect coastal landscapes against the influence of hazards or whether we need the capacity to mitigate the effects of hazards by financially supporting those affected by the hazards. At the same time, coastal management, and global agreements to which most countries have signed up, have to ensure that biodiversity is protected and the management is sustainable in the long term. In particular, of course, we have the technological means to reduce the vulnerability and thus risk to the effects of change, for example climate change such as building defences but this is an expensive action. Underlying all of this, again of course, is the need/requirement to protect economic goods and services such as infrastructure and urban areas, while at the same time protecting the natural system, the delivery of ecological goods and services. Hence while we have the capacity to engineer the coastline to protect it from hazards, this would be at the risk of creating a non-natural system, thus in contravention of nature conservation agreements and laws.

Natural phenomena that can create risks for society and the environment can be divided into two main categories depending on source of the causes: *endogenous* phenomena and *exogenous* phenomena in relation to their source within or on the Earth's surface. Endogenous causes, for example, include those which can release huge amounts of energy from seismic or tectonic events, and thus are seen as earthquakes and volcanic eruptions and the tsunamis, wrongly termed tidal-waves, which emanate from these. Exogenous phenomena, such as landslides and floods, accelerated erosion (of beaches and river beds) are often, but not necessarily linked to extreme meteorological events and act on the Earth's surface, tending to modify the landscape. Of course, the nature of the landscape has to be such that it cannot accommodate such forces without resulting modification, for example flat landscapes will exhibit greater change by flooding than ones with greater elevation. Such phenomena are clearly an expression of the internal and external geophysical dynamics and represent the natural evolutionary processes. However, by interacting with societal components (population, settlements, infrastructure, etc.) they frequently determine risk conditions (ISPRA, 2007). It is emphasised here that, while natural systems have the capacity to adjust to such natural changes, it is only when the natural and societal aspects interact that we see hazards and risk, both terms being used in relation to human uses of the geographical space.

Floods, landslides, the instability of the coastline, abrupt subsidence and substratum failure due to the presence of cavities in the subsoil are all either the cause or effect of natural events which are generally grouped together as *hydrogeological phenomena*. These changes are the result of interaction between meteorological events and the geological, morphological and hydrological environment, in which humans either play an important role by making the landscape more susceptible to change or are greatly affected. Clearly, natural phenomena can cause disasters but more often human actions make them more severe. For example, in assessing the causes and consequences from the Katrina hurricane in August 2005, Austin (2009) showed that the situation was made worse in Southern Louisiana because of its history and features. These included its often poor human population being less able to withstand the changes, a long history of coastal modification by natural and man-made levees and other modifications through canal construction and the oil exploration and extraction industries. In essence, the loss of coastal wetlands removed a capacity to cope with natural events such as hurricanes, a poor and poorly prepared population were unable to cope with the after-effects and a large amount of city infrastructure then increased the repercussions of the hurricane.

The language of hazard and risk includes emotive terms and hyperbole more relevant to popular journalism than scientific articles. However, as hazard and risk relate to the societal use of the landscape then such terms have to be used here. For example, a disaster can become a catastrophe because of anthropogenic factors and/or inadequate risk management and a lack of preparation. The geological formation of an area, for example, can be considered the underlying cause of hydrogeological risk and serious damage although added to this, however, should be factors linked to human activities. These include the failure to maintain slopes and cliffs through drainage works, the presence of settlements on flood plains or on unstable terrain, and the intense exploitation of the coasts for tourism and industry; for example the weakening or removal of sand-dunes to create bathing centres, vacation resorts and marinas for pleasure craft.

Against this background, the environmental 'disorder' resulting from increasing exploitation of the coastal strip is periodically exacerbated by adverse meteorological events. For example, heavy rains, swollen rivers and marine surges (either by tsunami or tidal), all increase the deterioration not only of the coastal strip but also inland. Events that the mass media often portray as natural catastrophes – unpredictable because of their 'exceptional' nature – are indeed catastrophic in societal terms, but not exactly 'unpredictable' as they will occur but we just do not know when. For example, in the last 40 years, these phenomena have become increasingly frequent in the Po River plain – the Polesine

Table 17.1 Types of hazard in coastal and coastal wetland area

Surface hydrological hazards
Surface physiographic removal – chronic/long-term
Surface physiographic removal – acute/short-term
Climatological hazards – acute/short term
Climatological hazards – chronic/long term
Tectonic hazards – acute/short term
Tectonic hazards – chronic/long term
Anthropogenic microbial biohazards
Anthropogenic macrobial biohazards
Anthropogenic (introduced technological) hazards
Anthropogenic (extractive technological) hazards
Anthropogenic (chemical) hazards

flood of 1951, the destruction of the Venetian *murazzi* (sea defences) in 1966, the exceptional 'high waters' in Venice throughout the 1960s – a set of notable events in a long period of generally bad weather. In turn these destabilised the coastal strip, which has clearly been affected by the periodic variations in climatic conditions but also by the ever-more intense anthropogenic impact on the natural environment.

Within these considerations, we should not ignore the movement of populations from the interior and thus increasing urbanisation, hence coastal populations are increasing exponentially worldwide causing an increase in the number of urban areas centred on estuarine, wetland and coastal areas. This therefore increases the potential to risk, the vulnerability of areas and thus the potential for disaster. Hence the hazard will have an actual and/or perceived magnitude which in turn will have a spatial and temporal dimension and of course the perception by society may be greater than the actual, measured extent. Hence there is the need to determine the extent (as the spatial dimension) and the duration (as the temporal dimension) of the hazard and the effect, to people, to goods and to the environment (Smith and Petley, 2009). In turn, the hazard and its consequences may be acute, and thus operating over a very short time, or chronic, and thus occurring over a long period – these are features used to define categories of hazard (see Table 17.1).

Of course, all societies have adapted to coastal hazards and thus either have accommodated risks or tried to minimise them for the benefit of living in coastal areas. Klein *et al.* (2001) indicate that technologies can incorporate adaptation although this requires to be communicated and populations need to be made aware of their vulnerability, for example populations living on low-lying and threatened coasts. Coastal managers then need to design and implement adaptation strategies, even if these are not societally desirable, for example the UK has a present policy of protecting large urban areas and industry in the national interest but not protecting farmland where there is not an economic justification for protection – while this may not be desirable by small and isolated residences or farms, it is a pragmatic approach. The cost of protecting coasts may be £2M (at 2009 prices) per 100 m and possibly considerably more expensive than moderate quality coastal farmland. Klein *et al.* (2001) further consider important the adaptation strategy of relying on soft engineering, the use of better information and awareness systems, and site-specific and local adaptation.

Hazards and the risk from them can be categorised along a set of gradients from those which are natural to those man-made and from the spatial dimension of their impact and intensity ranging from widespread and diffuse to point-source (Fig. 17.1). They can also be ranked

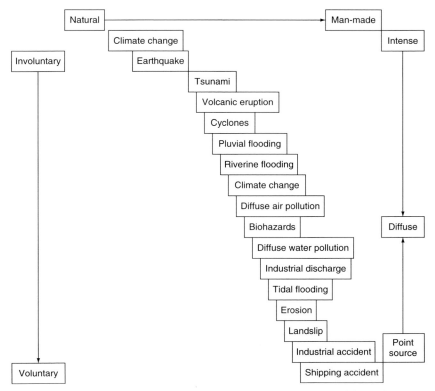

Fig. 17.1 A gradient of natural and anthropogenic environmental hazards covering spatial scales from the global to the local (greatly modified from a concept in Smith and Petley, 2009, see text for explanation)

according to whether society has any control over them – in the figure *'voluntary'* relates to the degree of human control and therefore causation whereas *'involuntary'* indicates that the community has no control and must only try to respond to the consequences of the event/activity. The axis *intense*, *diffuse* and *point-source* relates to the extent of the hazard. In Fig. 17.1 we have identified climate change at various points depending on whether it is regarded as an anthropogenic change and whether it consequently affects other hazards such as the introduction and spread of biohazards.

17.2   Types of coastal hazard

Table 17.1 indicates and summarises the types of hazard within the coastal zone and this chapter aims to give a description, an explanation and examples of these and to indicate solutions. Where the term anthropogenic is used in the table and text this implies a self-inflicted hazard where in-situ responses may be sufficient to minimise, mitigate or control the hazard.

17.2.1   *Surface hydrological hazards*

The most frequent and often widespread hazards at coasts and adjacent lands are caused by surface flooding from regular high tidal events, albeit often around spring tides and equinoxes. The low-lying surfaces most at risk will be in macrotidal estuaries, flat coastal areas, deltas and natural floodplains. These therefore will be in open coastal areas away from non- or micro-tidal enclosed or semi-enclosed seas and away from amphidromal points. They will have catchments conducive to flash-floods and perhaps with that flooding being through channels to cause high energy run-off. Consequently there will be infrastructure effects, for example bridge damage as occurred at the Ponte de Ferro bridge March 2001 in the Douro River near Porto in Northern Portugal killing 70 people. As a coastal river example, the Tararu and Te Puru creek bridges in New Zealand exacerbated flood run-off from heavy rain which resulted in a loss of life in 2002. A response to this type of hazard is shown by the establishment of the Thames Coast Project, covering London and the adjacent areas and which includes a multi-agency catchment management plan, flood risk plan and hazard mapping, provision of new 'sustainable' infrastructure and a policy of property retirement in high risk areas. The surface flooding may be related to changes in global weather systems such as the North Atlantic Oscillation – ENSO events.

17.2.2   Surface physiographic removal – chronic/long term

Surface and shallow geomorphological features will focus in the continuous, long-term and thus chronic removal of the substratum. The erosion of soft rock or clay/till material or of regular cliff failure may be caused by wave undercutting or, for soft sediments, slumping due to waterlogged sediments (see Box 17.1). While the failure of soft or hard rock cliffs may be more spectacular, the constant and continual removal of soft sediment leads to a greater impact on coastlines. For example, in parts of Sicily 70% of its coastline is at risk of erosion and parts of this are critical given that the island's coasts have retreated visibly in the last thirty years and an average of 60 m of beach has been removed by the sea.

The creation of coastal infrastructures that affect longshore drift (wharves, ports, sea walls, emergent breakwaters) have the potential to starve adjacent areas of sediment from the beach and thus increase the hazards and risk in those areas through erosion. Similarly, human activities have reduced the flow of sediments from watercourses through building dams, creating diversions, dredging of the river beds, structures to counteract soil erosion and the paving over of roads and other surfaces. Urbanisation has led to the dismantling of natural defence structures (*Posidonia* and other sea-grass meadows, sand dunes, coastal vegetation). The destruction of the coastal dunes and related psammophile vegetation, caused by the building of roads and dwellings, has also reduced the resilience of habitats to erosion processes. The high demand for coastal space has grown and has accentuated the periodical or seasonal retreat of the coastline thus paradoxically increasing risk to the communities creating the problem.

In addition to the removal of sediments or the interference with sediment processes through barriers and dredging, risk has been increased through land sinking either by isostatic rebound or the extraction of coal, hydrocarbons and water in areas too close to the sea. The latter has occurred for example in the northeast coast of England, the Po delta and the Lagoon of Venice (see below). These in turn have led to the rapid destabilisation of the coastal environment.

17.2.3   Surface physiographic removal – acute/short term

Intermittent, irregular and thus unexpected cliff failure either along fault lines or due to an unexpected failure of other types of substratum may present a greater risk and thus an unexpected hazard. Thus it is particularly difficult to prepare for this type of event. An example is the land failure at Holbeck in North Yorkshire in 1993 (see Box 17.2).

Box 17.1 *Chronic and long-term hazard – coastal erosion – Holderness coast*

The Holderness coastline in eastern England is arguably the fastest-eroding coastline in Europe being composed of glacial tills and clay with occasional moraine areas (Metheringham, 2008). The present rate of 1–2 m per year has probably been occurring since the last ice-age and consequently villages have been lost to the sea – an example of chronic risk and hazard (see Fig. 17.2). The area has historically employed adaptation and voluntary 'roll-back' – a policy now enshrined in the present municipal response whereby building is discouraged within a 100 yr erosion safety limit. The erosion is through cliff slumping as opposed to the more classical type of erosion via cliff failure. As such the 'erosion' is characterised by a series of rotational slumps of the boulder clay cliff, caused largely through pluvial/groundwater permeation. The base of these 'slumped' areas of cliff is then readily removed by wave action. This type of erosion results in a 'scalloping' of the cliff line, with short reaches of perhaps 10 m–100 m seeing an annual erosion rate of over 10 m per year, with other adjacent sections seeing little or no erosion, and with a net retreat of 1–2 m per year. The local population has a continuing assumed perception of risk through hazard to their buildings even if lives are not threatened. However, this has not stopped the desire for development. A technological response is possible, e.g. the building of devices to create beaches, but this is both expensive and there are doubts regarding the repercussions of interfering with natural processes. In particular stopping sediment movement down the coast and the sediment supply to the adjacent Humber Estuary and the Wash estuarine areas which in turn would increase the risk of flooding there; most notably the city of Kingston-upon-Hull within the Humber, could be at risk. Furthermore, increased hazards from sea level rise and storm surges could result from interfering with the sediment supply. This example also shows the importance of management according to sediment and hydrographical systems – in the UK this is through management responses using Shoreline Management Plans.

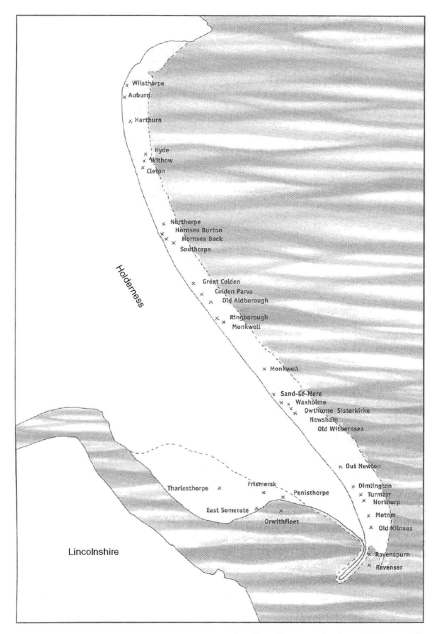

Fig. 17.2 Holderness coastline, eastern England, indicating the loss of historically recorded villages due to erosion of the glacial clays

Box 17.2 Coastal landslip – Holbeck Hotel hazard

The Holbeck Hall Hotel was built in the late 1800s on South Cliff, Scarborough, Yorkshire, eastern England, 65 m above sea-level with views over the adjacent coastline. It was built on glacial till (boulder clay with some sand horizones) which in 1993 had suffered small-scale historical movement. Following a period of heavy rain, cracks were observed in a tarmac footpath running up the cliff side, and around 6 weeks later (by June) a large area of fronting garden 'disappeared' with subsequent landslides following over the next 24 hours, culminating with part of the hotel collapsing the following day. The landslides were rotational slumps which regularly occur in steeply shelving areas of glacial till along the Yorkshire coast, but with conditions exacerbated in this area by several dry summers (allowing cracks in the clay to develop), followed by a period of heavy rain and modifications to slope drainage, leading to a catastrophic build-up in pore pressure. The municipal and national authorities were then required to respond rapidly under emergency works orders in order to stabilise the cliff and prevent further damage (see Fig. 17.3).

Fig. 17.3 Holbeck landslip, Scarborough, North Yorkshire, UK – at the start of the stabilising works following the landslip

17.2.4 Climatological hazards – acute/short term

Acute, erratic and short-term hazards may be the result of climatological conditions in which several phenomena coincide. For example storm surges linked to the tidal conditions and physiography of the area, and cyclones, hurricanes and tropical storms produce hazards and thus the risk to infrastructure and populations. These may be caused by fluctuations and sequences in sea surface temperature, wind patterns and even the influence of NAO/El Niño/La Niña on weather patterns. These will influence riverine run-off or even the retention of freshwaters due to tidal pumping inland which in turn leads to estuarine and wetland damage. For example the Sundarbans mangrove area of Bangladesh is subject to tidal, fluvial and pluvial flooding and with an increased hazard during the tropical storm and monsoon season. The low-lying area suffers from natural hazards but also, because of its rich fishing and other resources, supports a large human population (Haque and Elliott, 2005). Accordingly the area exposed to high risk is large and the consequences from the hazards are considerable (Smith and Petley, 2009; Brammer, 2000). Despite this, the societies in countries such as Bangladesh have a long history of tolerating and adapting to these natural events.

In macrotidal, shallow and semi-enclosed areas this type of hazard includes storm surges (see Box 17.3). A combination of a period of high tide (spring or equinoctial), sufficient fetch and wind direction, low air pressure (to allow the water level to rise) and basin shape can all conspire to produce hazardous and potentially catastrophic conditions (Baxter, 2005).

17.2.5 Climatological hazards – chronic/long term

A rather more insidious loss of coastline, and thus a hazard to those inhabiting the coast, is caused by global warming and the resultant sea-level rise. While this may be gradual and thus the local populations can adapt to the risk or even move away, it can result in large-scale coastal changes especially in countries too poor to respond with hard engineering, for example the Maldives and Bangladesh where only a modest rise in sea level, and it is predicted to be 1 m during the current century, will remove a large amount of land. Furthermore, and again in Bangladesh this will be accompanied by the ingress of seawater and thus saline incursion into the mangrove areas, estuaries and deltas. Unfortunately, in Bangladesh the effects of this may also be exacerbated by the removal of fresh water and dam building in the Indian catchments of

Box 17.3 Development of a hazard – the 1953 storm surge

In 31 January/1 February 1953, a combination of factors produced a storm surge with catastrophic effects. The south-westerly winds in the north Atlantic pushing water into the northern North Sea, a high spring tide, a low pressure system over the southern North Sea, the shape of the North Sea which funnels the water mass into a shallow and narrow area, and the underlying anticlockwise gyre in the North Sea, in itself the effects of Coriolis force, all combined to produce a storm surge. This moved down the western edge of the North Sea (the English and Scottish east coast seeing a surge height of almost 3.0 m) and then up the eastern continental coast (Belgium and the Netherlands where the surge was over 3.3 m), across low-lying coastal areas and thus leading to the overtopping or breaching of the defences. This resulted in 307 deaths in the UK and 1835 deaths in the Netherlands and the flooding of *c.* 300 000 ha of land. This was a 1-in-250 year event and sea defences in the immediate post-war period were not designed for such events. The disaster led to the construction of greater defences including the barriers across the River Hull in the Humber and across the Thames estuary and in particular the Dutch Delta works (Nienhuis and Smaal, 1994) – the latter is a system of closed estuaries and barriers across the Rhine-Meuse delta area whereby the large-scale geomorphology of the southern Netherlands was changed dramatically. Baxter (2005) concludes that no one was to blame for the unpreparedness of the areas which were flooded, and that the austerity following the Second World War exacerbated the problem. As long as this disaster is within the public consciousness then funding is easily allocated to solving it. whereas once the public no longer remembers the disaster then it may lead to an unwillingness to act. Despite flood defence improvements, there remains a potent surge risk in this region, as relative sea-level rise is a problem in south-east England and the low countries, with increased storminess also predicted due to climate change. In addition, isostatic rebound is apparently causing the land to sink in these southern North Sea coasts, again exacerbating the effects of such a surge. As such, it is postulated that the frequency of such events (a 1-in-250 year occurrence in the 1950s), could be more than 10 times more likely by the 2080s.

their deltas. As an indication of the interlinked nature of these hazards, the ingress of seawater could adversely affect the mangroves of the Sundarbans, in itself which acts as a method of protection against typhoons, tsunamis and storm surges.

As is emphasised throughout this chapter, we have to consider the interlinked nature of the factors which increase coastal hazards. For example, Thornton *et al.* (2006) showed that in Monterey Bay, California, the episodic erosion events which occurred when storm waves and high tides coincided, by eroding the sand-dunes, appeared to be linked to the occurrence of El Niños. They estimated that the dune loss in the Bay during the 1997–98 El Niño winter was 1.82 million m^3, which was seven times the long-term annual dune erosion rate.

Climate change can be regarded as an '*exogenic unmanaged pressure*', that is when we are managing local areas, we are not *managing* climate change; we are merely managing both the *consequences* of it and our *responses* to it. Climate change can have a well-defined set of consequences – from relative sea-level rise and increased storminess to the responses by organisms in adapting to new temperature regimes or even changing distributions. Sea-level rise both affects the coastline and may result in coastal-squeeze where the low water line is rising but the high water one may be fixed by infrastructure. It may lead to erosion especially where it is accompanied by increased storminess. For example, in the long term, whereas there is no indication of increased storminess in the North East Atlantic, a steady increase of the significant wave heights in the last 30 years by about 2 to 3 cm per year was demonstrated by Storch (1996).

17.2.6 Tectonic hazards – acute/short term

The proximity of coastlines to seismically active areas such as subduction zones or transform faults increases the potential hazard due to earthquakes and tsunamis. While actually or potentially catastrophic, these are acute but short-term hazards even though the effects may last for years if not decades. For example, the tsunami produced in December 2004 in Indonesia devastated large areas of coastline (Thanawood *et al.*, 2005) although the effects were exacerbated by the removal of large areas of coastal and wetland vegetation which otherwise would have provided protection against the inundation (see Figs 17.4a and 17.4b). Of similar concern are reports of the underlying geology and the seismic activity in the central Atlantic suggest the potential for geological failure on the island of Tenerife causing a

(a)

Fig. 17.4 The effect of vegetation clearance in reducing protection from storm surges and tidal waves/tsunamis – Gleebruk Village, Indonesia. (a) 12 April 2004 vs. (b) 2 January 2005 (from http://www.digitalglobe.com/images/tsunami)

tsunami across the northern Atlantic and especially the Eastern US and Canadian seaboards. Given the very low frequency of such events, however, it is not surprising that the population and authorities in the receiving areas are unprotected and unaware. However, in the case of SE Asia, it is unlikely that any protection could be deployed even though a result of the 2004 Indonesian tsunami was to ensure that an early warning system for the Pacific Ocean was implemented (Thanawood *et al.*, 2005).

17.2.7   Tectonic hazards – chronic/long term

Tectonic hazards on the coast may develop over a long term rather than being the catastrophic events and can be the effects of past events. For example, the influence of sea level rise is more affecting the low-lying southern North Sea coastlines that are sinking because of isostatic rebound which has been occurring since the last ice-age (Ducrotoy and Elliott, 2008). The removal of the weight of ice since the last glacial

(b)

Fig. 17.4 Continued

period has allowed the crust to rise in some areas and correspondingly sink in others, thus the Baltic and northern British Isles' areas are rising (Flint, 1971). A general sea-level rise of 50 cm in 2100 has been suggested for the North Sea by the International Panel on Climate Change (IPCC). The spatial pattern over the region depends on eustatic movements provoking a tilt of the European landmass. Weaker or even negative trends in sea-level rise have been observed in the north (Scotland, Sweden). The southern part of the region, especially the south-eastern coast of England, and parts of the Netherlands and Germany are undergoing isostatic rebound. In essence, the land is sinking thus causing a greater sea-level rise in contrast to most of the Baltic countries which are rising and so sea level is less of a problem there (Ducrotoy and Elliott, 2008).

The remaining hazards all relate to materials, whether solid or liquid or biological, physical or chemical. The addition of materials which may or may not be hazardous is regarded as contamination whereas any resulting likely or actual biological effect is regarded as pollution (McLusky and Elliott, 2004; Clark, 2001). In this respect, hazard is regarded as the potential for an adverse change to the biological system whether at cell, individual, population, community or ecosystem level and also including humans within the biological system. Contamination of the seas, coasts and estuaries is defined as an increase in the level of a compound/element (as the result of Man's activities) in an organism or system which not necessarily results in a change to the functioning of that system or organism. In the case of hazards, however, pollution is regarded (i) as a change in the natural system as a result of Man's activities; or it (ii) has occurred if it reduces the individual's/population's/ species'/community's fitness to survive. It includes the introduction by Man, directly or indirectly, of substances or energy into the marine environment (including estuaries) resulting in such deleterious effects as to harm living resources, hazards to human health, hindrance to marine activities including fishing, impairment of quality for use of seawater, and reduction of amenities (McLusky and Elliott, 2004).

17.2.8 *Anthropogenic microbial biohazards*

With regard to biological entities, biohazards, contamination is then translated as *biocontamination* – the introduction of species without noticeable effects (e.g. microbes which are killed immediately by natural conditions). Following this, *biopollution* is regarded as the effects of introduced, invasive species sufficient to disturb an individual (internal biological pollution by parasites or pathogens), a population (by genetical change) or a community or ecosystem (by increasing or decreasing the species complement). This type of hazard can produce adverse economic consequences.

In the case of microbial biohazards, the long-held practice of coastal anthropogenic introduction of microbes (through sewage thus leading to disease) is an indication of biological pollution which can be prevented by treatment such as ozone or chlorination disinfection of waste waters. The long-established practice of discharging sewage into the sea, since the 1970s through long-sea pipelines, has used the sea's characteristics of being saline, cold and with high UV levels to kill sewage pathogens. While this strategy is considered suitable for controlling and acting as treatment for sewage pathogenic bacteria, it is considered less effective for viruses (see, e.g., Efstratiou, 2001).

17.2.9 *Anthropogenic macrobial biohazards*

The concept of biological pollution (e.g. Elliott, 2003) whereby introduced or invasive species create problems and thus hazards for the biological system, can be applied to macro-organisms as well as micro-organisms. With an increased movement of materials and vessels around the world, and thus the movement of ballast-water, there is an increased chance of organisms being moved and thus creating hazards. For example, the introduction into Europe of the Chinese Mitten Crab, *Eriocheir sinensis*, early in the last century has now created populations in estuaries and rivers from Portugal to Scandinavia. The crabs burrow into dykes and thus increase the risk of dyke failure and thus flooding. In addition, climate change will lead to organism distribution range change or expansion, again increasing the risk of adverse effects in an area. Such effects can relate to human health such as the increased incidence of Paralytic Shellfish Poisoning as the result of the introduced red-tide forming organisms or merely a reduction in amenity through recreation beaches being populated by non-native oysters such as *Crassostrea gigas* in northwest Europe. Ballast water controls, such as treatment or prevention through the International Maritime Organisation, are advocated to minimise the likelihood of risks from introduced species although these require maritime nations to ratify the controls.

There are many terms and concepts for alien and introduced species (e.g. Occhipinti-Ambrogi and Galil, 2004) and suggested protocols for identifying the size of the hazard (Olenin *et al.*, 2007) and assessing the risks (Panov *et al.*, 2009). Rapport *et al.* (1998) and Boudouresque & Vaerlaque (2002) indicated the concerns involved in assessing ecosystem health. Ruiz *et al.* (1997) were among the pioneers identifying the size of the hazard but whereas there are good data regarding the vulnerability of and risk to ecological systems (e.g. Zaiko *et al.*, 2007), there are few studies defining the risks to human systems. Despite this, countries are increasingly requiring mechanisms to deal with what is likely to become an increasing hazard, thus often termed *biosecurity*. For example, the Central Science Laboratory (2008), Genovesi and Shine (2004), Reise *et al.* (2006), and Hewitt and Campbell (2007) give the national strategies for identifying and controlling the level of hazard in the UK, Europe and Australia/New Zealand.

Panov *et al.* (2009) considered that risk analysis for this problem as being four steps: (1) the identification of the problem; (2) the assessment of the likelihood of introduction, establishment, dispersal and impact; (3) the management of the problem; and (4) communicating the problem. Hewitt and Campbell (2007) in discussing a biosecurity policy for Australia and New Zealand concluded, as is expected in areas with both a unique and formerly isolated fauna and flora, that

413

the policy of minimising risk and thus reducing the hazard should concentrate on prevention by first developing Import Health Standards and deciding on the acceptability of intentional introduction. Second, it needs to determine the likely species of concern (the 'next pests') and the high risk entry locations such as ports and international harbours. Third, this in turn aids the monitoring and rapid response efforts aimed at eradication. Fourth, they suggest determining which vectors of greatest concern. However, it is suggested here that this action should perhaps be the first in determining the risk and thus the control mechanism.

17.2.10 Anthropogenic (introduced technological) hazards

Given the above definitions for pollution then it is possible logically to take the view that adding large structures into the sea and on coasts and which will have an adverse impact and thus lead to the potential for hazards is also pollution. An increased coastal infrastructure and possible failure, such as from bridges, thus increases hazards and risk. Leavitt and Kiefer (2006) showed the interrelationships between the effects of hurricane Katrina in New Orleans in 2005 and the existing city infrastructure. While the presence of the infrastructure made the consequences of the hurricane much worse, it also added to the cause of the problems by removing natural defences. They conclude that any assessment of risk and vulnerability and hence the response to such hazards required a flexible approach which included '*coordination, cooperation and communication*'.

17.2.11 Anthropogenic (extractive technological) hazards

The extraction of physical materials has the potential to both cause hazards and increased risk and exacerbate the effects of other hazards. For example, the extraction of nearshore sand as aggregate for building removes the natural defences such as beach or sand dunes and thus makes storm surges potentially more damaging. For example, Thornton *et al.* (2006) showed that in Monterey Bay, California, an annual average removal by mining of $128\,000\,\text{m}^3/\text{yr}$ equated to half of the estimated sand dune loss over a large part of the twentieth century. Coastal erosion rates of 0.5–1.5 m per year were influenced by the mining and stopped in some areas after the cessation of the mining. Similarly there are incidences of physiographic change due to surface and subsurface extraction; for example in northeast England, subsurface

414

and undersea mining of coal over many decades caused subsidence which in turn increased wave erosion on the adjacent shores (Humphries, 2001). Similarly, the extraction of aquifer waters under Venice increased subsidence and thus flooding in the city while the upstream withdrawal of water and damming of the rivers entering Bangladesh will increase saline intrusion and could exacerbate the effects of storm surges.

17.2.12 Anthropogenic (chemical) hazards

Chemical inputs can be both planned, and thus licensed, but also accidental. They include point source discharges, from boats and pipe-lines, and also diffuse inputs from run-off of land and hard-standing structures (see McLusky and Elliott, 2004 and Clark, 2001 for more discussion of this very large topic). While most countries now have legislation to control the adverse effects of chemical discharges, fewer have legislation requiring companies to have environmental management systems which both reduce the chances of chemical hazards and require a contingency plan for a response to hazards once they do occur. Of course shipping lanes or port estuaries with a high volume of shipping transport increase the risk of hazards occurring and also, because of the sensitive nature of habitats in those areas, increase the consequences of oil-spills.

17.3 Increasing risk and hazard – anthropogenic coastal erosion

The underlying geomorphology is the largest factor determining hazard, for example beaches become both a source of problems such as coastal hazards and part of the solution. They have economic benefits in terms of supporting recreation and tourism and the organisms fed on by commercially-fished species but their desirability and production of such economic and social benefits increase the effects of hazards. Their form is the result of the prevailing hydrophysical conditions and they may be eroding or accreting even at different seasons, hence they may provide differing degrees of protection from marine-sourced hazards. In the context of hazards, they provide further economic goods and services including protection by dissipating energy, hence the policy of beach nourishment to provide protection or by building groynes to trap sediment, create a beach and dissipate energy. Hence they may be in a delicate equilibrium between the action of the sea and the availability of sandy sediment along the coast. This equilibrium is particularly sensitive and thus at risk from the constant anthropogenic pressure on the coastal strip and its economic assets.

Given the above features, it is valuable to focus on the nature of the hazards and risks and the consequences at spatial scales, for example both regionally and nationally – as an example, Boxes 17.4 and 17.5 indicate the challenges faced in Italy. As shown here, erosion affects many coastlines; for example the coast on the Ionian Sea adjacent to Puglia, Southern Italy, is highly compromised and retreating as the result of a deficit of material from reduced inputs from the main water-courses. On the main rivers 18 dams and weirs have been constructed with the aim of trapping and storing water for agricultural, industrial and civil use. In some areas, for example large areas of Puglia and the Adriatic Coast, the morphology has been compromised both through an unstable coastline but also intensive exploitation for tourism (Refolo *et al.*, 2007). This has even included tourism operators systematically flattening the dunes, reducing their area and leading to the disappearance of psammophillic vegetation. This in turn removes some of the protection for the coast thus both increasing the risk of further damage by waves and lessening its ability to cope with any other surges.

The above examples emphasise that the causes and thus also the responses to coastal hazards such as erosion have to include economic as well as environmental considerations. The local population may require their amenities to be defended even if this requires expensive engineering solutions. It is the prevailing wisdom, however, in many areas to work with natural processes rather than against them where the latter may either be environmentally or economically unsustainable. An example of this is shown by Spurn Point in eastern England (Box 17.6).

17.3.1 Solutions and response for reducing risk and hazards from erosion

The societal adaptation to hazards, thus allowing minimising of risk, may be by engineering as described above or by behaviour, or by statutory or emergency action. Again, coastal defences or the improved structure of buildings, such as being raised or floating, become engineering options. Behavioural changes in society may be induced by legislation or economics, for example the policy of 'roll-back', whereby permanent human occupation of the coastal strip is discouraged, and by voluntary agreement or enforced by spatial planning. The East

Box 17.4 A national perspective – the Italian example

Recent studies indicate that for *c.* 30% of Italian territory the erosion risk is above tolerable levels especially as 20% of the Italian coastline (8350 km) suffers clearly from erosion and is at risk of flooding. Since the 1970s sandy coasts have been in retreat and currently about 1500 km of the 4600 km of low-lying coasts (including coastal plains) are threatened by rising sea levels, erosion and flooding. Italy is heavily affected by natural events, especially those associated with hydrogeological risk (landslides, floods), which are second only to earthquakes in terms of the damage they cause (Barberi *et al.*, 2004). The Italian 'hydrogeological disaster' is exacerbated by demographic and socio-economic growth in a way that ignores the characteristics and the delicate hydrogeological equilibrium of the land mass and especially the coastal zone. The process of urbanisation and the uncontrolled growth of residential and industrial areas in low-lying regions in the post-war period has had undeniable socio-economic benefits but has led to large areas being concreted over, with increasingly invasive structures (dykes, dams, canals, drainage systems and walls), and has thus interfered with natural processes. This appears to be yet another example of 'once areas are managed then management has to continue otherwise the area tries to return to a (societally) less-desirable state'. The degradation, especially of a country heavily dependent on tourism income, of the coastal environment is increasing and shown by the retreat of the coastline and increasing risk of erosion. Hence this has major effects on sea-coast interactions and creates the conditions for a new dynamic equilibrium that is quite different from the natural state before Man's intervention. In addressing such an increased risk, the authorities appear to forget that the coastal environment is a highly complex system, closely linked to the river network which supplies the beaches with solid material, thus compensating for the destructive action of the sea. A well-documented example of this situation is the coastal strip of the northern Adriatic, which is affected by progressive degradation, as shown by the retreat of the coastline. This coastal destabilisation is generated mainly by the wave-action but additionally compromised by intensive human activities along the coast and the rivers that flow towards it. Such activities have resulted in harmful interference with the natural environmental equilibrium, a phenomenon which began to have devastating consequences in the 1950s and 1960s after a long period of stability of the coastal area (Marabini, 2000).

Box 17.5 A case study: *Casalabate in the province of Lecce*

Casalabate, in the north of the Municipality of Lecce, Puglia, is a noted example of an area affected by serious hydrogeological disturbance. The coastal area has been heavily affected by human activities since the 1950s, and most buildings were constructed without authorisation within a flat physical landscape. There are two distinct sub-areas – a higher one 12–15 m above sea level and divided from a lower area by a clear escarpment running roughly parallel to the current shoreline. The whole of the urban area of the resort of Casalabate slopes down gently towards the sea, from a height of 15–20 m above sea level inland to less than 1 m above sea level near the shore. The lowest-lying areas are covered with beach deposits, together with the remains of the dunes and marshes, all of which are affected by erosion or removal by human actions. Consequently the original karst features have been partially re-exposed. In areas close to the shoreline, the human modifications over the last 50 years have largely obliterated the natural morphology of the area, which today is clearly visible only in very small patches. The shore now has only sandy beaches and with just one line of dunes, in many places deliberately demolished, at the foot of which is a modest escarpment, shaped by the action of the waves. The crest of this residue of dunes, partially eroded, is a few metres above sea level. The mainly carbonatic composition of the underlying rock (which outcrops in places) has produced karst features in the deeper Mesozoic calcareous rock and para-karst features in the quaternary calcarenite rocks closer to the surface. The most important environmental sea and karst processes affect the strip closest to the shoreline and are conditioned by the intense anthropogenic pressure, which is neither coordinated or planned but which has put the area at risk. In the urban districts closest to the shoreline there is a high risk of subsidence due to the presence of cavities and hydrogeological pressures. The main causes lie in the obstruction of watercourses, the poor functioning of the drainage network, and the widespread problem of hydrogeological disturbance arising from unregulated building. The area is at risk through intense coastal erosion and serious damage to buildings from continuous subsidence in the last decade hence many buildings have been abandoned and declared unsafe. Significant soil subsidence due to collapsed underground cavities was seen in Casalabate in 1993 and 2000 which affected some civil dwellings. Hence the morphology of this area is compromised due to the general instability of the shoreline, which tends to be most serious in tourism areas. To this may be added the poor drainage in Casalabate hence rainfall directly enters the subsoil through wells in the surface thus increasing subterranean erosion, especially where the calcarenite rock is particularly crumbly (e.g. fossil dune deposits). Although the current data are insufficient to numerically model these phenomena, there is a good understanding of the effects of erosion and new structures; the coastal system linking the beaches, the dunes and the area behind them has become less flexible due to widespread urbanisation and this has reduced the capacity of the system to adapt to new environmental conditions.

Riding of Yorkshire in northeastern England has adopted such a policy in order to minimise future safety or economic issues. Even if this has not been implemented by statutory authorities then it could be effected by insurance companies, i.e. 'you can build on an eroding coastline but do not expect your property to be insured'.

Erosion of coastlines is not a problem until human inhabitants get in the way – without these the coast would naturally adjust, the natural features of an eroding coastline will be the same in 100 years except that it may be many metres further back. Hence there may be environmental and economical repercussions. This could be contained by means of three types of engineering intervention:

- *high geo-environmental impact* (with the use of barriers and breakwaters set at right angles to the coast; construction of sea walls for the diffraction of wave motion and coastal currents)
- *medium geo-environmental impact* (with beach nourishment on coasts subject to erosion by distributing sediments taken from elsewhere)
- *low geo-environmental impact* (including the construction of submerged breakwaters, i.e. artificial barrier systems, and the recovery of typical vegetation along the backshore to act as a sediment trap and energy dissipator).

The responses for protection/preparedness for a disaster event versus the recovery from it can be grouped into three categories:

Box 17.6 *Balancing of economic and natural risks*

Spurn Point on the Yorkshire coast (northeast England) is a peninsula landform, consisting predominantly of sand and gravel, with an area of cobble lag deposit at its tip. It is a dynamic feature, subject to movement as a result of wave, wind and tidal action on a seasonal basis. Over the longer-term, it is undergoing an inward movement, tracking back with the retreat of the more solid boulder clay landform of Holderness to which it is connected, this boulder clay feature being subject to an annual erosion rate of 1–2 m (see Box 17.1). Spurn Point was the base for national defence structures during World War I and World War II and, although these have since been removed, it remains a base for navigation and safety provision for the adjacent busy shipping channel of the Humber Estuary (lifeboat, pilotage and vessel traffic management). These activities thus require road (and previously rail) infrastructure along the landform to the tip. The nineteenth and twentieth centuries saw a range of coastal protection measures applied to Spurn Point, in order to maintain the infrastructure linkages; however, these structures meant that the peninsula had been held in effectively the same spatial position for over 100 years, while the adjacent coast had continued to erode. Effectively the neck of Spurn had been held in a position considered stable during the Victorian age (late nineteenth century), but was in fact later identified as being considerably dynamic. By the late twentieth century it became evident that the current position of the neck of the peninsula was being held in an unsustainable position compared to the adjacent coastline and was at immediate risk of a catastrophic breach and it was therefore necessary to decide the future management of the peninsula. The principle of 'working with coastal processes' was agreed by many of the management group, which meant that the peninsula would not be actively protected from wave action in the future, but with the need to maintain the navigation and safety provision (and associated access) also a necessary and valid management aim. A solution was found that allowed the infrastructure (roadway) to be maintained, through the use of an interlocking concrete block system, which provided a sufficiently robust roadbed for the limited vehicular movements (Fig. 17.5). Notably this could also be moved with relative ease, allowing the neck of the peninsula to move with natural processes and the roadway to be moved with it on future alignments.

(a)

(b)

Fig. 17.5 Erosion at Spurn Point, eastern England: (a) loss of the roadway; (b) replacement with a flexible solution of a movable roadway

- mitigation – disaster aid (or compensation for those affected)
- protection – environmental control, design of buildings, sea defences
- adaptation – community preparedness (civil defence), forecasting and warning system (e.g. North Sea storm surge warning).

The vulnerability to a hazard, and thus the amount of risk or the perception to risk and hence the eventual consequences (even disaster) relates to the nature of the area and the degree of preparedness. There are technological approaches for dealing with coastal hazards and for minimising the risk plus reducing the vulnerability of the receiving populations. For example, coastal defences can be engineered, by using either soft or hard engineering (French, 1997; Elliott *et al.*, 2007) to minimise or even remove the risk and so protect the local populations although of course this has an economic consequence. Hard and soft engineering approaches each have different economic and environmental consequences. Hard engineering includes concrete seawalls and very often the fixing and possibly even advancing the coastline which in turn has little regard to the natural system and functioning. In contrast, soft engineering may involve beach nourishment, by taking sediment from the sublittoral areas and redistributing it onto beaches in the knowledge that although this confers initial protection, it will be removed and have to be replaced in time (thus maintaining the line of the coast). However, increasingly solutions may include realigning and even retreating the coast in order to produce wetland, controlled flooding areas or water storage areas which both afford protection and create (and possibly replace) valuable wetland habitats.

More specifically, measures to be implemented may include *protection of inner coastal areas* by fencing off wetlands, protection of coastal dunes by setting up Nature Reserves or Protected Areas, and planting to form sediment traps. A fundamental measure to reinforce the coastline consists of the recovery of the ancient line of dunes. The dunes are reconstructed by deposition of suitable sand and consolidated by transplanting large quantities of grasses and shrubs, especially psammophile plants and tamerisks, characteristic of coastal areas.

Protection of beach areas to reduce the hazards can occur through beach nourishment or using barriers or groynes and jetties i.e. piles of blocks or 'armour units' (rarely cemented together), attached and usually perpendicular to the shore. For example, areas adjacent to the Venice Lagoon lost beaches thus exposing the coastline to high risks, such as seawater flooding and damage to the rocky shoreline. To counter this, a series of reinforcement measures were adopted which included the creation of a new, wide beach, more than 9 km long, using *c.* 5 million m^3 of sand in beach nourishment. The new beach is protected by 18 groynes set perpendicular to the coast, connected to each other by a submerged breakwater running parallel to the coast, 300 m from the shore, along the entire 9 km of coastline. Other measures include breakwaters composed of lines of armour units such as 'tetrapods' a short distance offshore running parallel to the most frequent wave front to ensure the *dissipation of the wave motion.*

Traditional rigid structures, such as rubble-mound breakwaters and sea walls, have proven to be inadequate in providing comprehensive solutions to the problem of erosion. Traditional heavy structures such as sea walls and breakwaters entail high maintenance costs and do not always succeed in preventing the erosion of the coastline; on the contrary in some cases they even accelerate it. Hence, in many European areas, national and regional authorities have taken the view that building artificial barriers to prevent natural erosion is neither cost effective nor sustainable. Hence the policy of roll-back, which consists of gradually reducing the presence of human activities in those parts of the coastal strip liable to erosion/flooding. This may be accompanied by 'managed realignment' in which dykes are moved back and wetlands created as a method of soft-engineering to minimise risk through erosion and coastal flooding thus aiming for a win-win-win situation of benefits for human safety, economy and the ecological system (Elliott *et al.*, 2007; Edwards and Winn, 2006). In the regions in which managed realignment is not practical (for example in areas of high economic or historic value), the authorities have frequently opted for light coastal protection instead of traditional dykes and breakwaters.

In the Flanders region of Belgium, the authorities are trying to adapt the management of the highly built-up coastline to its natural dynamics to minimise hazard and risk. Where possible, they are trying to manage the problem of erosion in a more subtle way by replacing the protection barriers with, for example, sand dunes covered in vegetation that are able to naturally absorb the energy of the sea. This solution is also being adopted for the Adriatic coast of the Salento in southern Italy. In this example, prevention of coastal erosion and the safeguard of the beaches involve drainage to lower the water table near the shoreline together with the stabilisation of the sand and a noticeable reduction in backrush, thus favouring the deposit of sediment on the seashore.

The North Sea states to date have used traditional solutions to the problems of coastal change, erosion and sea-level rise. This has included hard engineering solutions such as sea defences and barriers and barrages such as across the Thames and Oosterscheldt to combat the effects of tidal storm surges moving down the North Sea. There is now an increase in soft-engineering such as beach nourishment, set back or managed realignment (depolderisation) in order to protect areas (Edwards and Winn, 2006; Elliott *et al.*, 2007). Of course, some areas have to be protected by engineering but not all areas. The UK strategy that has evolved is to protect large urban areas and industry in the national interest, hence the protection respectively of cities and coastal gas terminals, but, because of the low cost of agricultural land then that would not be protected. This in turn has led to policies, plans and strategies for dealing with that habitat change not only flood-risk management planning but also habitat planning and managing carrying capacity (Costanza, 1995). Consequently science and management now relates to how do we regain carrying capacity, how do we maintain it? How do we create it? This is a challenge particularly for the North Sea coastal areas (Elliott *et al.*, 2007).

As a precursor to management actions and thus possible solutions, the assessment and quantification of risk involves a definition and quantification of the hazard, the determination of the elements at risk, and an analysis of the vulnerability of those elements to change (adapted from Smith and Petley, 2009). Risks may be deemed by society to be *unacceptable*, *tolerable* or *acceptable* thus using the ALARP framework – in this risk is managed to be '*as low as reasonably practicable*' (Melchers, 2001) which in itself infers a governance element (the *managed* aspect), the societal demands (the *reasonably* aspect) and technological and economic aspects (the *practicable* aspect). Unacceptable risks have to be addressed almost irrespective of the costs given society's high concern. Tolerable risks then require to be tackled using the ALARP principle in that society will address them as long as the finances and benefits warrant it. Acceptable risks may be those which society will decide not to address given that they consider the benefits do not warrant the costs (Smith and Pedley, 2009).

Risk management relates to the ability to adjudge and identify hazards, leading to protection or removal of the elements at risk and therefore a means of reducing vulnerability, i.e. as an action, incorporating an evaluation of social consequences against the probability of such events. The role of science is to determine risk in which it is possible to evaluate the likelihood of an event. This leads to preparedness, e.g. for the design of coastal defences according to, for example, a 1-in-250 year wave height. However, a cost–benefit analysis would have to determine whether only a 1-in-100 year event can be prepared for as this would be less expensive than the longer event return period. This may apply, however, to locally-caused changes and acute events whereas society has to respond to the gradual changes caused by climate change. Climate change is regarded as a hazard but more importantly is an *exogenic unmanaged pressure* in which the probability of effect cannot be reduced at a local scale, i.e. requires global action, but the response by society has to be to the consequences and thus can be at a local scale to reduce risks.

Risks may be separated into *involuntary* and *voluntary* ones (Barnett and Breakwell, 2001; Mai *et al.*, 2008). An involuntary risk is one imposed from outside and is one in which the stakeholder has no influence. For example, society has no control of the presence of a soft, low-lying coastal area which is liable to landslip/coastal erosion and as such is an involuntary risk. However this becomes a voluntary risk that the stakeholders, at least those occupying the area by their actions, have created and thus put themselves at greater risk. Therefore, an involuntary risk can become a voluntary risk, i.e. one that the players can influence, by building on land close to the danger area such as on an eroding coastline. Within this there is the need to determine at what stage is a risk perceived or does society consider that vulnerability not an issue.

This chapter has shown that some hazards relate to many coasts worldwide, both temperate and tropical, such as storm surges and waves, coastal erosion, flooding, saline intrusion (acute by typhoon tidal waves but also chronic by sea-level rise) and withdrawal of waters from the catchment by inland communities (such as Bangladesh rivers becoming more saline through damming by its neighbours), and building damage. Of course, many solutions and responses to coastal hazards require cross-disciplinary action and especially the need to engage with local society rather than imposing actions from outside. It is axiomatic that solutions to coastal problems usually have a greater chance of success if the local society is fully a part of the responses. For example, initiatives to restore habitats on vulnerable coasts and thus contribute to protection and which involve local people will increase the chances of success as well as increasing awareness in the community (Box 17.7).

17.4   Concluding comments – challenges and changes

Of all the issues relating to the defence of the coastal strip, that of marine erosion – together with the measures for the reconstruction of the coastline that it requires – is one of the most complex, in terms of the environment, economics and the law. It is likely to become even more important in the future, due to the growing frequency of

425

Box 17.7 *Responses on vulnerable coasts – positive action*

As certain habitats confer a high degree of protection to coastal areas then action is required to maintain those habitats. For example, offshore coral reefs and coastal mangroves occur in appropriate areas and produce protection against the effects of tropical storms and cyclones. In addition, these areas produce ecological goods and services and support biodiversity which in turn deliver economic goods and services. The negative impacts to people's livelihoods only arise after the damage has been done. For example, coasts without coral reefs or mangrove forest appear to be much more vulnerable to extreme weather than coasts protected by intact natural areas. In addition, there are economic consequences as fish catches are decreased considerably in coastal zones where coral reefs or mangroves have been destroyed. As an indication of positive action, *Wetlands International* works in Africa and Asia to protect and restore these threatened and degraded coastal zone ecosystems. It works together with local communities, to replant mangroves and other coastal forests and clean up coral reefs (see http://malaysia.wetlands. org/WHATWEDO/VulnerableCoasts/tabid/516/Default.aspx)

---

floods and storminess and rising sea levels linked to climate change (Garzia, 2007). Hazard removal and risk reduction requires an integrated approach linking environmental sustainability, economic reconstruction of the coastal strip and actions on other coastal uses and users, for example tourism and coastal navigation and maritime traffic. In legal terms the complexity derives from the need to tackle the problems at an international level and from the plurality of interests (public and private) affected by and affecting shoreline developments. This requires a good knowledge of the behaviour of the coastline and greater awareness and realism amongst the general population regarding the environmental impact and what is possible and what is not possible to reduce the coastal hazards. Taken together, the various forms of reducing vulnerability involve significant retreat of the coastline and serious environmental and economic damage. However, the risks are common to many coasts and require coordinated, comprehensive and long-term intervention strategies to conserve and protect a habitat that is increasingly fragile and at risk.

Coastal protection and the minimising of hazard and risk is central to measures adopted under Integrated Coastal Zone Management Plans, which represents the main means by which authorities are attempting, for example in line with European guidelines, to comprehensively tackle the many problems that affect the coastal system. ICZM should aim to steer all coastal and marine activities towards full environmental sustainability and hence concerns not only erosion but also marine pollution, protection of the typical natural habitats of the marine areas, infrastructure, residential areas and tourism. Hence, a four point strategy to tackle erosion, for example, would include *Restoring the sediment balance and providing space for coastal processes*, but also to *make responses to coastal erosion accountable*. The management has to move away from piecemeal solutions towards a planned approach based on proven principles, above all by optimising investment in the items at risk, increasing the social acceptability of the measures and keeping options open for the future. This approach should be guided by the need to restore coastal resilience and equilibrium which should include a Coastal Sediment Management Plan. A further recommendation is to *internalise coastal erosion costs and risk in planning and investment decisions*. Finally it is just as important to *strengthen the knowledge base of coastal erosion management and planning*. Basic knowledge of the planning and management of coastal erosion needs to be enhanced via the development of strategies for managing information. These should include the dissemination of 'best practice' (including what works and what doesn't), promoting an active approach to data and information management, specifying the officers that are responsible on a regional level. As an example of this, the management of the problems and risks of coastal erosion in Italy requires the drawing up of a Strategic National Plan for integrated coastal zone management. Of course, coastal disasters cause a rethink and perhaps re-prioritisation of measures to protect the coast, even by working with nature rather than trying to over-engineer the coast. Pilkey and Young (2005) emphasise that the hurricane Katrina must cause a rethink of the way shoreline management is carried out, the building of infrastructure close to or on the coast and the way we engineered coasts.

In previous papers (e.g. Elliott *et al.*, 2007; Mee *et al.*, 2008) we have suggested that the successful and sustainable management of environmental problems has to follow an interlinked set of *7 tenets*. These relate to actions which ensure the delivery of economic goods and services while at the same time protecting ecological goods and services; in this way societal aspirations will be delivered. These 7 tenets can then be re-interpreted according to responses to coastal hazards and risk (Table 17.2). McLusky and Elliott (2004) give further details of the

Table 17.2 The 7 tenets of environmental management (adapted from Elliott et al., 2007; Mee et al., 2008) as related to coastal hazards and risk

Tenet	Meaning	Comments for hazards and risk prevention and response
Environmentally/ecologically sustainable	That the measures will ensure that the ecosystem features are safeguarded	That the natural ecology is maintained where possible
Technologically feasible	That the methods and equipment for ecosystem and society/infrastructure protection are available	Flood barriers, shore protection, treatment plants of chemical pollutants, mechanisms to prevent inflow of biological organisms
Economically viable	That a cost–benefit assessment of the environmental management indicates sustainability but that adaptation to hazards is within financial budgets	Compensation schemes for those affected; that industry in the national interest and large urban areas are protected
Socially desirable/tolerable	That the environmental management measures are as required or at least are understood by society as being required; that society regards the protection as necessary	The society is educated regarding the effects and implications of coastal hazards and thus has a high level of preparedness
Legally permissible	That there are regional, national, European or international agreements and/or statutes which will enable the management measures to be performed; that either under regular or emergency statutes the hazard protection can be achieved	International agreements for aid and minimising hazards or the consequences of it; national laws and agreement allowing regional and national bodies to act even in emergencies
Administratively achievable	That the statutory bodies such as governmental departments, environmental protection and conservation bodies are in place and functional to enable the successful and sustainable management	Flood management schemes, erosion protection schemes, shoreline management plans; that there are contingency plans showing the command structure to respond to hazards and disasters; that there are bodies to carry out these actions
Politically expedient	That the management approaches and philosophies are consistent with the prevailing political climate	Pressure on politicians to carry out measures, that politicians are aware of the risks and the consequences of either not being prepared nor having suitable responses for the hazards occurring

responses to estuarine and coastal problems and Bell and McGillivray (2008) give an excellent discussion of the legal basis of environmental management.

In conclusion, in this chapter we have reflected on the size and number of hazards relating to the climatological, hydrographical and geomorphological conditions of coasts – the change of regime in rivers, polluting processes, alteration of water use, the subsidence caused, urban development, and cliff and beach erosion and shown both the interrelated nature of the problems and the solutions. We emphasise the distinction made by Zunica (2001) regarding natural and anthropogenic disasters and hence we indicate those over which society may have some control and those which it does not. Thus the reduction of risk may be achieved by preparedness and planning, by education and by good science to inform decisions. The increasing coastal population increases the risk and the effects of the hazards and so risk reduction may be proportional to the value of the assets at risk or the population at risk of harm. The degree of mitigation or adaptation will have to be determined by a willingness to pay and/or react to the hazard. We emphasise that there is the need for a greater understanding of processes to address the causes of these hazards and thus minimise risk. We also emphasise that a multidisciplinary approach is required thus incorporating the 7 tenets discussed above. Most importantly we need a system in which policy makers are educated to look and act across that multidisciplinary framework.

References

Austin, D.E. (2009) Coastal exploitation, land loss, and hurricanes: a recipe for disaster. *American Anthropologist*, Vol. 108, Issue 4, pp. 671–691.

Barberi, F., Santactrose, R. and Carapezza, M.L. (2004) *Terra pericolosa*, Pisa, Edizioni ETS.

Barnett, J. and Breakwell, G.M. (2001) Risk perception and experience: hazard personality profiles and individual differences. *Risk Analysis*, Vol. 21, No. 1, pp. 171–178.

Baxter, P.J. (2005) The east coast Big Flood, 31 January–1 February 1953: a summary of the human disaster. *Phil. Trans. R. Soc. A 15*, Vol. 363, No. 1831, pp. 1293–1312.

Bell, S. and McGillivray, D. (2008) *Environmental Law*, 7th ed., Oxford University Press, Oxford.

Boudouresque, C.F. and Vaerlaque, M. (2002) Biological pollution in the Mediterranean Sea: invasive versus introduced macrophytes. *Marine Pollution Bulletin*, Vol. 44, pp. 32–38.

Brammer, H. (2000) Flood hazard vulnerability and flood disasters in Bangladesh. In: Parker, D.J. (ed.) *Floods*, Vol. 1, pp. 100–115.

Central Science Laboratory (2008) The Invasive Non-Native Species Framework Strategy for Great Britain. Department for Environment, Food and Rural Affairs. London. Online at: http://www.nonnativespecies.org

Clark, R.B. (2001) *Marine Pollution*, 5th ed., Oxford University Press, Oxford.

Costanza, R. (1995) Economic growth, carrying capacity, and the environment. *Ecological Economics*, Vol. 15, pp. 89–90.

Ducrotoy, J.-P. and Elliott, M. (2008) The science and management of the North Sea and the Baltic Sea: natural history, present threats and future challenges. *Marine Pollution Bulletin*, Vol. 57, pp. 8–21.

Edwards, A.M.C. and Winn, P.S.J. (2006) The Humber Estuary: strategic planning of flood defences and habitats. *Marine Pollution Bulletin*, Vol. 53, pp. 165–174.

Efstratiou, M.A. (2001) Managing coastal bathing water quality: the contribution of microbiology and epidemiology. *Marine Pollution Bulletin*, Vol. 42, No. 6, pp. 424–431.

Elliott, M. (2003) Biological pollutants and biological pollution – an increasing cause for concern. *Marine Pollution Bulletin*, Vol. 46, pp. 275–280.

Elliott, M., Burdon, D., Hemingway, K.L. and Apitz, S. (2007) Estuarine, coastal and marine ecosystem restoration: confusing management and science – a revision of concepts. *Estuarine, Coastal & Shelf Science*, Vol. 74, pp. 349–366.

Flint, R.F. (1971) *Glacial and Quaternary Geology*, Wiley, New York.

French, P. (1997) *Coastal and Estuarine Management*, Routledge, London.

Galil, B.S. (2007) Loss or gain? Invasive aliens and biodiversity in the Mediterranean Sea. *Marine Pollution Bulletin*, Vol. 55, pp. 314–322.

Garzia, G. (2007). L'erosione costiera e gli interventi di ripascimento del litorale: il quadro giuridico attuale e le prospettive di riforma. *Federalismi.it*, No. 15, pp. 1–17.

Genovesi, P. and Shine, C. (2004) European Strategy on Invasive Alien Species: Convention on the Conservation of European Wildlife and Habitats (Bern Convention): *Nature and Environment* No. 137, Council of Europe Publishing, Strasbourg.

Haque, E.M. and Elliott, N. (2005) The Sundarbans bangrove ecosystem of Bangladesh: high biodiversity, resources and protection. *Bulletin of the Estuarine & Coastal Sciences Association*, No. 48, pp. 7–11.

Hewitt, C.L. and Campbell, M.L. (2007) Mechanisms for the prevention of the marine bioinvasions for better biosecurity. *Marine Pollution Bulletin*, Vol. 55, pp. 395–401.

Humphries, L. (2001) A review of relative sea level rise caused by mining-induced subsidence in the coastal zone: some implications for increased coastal recession. *Climate Research*, Vol. 18, pp. 147–156.

ISPRA (2007) Istituto Superiore per la Protezione e la Ricerca Ambientale. *Annuario ambientale*. Online at: http://annuario.apat.it; *Environmental Data Yearbook*. Online at: http://annuario.apat.it/annuario_en.php

Klein, R.J.T., Nicholls, R.J., Ragoonaden, R.J., Capobianco, M., Aston, M. and Buckley, E.N. (2001) Technological options for adaptation to climate change in coastal zones. *Journal of Coastal Research*, Vol. 17, Issue 3, pp. 531–543.

Leavitt, W.M. and Kiefer, J.J. (2006) Infrastructure interdependency and the creation of a normal disaster: the case of Hurricane Katrina and the City of New Orleans. *Public Works Management & Policy*, Vol. 10, No. 4, pp. 306–314.

Mai, C.V., van Gelder, P., Vrijling, J.K. and Mai, T.C. (2008) Risk Analysis of Coastal Flood Defences – a Vietnam case. *4th International Symposium on Flood Defence: Managing Flood Risk, Reliability and Vulnerability*, Toronto, Ontario, Canada, 6–8 May, paper 93, Institute for Catastrophic Loss reduction, the Netherlands.

Marabini, F. (2000). Effetti sull'erosione costiera dei fenomeni climatici recenti: l'esempio del litorale Nord Adriatico. In *Mare e cambiamenti globali*, ICRAM, Rome, pp. 119–134.

McLusky, D.S. and Elliott, M. (2004). The Estuarine Ecosystem: Ecology, Threats and Management, 3rd ed., Oxford University Press, Oxford.

Mee, L.D., Jefferson, R.L., Laffoley, Dd'A. and Elliott, M. (2008) How good is good? Human values and Europe's proposed Marine Strategy Directive. *Marine Pollution Bulletin*, Vol. 56, pp. 187–204.

Melchers, R.E. (2001) On the ALARP approach to risk management. *Reliability Engineering & System Safety*, Vol. 71, Issue 2, pp. 201–208.

Metheringham, V.E. (2008). The Socio-economic Implications and Management of Coastal Erosion along the Holderness Coast, its history and its future. Unpublished MSc Thesis, University of Hull, UK. Online at: http://www.hull.ac.uk/iecs

Nienhuis, P.H. and Smaal, A.C. (eds) (1994) *The Oosterschelde Estuary (the Netherlands): A Case-study of a Changing Ecosystem*, Kluwer Academic, Dordrecht.

Occhipinti-Ambrogi, A. and Galil, B.S. (2004) A uniform terminology on bio-invasions: a chimera or an operative tool? *Marine Pollution Bulletin*, Vol. 49, pp. 688–694.

Olenin, S., Minchin, D. and Daunys, D. (2007) Assessment of biopollution in aquatic ecosystems. *Marine Pollution Bulletin*, Vol. 55, pp. 379–394.

Panov, V.E., Alexandrov, B., Arbaciauskas, K., Binimelis, R., Copp, G.H., Grabowski, M., Lucy, F., Leuven, E.S.E.W., Nehring, S., Paunovic, M., Semenchenko, V. and Son, M.O. (2009) Assessing the risks of aquatic species invasions via European Inland Waterways: From concepts to environmental indicators. *Integrated Environmental Assessment and Management*, Vol. 5, Issue 1, pp. 110–126.

Pilkey, O.H. and Young, R.S. (2005) Will Hurricane Katrina impact shoreline management? Here's why it should. *Journal of Coastal Research*, Vol. 21, Issue 6, pp. iii–x.

Rapport, D.J., Costanza, R. and McMichael, A.J. (1998) Assessing ecosystem health. *Trends in Ecology & Evolution*, 13(10): 397–402.

Refolo, G., Sterponi, L., Moschettini, F., Urrutia, C., Ciurlia, S. and Perrone, R. (2007) *Sistema di monitoraggio satellitare delle aree costiere della Provincia di Lecce*. Online at: http://digilander.libero.it

Reise, K., Olenin, S. and Thieltges, D.W. (2006) Are aliens threatening European aquatic coastal ecosystems? *Helgoland Marine Research*, Vol. 60, Issue 2, pp. 77–83.

Ruiz, G.M., Carlton, J.T., Gorsholz, E.D. and Hines, A.H. (1997) Global invasions of marine and estuarine habitats by non-indigenous species: mechanisms, extent and consequences. *American Zoologist*, Vol. 37, pp. 621–632.

Smith, K. and Petley, D.N. (2009) *Environmental Hazards: Assessing Risk and Reducing Disaster*, 5th ed., Routledge, Oxford.

Storch, Von H. (1996) *The WASA Project: Changing Storm and Wave Climate in the North East Atlantic and Adjacent Seas*. GKSS 96/E/61.

Thanawood, C, Yongchalermchai, C. and Densrisereekul, D. (2005) Effects of the December 2004 tsunami and disaster management in southern Thailand. *Science of Tsunami Hazards*, Vol. 24, No. 3, p. 206.

Thornton, E.B., Sallenger, A., Sesto, J.C., Egley, L., McGee, T. and Parsons, R. (2006) Sand mining impacts on long-term dune erosion in southern Monterey Bay. *Marine Geology*, Vol. 229, pp. 45–58.

Zaiko, A., Olenin, S., Daunys, D. and Nalepa, T. (2007) Vulnerability of benthic habitats to the aquatic invasive species. *Biological Invasions*, Vol. 9, pp. 703–714.

Zunica, M. (2001) *Ambiente costiero e valutazione d'impatto*, Bologna, Patron (ed.).

18

Postscript – an epilogue

William Ritchie
Aberdeen Institute for Coastal Science and Management, University of Aberdeen, Scotland, UK

18.1 Conceptual basis

Normally, coastal zone management is preceded by the word 'integrated' to add a sense of 'wholeness' and 'merging' of different components. Coincidently, both coastal and marine spatial planning (MSP) are now being discussed in the context of 'the ecosystem approach' which implies the interactions between a (biological) community and its non-living environment and is also inherently holistic and integrated. Setting aside the ongoing debate on the boundary between 'coastal' and 'marine', the remaining term in ICZM is management which appears to be a self-evident process and therefore has no further need for definition or development. Management, however, is the critical element in ICZM or CZM or MSP for several reasons, including the belief that the coastal zone (using a working definition of areas of seas and estuaries, that are relatively close to the inter-tidal zone) is already managed, normally on a sectoral interest basis, or, being part of an historic common estate, has no need for any or more managerial interference. Similarly, in many texts and academic papers, a notional 'coastal manager' or 'coastal practitioner' appears and, often prompts the question 'who is this person?' – a planner, a coastal engineer, a conservationist, an agency, a national body, or government at several levels and many more. In reality no such person exists – and, perhaps, it is this lack of leadership and the tangle of overlapping functional arrangements, some of which are historical, that initiated 'a real or perceived need for ICZM in the 1960'. It is a short step from this tangle of particular needs to assert that ICZM will solve existing or potential 'conflict'; conflict which is claimed to be based on an irreconcilable situation where there is more than one demand being made on the same coastal space whether two-dimensional – the surface, or 3D – including the water column. What might be emerging at this time, however, in addition to conflict resolution reasons for ICZM, is a more cogent argument that is based on the optimisation of the marine resource either on the premise of sustainability or, realistically, in relation to making the best use of those resources which are inherently non-renewable, and some of which are unique to the marine environment and some of which are needed increasingly to replace terrestrial sources of the same or similar assets. Arguably, both sustainability and optimisation of the marine and coastal resource base are strong arguments in favour of adopting ICZM principles.

18.2   Current developments

In the context of this volume, the existence, application and use of integrated coastal zone management as a means for better coastal management at a time of undoubted pressure for a growing list of demands on coastal and marine systems – renewable and non-renewable – is accepted for both conceptual and pragmatic reasons. In many coastal areas ICZM exists, in others it is presently taking the form of guidelines or advisory statements. It is also more than obvious that human activities in myriad ways are increasing at inexorable rates as world population grows and, that proportionally, the movement of people with their economic activities, their social requirements and their economic needs are shifting seawards. This is not a new revelation; it is the scale and range of demands, some of which might be crossing critical thresholds of sustainability, that are in conflict with the capacity of coastal seas and estuaries to absorb these rapidly escalating demands.

18.3   Content

The design of the chapters of this book is essentially practical and is based on the reasonable premise that ICZM exists or it will develop soon in some form or another, globally, nationally and regionally. In places, it will occur by an extension of land planning principles and practices seawards. Alternatively, in contrast, marine spatial planning will extend landwards into the coastal zone. To a degree, this distinction is irrelevant to the aim of the chapters in this book because good management in all situations requires an understanding of relevant factors, and causes and effects. Techniques for data handling and modelling, prioritisation of needs and risks are also essential skills to assist the process of understanding. Although the term is often over-used, there is a current need for capacity building not just with planning practitioners and potential decision makers but also to those identified in the Preface as 'the wider coastal community' i.e. those at the receiving-end of the managerial decision. The range of topics and chapters cannot be wholly comprehensive but most of the key scientific disciplines, current economic social and conservational issues, contextual factors and techniques are all communicated in non-technical language to a prospective wide readership. Realistically, the book should do more than stimulate 'discussion' but, as also stated in the Preface, provide readers of all backgrounds with a grounding in the 'fundamentals that will perhaps not date too quickly'.

18.4   Retrospective review

An epilogue is a short postscript at the end of a book and, being the last element in the compilation and editorial process can comment on the relevance of its aims and objectives. Strengths and weaknesses of content might also be identified as a consequence of different styles, possible overlaps and gaps in what might be regarded as the full list of topics to justify the claim for this to be a book that is intended for use as an introduction to the fundamentals, or course reader. But this is unfair for several reasons. First, it is an introduction rather than a comprehensive text. Second, the subject matter is too large to be encompassed in other than an encyclopaedic volume. The range of relevant subject material that could be included at both global and regional scales is far too great. The content has to be selective and, perforce, the selection is to some extent an individual editorial process but, in this instance, it has been guided by prior consultation with reviewers and academic colleagues. It would not be difficult to suggest additional topics for inclusion but, inevitably size and space constraints must prevail.

In contrast, the approach taken has the great strength of considerable in-depth expertise and knowledge by a range of individual experts. All chapters have been presented in an accessible, readable, relatively non-technical form. Unlike other publications, especially conference transactions, it is relatively free from a proliferation of case-studies. Regional and local examples are included but are normally used correctly in order to illustrate and to explain general principles and information. It is also features impressive reading lists for further reference and study at the end of each chapter.

The list of chapters provides adequate cover of most aspects of the science base although the biotic resource base and its exploitation could be developed further. Planning, legal problems and management issues are well-represented in a range of different contexts, including regional and cultural differences. Modelling and data handling are also included both in special chapters and are also embedded in some other sections of the volume. Risk, vulnerability and the difficult topic of economic appraisal are also well-covered. Many chapters contain implicit reference to the insoluble equation of trying to distinguish between qualitative and quantitative measures of the value of coastal resources and the beneficial or deleterious impacts of different types of use on the biotic and abiotic resource base. The format and length of each chapter have permitted ample depth of information, discussion with useful signposts to further reading. Although designed as an introduction to the topic, there are numerous sections which pose fundamental questions about the underlying meaning of the underpinning principles which lie at the heart of the conceptual development of integrated coastal zone management which, arguably, emerged during the 1960s and spread quickly, often stimulated *inter alia* by the facility of global communication to broadcast coastal 'events' such as coastal disasters, both natural and man-made, and by national and international agencies demonstrating unequivocally the accelerating rate of depletion of the renewable and non-renewable coastal and marine resources. The lengthening shadow of climate change (which is most frequently illustrated in popular and scientific presentation by future scenarios of coastal flooding and increased storminess) is also an important factor. Finally, our individual perceptions that the former empty spaces of sea and coast, with their untapped potential and richness, are no longer as 'empty' or 'unused' as they had been for earlier generations. Three further specific issues could claim to have raised the level of awareness of societies and government to the importance of our seas and oceans – and there are others. These are the shift of sources of energy (oil, gas, winds, tides and waves) to the offshore and nearshore zones; the near extinction of a large number of populations of one of the main sources of protein for many societies – fish; the wider understanding (although the fact has been well known since the nineteenth century and is not a concern that has come to prominence solely in the context of climatic change) of the vital

436

coupling of seas, oceans and atmosphere as the fundamental driving force of global patterns of weather.

18.5   Timing and implementation

Over the last decade, the introduction of ICZM into national legislation and planning frameworks has gathered pace, sometimes in its own right, sometimes as an extension of marine planning. This is exemplified within the European Union where guidelines for the introduction of the principles and good practice of ICZM have developed relatively quickly. Different nation states have moved at different rates to implement these EU recommendations. Many regions have developed regional pilot and demonstration schemes. European funding, particularly the INTERREG programme have supported international co-operation and co-ordination to promote and exchange experiences in ICZM based coastal management and spatial planning. In the United Kingdom, a Marine Bill is at the last stage of its progression into legislation. In Scotland a separate Marine Bill is in the final consultation stage (which ended in October 2009) and will make its way as a Bill through the Scottish government.

Without exception, the adoption of ICZM, either in its own right, i.e. strictly coastal (often defined by the three nautical mile limit or similar specifications), or as an extension into coastal waters from the more distant marine environment, is happening now and its adoption will not be reversed. During the consultation stages for the development of some form of coastal management legislation, consensus was reached relatively easily at all levels – European to regional – and can be summarised succinctly in the statement from the DEFRA (2009) (UK Department for Environment, Food and Rural Affairs) website in January 2009 as follows.

ICZM is the adoption of an integrated or joined-up approach towards the many different interests in both the land and marine components of the coast. It is the process of harmonising the different policies and decision making structures, to encourage concerted action towards achieving specific goals.

Successful ICZM may involve adopting the following principles

- A long term view
- A broad holistic approach
- Adaptive management

- Working with natural processes
- Support and involvement of all relevant administrative bodies
- Use of a combination of instruments
- Participatory planning
- Reflecting local characteristics

We expect to embed these principles within all planning and decision making processes affecting coastal areas.

Noting some of the conditional phrases in this policy statement, few advocates would deny that this is a fair summary of the principles, practice and pathway to implementation for ICZM at regional and national levels. There are, of course, negative views, two of which continue to be widely held, in that ICZM is not needed and the so-called problems of multiple use and conflicts have been exaggerated and could be resolved by existing legislation and practices. Moreover, although, the principles are sound and welcome, in the end it will just add another layer of bureaucracy and therefore be self-defeating.

Irrespective of the continuing debate and the precise timing for practical implementation, this book is being published with perfect timing and it will therefore contribute significantly to the process of understanding the key environmental, cultural, historical, social and economic factors, without which the desired managerial outcomes will not be easily achieved.

Reference
DEFRA (2009) http://www.defra.gov.uk/marine/environment/iczm.htm

Index

Page numbers in *italics* denote figures.

439